A Mingled Yarn

Also by Russell Fraser

The Language of Adam: On the Limits and
Systems of Discourse

The Dark Ages and the Age of Gold

An Essential Shakespeare

The War Against Poetry

Shakespeare's Poetics

Russell Fraser

A
MINGLED
YARN

The Life of

R. P. BLACKMUR

New York and London

Harcourt Brace Jovanovich, Publishers

Library of Congress Cataloging in Publication Data
Fraser, Russell A.
A mingled yarn.
Includes bibliographical references and index.
1. Blackmur, R. P. (Richard P.), 1904–1965.
2. Authors, American—20th century—Biography.
I. Title.
PS3503.L266Z64   801′.95′0924 [B]   81–47554
ISBN 0–15–160138–0   AACR2

Printed in the United States of America

First edition

B C D E

For M N Z

And many a poor man that has roved,
Loved and thought himself beloved,
From a glad kindness cannot take his eyes.

As it is a condition of life to die, it is a
condition of thought, in the end, to fail.
Death is the expense of life and failure
is the expense of greatness.

Contents

Illustrations

Preface

R. P. BLACKMUR was our best American critic, a good poet, and a great man. This seems enough reason to write his life. He left five finished books of criticism: *The Double Agent* (1935), *The Expense of Greatness* (1940), *Language as Gesture* (1952), *The Lion and the Honeycomb* (1955), and *Eleven Essays in the European Novel* (1964). He had planned a sixth book and didn't complete it. What he did complete was published after his death as *A Primer of Ignorance* (1967). The collection of essays he called *New Criticism in the United States* (1959) is off-the-cuff writing, a transcript of informal lectures he gave in Japan, and doesn't make a finished book.

Blackmur's poetry is collected in three volumes and has recently been republished by Princeton (1977). *From Jordan's Delight* (1937) is his first and best volume. He got the title from an island in the Bois Bubert Quadrangle off the coast of Maine, where he lived summers for more than twenty years. *The Second World* followed in 1942, then *The Good European* (1947). He wrote plays and short stories, mostly young man's work. A side of him wanted to write novels, Robert Lowell said. This was "because he remembered everything and felt things most critics can't—people." Sometimes, in his two novels, he got the feeling down on paper, but the novels remain unpublished.

The principal labor of his life was the biography and critical study of Henry Adams, in whom he saw himself and with whom he wrestled in love and torment from his early twenties until he died. His last editor called the Adams "the most famous unpublished book" in America. Richard was dead fourteen years before an abridged version was published. He himself would never have let the manuscript go. He thought it unfinished or he didn't want it finished. It is a piece of luck that the decision to publish was taken for him.

Though literature was his appointed study, he isn't exclusively a literary man. Of all forms of purity the least possible, he said, was that a man should be "purely an artist." In his impurity he touches the life of his time at every point, and almost "everyone" in his time participates in his story. "A study of Dick Blackmur that amounted to anything," said his friend Sidney Monas, "would *have* to be a social commentary." His life provides this kind of commentary, from the jingoism of the twenties when he began, to the Cold War when he died. As that is so, essential Blackmur is more than what he published. He endures as a character, gravid or deeply cut, not one of nature's noblemen exactly, but a powerful presence who stands out against his time and is still vividly present, even to friends who never read him. What he said of Adams holds for himself: "He was something besides all his professions."

Blackmur's skepticism ran deep, and he went on to say that what Adams was or what he failed to be is his mystery. Literary biography seemed to him a contradiction in terms. He supposed that a biographer could "do little but dilute, or perhaps misinterpret, the work," as by writing a bad novel or creating a mischievous legend. But after the poet John Brooks Wheelwright was killed, he looked at this friend's life and sought to bring all that had appeared "fragmentary, adventitious, disorderly, generally out of bounds," within the bounding lines of death. He said how character emerges "when the flux has been arrested." The principle of discontinuity bemused him, but in an early story he asserted that we might "cross the horrible gap from one moment to the next." Dwelling in memory was how we crossed the gap. Only then did "the surds of change merge and seem continuous. . . . Always we live in the midst of memory, and if our shelter topple—so must we." From these gingerly phrases, his biography takes its charter.

Memory offers ambiguous testimony, though. Blackmur was many things, often contradictory and not always becoming. Shakespeare, venturing a metaphor, suggests how this resembles him to the rest of us: "The web of our life is of a mingled yarn, good and ill together." You can apply to him the words he used for Baron Corvo, a failed esthete of the period just before his own: "At all times he found himself persecuted and betrayed; had mountainous pride and a genius for self-torture and humiliation. . . . He was domineering and self-obliviating. . . . A marvellous monologuist, an amateur of words and pretender to knowledge." He was all this and more besides. What he was besides, his biography undertakes to show. Because the showing is necessarily partial, the life remains mysterious. But Blackmur in word and deed comments amply on the life, and so resolves a corner of the mystery. This obviates—anyway in hope—the writing of bad fiction and the propagating of mere legend. Like Thomas Mann's hero, "He is his own foil; he shows off clearest against himself."

Blackmur wasn't especially prolific as a writer, and so the sum of what he published is less than the array of titles against his name. Like a good Scot he pillaged all his books, squeezing them for every cent he could get. *Form and Value in Modern Poetry* (1957), the book most readers are likely to know, is a scaled-down reprinting of *Language as Gesture*. But this was partly a reprinting, too, and incorporates more than half the essays that made up *The Double Agent*. And so on. Excepting the life of Adams, this writer never wrote one wholly integrated book. Much of his achievement is work in progress, always in the offing. The big projects he talked about—his poetics, a book on James, another on Dostoevsky— ended up as fragments. Santayana, whom he was always quoting, has this to say, however: "To be miscellaneous, to be indefinite, to be unfinished, is essential to the romantic life." Blackmur was a Romantic and he thought and said that the only things you could rationalize altogether were things you couldn't experience—dead things.

In his lifetime he got his share of adulation, but he wasn't a success as success is commonly measured. The hermetic critic hungered after an audience. Partly, that is why he took up teaching. He said he knew himself to be "better than I am," but the knowledge didn't bring consolation. "I have a mind, only, to give, and not many have need of that," he wrote in his thirties. "It is a terrible rejoicing I must do in my works." He liked to tell himself that "books of my kind . . . sell better in England than here," but English publishers didn't think so. They said agreeable things: "The book has undoubted attractions," etc., and they turned him down. One English publisher to whom he applied called him "a very intelligent critic —too intelligent probably to have much of a sale." *Language as Gesture* was his best book of criticism and tenably the best criticism ever published in America, but in 1958 it sold just forty-two copies in America and the next year it was remaindered. "If I were a rich man," Richard wrote to his publisher, "I would simply ask you to ship to [me] . . . at your best price such copies as you may have still on the market." But he wasn't rich and had to pass up the chance. He said that in the future his books would be needed. This was bravado but prophetic of the truth. Maybe he sensed this vindicating truth and was willing to possess his soul in patience.

"Blackmur's patience will be rewarded," Kenneth Burke said, when "we come to realize that the morality of one's craft is close to the source of all morality." His view of himself added up to failure, however. Superficially he resembled his friend Delmore Schwartz, whose life was a long running down. Richard also was a ruin at the end. This means that suspense, the kind in which melodrama involves you, is off the point. But he wrote in his twenties, when the gloomy writing was already on the wall: "All of us are strewn with our dead pasts—dead successes as well as failures. Occasionally a man has the strength, or the luck, to become a kind of strange necromancer, and pull himself up from the dead." The important question is all but put in these phrases, and is critical for the life. Writing in his early days on John Wheelwright, he had this prescient sentence: "One is the product as well as the victim of the damage of one's lifetime." The damage is painful, and the way he was victimized by it is the day-to-day story of his life. But after all, his story is genuinely suspenseful. Did he build on his ruin, and if he didn't fail, what is the nature of his triumph? The question worth raising and trying to answer is not how he died, but how he lived before he ran out the tether.

For the first and last time in this book, I must use the first-person pronoun and say something of myself in relation to Richard Blackmur. We were friends and colleagues the last nine years of his life, and when he died in 1965 I supposed that someday I would write a personal memoir. What I have made is something different and concerned substantially with matter of fact. On the other hand, Richard says in his "Critic's Job of Work": "No approach opens on anything except from its own point of view and in terms of its own prepossessions." He says also, apropos of his own biography of Adams and the "touchy family" he had to placate: "One should write lives only of those of Virgin Birth and Virgin Families." To some of Richard's friends and some of his detractors, my particular point of view will likely seem inadequate. Estimating this equivocal hero "in the buff life" (as he used to put it) entails a proprietary attitude, though. I don't mind bearing witness to the hokum that went with the greatness, and I don't see it as diminishing either.

My book is composed in three parts, with a coda. The first three chapters deal with Blackmur's early years and the next three with his writing, though this runs, inevitably, all the way through. The final chapters locate him in Princeton. In telling his story, I have tried to tell it chronologically, beginning at the beginning and going on to the end. But his need to write poetry and fiction and criticism, though more or less intense from one year to another, was only appeased with his death. So the chapters overlap and the linear pattern is topical, too. To help the reader who wants to know what happened from year to year, I have offered a time line or chronological account.

Blackmur's biography depends on his published writing, his correspondence and unpublished writing, and the recollections of his contemporaries. I have had inestimable help from many who knew him personally and some who knew him only in his work. Here is a list of people who helped me:

John W. Aldridge, A. Alvarez, William Arrowsmith, James Atlas, Bernard Bandler, Stringfellow Barr, Jacques Barzun, Mrs. Montgomery Belgion, Saul Bellow, G. E. Bentley, Bruce Berlind, Mrs. Kate Berryman, Cyril Black, Elizabeth Blackmur, Marvin Blumenthal, Mrs. E. B. O. Borgerhoff, Julian P. Boyd, Mary Bretagne, Cleanth Brooks, Katharine Brown, Gertrude Buckman, Frederick Buechner, Kenneth Burke, James Burnham, Eleanor Clark, Walter Clemons, Florence Codman, Earle E. Coleman, Edward T. Cone, George Core, James Gould Cozzens, Malcolm Cowley, Louis Coxe, Margot Cutter, David Daiches, R. D. Darrell, Susan Davis, Harold Dodds, Denis Donoghue, Harry Duncan, F. W. Dupee, Mr. and Mrs. Richard Eberhart, Leon Edel, Mrs. Murray Eden, Arthur Efron, Albert R. Erskine, Jr., Lincoln Faller, Francis Fergusson, Leslie Fiedler, Maurice Firuski, Doris Fish, Mrs. Dudley Fitts, Robert Fitzgerald, Richard J. Foster, Joseph Frank, Northrop Frye, Robert Fuller, Paul Fussell, Edgar M. Gemmell, Cedomil Goic, William B. Goodman, George T. Goodspeed, Ernest Gordon, Clement Greenberg, Albert Guerard, Jr., John Haffenden, Jay Gordon Hall, Mrs. William Hamovitch, Henry W. Hardy, James B. Harrison, Robert Hartle, J. William Hess, Robert Hollander, Janis B. Holm, Mr. and Mrs. Philip C. Horton, Irving Howe, W. S. Howell, G. A. M. Janssens, E. D. H. Johnson, Robert Johnson-Lally, Matthew Josephson, Joan Jurow, Ralph Kaplan, R. J. Kaufmann, Alfred Kazin, E. L. Keeley, Robert V. Keeley, Robert Kent, Lincoln Kirstein, Arthur J. Krim, Louis Kronenberger, Mark L. Krupnick, Roy Larsen, James Laughlin, Phillip Leininger, Alexander Leitch, Aaron Lemonick, A. W. Litz, Jr., Robert Lowell, Richard Ludwig, Mary McCarthy, David McCord, Dwight Macdonald, Archibald MacLeish, Norman Macleod, Hugh McMillan, Jr., Veronica Makowsky, John Marshall, Mary Gardner Marshall, Jay Martin, A. Hyatt Mayor, William Meredith, W. S. Merwin, Sidney Monas, Frederick Morgan, Oskar Morgenstern, Harry Murray, Howard Nemerov, Alan Newman, Sean O'Faolain, Paul Oppenheimer, George Orrok, George Anthony Palmer, Phoebe Palmer, Mr. and Mrs. A. Lincoln Pattee, John Pell, Leland F. Perkins, Serge Perosa, Stow Persons, William Phillips, Rose A. Pollard, Kenneth Wiggins Porter, Victor S. Pritchett, Peter Putnam, Philip W. Quigg, Isidore I. Rabi, Gordon Ray, Franklin Reeve, I. A. Richards, Alfredo Rizzardi, Richard de Rochemont, Sigmund Roos, Charles W. Rosen, Peter J. Rosenwald, Philip Roth, Elinor Rowe, Louis Rubin, Muriel Rukeyser, Stephen L. Schlesinger, Carol K. Scholz, Alfred F. Schwarz, William Shellman, Charles Scribner, Daniel Seltzer, Karl Shapiro, Eileen Simpson, B. F. Skinner, William Smith, Louise Solano, W. M. Spackman, Robert Speaight, Mrs. Harold Sproul, Donald Stanford, George Steiner, Holly Stevens, Alan M. Stroock, Allen Tate, Olive M. Thayer, Harry Thomas, Virgil Thomson, Willard Thorp, Ludmilla Turkevitch, Mrs. Leonard F. Van Eck, Rita Vaughan, Fred B. Wahr, Alan Wald, Anna Walsh, Austin Warren, Robert Penn Warren, Mary Blackmur Waterbury, René Wellek,

Leslie Westoff, Christine Weston, William W. Whalen, Marina von Neumann Whitman, Richard Wilbur, Lucius P. Wilmerding, Geoffrey A. Wolff, Hortense Zera.

I could not have written the book as written without Tessa Horton, Rob Darrell, and Betty Blackmur, and my chief thanks goes to them. I am grateful also for the support of the National Endowment of the Humanities, the University of Michigan, the Institute for Advanced Study, and the Rockefeller Foundation.

Far and away the most important collection of Blackmur material is that in the Firestone and Mudd libraries at Princeton, which also houses the Scribner Collection and some of the papers of Allen Tate. Other notable collections are those in the Beinecke Library at Yale (more on Tate, letters of Delmore Schwartz, the *Hound & Horn* Archive, the *Southern Review* papers), the Regenstein Library at Chicago (the *Poetry Magazine* Archive, the papers of Morton D. Zabel,), and the Houghton Library at Harvard (correspondence relating to Blackmur's Adams, the Sherry Mangan letters, and—a recent acquisition—Blackmur's letters over many years to his cousin George Anthony Palmer).

There is additional correspondence and relevant factual material, some of it voluminous, in the New Directions Archive; the University of Delaware; the offices of Harcourt Brace Jovanovich; the Maine Author Collection in the Maine State Library at Augusta; Bowdoin College; Washington University; the Rockefeller Archive; the Guggenheim Foundation Archive; Columbia University; Northwestern University; Middlebury College; the Berg Collection of the New York Public Library; the Newberry Library (the papers of Malcolm Cowley); the Huntington Library (the papers of Conrad Aiken and Wallace Stevens); Bryn Mawr College; the Archives of the American Academy and Institute of Arts and Letters; the John Hay Library at Brown University (letters of J. B. Wheelwright, and Winfield T. Scott); the University of Pennsylvania; the University of Illinois (*Accent Magazine*); the University of Minnesota (the papers of John Berryman); the Archives of the Institute for Advanced Study; the University of Massachusetts; Syracuse University; Kenyon College (the papers of John Crowe Ransom); the University of Iowa; the Johns Hopkins University; Rutgers University (the *Partisan Review* papers); and the Library of Congress.

Private holdings include, first and foremost, the R. D. Darrell papers; and the papers of John Marshall (and his heirs), Rose Dickson, Mrs. Montgomery Belgion, Mrs. Murray Eden, Mr. and Mrs. George Orrok, John W. Aldridge, Maurice Firuski, and Hugh McMillan, Jr. I record my thanks for access to all this material, most of all to the staff at Princeton, where any study of Blackmur's life begins. I am grateful also to the editors of the *Southern Review*, the *Sewanee Review*, the *Michigan Quarterly Review, Salmagundi*, and *Canto*, where earlier versions of some of my chapters first appeared.

RUSSELL FRASER

Ann Arbor and Limerick, Maine, 1980

Chronology

1904   (January 21) Born Springfield, Mass. to George Edward Blackmur and Helen Palmer Blackmur.

1905   Moved with family to New York City, where George Edward worked as a stockbroker on Wall Street.

1906   Edward Benson Blackmur (Ted) born.

1908   George Watson Blackmur born.

1910   Family returned from New York to Cambridge, Mass., settling after a year at 52 Irving Street.

1910–13   Kept at home by his mother in the boarding house she operated, and tutored by her.

1910   Helen Blackmur born.

1913–16   Attended Peabody Grammar School, Cambridge.

1914   Elizabeth Blackmur born.

1916–18   Attended Cambridge High and Latin School. Choirboy at Christ Church Episcopal, Cambridge.

1918   Expelled from high school after quarrel with headmaster.

1918–25   Blackmur on his uppers: stirred sodas, clerked in Cambridge book stores and for the Widener Library, Harvard.

1922   George Munroe Palmer, Blackmur's favorite uncle, a suicide.

1925–26   Partnership with Wallace Dickson in Dickson & Blackmur, Sellers of New and Used Books, 87 Mount Auburn Street, Cambridge.

1927–28   Secretary to Maurice Firuski and clerk in Firuski's Dunster House Book Shop on Mount Auburn and Holyoke streets, Cambridge. Contributed essays to R. D. Darrell's *Phonograph Monthly Review*.

1928–30   Editing manager of *Hound & Horn*. Fired in 1930, but continued as contributor until demise of magazine in 1934.

1928–40   Free-lance poet and critic.

1930   (June 14) Married the painter Helen Dickson.

1930–33   Lived in Belmont with his mother-in-law and her family.

1933–40   Lived in apartment on Chambers Street in the West End of Boston. Spent summers in the Dickson farmhouse near Harrington, Maine. Years of intense poverty.

1935   Published *The Double Agent*. Began work on the biography of Henry Adams.

1937–38 Awarded Guggenheim Fellowship for the Adams book; award renewed, 1938–39.

1937   Published *From Jordan's Delight*.

1940   Signed contract with New Directions for critical book on Henry James. Published *The Expense of Greatness*. Accepted one-year appointment at Princeton University as "associate" to Allen Tate in program in Creative Arts. George Edward Blackmur died at 79.

1940–43 Lived at 43 Linden Lane, Princeton.

1941, 1942 Taught summers at Cummington School, Cummington, Mass.

1942   Published *The Second World*.

1943   Appointed Alfred Hodder Memorial Fellow at Princeton for 1943–44. Moved to 12 Princeton Avenue.

1944–46 Fellow of the School of Economics and Politics, Institute for Advanced Study, Princeton.

1946–48 Resident Fellow in Creative Writing, Princeton.

1947–48 Awarded Rockefeller Fellowship in Humanities. Published *The Good European*.

1948–51 Associate professor of English at Princeton.

1949   Inaugurated Princeton Seminars in Literary Criticism, reconstituted as the Christian Gauss Seminars in 1951.

1951   Appointed full professor with tenure. Divorced.

1951, 1952 Taught summers at School of Modern Critical Studies, University of Vermont.

1952   Published *Language as Gesture*.

1952, 1954, 1958, 1959 Taught at Indiana Summer School.

1952–53 Fourteen-month leave from Princeton. Traveled in Italy, England, Germany, Egypt, the Near East.

1955   Published *The Lion and the Honeycomb*.

1956   Elected to the National Institute of Arts and Letters. Lectured at the Library of Congress, January 9, 16, 23, 29. His lectures published as *Anni Mirabiles, 1921–1925*.

1956–57 Eight-month leave from Princeton. Traveled in Europe, the Near East, and the Far East. Lectured at Nagano, Japan, July 30–August 18, 1956.

1957 Published *Form and Value in Modern Poetry*.

1957–58 Appointed part-time at Rutgers, replacing Francis Fergusson.

1958 Awarded Rutgers Litt.D.

1959 Moved to 53 McCosh Circle, Princeton. Published *New Criticism in the United States*.

1960 A second part-time appointment at Rutgers.

1961–64 Honorary Consultant in American Letters, Library of Congress.

1961–62 Pitt Professor of American History and Institutions and Fellow of Christ's College, Cambridge.

1961 Awarded Cambridge M.A.

1962 Resident at the Villa Serbellone, Bellagio.

1963 Helen Palmer Blackmur died.

1964 Elected to American Academy of Arts and Sciences. Published *Eleven Essays in the European Novel*.

1965 (February 2) Died in Princeton. Funeral services in Princeton on February 5; burial in Pittsfield, Mass., February 6.

1967 *A Primer of Ignorance* published.

1976 (March 13) Helen Dickson Blackmur died.

1977 *Poems of R. P. Blackmur* published.

1980 *Henry Adams* published.

A Mingled Yarn

CHAPTER ONE

Past and Present

WHEN RICHARD was thirty-eight he got a letter from his friend John Walcott, wishing he would write a portrait of his Cambridge childhood. This portrait remained a blank except for private admonitions from the sitter to himself. Like his model writer Flaubert, Richard hid himself in his achievement. As he saw it, laying out his plan for a book on Henry James, there was no biography except what went into the books. In describing his author's life, he proposed to offer nothing beyond the barest facts. He said that he regretted all objective reports of himself. When they weren't objective, he tended to approve. A crank having assured him that Bacon wrote Shakespeare, he saw possibilities in this idea. He said how he himself had the honor of being a direct descendant of the Honorable Lord. That was what his genealogical uncle had told him. If Bacon was Shakespeare, Richard claimed an ancestral part in the work. The face he turned to the public, as regards the real information it conveys, is as vacant as Shakespeare's, however. Photographs put him off. He thought you shouldn't wear your face on your sleeve. As a young man he insisted, "I have no biography." Though he wrote and rewrote entirely in longhand, that wasn't because typing was impersonal or cold. The less personal, the better. His handwriting was stingy—the Freudians would say it was anal. Even the way he signed himself is close to the vest. "I've grown so used to R.P.," he said, "that anything else seems a monstrous egotism." He was chary of egotism and declined to spread himself. The other side of the coin is arrogance, of course. "Not to know me argues yourself unknown."

During his lifetime he received numerous requests for biographical information. Generally his replies went like this one to the students at McGill: "I have a firm belief that a small amount of expression in these matters goes a long ways." The entry against his name in *Twentieth-Century Authors* reproaches him for reticence with his own publishers and the publishers of biographical dictionaries. His reticence was deliberate, also involuntary. Toting up the ten thumbs of memory—his phrase—he could discover no pattern in his story. Like Hamlet he was "all asea; a kind of fighting in my heart." At twenty-two he wrote in his journal: "I am identified only in company. . . . I am ego only as an accumulation." Consciousness was a mirror which reflected ambiguous things. Thinking was an act of mystery. "Hence I understand least and most adore my own thoughts." Sharing your life with someone else was out of the question, and the incapacity of the human being to believe this begot more tragedies than he was able to count. "We dream the difficulty is escaped when we communicate by art or other convention." Communication wasn't communion, however.

A reviewer had censured him because he lacked a single point of view, and he concurred in this censure. He confessed that his imaginative faith was "various, selective, and oscillating." It didn't proceed to the authority of conviction, and he doubted if the welter of convictions or obsessions which described him sounded much of a name or made much of a face. The only unity he detected in himself was "the suspicion of an ultimate unity of fragments." Then he turns, maybe, to his biographer, a comical figure who is looking for the pattern in the carpet. "Unity of personality," he observed, calling all biography in question, "is a specious, imagined thing, a name upon a waste, a face upon a void, for others to speak and see."

As a young man, Richard wondered sometimes if his body were even there. "Substance is always dubious," he said. He attested the functioning of this occulted substance, no one more acutely, but he never knew for sure how the effect related to the cause. So he despaired of what he called his sense of being. In the end this despair defeated his art, first in poetry, then in the criticism of poetry. But it nourished his art in the beginning. Failing to discover a coherent self, he imagined a self. This is an additional reason for his reticence in communicating matter of fact. "To appropriate one's own past," he wrote at eighteen, "is one method of securing an intelligible life. . . . If I know that which I have been, I may then know what my present *should* be." This cuts both ways. It sanctifies fact and allows for the displacing of the mere fact. What Richard had been was a lonely and unprepossessing young man whose family had come down in the world. His colleague on the *Hound & Horn*, Bernard Bandler, described this family many years later as marked by ancient "gentility run very much to seed." His young life was humiliation and opened the gates of hell. More than once he quoted Gide: "L'humilité ouvre les portes du paradis;/L'humiliation, celles de l'enfer." What he should be was the artist as hero. So he appropriated his past.

Read him on Poe—Edgar Poe, Richard called him, asserting a personal claim—and you get the impression that his own house was haunted like Roderick Usher's. Or this house was a mansion from whose windows you looked out at Irving Babbitt's house "next door." That was where Austin Warren, who knew the young Blackmur slightly, located him. Other near neighbors in this moralized landscape were the Harvard philosophers Will James and Josiah Royce, Walter Cannon the physiologist, and Charles Eliot Norton, the president of Harvard. They made a fraternity, Richard among the Sanhedrin. When he went coasting in winter, it was in "Norton's Woods." Santayana might have waved to him there. He saw Santayana plain and appropriated him, too. His house took luster from the white house on the corner where Zechariah Chafee, the famous law professor, lived. At Christmas the tall French windows shone with candles. The neighbors were real, their proximity was Richard's idea. He makes you think of Yeats, assimilating himself to Burke and Goldy and the Dean.

"Last week," Delmore Schwartz wrote to Richard in 1942, "Gertrude and I walked down Irving Street from the lower to the upper middle class, wondering which was your house, which Cummings', and which Babbitt's." Richard lived on lower Irving Street. On the upper street were the houses of the well-to-do and that is where he lived in his mind. He said he had been born—this in a fantasy he concocted at sixteen—of "wealthy and respectable parents from whom I inherited wealth." Later, when the fantasy was no longer tenable, he dwelt on the difference between being well born and well bred. Who cared about being well born? E. E. Cummings, ten years his senior, grew up in the same neighborhood just north of the Harvard Yard and attended the same public school. But the milieu which nourished Cummings made all the difference: "good manners, tea parties, Browning, young women with their minds adequately dressed in English tweeds," an admired and distinguished father who was Harvard '83. Richard hated his father and lived in a dismal boarding house full of other people. He had a little room in the garret. So he took Cummings's milieu for his own.

The need rankled, however. Cummings became, even obsessively, the object of his critical scorn. "He is primitive, almost prerational, and his intellect is dull. . . . He boasts of despising the very functions and talents of man which I most hope to acquire and preserve." This was Richard at nineteen. Later he went after Cummings in print. Allen Tate thought his essay in denigration "thorough and brilliant." But he said: "It is too bad that it is about Cummings at all. You have opened a powerful artillery on a jay bird." There wasn't any help for this. The arriviste was getting his own back.

After he left Cambridge, other versions of his early life were offered. They were contradictory but glamorous and he let them stand. He had been a carpenter or else a lobsterman on the coast of Maine. No doubt he drove a nail or two in his time, and had pulled a lobster trap for fun when he went sailing with the locals. Edmund Wilson used to say that Richard "had something of the old sailor in him, which he traced back to his Newburyport origins." Mary McCarthy, from whom this reminiscence derives, inquired in an aside: "It was Newburyport, wasn't it, or was it Gloucester?"

Richard Blackmur was born in Springfield, Massachusetts, on January 21, 1904, the oldest of five children. His father, George Edward Blackmur —sometime in the past the family had dropped the *i* from the more familiar spelling—was British, born in London about 1861. This provenance comes as a shock. Richard all his life never mentioned his father, and when George Edward died in July 1940 at the age of seventy-nine, his son spoke no regrets and didn't return for the funeral.

Blackmur men were officers in the British Army. Their given names were often Richard or Edward or George. Richard Blackmur's grandfather was Edward or George Edward, also a Londoner. He came to New York City before the Civil War. His older brother Horace, Richard's great uncle, emigrated, too. Horace was an early version of the remittance man. His arrogance offended his well-connected family, so the family sent him away. He arrived in America accompanied by a man servant and set about retrieving his fortunes. He made and lost three fortunes and he married three wives. Before the Civil War he lived in Richmond, Virginia, and when his slaves were freed he moved to New York City. He died in New York and is buried in Brooklyn. Horace was a gay old boy, Richard's sister Betty said, and had several wives mourning at his funeral.

Richard's grandfather took his wife with him when he went back to London on visits. On one of these visits, their son George Edward was born. He remained a British subject, and as a small boy he crossed the ocean with his parents several times. Shortly after he died, his son Richard "became fascinated with the possibilities of using the phase Between Two Worlds in or about the title" of a book he meant to write. George Edward, like Richard, was at home in two worlds but always in provisional ways. You get the sense that his bags were never unpacked. Also like Richard, he was the child of an unhappy marriage. His parents divorced and he shuttled from one boarding school to another. At the age of eleven he was sent to the Allen School in West Newton, near Boston—Harriet Beecher Stowe had preceded him there—then to the Mawry-Goff School in Rhode

Island. At St. George's in Newport—an Episcopal academy and, like Groton and St. Mark's, the embodiment of *noblesse oblige*—he mingled with the sons of the wealthy. By his father, George Edward was destined for wealth. But he quarreled with his father and refused to go to college. The break between them was permanent. Richard's future course is adumbrated in his story. "What's past is prologue."

At seventeen, George Edward confronted the world on his own. He had no formal credentials. "He was a free lance"—quoting from Henry Adams, his son's sacred book—"and no other career stood in sight or mind." Through Bishop William Lawrence, a powerful prelate in the Episcopal Church of Massachusetts and the son of a pious and successful woolen merchant, he got a job with the old firm of A. & A. Lawrence, makers of dry goods. George Edward was in his thirties when the firm passed him over for promotion. He gave notice and never held a permanent job again.

For the next ten years he lived in Auburndale, a part of Newton. He lived like a transient in the old Woodland Park Hotel. He played tournament golf and had the run of the golf course, even though he wasn't a member. What he did otherwise isn't known. About 1901 he met Helen Palmer, a schoolgirl in Cambridge. He was over forty when they married.

During the years of his marriage George Edward moved from job to job, and one by one his jobs failed. The Cambridge City Directory lists him as a broker in 1919. A year later he was making children's toys. This venture failed. He became a salesman, going between toy manufacturers and department stores like Jordan's and Filene's in Boston. He could remember those two stores when they were housed in a one-story building on the corner of Washington and Summer streets. The horse cars ran up and down Washington then. George Edward's job was lucky for his children. They could count on toys for Christmas if they couldn't count on anything else. He was a man for silver linings.

When he came home from work, he brought the children cake and ice cream. On holidays he never failed to bring his wife a box of candy from Bailey's on Temple Place. The boxes were painted with colorful scenes of old Boston. George Edward was proud of his wife's beauty and liked to take her out to dinner. They dined at Young's Hotel and drank wine with their meals. This made Helen dizzy, though. When they went canoeing, it made her frightened. After a while, she wouldn't go with him anymore. George Edward loved canoeing and walking in the woods. Before his fortunes fell he played tennis and golf, and the house on Irving Street was filled with his trophies. When the children were young, he flew kites with the boys and took the whole family for walks along the Charles on Sundays. They floated little boats in the river. He loved to read Dickens. He didn't have the money to do anything else.

Though he was poor, he honored his priorities. He gave his family the appurtenances of things. For years he took the boys on summer holidays to Bridgton, a pleasant resort town near Lake Sebago in southern Maine. When the girls were born, he managed to get them away in the summers. He sent them with their mother to Lanesboro in the Berkshires, where Helen's father lived. Richard as a child looked forward to these vacations with Grandpop. He looked forward also to summer holidays in Maine, and until he was sixteen he went with George Edward to Bridgton. Then they quarreled and he never went again. You could glimpse Richard in his father, in the smallness of stature, the courtliness and patience, and the turn for caustic speech. George Edward was a tart little man and had an eye for the ladies. When pretty girls came to visit, he always sparkled a little.

The depression that followed World War I took the wind out of him, the crash of 1929 destroyed him. He went to Bridgton for the last time a year later. Flourishing was beyond him after that. George Edward at sixty had a wife who was still young and five children to raise in hard times. He did his best and it wasn't enough. He sold fireworks on the side. He had a friend with American Fireworks in Boston and he got his daughter Helen a secretary's job with the firm. This connection was lucky, too. On Bunker Hill Day and the Fourth of July, George Edward brought home fireworks and he and his sons shot off rockets at night. For his girls, Pink and Pudge, he brought home squibs and sparklers. But he failed to make ends meet. "He cannot sell fireworks anyhow," his wife wrote scornfully to her oldest son. To buy them he needed a special license, to sell them he needed insurance; he couldn't afford either.

He worked, when he found work, until he was over seventy and suffering from heart disease. But his wife paid the bills—otherwise the family would have starved. So George Edward fell silent, except when he blustered. He sat in the back parlor—"he did *almost nothing* but sit in the parlor"—where Richard's friend George Orrok first encountered him. He *would* have been an Englishman, Orrok thought, "because he spoke very nicely." Another friend recalls him as a kind of adult dropout who quit work and spent his time walking around Cambridge. His presence waned as he got older. Taciturn was how people described him. For years he and Richard didn't speak. In an autobiographical story Richard wrote at twenty-two, he depicts his hero's father as "a silent man" who "spent hours looking into the corner where the steam pipes came out of the floor." The young hero in another sketch for a story feels that his own small fund of knowledge is useless: "he could never reveal it to his father." This wasn't from fear. "Although there was no great affection between them Bill was too kind, or perhaps too cowardly, to crush . . . [his father] completely." The only course of action open to this hero was to "live and wait."

A scrap of paper Richard kept for forty years is headed: "My Parents: 1925." He cannot remember when his mother lost her beauty, but only "that my father was once more jealous than he is now." He goes on: "My father is nearly 65 I think. Whenever he hears that one of his children has earned so much as a dollar, he lectures vacantly on the virtues of thrift and economy. His strictures grow more harsh and more comic with each month. Looking at him or thinking of him, I wonder always how soon he will die."

Richard's mother, Helen Palmer, was born in Lanesboro, outside Springfield, Massachusetts, on January 23, 1882. She was only twenty-two when she delivered her first child, and she died at eighty-one, only two years before his own death. Awareness of her family's distinction aggravated her sense that life hadn't turned out as it should have. Her gentility was affronted by the miscellaneous neighborhood she lived in most of her life, populated by "cheap Jews or Italians, the sort who stand on corners and chew gum." Her family tree had brought forth a Royal Councillor, a deputy governor of Massachusetts, a passenger on the *Mayflower*. Her ancestors were called Hezekiah and Abigail, Patience, Thankful, and Remember. Soldiers were conspicuous among them. They fought in the French and Indian Wars and in the Revolution. One of these ancestors was Jonathan Prescott, whose statue stands on Bunker Hill.

Helen's paternal grandfather, James Monroe Palmer, was a Congregationalist minister born in 1822 in the dairy farming country around Fairfield, Maine. In creating his own sense of the past, Richard elected him, and not the city-bred Blackmurs, as Founding Father. To himself, Richard was always a State of Maine man. James Monroe Palmer talked a lot and this blighted his career: he developed "minister's throat." When he couldn't deliver sermons, he turned inventor. The family gave him credit for inventing the air conditioning in Pullman cars. He was an improvident inventor, though; he held no patents and he never made a cent.

His son Charles James was improvident, too. He considered the lilies of the field. His obituary reckons him "a scholar and a saint." He gave himself to God and antiquarian research. To his daughter Helen he gave little but the odor of sanctity. Charles James Palmer was born in Kendall's Mills, at that time on the outskirts of Fairfield, on November 4, 1854. He graduated from Bowdoin College in the class of 1874. He did a postgraduate year at Bowdoin, then went down to Cambridge to study in the Protestant Episcopal School. A year later he entered the General Theological Seminary in New York City, which awarded him the Bachelor of Sacred Theology in 1882. Following his ordination as an Episcopal minister, he held a succession of brief pastorates, one of them in New York. His daughter Helen, when she married, retraced her father's steps. She couldn't live with him in Springfield, or not for very long. So she went to New York City to live, entertaining his aggressive presence at a remove.

In 1880 Charles James Palmer settled in Lanesboro, in the white clapboard house where Helen was born and where he lived for the next sixty-three years. To this house, a generation later, young Richard and his brothers and sisters came on visits to Grandpop in the summer vacations. The old stone church over which the Reverend Palmer presided—St. Luke's, built in 1836—is now a historical site. In old photographs its pastor looks like a hectic version of his grandson. He was a muscular Christian, and in his career he dramatized the injunction to go out upon the roads. He preached in every church or chapel in Berkshire County. Also he kept a herd of cows, and on Sundays he paid them his respects. "Grandfather had many amusing tales to tell," Richard's mother said. "I wish that I had gumption enough to work them into stories, for they are the real article, gay and sad, tragic and absurd."

The long life of Charles James Palmer is his best story. Even when he was blind and verging on ninety, he continued to visit the local schools and the jail house. He was a linguist who knew French and German. Also he wrote town and county histories. For years he served as secretary to his Bowdoin class. The *Boston Herald* in 1908 called him the busiest minister in Massachusetts. By then he had resigned his pastorate to become a county missionary, preaching the gospel in isolated hamlets. In this role he was subsidized by wealthy parishioners, and he continued in it for nearly thirty years. "Spiritual messenger of the Lenox millionaires to the lonely souls of the hidden villages"—that is how the story in the *Herald* began. "No matter how stormy is the weather, no matter in what condition are the roads, the Rev. Mr. Palmer always keeps his preaching engagements." Up at dawn, walking two miles to the trolley, preaching in as many as four towns a day and covering as many as fifty miles, he hardly got home before midnight. In ten years he delivered more than two thousand sermons. Some of this diligence might have rubbed off on Richard Blackmur, but didn't. Richard, by his own frequent and understated admission, was a monster of sloth. His grandfather exhausted whatever energy the family had to burn. On the other hand, Richard loved duties and this part of his legacy came down unimpaired. "At least in his more Mittyish moments," said one early friend, he saw himself as cut out for a preacher.

For Charles James Palmer, allegiance to duty was the governing imperative. It governed also in the life and writings of his famous cousin, the philosopher George Herbert Palmer, whose picture hangs over the stairs in Emerson Hall at Harvard. From these progenitors, Richard Blackmur derives in more than linear ways. George Herbert Palmer said: "Ally your labor with an institution." He did, for half a century. Duty, as he defined it, was the call of the whole to the part. Its one absolute law was that "there shall be law." On these formulations the successful labors of the philosopher and the clergyman depended. Richard in his later years took them to heart. Their impact for him, the outsider who knew nothing of institutional loyalty or absolute law, was equivocal and in the last resort subversive. The philosopher and the clergyman, like Richard's mother, lived to a great age. Longevity ran in the family. Jonathan Palmer, Richard's great-great-grandfather, born during the Revolution, outlived the Civil War. So the auspices for Richard were good. That he died when he was just sixty-one comments on his life and the desperation in which it involved him.

The Reverend Palmer married three times. He took his third wife in his sixties. His first wife, Helen Watson, survived her marriage to Charles James by only thirteen months. This was Helen's mother. Her death left Helen to a stepmother's care. Helen, before poverty overtook her, was beautiful. She was also the younger woman, and Gertrude, her stepmother, was insanely jealous. So Helen fled Lanesboro for Cambridge. She was still a girl, and except for two brief interludes she lived in Cambridge the rest of her life. In her unhappy story, her son's early story is predicted. The failure of her marriage is predicted, too. Helen's childhood resembles the childhood of her future husband, the offspring of a broken marriage and the butt of his angry father's disappointment. Helen and George Edward were fatal opposites. They felt cheated by the past and alone in the present. Each wanted to redress the past in the future. So they gambled away the present and ensured the waste to come. Richard's sister Betty wondered if her mother and father were not looking for too much from each other when they married—"and then came Dick, my mother's favorite. The rest is fantasy."

When her mother died, Helen gave her love to her father's sister Caroline, Richard's Great Aunt Carie. But Carie went to Japan to disseminate the gospel. In the East she met Charles Graham Gardner, an Englishman, an Episcopal minister, and a missionary like herself. They waited out the six-year period to which they were committed, then they married and came home by boat around the Cape of Good Hope. Their return made Helen happy. She had loved Aunt Carie, now she included Uncle Graham in her love. When the Gardiners left America to settle in England, she wrote to them faithfully. Later she wrote to their daughter Beatrice, too. Helen had a great fund of love, but the object of her love was always receding. Again, she makes you think of Richard.

As a schoolgirl, Helen lived with the Bartletts in the yellow house on the corner where Irving Street and Cambridge Street cross. Number 52 Irving Street was only Mr. Whitman's house then. She passed it often and it is hard not to see her as walking on her grave. But she had a lot of fun, living with the Bartletts. Dan, the Bartlett boy, made her welcome. So did Aunt Nanny and Uncle George Palmer, her father's younger brother. The Palmers lived on Ware Street, two blocks away. Helen moved in with them when she entered high school. For the next six years, until she left college, they were like the parents she had lost. Uncle George was a medical doctor, cultivated, charming, a linguist, a traveler. He was happily married, his social life was full. When he and his wife entertained friends for bridge, they spoke only French. But Aunt Nanny died still young, and ten years later Uncle George took his own life.

Helen had wanted to be a medical doctor. In the end she settled for training as a physical therapist. It was as close to medical training as a young woman at the turn of the century could come. After graduating from Cambridge High and Latin School in 1900, she enrolled in the Sargent School for Physical Education. Dudley Allen Sargent had created this school at the urging of the Society for the Collegiate Instruction of Women, known then as the Harvard Annex, subsequently as Radcliffe College. In the old building on the corner of Everett Street and Massachusetts Avenue, Helen Palmer learned remedial and preventive exercises. Dr. Sargent insisted on more than his pupils really had to know. He taught Helen the names of all the bones in the body. Though she wasn't a nurse, she got the rudiments of nursing. Her children never needed a doctor when they were young.

One friend stands out from these years. This was her roommate, Mary Blackmur, George Edward's cousin and the daughter of his Uncle Horace. "My mother had a bit of fun with Mary Blackmur," Betty said. They used to stay up after hours, putting a mitten over the light. The mitten got hot and of course they were caught. They were always in trouble and always getting caught. Helen didn't know George Edward then; and Richard didn't know his future wife, also named Helen, when he went into business with her brother Wallace. Comparing small things with great, there is almost a sense of Atredeian fatality in the story of this mother and her son.

Dr. Sargent was at Bowdoin with Charles James Palmer and at Harvard with Helen's Uncle George. It was George who decided her choice of career and then fortuitously helped to abort it. She never taught physical education. She was attending the Sargent School when Uncle George introduced her to his friend, George Edward Blackmur. Helen was still in her teens. A year later she graduated and she and George Edward were married.

Richard's parents were living at 375 Main Street in Springfield when he was born there in 1904. As a boy, he wrote stories about his parents and their tormented life together. In one of these stories his young hero has learned what marriage had meant to his mother, learned "that his father hadn't worked during the first ten years, that they had spent Grandfather Manley's money, lived in his old house, eaten off his old silver, slept between his old sheets. She'd never had a home that was really hers; everything was second hand. The old bruises came up again too where Mr. Manley had beaten her in jealous rages. He saw how her mind had been subjugated, how she was forced to think what her husband thought, do what he did. All these things helped to explain her condition, but being aware of them wasn't a cure."

Richard was still an infant when his parents left Springfield for New York. They welcomed this move as a fresh start, not understanding yet how the past is prologue. George Edward got a job as a broker on Wall Street. He found lodgings for his wife and son on Central Park West, later on Riverside Drive. They shared the rental of these apartments with other tenants, among them Katherine Lee Bates, who wrote popular fiction. When Mrs. Bates entertained, she included Richard's mother in her parties. The famous people Helen met at these literary parties nurtured her self-esteem. Life in the city was exciting, she thought. She remembered the imposing doorman outside the apartment house, and walking in Central Park with young Richard. But already she was pregnant again, first with Ted, then two years later with George. Helen was nearing thirty, the bloom was off her marriage, and she had three boys to take care of. George Edward was amiable. When Helen was pregnant with Ted and George and after she delivered, he had a maid in to help. Nights, he cared for the children himself. To his wife in her second confinement, he wrote to tell how Dick missed her and was restless in his sleep. He said he missed her, too. For his wife and children, nothing was too good. This was if wishes were horses. He had a high taste and bequeathed it to his son. When the boys needed clothing, he took them to Best & Company on Fifth Avenue. As they got older, he took them on excursions. They went to Asbury Park in New Jersey. Richard remembered Asbury Park. In a short story he published at twenty-three, he looked back at the queer ungallant youth he had been and at the little boy revolving "so many things" in mind, full of fears but full of curiosity too, self-blinded, walking with his eyes all wrinkled up shut, arms out, fingers quivering like antennae, endlessly searching down long stretches of boardwalk.

The move to New York, like the move to Springfield, ended badly. Money dwindled and the wife took stock of her husband. George Edward got a whimsical postcard that tells the story. It came to him at 69 Wall Street with a picture of his sons, Dick and Ted. The inscription read: "Results of your earliest efforts." The date was 1909, when Richard was five; that year the family returned to Cambridge. They lived first in Felton Hall, a dark red brick building near the Cambridge Library. From Mrs. Bartlett, Dan's sister-in-law, they rented a small housekeeping apartment, and they took their meals with other tenants in a central dining room. A year later they departed this communal indignity for Oliver Street, where Helen's fourth child, named for herself, was born. Then they moved to Irving Street, back to the beginning.

The three-story frame dwelling at 52 Irving Street was big enough to accommodate the children and then some. Richard's mother took in roomers, most of them Harvard students. Often they were difficult when it came to paying the rent. Some of her roomers were celebrated, among them the critic and art collector Leo Stein, Gertrude's brother—"a peculiar sort of chump," Helen wrote to Richard, like "a dug up holy ghost." She said she didn't care for him. She cared even less for her role as "high-class chambermaid." In time this role ruined her health. Her beauty faded, until with pathetic vanity she refused to let friends take her picture. She grew frail, like Richard in his youth, and in middle age showed the effects of malnutrition. But even in middle age her voice on the telephone remained fresh and girlish.

In an undated fragment from his adolescent years, Richard describes his mother. He covers his tracks routinely, making her fat where she was thin. "She was raised in a strict Presbyterian family, raised as a young lady should be. Her fun hadn't started until she reached college, and then marriage had ended it all." Her son Bill, who has learned to take advantage of her talkative moods, wonders as he listens if she will reveal something new. He waits on these revelations. She is praising the Charleston now and the Black Bottom. " 'They were so much fun.' She stepped away from the sink and started to Charleston humming 'Sweet Georgia Brown' as she danced. . . . Bill joined her, a sad smile on his face. 'Aren't we silly?' she asked. Tiring soon, she went back to the sink. 'Your father would think we were crazy. He's so conservative, won't do anything that makes him look the least bit undignified.'" The son's impotence before his mother's misery hurts him more than anything else, "more than the unkempt house, the insults, the embarrassment when his friends came in at the wrong times." So this elegiac tale is for Richard no less than his mother. When he looks up, he sees that she is crying. "She pressed her distended stomach against him. Her wet soapy arms clutched his neck. . . . 'I'm sorry,' she said. . . . 'I promise, I'll stop, so sorry.'" Climbing the stairs to his room, "Bill tried to remember whether that was the second or third time this month."

As Helen's life coarsened, her character changed. Self-pity rose in her. She had almost no social life of her own. Friends asked her out and she was always "too busy." One night Helen Dickson and her sister Katharine came by the house. They had made up their minds to give her a good time and they wouldn't take no for an answer. But this mother was obdurate. She summoned Betty, a high-school freshman, and pushed her out the door in her place. For the children she was willing to lay down her life. This is what she did. But she made their lives a casualty of her unrelenting affection. The affection was tempered by malice. Until Betty was in her forties, she would hear her mother say: "My daughter will do nothing for me!" In the house the children walked warily, forbidden to touch. The girls mustn't cook, the kitchen was hers. She ruled in the kitchen and spent her days killing bugs, scrubbing toilets with chlorine, redoing rooms, removing stains, sewing Ted's pants, cleaning the typewriter with carbona. Washing was a ritual and went on forever. She lived in dread of sickness. In her letters she dwelt incessantly on plasters and iodine, nerve tonics, laxatives. Her great subject was money. "Love and thanks for the five," she ends a letter to Richard.

Money was George Edward's great subject, too. He wouldn't allow his wife an adequate light in the kitchen. He "never has allowed one since we have had electricity—although before then, he used to sit out here evenings to read. Well, this week he has not been able to get into the dining room, and so he goes out to the kitchen, where there is but one, high light, and reads there, and then complains of how his eyes are bothered." The family fortunes sagged lower, and the complaining turned to petulance and self-justification. "I guess Father has an *inferiority* complex—for he is forever talking about *his brains* and how *he* never yet saw anything that *he* couldn't do." Always he is shouting at her, putting her down. To his unhappy mother, Richard played Hamlet—"Assume a virtue if you have it not"—admonishing his mother to avoid his father's bed. "You say you should think I would like to get away from the same bed etc etc—Well, I wish that I might go away and never see this house or furniture or street or Father again. I'd like to go to a brand new place with you children and not be jawed at for *every*thing."

In 1933 the family moved to Wendell Street, only a few blocks away, and it was hardly the brand-new place Helen craved. The quarrels persisted or they grew more intense, tragedy meeting comedy. "My Pussy —Father calls him 'LITTLE PUS' "—having escaped from the house, Helen filled a dish with cat food and went outside and howled. "Father went forth, and in sort of an imitation of me, howled also. . . . Both boys acted like madmen all the afternoon; I shudder when I look forward to spring and open doors." Richard at seventeen wrote of his parents that "they knew not what they did." In a letter he said how he had forgiven them. To himself he said, however: "In my family the males not only master their wives; they frustrate their souls. Did he understand my mother, my father should kill himself from shame."

The agony ended when Richard was thirty-six. He was living in Maine and got a letter from his mother. "Father died at about 8 this A.M. Fell downstairs yesterday. . . . Now, you must not think of coming." George Edward was cremated and his ashes were scattered in the Charles River. The funeral service was conducted with "utmost privacy—simplicity and lack of expense." There were no flowers.

Until he left in 1930, Richard lived at the center of the pulling and hauling in his parents' house. His mother took his side when he quarreled with his father. She had wanted something—who can say just what—and George Edward had failed her. Richard bore the brunt of his mother's disappointment. To this better version of her husband, she confided her hopes and poured out her unhappiness. "My mother idolized Dick," Betty said, "and although she mothered us all, he was her first and most precious, and somehow she kept him to herself."

Richard at twenty-six was still his mother's boy. By then he was married, but he came to see her faithfully twice a week. Tuesday nights he came for supper, Friday afternoons he and his mother spent together and alone. Then he discovered music and the Friday concerts at Symphony Hall, and this was another reason for his mother to complain. Helen Dickson, when she and Richard were courting, tried hard to please her and didn't. She was the younger woman who had taken Richard away. After the marriage Richard's mother said morosely to her youngest child, "Now you may talk to me, I don't have anyone." When Richard went to Princeton, she lived for his letters and read them aloud to his brothers and sisters. "I always felt I knew some of his friends whom I never met," Betty said. Present or absent, he was the cynosure.

Helen Dickson, when her marriage to Richard was failing, complained bitterly that he wrote his mother every day of his life. Maybe she exaggerated. He didn't flag in her service, though, and his wife took second place. When he was in his fifties you find him hunting a photograph "for my ancient mother," or begging off an engagement with Conrad Aiken "because I must be in Cambridge for five days of the week." This was his vacation and he devoted it to her. In her letters she addressed him as Dear Doggie or Blessed or Dear Beautie or Little Boy. This made him squirm. She said: "Look disgusted if you like, but you are still my baby." If he was sick she prayed that, should he need an operation, God would guide the doctor's hand and mind. She supposed the doctor would scoff at that, also "some, in fact, most, of your associates." Maybe when they were older they would "find out how silly and empty they seem." She had heard them poke fun at religion, wedding rings, etc. To her they sounded as though they had never grown up. She said to her son, "I do not include you, entirely." Richard was then thirty-five.

It was different with the other children. Helen scrimped and made their clothing and enlivened their nights with storytelling. But she enjoyed Richard separately. Keeping him to herself, she kept the children apart. Richard learned remoteness at his mother's knee. So did Ted, her second son. Ted resembled Richard in his smallness of stature, and he felt this to his mortification. He liked women but could never get close to a woman, and the relationships he made were mostly stormy. In Cambridge as a young man, he was often taken for his older brother. They walked alike, their shoulders hunching a little. Ted was a wizened and miniature Richard and sometimes when he passed, friends thought that Richard had snubbed them. He admired Richard greatly, or said so. In Mrs. Blackmur's house that was taken for granted. "We were all very proud of Dick," Betty remembered. "He had a life apart in his literary world, and we loved to hear stories of his doings and his friends." These stories made the rounds and came back to their source. At Princeton in the fifties, Richard got a letter from a self-anointed poet: "I am, indeed, glad to have heard, from your brother, that you are interested in Poetry (and Literature); and have had many of your own works published!" So Ted was talking again. He was an enthusiast, but by fits and starts. He felt that he couldn't live up to his brother. Sometimes he plucked up courage and argued with Dick about education. He had his own ideas and he urged them shyly but stubbornly, too. He loved literature and kept returning for courses at Harvard, but he wouldn't write the required papers and he never took a degree. Ted wanted to go on learning, not be finished with learning. This might have won Richard's approval.

George, the youngest boy, favored his father. The day he left high school he found work with the Canadian National Railroad. He didn't go back to school after that. He spent his adult life as a passenger agent, traveling from city to city. George stood in Dick's shadow. But Ted eclipsed him, too, and so did his sisters. He used to tell Betty that she looked like a Radcliffe girl and that Radcliffe girls would never look at him. He got married when he was young, but his wife left and took their daughter with her. When he died in Detroit, he was only fifty-one. "The last time," his mother wrote on a card he had sent her.

Ted and George had newspaper routes when they were boys. They worked for Amee Brothers on Brattle Street in Harvard Square. Christmas mornings the family opened their presents when it was still dark, so the boys could get the papers delivered. Ted's early morning hours horrified his brother Dick, a night person who was only half awake by noon and not completely awake until evening. When Mr. Amee retired, he left the business to Ted. But Ted, like his father, wasn't much of a businessman. He sold out and took a job with the *Christian Science Monitor*. Later he taught radio at an adult school in Boston. He liked to monkey with the radio and he had his own transmitter. Athletics absorbed him. He spent a lot of time at the Boston Skating Club. His life, said Richard coldly, venturing a rare personal comment, turned around the Bruins and the Celtics. Richard shared the Yankee view that blood is thinner than water.

When the family lived in Springfield, Richard was still the only child. Looking back, he doubted if he could understand what had happened to him during this period. "The assertion of understanding is our great metaphor," he said. Truth was pre-conscious and aloof from understanding. On the other hand, the whole object of criticism was to make "the pre-conscious *consciously* available." So he sought to recapture the unified state he identified with his earliest days: babies know best. A chance encounter at seventeen led to this depressing conclusion. He had almost knocked over a baby carriage in the street. Stopping to apologize to the nurse, "I became aware that the child was gazing serenely through me: there was a terrible, unutterable wisdom in its calm, unconcerned glance. . . . I believe, somehow, that babies are the embodiment of the wisdom of all time, which knows all and remains indifferent to all, perceiving all to be illusion."

Perhaps he could find his way back to the womb. "If as I think memory works like prophecy pushing from known things to things unknown, only backward rather than forward, why then may I not reach even across the gap of birth?" The gap was decisive, though. Parturition, "as ghastly for the son as for the mother," destroyed forever "the possibility of perfect knowledge" by imposing on the body "the burden of personality." The seedling, before the "cutting off"—this was Richard's phrase for emergence from the womb—was complete in its germinative existence, not compelled yet to the odious "declaration of personality." The perfect truth it possessed, "all sense and no senses," was perfect because remote from deliberation and purpose. "Then, as never after, thought and its object, action and reaction, were one and the same. There was no occasion to dramatise because everything was drama." Afterward came the "terrible deprivation" of birth. "The knotting of the navel cord was the first final action I suffered." Blessedly, it was succeeded by immediate amnesia which gratified the infant's need—"a need I still feel, to experience nothing at all."

So the blankness that followed birth, Richard thought, was like death, the last and best action which is the negating of action. All the interim, between the first torpor and the last forgetting, belonged to the fatal differentiation of consciousness. "Henceforth the universe was a wilderness of signs, most of them meaningless and all of them misleading, which yet must be followed . . . so long as life endured." No wonder the infant lost its serenity. Its squalling was taken as a healthy sign of life, a love of action, but that was a mistake. "The squall was full of terror and hate and rebellion, the first sign that the flesh had recognized, in the flowering of separate life, the seed of separate death." Richard asked himself: "How else can it be when I wake in the bottom of darkness that I find myself screaming?" He was in his twenties when he entered these gloomy questions and gloomier answers in his private journal. Resuming the past, they predict the long future. Much later he wrote how "all knowledge is a fall from the paradise of undifferentiated sensation." His life on one side describes a straight line from the beginning.

Boyhood aggravated his infantile fears. He went back in mind to New York City and imagined the small boy he had been, "lying on his belly, naked under the bedclothes, naked within his nightshirt," aware of his body but more aware of his defenselessness. "He lay in the state of being threatened, he lay about to be touched. There was no safety for him in the body in which he hid." He thought "the shelter might crumble under the pressure of the outside, the foreign, the unknown." He had to deal with the unknown "whenever he shut his eyes or the lights were put out." At eighteen he said how the presence of any mass, especially at night, came to rest on his shoulders. It wasn't simply that he felt this presence as fact but that it seemed to him alive, "a kind of terror impending." From the looming mass, tentacles reached out for him and he lay rigid, unable to move. This he called "the grey evil of the night." Against it he sought a hut that would save him, and "if he felt himself going to sleep he felt a cubby just his own shape being built upon him." But his body offered no protection. "The body was the very seat of terror." What frightened him was not the chance of death but "what might happen to his life in his body." For the body, as he acknowledged, was his master. In all his thoughts, in all his feelings, he sensed an antecedent thought and feeling he couldn't know. This was his ancestral being, "an accumulated allegiance" which consciousness was unable to utter, "but which controls and deeply qualifies the specious utterances" that all of us take for true. "In speaking, in thinking, in writing, we forget not only the body, but that our words, willy nilly, interpret the body."

The Pyrrhonist or total skeptic is already nascent in these early reflections. He admonished himself how every trembling hand—remembering Wallace Stevens—can "make us squeak, like dolls, the wished-for words." This is the body's revenge on the self-conscious intellectual. Blackmur, accepting it, is the critic as dilettante, one of the fops of fancy. He fought against it, though, and toward the end of his life, in an outburst of polemical fury, he wrote essays dedicated to coercing or denying the dark ancestral forces he felt moving inside him. His life dramatized the contention between the voices of unknowing and the yea-sayers who set themselves to know. He was Pyrrho the skeptic and Pater the solipsist. At the same time he was Aristotle preying on the world, and Freud reclaiming the turbid waters of the Zuyder Zee. He sought to accommodate these radically different psychologies, "to make of my philosophy a house in which to live, with one or two rooms in which to retire, but all the rest for public or social life; above all to have such a house that I would not be lonely in it, and would think it a good place to die."

So he labored at building a house for his spirit, and though it was divided against itself he made it stand. He considered that bewilderment was the terminus of all thinking, but resolved to push on to "the maximum degree of bewilderment" in order to awaken and clarify his knowledge, however circumscribed in last things. "One must know what it is that reaches the state of bewilderment." On this imperative, fearfully limited but also heroic, his poetry and criticism depended.

Early boyhood in Cambridge begot in Richard his fatal lassitude, his conviction of apartness that fostered helplessness no less than independence, and his willingness to let someone else do it. Mostly, "someone else" was a woman. The surprise is that this writer got anything written or that this celebrated traveler got beyond the front door. Until he was almost nine, his mother kept him from school. She was his tutor and his companion. She took him to the Cambridge Library and the librarians raised their eyebrows at the titles he asked for. He was precocious but stunted. Mrs. Blackmur held him so close he couldn't breathe.

In the fourth grade he entered the Peabody Grammar School. To his schoolmates he seemed a dim presence. "The name is familiar"—that is how they recollect him. In 1916, when Richard was twelve, he enrolled in his mother's school, Cambridge High and Latin. He didn't cut much of a figure there either: once more he is a name, but no face to go with it. One acquaintance remembers him. "He was, of course, the bookworm," said Richard de Rochemont, afterward a motion-picture and television producer. In his reading, Richard mixed good with bad. Joyce and Max Bodenheim were about on a par. The "innumerable felicities" of Cabell's *Jurgen* delighted him. So did the style of W. H. Hudson as it rested "not upon the content, but upon the beauty of the sound." Technique was his principal study. Smollett and Fielding had nothing of technique (Smollett remained an enthusiasm, though), and there wasn't much he could use in Sinclair Lewis, but he found what he was looking for in Ford Madox Ford. Later he understood how Ford was like himself in perilous ways, and that was the end of his allegiance. He admired Hardy's novels, all that stagy pessimism, poor Tess and the President of the Immortals. Conrad was even better than Hardy.

His great master was "the glorious Henry." James had what no other novelist had: "a sensuous knowledge taken at its own so high value." Even in his teens, he had got the style pat. He was an esthete. The artist was the enemy of society, he said, and "not merely this. . . . whatsoever is charming in society has been produced and persists through art. . . . the rest is blather."

De Rochemont went often to the house on Irving Street, "where Mrs. Blackmur rented rooms to students and Mr. Blackmur was not much in evidence." In the room at the top of the house, covered with scenes from Dante's Inferno, Richard conducted chemistry experiments—"a boom and an awful smell" and his mother materializing out of the smoke. There also he carried on experiments in the conservation of semen—his own, de Rochemont gathered. Sometimes he was Shelley's romantic hero Prince Athanase and sometimes P. T. Barnum. With de Rochemont and "a sturdy lad" named Harry Goodwin, he "planned such aesthetic and unrealized projects as a minstrel show or a vaudeville act." Of the three of them, said de Rochement later, Richard was the only potential intellectual. "Even if I had stayed in Cambridge I know Dick would have lost interest in me and in Goodwin as not being on his level of culture. We respected him as bright and different."

Without question, he was different: a prodigy who stood "seven thousand feet higher than the rest of mankind" and was lower than all the rest in his dejection, an atheist for whom Christianity was "antagonistic to all forms of intelligent life," and a superstitious Christian who crossed himself in fear, a loner with no friends and only a few acquaintances—his own characterization, in which complacency participated. He was hated, he said, "because I have always had the disgusting habit of attempting to speak the truth." Another habit was playing on his senses. He speculated that it would be easy to go mad "in the surge and swoon of sound." He practiced shutting his eyes and letting the silent roar of sound overwhelm him, creating what he thought was new knowledge and a new ecstasy. "I tried this in the public library the other day," he wrote to his cousin, George Anthony Palmer. "The table began to shake, and I thought I should have arisen and torn it in nine pieces. Something must have happened to my eyes, for I saw something very like fear in the eyes of a young lady who was looking at me."

He cultivated fear in others and amused himself by shooting blanks at sacred totems. (This species of amusement persisted.) "God is like a fart; he exudes, and is gone—leaving a circular acridity, and a sense of relief." Bernard Shaw was a sympathetic prophet to his immaturity, and this allegiance persisted, too. A letter to his cousin begins with the heading: "Anno odi," and plunges at once into what he hoped were shocking aperçus. "Reflecting, savagely": "man is . . . a degradation. . . . Progress consists of the interpolation of extraneity. . . . Love is the immortalising core of despair; a grand despair is a great glory." He was a Byronic hero who, wanting "to live vividly, vitally," was reduced to cold pronouncements, having got through all experience and found it a cheat: "Masturbation is less felicitous than coitus, since one escapes the huge ecstasy of disgust." His letter ended: "I can keep this up all day."

Betty Eberhart, Richard's choirmate at Christ Church Episcopal, where he sang with Ted and George on Sunday mornings, remembers him in those days as "an unathletic sort . . . with a definite opinion brooking no opposition on a variety of subjects. You bring up the chemoreception of butterflies and Dick would be off explaining." He was "a hopeless know-it-all," Mrs. Eberhart thought. But he was lovable too, in his character of polymath. Also he was a gourmet, anyway in hope: cold artichokes with French dressing made a tolerable repast.

Elizabeth Gilbert, the younger daughter of the composer Henry Gilbert, fell in love with the adolescent pontificator—"Though young in years his word was that of God"—and when he got older she sent him a rueful sonnet.

> Now that he's grown, he's dropped the tone all-tragic
> The smile of grave profundity is gone;
> He steps out forthright—in his eye is magic,
> Forgotten is the attitude forlorn.

The sonnet concludes:

> But now the merry air's become elective
> I'm almost sure the pose was more effective.

The forlorn attitude wasn't a pose, though, and if Richard was young Mauberley, partly a comic figure, he was also young Pound, an ambiguous hero. "Words have our glory in keeping," he wrote. But the glory he had in keeping was intermittent and perhaps an illusion. The world outside the self was real—he wasn't a solipsist—and read him lessons in "what seems almost certainly to be the tragedy of my life." He tried to run away to sea and the recruiter brought him home again. Against the gentility by which his parents set such store—they were in the Blue Book then—he chose for his companions a gang of young toughs. Ten or twelve years later, he thought about them and what they were doing. "Fred [Lamkin] is a bartender at the NE Press Club and is sore because he can't steal out of the till. Eddie Haran is at Deer Island for six months and is then to be returned to Cleveland to finish five years for robbery. Jack White has just finished five years for burglary. . . . Shep Lee is at present in a Virginia Prison for robbery and has served time variously for forgery and check-kiting. . . . These were the boys with whom I associated from 15 to 17."

The associates dropped away or they were put away. From the high-school years, three friends remained. George Anthony Palmer, Richard's cousin by adoption, was the closest of these friends. He and Richard played at being *poètes maudits*, and one was more successful than the other. "The guy who really suffered from intellectual jealousy of Dick was his cousin," said the musicologist Rob Darrell. "George Anthony made a better living than Dick for years but could never make the grade as a poet." He did all the indicated things. Just after the war Pound's Cantos were coming out, and he sacrificed two meals a day to buy the most recent volume and hurried off with it to Irving Street. Cantos V, VI, and VII were especially dazzling, in part because they defied understanding. "This," said George Anthony, "was the way we wanted to write." His exemplary poem called "Portrait: R.P.B." reads like inspired parody, but that wasn't how he meant it.

> The austere head emerges
> From the medallions in haze,
> As from the narrow lips
> The austere, burnished phrase.

There were a couple of Greek words in what followed.

"Way back," said Tessa Horton—she was the older sister of Elizabeth Gilbert, and Richard's first love—"George Anthony wrote a book of poems, and it was the most pretentious thing, it was terrible. He wanted desperately to be a poet but he didn't have the ability." This tells only half the story. "He became a good poet . . . by sheer *working* at it." There was the poem he wrote about the sea at Montegan. "You have a sense that he sat and watched the sea endlessly. He has the spirit and the very essence of the sea in that poem." In his youth with Richard, he was dapper in dress and erect like a foil. In later years he was small and frail with a wispy moustache, and the part of his hair fell away sharply and showed a great domed forehead like Shakespeare's. He made a proving ground of the years beween youth and age. "When he was young, he was absolutely awful. He was the kind who ordered waiters around. He would say, 'I wanted it *this* way.'" But he got better as he got older. He inherited money and had the use of money. This put him in a better frame of mind and he studied politeness, except to waiters. "I miss him," Tessa said. "I'm terribly sorry that he died." But he made a good death and ended on a rising curve.

Paul Rowe in his life showed first the incandescence, then the long subsiding. Like Richard, he hungered greatly. But other people and their claims took precedence, or you can say that his talent was less urgent. When his father died, Paul gave up Harvard to take care of his family. He became a composer. Nights he put himself through law school, and later he arranged Conrad Aiken's divorce, but he never practiced law. For forty-three years he served the *Boston Globe*. The life he had aimed at was better than this—he was a sympathetic student of the modern classics, and he got on to *Ulysses* just after it was published and kept the first edition hidden in his bedroom—but he bowed without complaining to the exigencies of things. "He was a very, very good friend," George Orrok said, a quiet man to Richard's marathon talker. Political activity absorbed him. For Richard, "it was more satisfactory to stay at home and curse." Paul was a lady chaser—"tall, dark, and ill favored, but amiable enough," said de Rochemont. He loved music; he and Richard lived for the concerts in

Symphony Hall. When Paul could afford it, he joined Richard and George Orrok at the ballet. "We saw the great Russian dancer Nijinsky. We saw Pavlova." Ballet was Richard's passion, and he wondered at nineteen why it hadn't taken root in American soil. "We have the dancers." But when his colleague Lincoln Kirstein answered to the need, he missed the point of what Kirstein had achieved.

Richard and friends were into everything in those days, Orrok said. They liked going to séances where they could be titillated and skeptical, too. Margery the Medium was popular then, and Paul and Richard went to see her in Emerson Hall. She had made contact with her dead brother Walter, and Walter titillated them by flipping doughnuts with his teleplasmic arm. In imitation of Margery, they tried to manage ectoplasm—Jerry Whiting, a Harvard student and subsequently a Harvard professor, became their star performer—and they marveled when the poet Foster Damon explained how ectoplasm was the mysterious First Matter hinted at by the alchemists. This was 1921, and Paul and Richard were Jonathan and David. They weren't ever going to get married, but whoever married first had to buy the other dinner at Frank Locke's on Winter Place. The friendship didn't die until they got married, and Paul's wife made him choose between her and his friends. But Paul's sister Elinor could see how their roads were sure to diverge. "It's as if he and Dick each had half of a wonderful life." Richard came up in the world and died childless. Paul lived in anonymity and was cherished by his sons and his grandsons. His sister grieved that he had missed the career his brains should have given him, "but he perhaps did not grieve for himself."

When Richard was fourteen and Lewis MacKay two years older, they discovered Ezra Pound. Richard had Pound's picture thumbed up on the wall. He was the god of their idolatry. Richard's mother laughed and said he looked like Jesus Christ. Paul and George Anthony sat before the picture, too. The four of them were junior prebends in a church of their establishing. Eliot was another of their idols. They had *Prufrock* by heart and they stayed up all night in Richard's room in the attic, reading the poetry aloud. Richard was the exegete. "He calls himself the foremost American exponent of T. S. Eliot," Paul Rowe told his sister. The high literary tone was too much for Lewis, and Paul didn't care for it either; after a while they tiptoed out the door. They were bored by the mentor, George Anthony said, but they didn't give up on the friend.

Lewis MacKay had a broad smile and a gentleman's manner. With Richard's mother, this assured him a welcome. "He would make a woman feel good," Betty said. Later he married Tessa, whom Richard loved and lost. His special talent was coping. He seemed "older than the rest of us,"

Rob Darrell said, and this difference was emphasized by the Harvard accent he affected. The Depression was a nuisance which he took in his stride; where others starved, he scraped a living. Working the mill towns as a cotton factor, he traveled the length and breadth of New England. Once in the Berkshires he asked a local lounger, "I say, my dear fellow, can you direct me to the depot?" This question getting no answer, he put it again. Finally he got an answer: "How would you like to be knocked on your ass?" He thought this story worth telling on himself. His friends were surprised when Lewis took sick—they could see no reason for it. He should have lived to a great age, dying at last "old, bald, and sere." But his life described a broken arc: he was thirty-four when he died of cancer.

Richard made a suspicious friend for whom betrayal was just around the corner. He wrote to his cousin, "More than five fingers make a monster, and more than four friends produce sore thumbs." He was wary of friends but lucky in them too, and they instructed him how nothing vital dies. Meeting Philip Horton for the first time—Phil was Tessa's second husband—he saw the shiny bald head just like Lewis MacKay's, and for days he lived in memory, his mind crowded with ghosts.

In the house on Irving Street there were five children now, in addition to the boarders who occupied the second floor. The children lived on top of each other—Ted and George by this time in the attic with Richard—but they didn't make a close family and their paths, then and later, didn't intersect. The more, the less merry. Eileen Simpson, who knew Richard as well as anyone, heard talk of a brother living twenty miles from Princeton whom he never saw. This was actually his sister Helen. Richard was six when Helen was born. She was a fat baby, so the family called her Pudge. For many years she lived in Bound Brook, New Jersey, with her businessman husband Leonard Van Eck. She might have been living at the Antipodes. "I don't hardly know Van myself," Richard said of the husband, "having hardly done more than exchange amenities with him ever." Leonard had a job with American Cyanimid, Helen was an active member of the DAR. Richard kept them in the closet. Once, Helen and Van had him over for dinner. She served a hot dinner right on the dot in the middle of Sunday, and no drinks to go with it. He regretted the drinks. Otherwise the event would have gone unreported.

Eileen Simpson thought that two women loved Richard unequivocally. One was his mother and the other his sister Betty. When Betty was a student at Radcliffe, she read her brother's books. His later books she found "somewhat complicated and difficult to comprehend." It wasn't to the books that she pinned her affection. Betty lived at home until her mother was almost eighty. "I was always there," she said, "being the youngest." When Mrs. Blackmur died and Richard came up for the funeral, he told Betty that everything she had done for their mother was right. Her career as a social worker realized the career that had opened briefly for Helen Palmer at the Sargent School long ago. Helen as a young woman had wanted to travel, then her wings were clipped. Betty traveled in the West and went on walking trips in Scotland. She climbed in the Alps. "My mountain-climbing sister," Richard called her. She loved the mountains and the countryside and "being close physically with my eyes, ears, and feet."

Like her mother, Betty idolized Richard, a remote and brilliant young man eleven years her senior. In his letters he always addressed her as Pink. She was like a pink carnation, he thought. When his cousin George Anthony stayed for the night, she carried coffee and toast to his room in the attic. Once Cousin George brought her mother violets in a brass bowl, and she treasured this gift as if it were hers; and once, in the bookstore near the *Harvard Lampoon*, she curled up to read a book and remembered Richard saying how it was far beyond her. Sometimes Tessa Gilbert, as she then was, put on a skit for the family with her sister Elizabeth. Betty was shy and gawky and she marveled at Tessa and her lovely high cheekbones on a slender face and her beautiful, dark arched eyebrows. When Betty was little, Richard let her come inside his guard. He was always good with children. He paid her a penny apiece to read Shakespeare's plays, and he wanted to know why she didn't read poetry. Yeats was the poet, he told her. Betty was just over the chicken pox when he took her to the circus. They looked into a barrel where a beautiful woman sat among crossed swords and she smiled up at him and he twinkled down to her. Richard was the rare man who did really twinkle when he smiled.

George Anthony wondered why Betty and Richard didn't meet when they got older. Richard had to need her and want her, she said. She felt it would never have entered his head to expect her to drop down for the weekend. One summer, when he was staying at Oak Point in Maine, he invited her to visit. This was Helen Dickson's place and Helen prompted the invitation. Betty was at camp only a short distance away at Bar Harbor. She raised a few mild objections: perhaps she wouldn't fit in with their group? Richard didn't press her and she didn't make the trip.

Word of Richard's achievements was meat and drink to Betty. Sometimes when she spoke of him, she called him RPB. She couldn't break through to her distinguished brother's life and she saw him only rarely on his own ground. His friends were often her friends. She had dinner with Phoebe and George Anthony Palmer, and when George read his poetry at

Pat Eden's apartment, they invited her to come. Richard's wife Helen was there—she was his former wife now. But Richard never came to these gatherings.

In the fifties Richard was "speaking some of T. S. Eliot's works at Boston College." Betty hadn't been asked; even so, she went to hear him. He was surprised and flustered to see her. He burst out that probably she hadn't understood a word. She thought "he must have been hurt inside and thought we did not care about his accomplishments." Like Thomas Mann's composer-hero, he was cold, aloof, and proud. This was "because of the great human pride," he said, "the temptation to re-create himself in his own fastness." This character was his legacy, and he gave of himself as he could.

As a freshman in high school, Richard studied English and Latin, Algebra and American History. He sang in the chorus. At Cambridge High and Latin they kept him up to the mark. He got a new book to read every week, sometimes a leviathan like *The Forsyte Saga*. When he was done reading, he wrote a thousand-word essay. He lost five points for every misspelling. Grammar drills were endless. Cecil Derry, who taught him Latin, knew seven ancient languages. He treated twelve-year-olds as if they were adults. This was progressive but implied great expectations.

At first Richard's grades were adequate to good. Algebra was his good subject. He got an F in Deportment, though. In the second year he went on to Geometry and he added French and Physics. He was strong in Physics but failed Latin and French, and he had to go to summer school to make up his failure. His attendance fell off steeply in his sophomore year, and again he failed Deportment. In his junior year he foundered completely and in the first term he dropped out of school. He was failing all his courses when he dropped, and in his two and a half years at Cambridge High and Latin he earned less than half the credits needed for graduation.

Years later he told Allen Tate that he had quarreled with the headmaster. His mother wanted him to apologize. He wouldn't, so he was expelled. One night he went with friends to the headmaster's house and defecated on the doorstep. He describes the headmaster, a granitic but foolish man, in a story he wrote at nineteen. "He was afraid of me when I called him a liar; he ought to have thrown me out of the window, and he only suspended me—for which 1 told him to go to hell . . . so he'd have to fire me. He did."

Richard's youthful rebellion acted out uncannily his despised father's past. He wrecked his father's hopes in him—he was George Edward, refusing to go to college and determined perversely to fail—and if his great refusal asserted his independence and accomplished his revenge, it left him wretched as well. When the truant officer came to the door, George Edward stormed and Helen grew defensive; while they quarreled, Richard sat crying on the stairs. His first-person narrator, in a story he began the year after he left school, expects to die "in nauseating terror, consuming wretchedness," and sees in his mind's eye his own rotting corpse. Later Richard annotated this story: "Written in the summer of 1920—aetat 16. Perhaps I was mad."

The high-school dropout was a hero to himself and subsequently to others, but he paid for his lack of formal schooling. Karl Shapiro, like Richard an untrained academic, was proud "that Blackmur and Kenneth Burke were in my category as 'honoraries,'" and Louise Bogan approvingly called him "a special case. He has escaped the taint of the academic approach by never going to college (or going only a little)." She thought this made Richard "really intuitive." He himself said bravely: "Colleges don't teach any more than correspondence schools." He knew better, though, or rather the precise discrimination eluded him. Edmund Wilson, his great opposite as a critic, "was fond of pointing out errors due to ignorance in some of Dick's analyses." He stressed the fact, Mary McCarthy remembered, that Richard was an autodidact. There was his mistranslation of a word in *Madame Bovary* and "then there was something about the name of Vavara Petrovna's house in *The Possessed*." Richard didn't know Russian, though it pleased him to transliterate a phrase. Like Harold Laski, who knew more than almost anyone else, he had to pretend to what he didn't know.

"He thought me," said Austin Warren, "an academic and a pedant; I thought him an autodidact and hence a charlatan. His early writings seemed to me to be dependent on the use of the dictionary, to which I as an educated man was superior. His style seemed obscure and pretentious —characteristic of the autodidactic." This pretentious style saved him from chaos. He became sovereign in his little world or *hortus inclusus*. From this enclosed garden he banished the vulgar, and he banished the avalanche that rushed upon him in his vertiginous dreams. Like Saint Jerome, the type of the hermetic writer, he treated words as talismans. Sometimes their magic worked for his readers; sometimes it was only mumbo-jumbo and efficient only in personal ways. He didn't always know the difference. He lacked the assured taste of the merely educated man, who was his inferior in every way but one.

In the early thirties he wrote to Morton Zabel at *Poetry* Magazine: "I more than anyone regret that I did not go to Harvard. I was meant to and

I wanted to mostly. First my eyes went back on me, then I was lazy and conceited; later, there was no money, my family having had a private and earlier depression." His regrets were largely that he couldn't teach. When he came to teach, it was by courtesy of Princeton. But he had no degrees and this put him absurdly on the defensive. He overvalued the Ph.D., often confounded pedantry and learning, and blundered badly in assessing the real credentials of his academic colleagues.

The unsureness that came with being self-taught is conspicuous in his early letters. He makes elementary mistakes. He spells his French authors as he heard them pronounced. His ideas are grandiose but want discipline. He thinks that in the past there may have been "summits of evolution, unknown to us, but all equal in essence of attainment." Who is going to tell him if this is so or only flashy speculation? "I have been trying to obtain books on the subject but can find none," he writes to his cousin. "I desired to go to Harvard; I find it impossible to do so." Accordingly, he has lost the chance to accumulate "a heterogeneous mass of particular knowledge." He had plenty of heterogeneous knowledge. Homogeneity was what he lost.

After Richard left high school, he emulated George Edward and drifted from job to job. He stirred sodas for Billings and Stover in Harvard Square and he clerked for Bill Tutin in the bookstore on Massachusetts Avenue across from the Widener Library. He worked as a stack boy in the Widener, and de Rochemont suspected that "he kept himself afloat by boosting volumes." He peddled the volumes to rare book dealers who sold them back to Harvard. Also, "he would filch from the secret files of the Widener books which we found excitingly pornographic." Much of the time he spent with Tessa Gilbert. At night he walked her home from the library when Bill Tutin wasn't walking her home. "He didn't get much salary, if any," Tessa said, "judging by the state of his finances, and the few ice cream cones he bought me."

He was strapped, he was lonely, and he wanted to go away—to China, to Chile. "I have a chance to go to Cuba," he wrote to George Anthony, "but shall have to refuse it, for lack of funds." This was bitter. In his new friend Jorge Mañach, he thought he had found the way out. Mañach was studying for the Ph.D. at Harvard, and he opened for Richard the prospect of a life and world beyond the boarding house in Cambridge. They talked poetry and politics—already Mañach was formulating the "Protesta de los 13" against the dictatorship of Machado—and they planned a triumphal progress to Havana. In time, the "vanguardia" and the rest of it got on Richard's nerves. At eighteen he discovered that Mañach had changed. "He seems coarser-fibred. We have fallen apart." A year later, when Mañach returned to Cuba, Richard stayed behind.

Staying meant humiliation. Poverty, a thickening tumult, beset the family. Richard, like his hero Eliot, saw behind this poverty the usurious Jew at the door. (Richard, unlike Eliot, wasn't an anti-Semite, but like most men and women from time out of mind he let the stereotype do his thinking for him.) "The damned jew who bought our house can't read or write; but he raises our rent from $75 to $125 a month." Betty remembered him saying, "We all had patches on our pants in those days." He wanted to visit his cousin in Lynn to watch the sun rise over the water, but even sixty cents carfare was beyond him. He badly needed someone to talk to, and would rather go down to Lynn than have George Anthony visit him in Cambridge, "for I much prefer your room to mine." But "I haven't a cent of money and perceive no opportunities of obtaining any." This refrain is a dreary constant in his letters until he died. "Tiens!" he wrote at seventeen in his character of Monsieur ―――――, the intimate of Axel, "My luck *may* change." Evidently it didn't. So his cousin had better come up. But "I shall have no blankets for you; no student brought any this year; so our whole stock is in use." Though it was January, maybe the two of them would be kept warm enough "by our combined overcoats and my shawl."

In this same year he went into the desert. Paul and Lewis and George Anthony ceased to exist. For weeks he looked at his navel. He dwelt "in an almost complete voluntary solitude," broken only by weekly visits to his adult friend James Leonard, a lame man who taught at the Cambridge high school and ran a class for retarded children on Broadway. The sense of isolation he associated with birth recurred powerfully: "each human organism is an absolute impenetrable solitude, a solitude which is horrible, inevitable, and irrevocable." At eighteen he was as bored "as the now certainly decayed cunt of Mary." He brooded on suicide and thought life "an infinite despair, a perpetual disaster." His identity was a trouble to him, also a lie. It masked the "solitude which is the given state of incomplete things, and which we feel only or most during some effort at communion." All effort at communion was futile. "What is the aim of passion?—to escape self." Still he hungered for communion and he tried to lose himself or find himself in sexual encounters. He had possessed fifty women (in his imagination) and had learned to despise them all. He was haunted by women seen from the window or in the street, dark flowers of streaming sorrow, showers of rain that freshen the senses. "Helen," he cried, "make me immortal with a kiss"—an extraordinary cry, never mind that he was quoting. A woman with naked arms smoothing down her long hair drove him to frenzy. He wanted to lie naked beside her, stroking her side like foam; he wanted to caress her legs and to run his hand between them and kiss them. In the Harvard library, when a girl was getting a book on the floor above him, he looked up and saw her legs. "Once I saw the crotch, and my lips stung for it." He added, "Pure form has its value."

Riding the Belmont bus, he enjoyed for twelve minutes the silent company of a young woman; Aphrodite was the name he gave her. "She sat close and under my arm. The warmth of her made a comfort that needed nothing but acceptance. I do not think I have ever, with a stranger, felt such benefit of blood-companionship, such deep sense of long-grown intimacy." Regret came later—"that in our society the bearer of such gifts must be and remain a stranger."

Beatrice, the daughter of Aunt Carie and Uncle Charles, was a stranger and his perfect, because unrealized, companion. In his youthful imagination she played a role like that of Dante's Beatrice. He sent her his photograph at the vicarage in Essex, and she responded in letters that were generous and sometimes poignant, one lonely adolescent to another. At first she thought him conceited and affected, and his grandiose reflections merely a pose. "The truth is I had never known anyone like you and I thought it couldn't be true that a person of only about eighteen could think like that." He wanted her to believe in the truth of his thinking and the beauty of his person. He told himself that he would "lop off a year of life to be sure possessed of a woman's love, to be 'attractive.'"

At night she came to him in dreams. "I kissed her hand, and then her mouth. She was very beautiful." He hoped that when he got to England, he might find in her "some instance of the ideal!" From her letters he knew her "thoroughly human and capable most wholly of a passion." But he wondered about himself. "Can I, who dwell so much alone and in the labyrinth of my mind, stir passion in another?" This was in private. In public, to his cousin, he ridiculed Beatrice as "our beloved Essex bitch." Stupid she was. He wrote her a ten-hour, six-thousand word letter in nine different styles and almost as many languages (George Anthony didn't know he "was so linguistically proficient"), and she replied that he needn't have gone to the trouble. Also she said that he lacked a sense of humor, and that being self-sufficient or pretending to be, he lost what society might have given him. This got him up on his high horse. For self-sufficient he substituted "the certainly more agreeable phrase, 'critical.'" Beatrice had granted him "keen perception and high ideals," but he couldn't take her compliment and had to mock himself and her. "Women speak best with their legs."

All the same, he wanted to see her legs. He felt it useless, though, to hope for more in a woman than "salivary or seminal" pleasure. There was a war in him between his conviction of apartness, beyond redress, and the "social illusion" that pretended to redress it. Reaching out, as in marriage, exposed one to hurt—he wasn't married yet, but the dismal record of the marriage-to-come is already written in these propositions—as one indulged the "impossible hope" of fusion with another human being. "It is only parts of men and women that are married."

When Richard was eighteen his world, already precarious, fell in pieces. His great uncle, George Palmer, the adult male to whom he felt closest, committed suicide. Richard never recovered from this blow, and when he was twice as old again he had not yet accommodated to the memory of it. He talked compulsively of Uncle George, not to friends who might estimate his suffering but to acquaintances—a random student at Princeton in whom he could confide only so far as he wanted. He didn't talk about the suicide but the living man. To Tessa Gilbert, whom he aspired to marry, he said nothing, and it was only years later that she learned what had happened. He was that way, she thought: he kept himself to himself.

George Monroe Palmer, born in 1863, was the favorite of Richard's mother, too. He had trained as a research chemist in the early 1880s at the Lawrence Scientific School, then a part of Harvard College. In 1892 he received his M.D. from Harvard Medical School and a year later he married. For two decades he practiced medicine. He and Aunt Nannie lived on Beacon Hill, and after that in Cambridge. He gave up his practice in 1910—arthritis had crippled him—and went back to more regular and less strenuous work as a chemist. Within two years, his wife was dead. He married his housekeeper, Lillian St. Onge, in 1916. She was, by an earlier marriage, the mother of George Anthony. In 1920 Dr. Palmer adopted George Anthony and moved the family to Lynn. He killed himself in 1922.

Shortly after his death Richard wrote: "If a young man should for long remember that most of the people with whom he is at all closely or affectionately connected will die before him, I imagine the proposition of suicide would compel some attention." This seems pretty cold. But the fact was only waiting to take hold of him: "the death of my uncle George . . . is *the* most terrible thing which has occurred to me. Mentally the effect is still palpitant; physically—I hardly know: the darkness perturbs me, and my throat and chest are still wrenched heavily."

The suicide of Uncle George figured in Richard's young manhood and in the years to come like the agonizing death by lockjaw of Henry Adams's adored sister: "Flung suddenly in the face, with the harsh brutality of chance, the terror of the blow stayed by him henceforth for life, until repetition made it more than the will could struggle with; more than he could call on himself to bear." The sum and term of education, for Richard as for Adams, was his discovery of the dominion of chance and the meaninglessness of all meaning. This vision at eighteen made nonsense of the commonplaces of religion and poetry. It made the world, which Richard had thought real, only a mimicry of his personal nightmare. It verified his nightmare. The stage scenery of his senses collapsed and he saw that life was—not inimical, as he had imagined in his melodramatic repinings —but a chaos of anarchic forces contending to no purpose, only a vibrating in a void. He never again found more than momentary comfort in what Adams called "the usual anodynes of social medicine," and such philosophy as he allowed himself was that of the stoic for whom the only recourse was to bite down hard on his pain. That was what he did thereafter when he entertained "the death of friends, or death of every brilliant eye"—no tears and no proffering or accepting of comfort. It was how he met his own death.

"What is this devil Christianity?" he wrote to Conrad Aiken nine years later. "Faith is reflexively blasphemy; and I thank God I am infidel." He had no option. Life he considered a tissue of "blind events replete with their own meaning." Only his writing sustained him. "If I cannot live," he said, "I will make life. I will make life into works; will make my works fire. May the fire love man."

In the weeks that followed his uncle's death, he took refuge in writing. He labored at a critical essay on W. H. Hudson. But his heart wasn't in it. He would sooner "play at ball than write essays." Fiction was what he wanted to write. He was big with ideas for stories. Writing poetry engaged him too, and a play on which he wanted George Anthony to collaborate. His novel in progress, "The Isolation of Bertram Thur, a Study in Purple and Green," fell in abeyance, though.

Inevitably, the casual jobs which kept him in pocket began to seem inadequate, to others if not to himself. When was he going to pull himself together? He wrote in his notebook: "I am thinking, apprehensively, of working. . . . Now that I have had two years of solitude the prospect is frightful." This was in August 1922. By September the die was cast: "Now, shortly, I shall be at work for the American Woolen Company"— presumably his father's old firm. Accepting a job meant accepting what he called the "tutelage of success—the applied doctrine of efficient imbecility." He wasn't efficient, the job didn't take, and when, a half year later, his nineteenth birthday came round, he was still an idle young man, and no other career than idleness "stood in sight or mind." He took a long look at himself on this birthday, "a festival to celebrate and to suffer." Literature, he had supposed, was to be his profession. He had counted himself prospectively among "the world's great artists . . . a true genius," and had put by the chance for a college degree and the living it might furnish him "in some kind of teacher's work." In his adolescence he had got "a wicked reputation and the name of queerness" as he diverged, "habitually and intentionally, from the common run."

Success was axiomatic. "I stepped out of the trend, and ignored the motive of my school generation. I stepped out alone; I was, utterly, sure of my victory, and made no measure of my loss." He was less sure now. He ended his meditation: "If it turns out that I fail as creative artist, then I shall know I have only a swim for a life ahead of me."

CHAPTER TWO

Breaking Out

THE IDLE YEARS ended when Richard was just into his twenties. He opened a bookstore in Cambridge. Wallace Dickson was his partner. First they were friends, then they were partners, and later when they weren't friends and partners anymore, they became brothers-in-law. Dickson & Blackmur, Sellers of New and Old Books, didn't set the world on fire. Within a year or so the bookstore was failing and the young partners were at sword's points. But the chance acquaintance Richard struck with Wallace Dickson cast a long shadow. It comprehended his unlucky marriage, also the real beginning of his literary career. Selling books put him in the way of Lincoln Kirstein and friends, who were creating at Harvard the best and most famous of the little magazines. So, as one thing leads to another, Richard found himself editor of the *Hound & Horn*. He wrote in his notebook: "Vocation is the right naming and right following of our nature." In his twenties he discovered his vocation and this was a lucky chance. Sometimes—to take a line from the poetry he was writing then—chance flowers to choice.

Wallace Dickson was a bundle of energy and no place to go. At nineteen he decided to go into business. He tried to work a deal with the publisher Harold Vinal, who owned the bookstore on Mount Vernon Street and wanted a partner so he could spend his time writing poems. E. E. Cummings made him immortal when he wrote how "Beauty hurts Mr. Vinal." Evidently Wallace Dickson was not the partner he had in mind, so Wallace started from scratch. He opened the Mermaid Book Shop in the Brick Oven community between Joy and Myrtle streets on Beacon Hill. His sister Helen, an aspiring painter, painted the mermaid that hung before the shop. Richard's taste in books, a friend remembered, was "for most anything new." The Mermaid specialized in modern first editions, and this was enough to flag his attention. He thought he saw a kindred spirit in Wallace Dickson. So Wallace was promoted to the circle of friends.

Richard wanted to set up as a bookseller too, but always it came down to money. Homer Pound, Ezra's father and an early correspondent, applauded his desire to start a small shop and said he might even take a share. Nothing came of this. Perhaps, Richard thought, Murray Borish could raise the money. Murray was boarding with the Blackmurs and gave Richard's mother fits when he didn't pay his rent. He wanted to help, but when he went to his family, the answer was no. So Richard turned to Norman Dodge, a bibliophile who wrote poetry and who published with Richard in Sherry Mangan's little magazine *larus*. By the beginning of February 1924, he supposed he was ready for business. In choosing a partner he sought out Paul Rowe, the friend from the old days at Cambridge High and Latin. They were going to call their bookstore the Crucible House, and they meant it to function also as a publishing house for poetry. The honor of inaugurating the Crucible House Pamphlets went to the poems of George Anthony Palmer. This was only fair—Richard put his cousin right up there with Marianne Moore—but it was politic, too: he and Paul were hoping George Anthony would join the firm.

Then Norm Dodge had second thoughts. The promised capital disappeared and the Crucible House died a-borning. Richard was disconsolate, but he was also primed and ready when Wallace suggested that the two of them club together as Dickson & Blackmur. After a year Wallace had got sick of the Mermaid: the grass was always greener across the way. He took off in a touring car with Bill Gurney, Helen's boyfriend. They toured Maine and New Brunswick in the dead of winter. This made the papers and for a while Wallace was content to sit still. Back in town and predictably restless, he made his proposals, Richard listened, and the friends indented formally. Richard was twenty-one and in business for himself at 87 Mount Auburn Street in Cambridge.

"They had a few beautiful books," George Orrok remembered, "and then they had the general shelves with second hand books, four or five thousand in all." They hoarded the good books in the back room and there in the back, when the store closed for the night, George Orrok and George Anthony and Wallace and Richard played penny ante poker for ten cents a chip. George Orrok had been to Harvard, but he was working as a time-clerk then at the Edison plant in Weymouth. He was bedrock poor, so were the others, and they picked each other's pockets and forgave each other's debts. "We made a rule," Orrok said. "You could never lose more than $2.50 a night."

For Richard, the bookstore was less business than pleasure, and as natural and necessary as breathing. These were his own words, and he applied them to the unstructured life. Like the Dunster House half a block away, and Goodspeed's, and Bill Tutin's in the Square, the bookstore functioned as his poor man's club. Gordon Cairnie used to boast that Richard received his entire education sitting in the armchair of the Grolier Book Shop on Plympton Street, overhearing conversation and reading the new books as they came in. Richard liked to eavesdrop, but more than this he liked to talk. When he went to the club, he traded literary gossip with Norm Dodge and other cronies who were part of the inner circle— Murray Borish, the poets Dudley Fitts and Sherry Mangan, and John Marshall and his roommate Jerry Whiting. All of them were Harvard, class of '25. "In a sense," John Marshall said, Richard "went through Harvard with my class." He could have attended Harvard like the others, Marshall thought, but the formal academic thing stuck in his throat. "The unofficial, the unregulated" regimen was best. He read to please himself and the bookstore was his college. Harvard College was an annex.

For Murray Borish, Harvard was the emblem and the means of success. Among Richard's early friends he presented the academic, not least when he grumbled about the academy. Murray was Richard as Richard might have been, the vestigial side he left behind or the unfinished man he completed. Later on Richard wrote the character of Peter Abelard and it was Murray to the life. "His power was that of the unaided intellect everywhere passionately equal to itself, everywhere calamitously unequal to the world in which it found itself." His weapon was a petulant temper, forged in his belief that the academy had conspired to cheat him of the use of half his talents. Richard considered Murray a genius—the finest mind he had ever encountered—and he tried to boost him with Robert Hillyer for a job in English A. "There was nothing you couldn't ask Murray." He knew so much he could tell you where the Encyclopaedia Britannica went wrong, as in dating the first edition of the Book of Common Prayer. He was authoritative and he liked to tell you. To Richard's sister Betty, Murray was a dear. He worried about his marks, though, and when he came home to Irving Street, he would always look for the penny postcard on the hall table. It was always an A. George Orrok said he was handsome and tremendous. Tessa Horton said he looked like a cadaver. The painter Kate Foster, Sherry Mangan's first wife, understood how clever Murray was supposed to be, but he was always Murray Boring to her. These conflicting impressions suggest a mutable man or a man not altogether made up.

His letters say that Murray was highfalutin, full of self-pity, prone to scatology, and obsessed with private fears. He called teaching Freshman

English a vagrancy or else an abortion. He had "twenty-five cherrywood blocks" in each of his four sections and he hated them all. In return they made him sick. "My piles are renewed with new vigor"; "I carry an evil influence with me"; "I am not enjoying myself"—he goes on like that. Richard goes on like that, too. Read him in his young man's notebooks, dilating gloomily on "the tales of human cruelty" or "the ghastly cumulus of circumstance," and you feel with dismay that the two friends were cut from one cloth. But this isn't true after all. We mind true things "by what their mockeries be," and that is why Murray is important for these years when Richard was coming into his force. They had in common their dyspepsia and neither was long on goodness, where goodness is purity without reference to the life which it surpasses. Paul Rowe was perhaps a good man. Richard wasn't blessed with goodness but he went on to learn wisdom and his wisdom, however flawed, is available and availing.

His more vigorous character—you can call it masculine, employing the old convention—acted on Murray like a lodestone to filings. This made him a difficult friend. In the later twenties, when Richard considered marriage, Murray raised the alarm. He had thought his own abhorrence of marriage—the "bourgeois" thing—chimed with Richard's, and now he wasn't sure. "What do your mysterious, cryptic remarks about marriage mean?" He feels like kicking himself for not having protested sooner, and he does his best to make amends. "Do not work too quickly," he implores his friend. "Let it itch a little longer." His letters to Richard are thick with erotic feeling—he plays Patroclus, adoring and abject, to Richard's high and mighty Achilles—but these are metaphors, and partly what they convey is his desire to mend his weakness by resorting to Richard's strength. Richard, who admonished himself, might be admonishing his biographer: "Experience is equivocal; its expression ambiguous; the moral full of duplicity."

What Murray desired is matter for conjecture, also how Richard responded. Here are stray clues, possibly false. Growing up in Cambridge, Richard flirted briefly with a group of homosexuals who played at being women. When they stripped naked and danced together, they hid their privates between their legs. Richard used to say, or sing, if you couldn't get a woman, get a clean old man. This was only if you couldn't get a woman. In a short story he wrote at twenty-four, he described a homosexual episode that involved a grown man and an acquiescent boy. In the end, the boy backs away. For him it was only an episode, and he had his own sufficient resources. The boy and the man figure Richard and Murray, bearing in mind that a story is a metaphor, though the metaphor lies like the truth.

Murray, down in the depths, begins "to feel refreshed in that I shall soon hear from you again." He is jealous of Wallace Dickson—why hadn't Richard taken Murray for a partner?—and is tempted to "chuck this business"—his academic career—and "fall in with you." A letter to Richard brings with it "all the convulsions of gestation." Silence is worse. It leaves him terror-stricken or it begets agonies or clutchings of the heart and brain. He tries to nerve himself—"Every hour of delay . . . is a thrust of pain to me"—but breaks off because "I am ashamed." Sometimes the worm turns. "You do not treat me well," he writes accusingly to Richard. "You make your words depend on mine; such hesitancy was not your wont." Then he loses his nerve. "Now when only the hollow echo of my own voice dins in my ear a few occasional words from you would be a blessing."

The words were not forthcoming, and ultimately Murray moved to the edges of Richard's life. He took his Ph.D. at Harvard. He married a bookish woman who carried her book to the bedroom when friends came to visit. World War II came and Murray enlisted. He was lost at sea in the second year of the war when his ship was torpedoed en route to North Africa.

The young friends had one passion in common: the literature of their own time. They found it in short-lived periodicals like *larus* and *Pagany,* then in *Anathema, Symposium,* the *Magazine.* These are honorable names. "Most of the enduring literature of our time has had its origin," said Allen Tate, "in the critical journal of unpopular standards." He thought the New Criticism "could not have arisen outside the Little Magazines," and he was willing to say that without them "American literature would have ceased to function." This sounds like hyperbole and probably isn't. In the years after 1912, most of the important writers in America published for the first time in the little magazines, among them Richard and his friends.

Eliot was their hierophant and his *Criterion* was Holy Writ. "The story of American letters cannot be told without mention of it," said Pound. They waited on the *Criterion,* but most of all they waited on the *Dial.* They made a class, Richard said, "of young men and women who devotedly went to school to the *Dial,* never missing an issue and always devouring each in toto, and developing a cross between passion and fury with regard to its chief contents." From 1920 on, they "haunted Felix' newsstand in Harvard Square for days before publication date on the chance that the next issue might blessedly be early." Among American literary periodicals, the *Dial* stood first. Not everyone knew this and when it died in

1929, the *Times* commented briefly—relegating the story to page seventeen, "It has been generally reported that the publication did not make a profit." Richard and his fellow scholars were indifferent to profit. They thought it enough to be "living in the first days of a renascent period"—the hectic vision of the little magazine *Seven Arts*. Before you had renascence, you had to have "disintegration: the destruction of the reality we want to forget." This was Creighton Hill, standing in for Richard's friend Elliot Paul as coeditor of *transition*, the most famous of the exile magazines. All of them were exiles, over the water or in their own country, and they flaunted their apartness: "The plain reader be damned." Some of them were certainly crazy. Even the craziest, Malcolm Cowley said, were saner than the Stock Exchange, though.

Their goal, Richard wrote, was to make "society possible from the point of view of the artist." The *Dial* adhered faithfully to this point of view. It sailed a tricky course between the learned periodicals, which detest literature, and the popular periodicals which want journalistic comment about literature, and not too much of that. Unlike the *Hound & Horn*, it had little interest in day-to-day politics, and Gorham Munson in the first issue of *Secession* (Spring 1922) mocked it as "this *Yale-Review*-in-a-Harvard-Blazer." But in 1922 the *Dial* published *The Waste Land*, a gesture transcending politics or a great political gesture. The *Dial* was Richard's forcing-house and it stretched his sensibility "and gave the effect of adding to its stature and intensifying its residual strength." He "learned the new writing and the new art, and, through the feeling of novelty mastered, became a part of them."

Malcolm Cowley in just these years was writing to Kenneth Burke: "The function of poetry is to make the world inhabitable." This, perhaps with a different bias, is what Richard and his friends supposed. Loving the world, they were vociferous in support of poetry and poets. "Has Robinson's *Tristram* appeared yet?" Murray wants to know. He can't wait to get hold of Hart Crane's *White Buildings*. He is eager for Yeats's *Tower* poems right after publication. This avidity describes the twenties and maybe it still exists. Looking back on the twenties, Richard didn't think so. "The old thing that made Harvard good was that you were on your own," he said. "The new thing seems to be that you are on nobody." Being on your own meant reading all night in your closet. After that you checked impressions with friends. Richard the young stay-at-home differed necessarily from his seniors Burke and Cowley—only a few years made the difference. He had missed the war. He was innocent of the Dome and the Closerie des Lilas, and later Kirstein and Mangan put him down as a provincial. Kirstein said he was "strictly from nowhere." But he made in his mind his own version of the greater world, and he located poetry at the center.

George Anthony wrote a poem and handed it to Richard. Next it went to Paul or Murray and on to Foster Damon, who had the final say. He was a poet-scholar and he looked the part—fragile but intense, Richard called him. Foster read the poem "five times straight through then perused it in relation to the notes"—you had to have notes, *The Waste Land* was the model—"then took it up line by line. He thought it "ineradicably obscure," Richard said, "enormously clever, and very fine." These terms were felt as making a concurrence.

After the perusing, there was talk at John Marshall's, "literary or otherwise." John presided over the Harvard Poetry Society. He and Richard had met first when each was eighteen. This was at a poetry reading in Boylston Hall where Richard was taking tickets. The friendship between them, being unlikely, flattered them both. Richard, said Marshall, lacked a disciplined mind. He progressed from the difficult to the simple—what was wrong with the other way round? Marshall, Richard thought, was a paragon of discipline. Murray Borish called him conscience-bitten, already the right man for the Rockefellers, in whose service he spent most of his life. When John married Mary Gardner and moved to Mount Auburn Street, he reserved for Richard's use the Queen Anne chair in the living room. Richard called it the "Bishop's chair." It was *"Dick's chair,"* however, and its occupant seemed like a bishop to his friends, "whether you imagine him in mitre or in gaiters." Until Richard died, he and John related to each other like fellow alumni, but it wasn't Harvard College that got their allegiance. Poetry got their allegiance.

At Marshall's undergraduate parties in Matthews Hall, Lucius Beebe was a frequent guest; later Beebe was famous as a bon vivant and arbiter of fashion. James Gould Cozzens also turned up. Marshall and Jerry Whiting served the friends tea and cakes, then they all trooped off together to the Athens-Olympia, where in deference to Prohibition the resinous wine appeared on the bill as aspirin. More than forty years later, Teddy the waiter still remembered Mr. Dick. Sometimes Ted Spencer and Foster Damon joined the friends for a plate of cheap Greek food at the Athens. "We could only afford one drink a piece," Tessa Horton said, "but even with a drink you could get out of there for about $3.50. We thought we were living high." On a tight budget, they re-created hopefully the world of Willie Yeats and his ribald companions of the Cheshire Cheese and his white women that passion had worn. It passed understanding, Sherry Mangan said to Richard, "how you ever avoid succumbing to the crowd of females with which you forever surround yourself."

Maybe the crowd of females lived mostly in the mind. But Tessa was real. She was the older daughter of Henry Gilbert the composer, and she was only seventeen when she entered Richard's life. Richard was Narcissus and getting ready to live, but Tessa was already there. She had heard that Cleopatra washed her hair in myrrh and frankincense—a potent aphrodisiac, according to her sources. Myrrh and frankincense were not to be had, so she washed her hair in cinnamon and nutmeg. The trouble was it made her smell like apple pie. Richard met her for the first time in the Cambridge Public Library. He was almost living in the library then, and Ellery Street where Tessa lived was only two blocks away. She decided that Richard was the man for her, and without preamble she let him know it. Patient Griselda wasn't one of her roles. Later, when she fell in love with Lewis MacKay, she sent him out one day for roses and strewed the petals on her bed—she said she was tired of her virginity. The petals turned brown, though, and they tickled her skin.

At first Richard didn't pay much attention to Tessa—he was young Shelley, rapt in his book—so she made him fudge and he condescended to eat it. He was telling himself in his notebook that life and love were just a succedaneum, but his body knew better. After that, he was her suitor and he came to call six nights a week. For the Gilbert daughters, he was the Poet. For himself, he was Henry James "presiding" (as he put it) over their little soirées. He wrote complacently to George Anthony how they used to beseech him "with all possible earnestness" to say whether "they might ever be 'cultured.'" One night the younger daughter "brought in some very decent cordial which casually we three consumed."

Richard and Tessa were polar opposites, so they made a pair: Tessa "a beautiful instance of vitality," Richard haunted by the vertigo that had its springs in his inward dark and against which he contended by studied ennui. Tessa lived in her body and rejoiced in the world. The body was Richard's torment, and he defined the alienated man. Richard subsisted on air and looked it: "pinched, stoop shouldered, extremely thin, the look of poverty and the look of someone who hadn't had enough to eat from the time he was a baby." Tessa was his Wilbur Bud, after the tiny chocolates shaped like an onion and wrapped in silver foil. She was always eating chocolates if she wasn't eating ice cream. Delmore Schwartz said that Tessa brought joy in her train. He called her his favorite woman, and years later he remembered Lewis stepping into the dish of ice cream hidden under the bed ("thus summing up all possible marriages to Tessa"), and he wrote to propose that if they lived a second time, he should be the first to step into her dish of ice cream. "What flavor?" she asked him. "Tutti-frutti," he said.

For three years Tessa and Richard kept company, and he stopped looking at his image in the pool. They gave each other gifts—to avoid failing her at Christmas, he had to touch his cousin for a fiver—and they exchanged fervent letters. Then Helen Dickson swept him up and he got what he called—making light of the business—"a melodramatic dismissal" from Tessa. She was humiliated and she said it was better if they didn't meet again. He kept this two-line notice for the rest of his life, but then what didn't he keep? Eileen Simpson thought that Richard identified Tessa with Molly Bloom, when he wasn't identifying with Molly himself. After it was too late and she was married to Lewis, he traveled with her to New York on the old Fall River Line. They shared a single stateroom to save on the fare and he wanted to sleep with her, but Tessa declined. She felt sorry for Richard—even this early, his marriage was a disaster—but she didn't find him attractive anymore.

Richard feared that the break with Tessa had canceled, "probably forever," his connection with the Gilbert family. That turned out not to be true. He continued to call on Tessa's father, the composer, in the fantastic house on Ellery Street where an ancient figure in a white nightgown and white mobcap was apt to materialize at the head of the old-fashioned staircase. "What the hell was that?" Rob Darrell inquired, hearing the high-pitched laughter for the first time. Henry Gilbert's mother wasn't altogether mad. Sometimes she came downstairs, the model of a lady with a ribbon in her hair. That was only when her son and daughter-in-law were out of the house. When their return was imminent, she hurried back to her room—"to await the Advent!" she said. In the second-floor studio, the aging composer sheltered himself in his music. His tremendous wife, dressed like a peasant with clothes on top of clothes and wearing a mangy fur hat, dictated long letters to relatives and friends in the dining room below. Her daughters were hounding their mother to death. This was the gist of the letters, and Tessa took down the dictation. Henry Gilbert—"porcupine-prickly," his biographer called him—saw the world from his own peculiar window. "He was our music's archetypal plain, rock-salty, crabbed, dryly ribald Yankee maverick—the poor relation, bad-boy truant from the New England School, thumbing his nose at the establishment." Once, disputing the proposition that falling bodies accelerated at the same speed, he summoned Richard to the rooftop and together they dropped a flatiron and a penny to the ground.

George Anthony was often there when Richard arrived. He was smitten with the Gilbert's younger daughter, "the fair Yolanda." Richard approved. He said he respected "every effort to overcome the horror of personal solitude." Communion with the other sex was good. If you didn't achieve it, "the penalty of failure . . . [was] a bleaching and ubiquitous exile." Then he lapsed in Victorianism: George Anthony had better not be a cad.

Elizabeth Yolanda Gilbert was a beautiful girl, "one of those kids who had so many talents she couldn't concentrate on any one of them." She played the piano and wrote reviews of music, she wrote plays and dabbled at poetry, and without any training she drew with a skill that made the working-at-it artists like her sister squirm with envy. Also she concocted plans, "none of them feasible." One plan was to evade her mother's suffocating presence by running away from home. This Elizabeth attempted. She was caught in New York, to Richard's chagrin. "If I had the money," he wrote to George Anthony, "I'd send the dear girl away again, where she couldn't be caught: she has to *live* with Madame G." Richard, who estimated Madame Gilbert with horrified awe—Bossy Gillis he called her, after the autocratic mayor of Newburyport—likened himself to her put-upon husband. How would it be if you were married to such a woman? He was thinking, but at a level below conscious thinking, of his own mother and his father whose vitality Helen Blackmur had drained. After a while he married such a woman. He got his revenge, though. His own wife was a primitive who echoed Hemingway's opinion that critics were the eunuchs of literature. He became a doyen of critics.

Rob Darrell gave a permanent twist to the criticism. Richard met him at the Gilberts on a spring evening in 1926. Rob was completing his last year at the New England Conservatory of Music. He had got in the habit of dropping by for tea—he had his eye on Elizabeth, too, and he brought daffodils when he came to call. Once a week Rob and Tessa and Elizabeth sang English madrigals together. Music was their common language and Richard yearned to speak it. He struck negligent poses sitting at the piano, but he couldn't play the piano and had no formal training in music. He played the gramophone, though—a cornucopia of beautiful sounds; already in his teens he makes you think of Hans Castorp, Thomas Mann's hero, surveying a world to conquer that was remote from the world of poetry, but tantalizingly similar if only you had the key. Like Hans Castorp, what he felt, "sitting there with folded hands, looking into the black slates of the *jalousies*" from which the music came, was the triumph of pure form at a remove from merely denotative meaning. He loved Vivaldi, in whose music there was "Nothing extra, nothing false."

Rob Darrell was a year Richard's senior. He had a mind of his own but didn't push it at you—his ego was strong enough not to need salving—and though he was prodigiously learned in the past, he didn't live in it. His taste in music was catholic and he consulted his taste. In what he liked, he moved easily between past and present. Richard became his fellow traveler. He learned "a new writing and a new art"—it was like going back to school to the *Dial*, except that the medium was different. What he learned he made his own and turned it to account in criticism and poetry, also in the criticism of life. In style and thought, he and Rob were opposites who completed each other. Rob on one side was like Norman Dodge, who spent forty-five years cataloguing old books. He wasn't a retiring man like Norm, but his gift was for taxonomy, too. Richard already was trying the high critical wire and Rob gave him what he needed: balance, a repertory of forms, and a way to address it.

The summer Richard got married, he wrote Rob proudly from Harrington, Maine: "We have morning concerts which must puzzle the seals." In that part of the world, the seals ordinarily heard only dance music, "save when the great yachts go yachting by." Rob by then was editing the first nontrade journal devoted to recorded music, and he asked Richard to contribute to his *Phonograph Monthly Review*. "I'm ignorant as an actor about music," Richard said, "and have no reason to write." He went on in his patented manner: "though I'm glad to lucubrate whenever you want." Writing about music was play—he had "a swell time," he said, "doing reviews where I have no responsibility"—but, as always, play for Richard was intensely serious. He opened a dialogue between music and the other arts, and between music and society. The French composer Satie was like those poets who worked a banal vein deliberately and made poetry from banality, as they knew what they were doing. Richard said how the new music made the auditor conscious of rhythms to which he had privately accommodated—just as, in the nineteenth century, Impressionist painters tutored the eye in the real colors of light on water and grass. Music "in the godly modes"—he was thinking of Gregorian chant—grew like a language "with profound accretions of meaning" out of the necessities of everyday use. This music was anonymous and communal, so "reprieved from the flesh that bred it." (Already, in that perception and expression, he attains his majority as a critic.) He came to see how the reprieve—not assenting to the world and not depicting it either, or not in slavish ways—constituted the function and privilege of art.

Richard liked what was old—the polyphonic music of the sixteenth century, Palestrina, Victoria—and he liked the very new. Modern music, he said, was "music looking for house-room. It demands hospitality." William Walton's *Façade* got his approval as it blended music and poetry —the poems of Edith Sitwell—in a harmony that baffled translation and had "at once no meaning and all the meaning there is in nonsense." This, he decided, was both "modern" and "poetic." He was on the way to saying, as in his essay on Wallace Stevens, that the charm of the rhymes was enough to carry you over any stile.

Academic critics, dissecting the arts, bet on morphology and statistics. Richard thought they lost their bet. A scholarly treatise analyzing the folk songs of the American Negro had its own value, he supposed, but didn't relate to artistic creation. Or the relation between them was like that of the pursuit of the chemistry of ivory to a study of the game of chess. Time was consumed and some amusement resulted. The scholia of the arts was full of such irrelevance, "for the very good reason that the substance of the arts themselves is actually inaccessible." The contingent phrase was tough talk and seemed to shut the door to criticism. He found how to get the door open again, and what he said thereafter in his own criticism was more acute for the limitation he assigned to all critical pronouncing.

Subjective art left him cold—the poetry of Edna St. Vitus, as they called her—and so did realistic drama and romantic melodrama. At bottom they were the same, as their business was reduction or representation. In music, and by extension in the other arts, the thing of price had no program outside itself but had a real interior program. "It is full of struggling feelings which originate in and are bound by the music and at the same time have an equivalence in the predicaments of the daily struggles of the soul." Stravinsky, for example, represented nothing outside the field of music—his material was the most objective of which music is capable —and yet he gives us an imitation of nature. Stravinsky's music jigged with hard, percussive feeling, but the savage wrestling it suggested was that of part with part, a formal contention. Art wasn't a replicating of nature, but there had to be "an underlying equivalence between the art and the complexity of what the artist, as man, had seen." Richard clinched his argument with a great phrase: Bach, the supreme technician, was an athlete of the soul.

In these formulations, the New Critic is predicted. Richard in his twenties was unraveling and recomposing "the chain of sensation, feeling, and emotion" that a work of art composed. He wondered how meaning figured in this relation, and especially "in a non-verbal realm such as music—a realm free of artificial meaning." Words, if you could paraphrase them, weren't equivalent to meaning, or not when they confronted "any difficult, really substantial experience." They missed too much in their spurious clarity, or they asserted too much and became "almost invariably empty portmanteaux." But he wasn't seduced by the dead-end esthetics of Jolas and *transition*, who wanted to annihilate the word as signifier. Reviewing the poems of his friend Conrad Aiken, he qualified Pater's dictum that all arts tend to the condition of music. Poetry, he said, "cannot altogether escape the meaning of its words." No doubt the meaning was only proximate. He concluded: "Approximations are a form of madness; but are sometimes divine."

So poetry, unlike music and painting, was inevitably if tenuously a language of signs. But the signs didn't comprise the poem, and meaning wasn't comprised in or carried by statement. When a poem didn't work, that was because "the material *between* the statements is not always forced into being." What carried meaning was rhythm, a cognate of form. Rhythm was "that meaning in music which persists after the words have stopped." Rhythm, or music, entailed whatever was palpable, as opposed to all that farrago of abstract things which are not really things. It entailed drama but not leading ideas. "The sense of drama, and the ability to represent it . . . gives the only full account of what mere ideas stand aghast at." So down with mere ideas or denotative meaning as the price of admission. Pound's ideas were suspect, but the virtue of his work was not in the expression of his private fervors and dismays. "What is personal in his work is the general tone infusing his various styles; and the ultimate value of his poetry should be in the adequacy of his methods and the freshness of his ways of feeling, rather than the novelty or truth of his substance." That is how to come to terms with the poet off his head: Pound the anti-Semite, etc.

For this perception of the primacy of rhythm and tone, or form amply defined as the index of value, the experiencing of music made the difference.

Most of the friends were, like Rob, small in stature. They made the best of this and called themselves the Seven Dwarfs. There weren't always seven of them and the group wasn't always the same. Richard presided over their court or he stood in the center of the circle. The friends stood around him and they comment, in their different characters, on what he was and what he lacked and what he might have become. For a few years Wallace Dickson belonged to the circle. He and Richard were born in the same year and were committed apparently to the same lofty purpose. The resemblance between them was only apparent, though, like that of the simulacrum to the genuine article.

Wallace at twenty-one was already footsore from chasing the American dream. Like Richard, he was going to be a great writer—he called the scrapbook to which he confided his hopes "The Citadel of Fame"—but unlike Richard his talents were less for writing than promoting. In high school he had edited the student paper, and at Boston University a new literary magazine. While still in his teens, he was helping administer the Peabody Play House. He wrote plays himself. Also he wrote musicals, songs, and short stories. He pasted his rejection slips in "The Citadel of Fame."

Sometimes his restless energy flowed over in violence. All of the Dicksons had a fiercely violent streak, Tessa Horton said, and when it showed, they were almost wild people. One night after a party Wallace followed Tessa home to her apartment. He got his hands on her throat. He pursued her around the apartment with a bread knife. When the police arrived, he pretended composure. He said you knew how it was with hysterical women. The police went away and he picked up the bread knife and resumed his pursuit. "Wallace when he got older became a very respectable citizen," Tessa said, "but I didn't think much of him when I was young."

Maurice Firuski didn't think much of him either. Firuski owned the Dunster House Book Shop on the corner of Mount Auburn and Holyoke streets, and it was partly from him that Wallace had got his stock of books for the Mermaid. Though he disapproved of Wallace ("a very slippery individual"), he had faith in Richard. So he agreed to sponsor Dickson & Blackmur. He supplied the initial outlay, and when it was gone he sold the partners what they needed at minimum cost and gave Richard books to sell on consignment. But the dingy storefront didn't draw many customers, and the bills piled up—some so minuscule as not to need mention, except that the partners couldn't pay them. Richard paid the bills after the bookstore failed.

To make ends meet, Wallace got a part-time job as a butler. Then he disappeared, having appropriated "either money or books from the business." Firuski thought it was both. Later Wallace turned up in New York, working for Brentano's. After that he was selling apples for a nickel apiece. Already, in April 1926, he had given Richard power of attorney over all his interest in Dickson & Blackmur. So Richard at twenty-two was left holding the bag. He had failed in business but he wasn't bankrupt— bankruptcy was the easy way and he didn't consider it. He owed Firuski two thousand dollars and badly needed a job.

Just then the bookkeeper at the Dunster House gave notice. Firuski offered the job to Richard at forty dollars a week. There was a proviso— he would have to take lessons in accounting and stenography and shorthand. Firuski paid for the lessons and he got his money's worth. Richard was meticulous—the other face of the vertigo. Like Hamlet, he wrote things down to hold himself together. "You remember his handwriting," Firuski said. He took to bookkeeping as to his crabbed journals. He served Firuski as secretary too, and did his turn as a salesman. He wasn't much of a salesman—"not pushy," said Bernard Bandler, "nor interested in selling books. He loved books." His love of books and what he knew about them made the Dunster House a good place to be. "There was an atmosphere for chatting and for browsing," Bandler said, "just a beautiful two-story bookshop."

The building itself, a Federal-period house built in 1798, was constructed in part of old brick brought over from England. A third story had been added after the Civil War, and this Firuski rented to students. The *Harvard Advocate* had its quarters on the top floor. Roy Larsen, subsequently a founder of *Time*, was business manager of the *Advocate* then. He and Firuski saw a lot of each other. Larsen never saw Richard, though, or not that he remembered. Richard in his twenties was still the young recluse whom classmates at Cambridge Latin had found it easy to forget. John Pell—later he wrote the life of Ethan Allen—was another student who lived over the bookstore. Pell was putting together a collection of Henry James in the original editions. This was thanks to Firuski but no thanks to Richard, who knew more about James than anyone else and wasn't about to say so. "My memory is blank on RPB," said John Pell.

With Bernard Bandler, his future colleague on the *Hound & Horn*, Richard was more forthcoming. "I went one day to the Dunster House looking for James—it would be about 1928," Bandler said. "And James had not been rediscovered at all. . . . But Dick knew James" and didn't grudge his opinion. Only he expressed it in that "chiselled way" he had, almost a lapidary manner. "There was no smoke in his discourse—everything was clear, like the clarity of Arizona before the air was polluted—such distance in the sky and air." Bandler had no sense of effort going into the thing. The style was always laconic. This didn't deny but reinforced the intensity of feeling behind it.

Harry Murray, the Melville scholar, met Richard often "within the surround of Firuski's superlative assemblage of books." They talked high talk, Richard having "no appetite for trivia or banter or platitudes." He was "less interested in selling books to customers than in prospecting through their pages." Murray liked that kind of man. He was a friend of poetry himself, and he and Conrad Aiken had put together a stake for the poet Kenneth Patchen, who did his writing at night and labored by day unloading heavy drums of raw rubber. Richard hadn't this flamboyance—he was visibly inconspicuous, Murray remembered, "an introvert born and bred, self-contained, silent, meditative"—but he came across as an uncommon man. "Some greatness was in him."

Firuski saw the greatness. Like Harry Murray, he loved Melville— *Moby Dick*, he said, was "the only book I've ever read"—and he assimilated Richard to the Customs House inspector, poor, solitary, and persistent. Richard's poverty distressed him, and his thin skin provoked ironic amusement. "You sweat too much over your reviews," Firuski said. Several years later he got a letter from his former employee, requesting the loan of three hundred dollars. Richard proposed to leave Boston for Maine, "where Helen and I can live . . . for just a hair over $65 a month." Living was writing, so a little money went a long way. Richard said: "I have written a good deal of verse which I think is pretty good. Within a couple of weeks I shall have written two plays. . . . I want to complete my novel. And that is what I want the next five months for." Firuski remarked the "exceptional honesty" of this. You honored your obligations, and Richard in course paid his debt. But probity in such matters was anyone's possession. Richard's greater obligation was not financial but impersonal. He was honoring his talents.

"Such gambles of the whole soul . . . constitute the heroism of ability and will and honesty." The phrase is Richard's and applies, though he didn't draw the connection, to himself. It wasn't his abundant intellect that set him apart, but a fiercer allegiance. He reminded Firuski of the poet Robert Hillyer and the poet and Blake scholar Foster Damon. They were teaching at Harvard but without benefit of formal credentials. Like Richard, they had more pressing business than the Ph.D.

The Dunster House clerk smoked a pipe and was always rubbing it against the wings of his nose. It was a cheaper smoke than cigarettes and it gave him the panache of a literary gent. Also, he was always worrying a bone of contention. Firuski supposed he would have made a teacher. "He was a somewhat shabby clerk"—this from Bernard Bandler—but the shabbiness was groomed and the faded clothing ornate. He seemed old for his years—another acquaintance thought he belonged to the generation of Wheelwright and Cowley—and Firuski feared for his health and didn't put his chances of survival very high. Looking at Richard, thin as a rake and with an awful complexion—a dark pallor, Firuski called it—he saw a sick man and marveled later that his young assistant had lived even into his sixties. He suspected that Richard was tubercular and guessed at the wretched childhood—never once, when they talked, did the family come into it. Courting Helen Dickson made Richard happy, but you sensed he was clamping down on all manner of ugly things. There was the frugal way he talked, the tiny pursed mouth which hoarded the elegant phrases. This went with the formality. "It was always Mr. Eliot, Mr. Adams, Mr. James." Even with people he liked there was a stiffness. Bandler couldn't imagine Richard as having had a childhood or adolescence. "I have a mental picture of Dick from the time he was born right until the time he died, without youth or age intervening."

Richard called his new job "the softest job in the world," but he supposed it wouldn't last and that he and John Clement, who clerked for Firuski too, were about to get the sack. "Another couple of weeks, and I'll be looking for work." This was wishful thinking. He didn't get the sack and after a while the soft job turned tough. "I had forgotten what work was like," he wrote to his cousin. The Dunster House was moving to South Street, across from the house where George Anthony used to live, and Richard was shifting cartons from eight in the morning and discovering muscles he hadn't been aware of. Still, it was a relief to draw a week's pay instead of making a weekly addition to his debts.

To eke out his pay, he hustled first editions like Pound's *Draft of XVI Cantos*. Homer Pound had sent him a copy to sell on commission and he found a buyer in Elliot Paul, a friend and drinking pal of Wallace Dickson's. "He felt called upon to drown his mentality in alcohol, I assisted him," Wallace said. Elliot Paul was only another unpublished writer hoping his luck would turn, when he came back to Boston after the war. *The Last Time I Saw Paris* was still in the future, so were the years with Jolas and *transition*. For the present he made his living, like Kenneth Patchen, at manual labor. "Horizontal Labor," Wallace said scornfully. He had a taste for books he couldn't afford, and Richard was glad to oblige him. Then his luck turned dramatically. He got an advance on his novel, and he and Richard hailed a cab and started north in search of liquor. These were the years of the Volstead Amendment and Richard thought he might do Scott Fitzgerald. He wasn't a poseur but he liked to pose. He said they drove through the night until they reached Montreal.

In the bookstore Richard played cicerone to Harvard students, some of whom were older than he was. Kirstein said you couldn't estimate his influence "on the boys of his time who bought books suggested by him." Rob Darrell remembered how one of his undergraduate pupils, a well-fixed young man who worked at the Dunster House just because it pleased him, was laying a fire against the morning chill "when Dick staggered in, half asleep as usual at that time of day." The undergraduate was used to this labor, he said, "since I've never been able to find a houseman who could lay a proper fire." Had Richard fared any better? This question delighted the impecunious clerk. Also it woke him up.

Excitement for Richard was when T. S. Eliot's mother dropped by and he touched the hem of greatness, or when the Watch and Ward Society got after Firuski for selling *Lady Chatterley's Lover*. The censor asked him triumphantly—he wasn't himself a fastidious man—"Did you ever see a pervert with dirty hands?" and he sat down "in personal rage" and wrote a straight-out polemic for the *New Republic*. "Dirty Hands" was the title he gave it. This tickled Ezra Pound. "One hears curious tales of Boston," he wrote Richard from Rapallo. "According to reports it is now the rival of Tennessee and Arkansas."

When business was slack, he scribbled stories on Firuski's letterhead. "Equanimity à l'outrance" was one of his titles, and typically forbidding. Otherwise he had his nose in a book. "Nearly all day Monday," he confessed to George Anthony, he did "nearly nothing but read." The popular writers of his own time came first. MacLeish was the Modern Man in Search of a Soul: "but not too much in search, nor for too much of a soul." There were good things in Hemingway—in *The Sun Also Rises*, the fishing trip in the Pyrenees—and "the dialogue is swell." But Hemingway's novel "is much more a method of recording things seen by the author than of developing a donnée." His own greatest talent was for absolute recording which, as it is absolute, transcends mere recording and is its own donnée. He might have written of Hemingway what he wrote about Frost: "This is observation which is equal to vision." But he was too much a Jacobite to see the equivalence—in Hemingway, not least in himself.

Scientific writing engaged him in imaginative ways. This was a life-long interest and brought together, as often in Richard, his patient brooding on things and his irritable desire to use them as a halfway house. He cultivated his passion for Santayana, too—in philosophy, he said, "I can sink most wholly into him"—and he swallowed without comment the curious mix in this philosopher of obdurate individualism shading into art-for-art, and a fatuous progressivism that negated art-for-art. He didn't comment because he couldn't—he was looking at one side of himself, the Tory anarchist who despaired of the kingdom on earth and nonetheless liked to offer solutions. Reading Mann and Conrad, he said how the declarative mode wouldn't do. Mann, who shied from simple statement, had been "more resourceful in his exposition of being than anyone in our time." Conrad, on the other hand, was content to depose, as in telling us that loyalty and disillusion were noble. Meaning was not established but only intuited. Returning to Conrad, who had occupied first place in his pantheon of writers, Richard found him out. Mostly what Conrad saw went unrealized, and what he knew "was not often invested in the language as its blood stream." Sometimes Richard

himself invested what he knew in the language as its bloodstream, and
sometimes he spoke *ex cathedra* or spoke in thin air. This dichotomy
persisted.

In 1927 Firuski bought a house in the northwest corner of Connecticut. He wanted to live away from the city and to work with his hands.
Before winding up the Dunster House and leaving Cambridge for good,
he wrote to Richard: "I've been a dirt farmer for three months, and at
night I find a victrola better than a book. Eventually we all find out
what we were meant for." Richard by then was finding out what he was
meant for. All his spare time went to writing, and finally spare time was
not enough. He advertised his desire to quit, and Firuski didn't stand in
his way. By the spring of 1928 he was teaching his successor how to keep
the books. By the end of the year, he was gone. He wrote to Sean
O'Faolain, who was studying at Harvard and living at Miss Beck's
boarding house on Irving Street, two doors below the Blackmurs: "You
probably remember I was leaving Dunster House for the *Hound & Horn*
the first of the year. At any rate, here I am."

His title was "editing manager" and he told Ezra Pound he hoped to
hold it for at least the next five years. Pound rejoiced in a friend in
power. He was plugging his favorites and he wanted Richard to enlist
the help of Louis Zukofsky ("a serious character capable of making a
place in ANY country in europe"). When Richard didn't come to attention, Pound wrote indignantly: "Look for yourself at your current number and ask yourself how much of it ANYONE will be able to read in
1940." The current numbers of the *Hound & Horn* in the years 1927–34
included fiction by Dos Passos, Erskine Caldwell, Sean O'Faolain, Kay
Boyle, Caroline Gordon, Katherine Anne Porter (it was Richard who
accepted her "Flowering Judas"); essays and reviews by T. S. Eliot (his
"Second Thoughts about Humanism"), Theodore Spencer, Yvor Winters, Archibald MacLeish, Valéry on Leonardo, Eisenstein on film;
poems by Allen Tate, William Carlos Williams, Rilke in translation,
James Agee (his first published work other than a schoolboy effusion),
Jack Wheelwright, E. E. Cummings, Eliot, and Pound himself. This is a
partial list.

We want "a center for action and reaction," said Foster Damon,
cheering his friend's appointment. "There is a great chance for someone
to step in and ride the whirlwind; I think that you can do it perfectly
well." He did it partly by badgering the best writers of his time, who
were not always the most eminent writers. He asked Malcolm Cowley for
an essay or review or "something else," if Cowley had rather, and went

after Kenneth Burke and published Burke's "Declamations." He counted on friends to turn good things his way, and was grateful when Cowley put him on to Matthew Josephson, whose poems he had read in *Broom*, and Allen Tate and Edmund Wilson. Hemingway, at his urging, promised a story, so did Jean Toomer, the gifted author of *Cane*. He said he was "freshened" when Wallace Stevens sent a poem, and he had the temerity to tell Stevens that everyone liked it, "some more than I."

The list of writers he got to contribute is more impressive for his own contribution. His essay on Eliot, spread over two numbers in 1928, dramatized his own principle that absolute patience—in personal intercourse, in coping with ideas, or in "the game of criticism"—was "the only operative agent for getting to know." Before the poetry and prose, he sat like Patience on her monument. This made his reputation. "You are already famous in Cambridge," an English admirer told him, "as the author of the only good criticism of T. S. Eliot." Allen Tate called the essays on Cummings and Stevens "the finest criticism of contemporary poetry in my generation." The number of the magazine devoted to Henry James (April 1934) was "the best thing of its kind" he had ever seen. For this number—"our masterpiece," Kirstein said—Edmund Wilson wrote an essay. So did Marianne Moore, Francis Fergusson, Stephen Spender, Glenway Wescott, others. Richard on James was incomparably the best of them.

He was good when he tried the high wire, better on finicking matters like diction, no one more finicking than he. He said how the Imagist poet H.D., using antipoetic diction, made you feel it as poetry (this was like Satie in music), also how poetic diction—what most readers called poetry—was only "fancy flatulence." The belletristic style got his hackles up. He disliked in Herbert Read the slack suavity that passed for good manners. "Live Language is always on the stretch," he said, "and covers the nervous metabolism it expresses." Reviewing Wyndham Lewis, he posited two ways of approaching experience. "One is the abstract and intellectual habit; the other is the concrete or intelligent." One aimed at delineating the scheme of relations, the other at registering wholes. His critical habit was intelligent, not yet intellectual. He attended to qualities, not to the scheme of relations. Many years later a perceptive reader called his criticism "the ripest fruit of the Crocean method." This was "a way of treating a poet as if he were, for the moment, only valuable as a rich and complete stasis in the history of art." There in a nutshell is the New Criticism. "Weather is all." This line from Richard's poetry makes a good rubric for the critical essays he published in the *Hound & Horn*. His province was ontology. He wished "to qualify the thing, to seize upon it individually" without plans or blueprints. When he said that Stevens' poetry was weather, he was praising his highest praise.

Stevens thought the essays "extraordinarily interesting" and wrote Kirstein to say so. The interest is permanent, as the eye is on the streaks of the tulip. Richard in the early work makes you think of early Hemingway, whose real merit he didn't divine. The great thing was to "see and hear and learn and understand; and write when there is something that you know; and not before; and not too damned much after." This taciturn stuff was not to everyone's taste. Conrad Aiken called it pedantic. "I think you sometimes read with your eye a little too close to the page, seeing enormous and separate syllables, each distinct and portentous." This is fair criticism and requires a codicil. "Just the same your analytic attack on the *texture* of a text ought to be damned useful as a preliminary to the something else." The something else wasn't always in train. Aiken didn't know that. "Art looks at things outside the self for themselves." That is Richard, reviewing his mother's old boarder, Leo Stein. The analytic attack—on a hostile reading, critical myopia— "advances no propositions and infers no truths." But it got you further along than the belletristic style—"I should have thought," etc.—or academic mugwumpery: "On the one hand, but then on the other."

Edmund Wilson didn't think it got you far along. He and Richard were friendly, but he wasn't one of the friends. He is like them, however, in presenting the background against which Richard shows his difference and his value. "Edmund Wilson did not care for Blackmur's criticism," Mary McCarthy said, "or for the whole school it represented . . . though he rather liked him personally." In 1929 Richard perhaps hadn't earned the right not to care for Wilson's criticism. He thought it would be "quite swell" to get a piece from Wilson on French Symbolist poetry, like the one he had written for the *New Republic*. Nothing came of this, Wilson being skeptical of the *Hound & Horn*. He said it was "infected by the tendency to be too abstract," and he wished that Richard in his own writing "would tell a little more about the author's style, about his 'atmosphere' and personality." What Wilson called "the philosophic criticism now in vogue" put him off, as it discussed literature "in terms of a sort of literary scholasticism." That is just right. The best of New Criticism is hermeneutical writing.

Wilson in his own discussion of literature was primarily the intellectual critic. When he confronted poetry he walked around it, never closing with the poem. *Axel's Castle* shows this. "The book is not written, it is written about." The thing itself was less important than the thing in its scheme of relations. No harm in that, Wilson supposed. The reader wanted the critic "to tell him what the book is like—that is to say, how it is written, what sort of temperament the author has and what sort of effects he produces." A critic like Richard, reacting against the impressionism of the day before yesterday, threw out the baby with the bath. Reading him, you searched in vain for "any intimation of what the work under consideration looks, sounds, feels or smells like."

This is the standard objection to the New Critical method and comes home more persuasively as it invokes the senses, while deprecating criticism couched "in abstract terms." But what makes Wilson sore isn't that New Criticism is too intellectual, but that it isn't intellectual enough. It doesn't "make any effort to understand the writer's point of view." Richard as critic, said Morton Zabel precisely, "respected Mallarmé's principle that literature is not written with ideas but with words." Ideas or point of view, disengaged and deftly placed—that is Wilson's métier. He is "a chronicler of his time," one reviewer wrote, whose critical technique "he borrowed from that old master of Nineteenth Century reviewing on the grand scale, M. Taine." You describe "the man and his environment, and then his works in their terms." No American writer has ever performed this function with greater mastery, but it isn't literary criticism.

Richard's notion of criticism boiled down, he said, to "exegesis tout court." The academy, when it got round to canonizing the New Critics took them to mean that exegesis said the poem, as when you explained all the recondite allusions in a poem by Yeats or Donne. Explanation had its uses—Richard was clear on that—so did the labor of analysis. You didn't shirk this labor—"I am timid of mistakes in a matter where I so wish to be correct," he wrote to Wallace Stevens—but you understood that it was only partial. What was plenary? No method was plenary or no labor all sufficing, for the substance of the arts was finally inaccessible —recalling the essays Richard wrote for the *Phonograph Monthly Review*. The inaccessibility didn't breed despair. "Our fiction that we understand one another and one another's poetry is convention; and convention when it is alive—that is to say intelligent—is the most daring form the imagination takes." So there was something to dare.

"On a huge hill,/ Cragged and steep, Truth stands, and he that will/ Reach her about must, and about must go." This was Donne's metaphor. He dared greatly and he thought you could win to absolute truth as you persevered in the ascent. His poem was declarative, though, like Joseph Conrad, and he took the wish for the deed. For Richard, "the game of criticism" was comprised in the ascent. You didn't get to the summit, and perhaps there was no summit or else it was impenetrably shrouded. Ambiguity, he said, is "the *explicit* virtue of poetry," and only by insisting on this would one ever learn "what the meaning in poetry is."

The move to the *Hound & Horn* was hatched in the Dunster House Book Shop. Bernard Bandler and Richard had "hit it off directly we met," Bandler said. His bent was for ideas and he was seeking to perfect a command of intellectual and philosophical abstractions. He liked the gloom and doom for which Irving Babbitt, his teacher at Harvard, was famous or notorious. Bandler wasn't "what you might call 'literary,'" Richard told Cowley, though "deo volente [he] will become so." In fact he became a well-known psychiatrist. Kirstein felt he might have been a rabbi or a priest, and when they talked for the first time, it left Kirstein exhausted for two days.

Whatever Bandler was looking for he found briefly in Richard, on the principle that opposites attract. He wrote how his thoughts reverted to Richard "when I am deeply moved and serious," and he waited anxiously on "tidings of your play, your novel, your poetry, your review." He knew that Richard's job crowded this activity into the corners, and he suggested to Kirstein that they find a way to take him on. "We needed someone to act as our business manager and oversee the editorial side"—Varian Fry, whose duty that was, had resigned in a huff when Bandler came in—"and I felt that the salary would free him from selling books and give him some opportunity for his own writing. I guess we were the first Guggenheim Foundation in Dick's life."

The *Hound & Horn* had "a certain modest affluence" supplied by Kirstein's father, a character out of Balzac who pretended to have a hearing problem when you wanted to get something from him. He was *the* power in Filene's, Firuski said, and like Richard a self-educated man, "the most interesting kind." When Harvard, making no distinction among princes and paupers, wanted to know if the Kirsteins could afford to pay their son's tuition, Firuski signed the bond which certified this family's ability to pay. The Kirstein daughter was Firuski's friend, too: she was Mina Curtiss, who wrote the life of Bizet and awoke a great ardor in Sherry Mangan. Richard was only three years older than Lincoln Kirstein, but the relation between them was that of master to pupil. Gradually this changed.

They met at the Dunster House in 1926—Jack Wheelwright was there, Kirstein remembered—and they talked about poetry. Kirstein must have seemed to Richard, who did one thing well, a modern version of the Renaissance man. He wasn't an artist, but he won a prize for freehand drawing at Harvard. He wasn't a pianist, but he played the piano better than most. He published a novel and a book of poems, and he wrote on painting and photography. He was an art collector and helped establish the Harvard Society for Contemporary Art, which gave birth to the Museum of Modern Art in New York. As a sophomore at Harvard, he began the *Hound & Horn*. This made him a focus of literary gossip. The college-boy hero of Richard John's story "Solstice," who becomes the darling of an amoral expatriate society, was supposed to be Kirstein. Gossip colored the magazine, too. The color was yellow, as of the Yellow Book or Yellow Nineties. "The *Hound & Horn* crew," said Richard's friend de Rochemont, "were a little too limp-wristed for me."

Many years later, Richard said how no one could be more American than Kirstein. "His many and long exposures to 'Europe' and to South America had only weathered him down to a native rock to which they had then administered a durable and variable polish. His glitter reflected many lights but his glow was his own—as much as his figure with its delicate balance a little off plumb and his walk that came straight from 'Alice in Wonderland.'" The great work of Kirstein's life was undoubtedly the School of American Ballet, which he created for the choreographer George Balanchine in 1934. This work put period to the *Hound & Horn*. The magazine didn't die from inanition, Richard said bitterly. "That great exponent of not criticism . . . A. Hamlet MacLeish" had represented to Kirstein senior that Lincoln was wasting time on what was "merely a critical journal." So Kirstein's father tied up his money bags, and "now Lincoln Kirstein can waste all his career on his school of the ballet." Eight years earlier, however, literature was still the engrossing thing for Kirstein. When he finished a poem, he sent it to the bookshop. No one except Richard was to see it. He said, "I wanted you to see it because I value your opinion on such matters higher than anybody I know." After a while, a thread of complaining appeared in his letters: "No word from you ever. I feel deserted." Then the letters stopped on both sides.

Kirstein, like Bandler, found resources in Richard he didn't find in himself. Richard hadn't been to college and perhaps, Kirstein said, "that was why he was so amazingly well-educated . . . ten times a Harvard Ph.D." College was a vacuum—Henry Adams had said "everything one can say about Harvard"—and the *Hound & Horn* was intended to fill it. Kirstein admired Eliot and Varian Fry admired Joyce, and both of them were conscious of Not Being Schoolboys Any Longer. One was twenty, the other nineteen. They had read Gertrude Stein and looked at Picasso and listened to Stravinsky, and they wanted to "hail the new and glittering world" these artists were creating. In 1927 they brought out the first number of their "Harvard Miscellany." The *American Mercury* furnished a model, so did the old *North American Review*. But the great debt was to the *Criterion*. Eliot's friend Monte Belgion "had quite a standing in the literary world" of the twenties, Malcolm Cowley said, and Belgion functioned as the liaison between the magazines. A received text for both of them was the polemical writing of Charles Maurras. He had led the rebellion against the vagueness and emotionalism of the Symbolist poets, and the editors listened respectfully when he summoned them to clarity and restraint. Partly that was the message of the horn call.

The first number of the *Hound & Horn* was "full of bad taste" and Kirstein meant this as a boast, "considering all the good taste we had crammed into our eyes and ears for four years at Harvard." From a poem of Ezra Pound's, "The White Stag," they took their title—" 'Tis the white stag Fame we're hunting, bid the world's hounds come to horn"—and they got their handsome cover and their colophon from Rockwell Kent, who gave them "children's prices." If you were in the know, you referred to the magazine as the Bitch and Bugle. Some people took it for a hunting magazine, and for the next seven years the editors got advertisements for prize beagles and Airedales.

The *Hound & Horn* was primarily artistic, a magazine of techniques. "Our standard for judging the arts is technical." (Richard was signaling the end of the purely Harvard connection.) "What we really ask of our criticism is that it be critical, that it should seize the central point of any subject, and discuss that with all the learning, logic, and insight it can command." In politics the bias ran to the left, with plenty of divagation. "What to do with the technique after you got it" seemed increasingly clear to Kirstein. But the more important bias was to make the magazine a repository of the accidental good. "We try as consciously as may be not to depend on our own taste," Richard said, rather "to elucidate a general taste not the individual property of any one of us." He hoped it might be thought "that the contributors collectively edited the magazine." Also the magazine did its conscious best not to hear America singing. None of its most memorable stories "could have been printed in the *Atlantic, Scribner's* or *Harper's*." That made Kirstein proud. In an intolerant country, said Sean O'Faolain, "an open arena . . . is a gift of God." He wanted the Hound to chase the Stag forever, like the folk on the Grecian urn, and he pleaded with Kirstein, whose eye was already turning to ballet, not to let the magazine down. "It is the best America has and nothing else to replace it." The *Criterion* shared this opinion. "From the literary and philosophic-literary point of view," the *Hound & Horn* was "the best magazine . . . of any in America."

The editorial announcing the first number sounded the hunting horn (from Brahms's E-flat Trio for horn, violin, and piano). It took off from Plato in the original Greek (getting the sense exactly wrong), and bade disdainful farewell to the old familiar contours. For the first number, Conrad Aiken stood in as editor. This was another point of access for Richard. Aiken was living over Gordon Cairnie's bookstore, and sometimes in the morning he gave Richard gin and criticism. No two poets were more dissimilar and each gave the lie to the neurasthenic idea of the poet. A heroic type of the ladies' man, Aiken talked freely about his adventures and his misadventures, too. There was the young woman he had failed to penetrate. "A clear case of synecdoche," he explained to his friend, "the part is greater than the whole." Richard the fierce recluse rejoiced in these stories. Also he valued Aiken's critical talent and the keenness of his critical grin. He said Aiken's reading of "my verse was the shrewdest and most sympathetic I ever had."

With subsequent editors Richard was on shakier ground. Varian Fry, who intended the *Hound & Horn* for college boys primarily, hated him, Kirstein said. Richard said that Fry made an excellent proofreader. After two years, as the magazine changed direction—according to Fry, as it went off the track—he got out and Richard replaced him. Bandler was now the formulating influence, and the chief props were Francis Fergusson and A. Hyatt Mayor. Both had come to the magazine from the American Laboratory Theatre. Mayor was Princeton and Oxford, his special competence was art, and later he ran the Print Room at the Metropolitan Museum. Francis Fergusson made his reputation as a critic of the drama. He wasn't Richard's kind of critic at all. He had tasked the great Eliot for depressing humanity in favor of literature and "form." Eliot presented "the spectacle of a man doomed by sterility in the effort to make art out of art." Richard looked at these strictures and wrote haughtily that "one sits somewhat in another corner."

Francis Fergusson went on to an academic career. For a while he and Richard were colleagues at Princeton, and you have to suppose that he smiled a little at the famous establishment figure. He remembered Richard in the *Hound & Horn* days as "starved, pale, thin, and subdued." Mayor, who encountered him a few times in "that tiny crammed office" on Massachusetts Avenue—the Harvard Coop is located there now—called Richard a force under compression. "He seemed cramped by the skimpiness of his past, tense to the point of explosion. His eye was fixed on the upper rungs of the academic ladder. Of course we were all in a turmoil over Sacco and Vanzetti, and the Depression was the air we breathed, but Dick Blackmur was straining so hard to advance that he had little energy left over for people or current events."

With this severe estimate Richard could live, so long as Kirstein was his friend and supporter. But the friendship went up and down. Kirstein gave Richard credit for being the original source of the magazine, and the whole energy behind it before Bandler joined the staff. "He was very clever, taught me about 'modern literature,' he was good to work with, a super-intellectual." The last was qualified praise. Richard wanted to learn Sanskrit (the Numen and the Moha beckoned seductively) and that was all right, but not having your eye on the academic ladder. Kirstein didn't like academics and when Richard became "a Princeton pundit," they never met again. That is Kirstein's version of the break between them.

After Richard's death Kirstein traced the rise of the poor boy who ended up a full professor. The key to the life and the "hideous overcompensating" that marked the last years was Richard's early poverty. He was saturated in poverty and struggled blindly to get free. "Blind energy makes you die." He made Kirstein think of a character out of Hawthorne—a joyless man, incapable of pleasure, a sexually bedeviled man who didn't like his own body. More than this: "He didn't bathe, he wasn't clean." Helen Dickson was pretty bad, too, and their wedding, which Kirstein attended, was a poor and miserable affair. The music was furnished by a victrola. Richard, Kirstein said, was a snob.

The poverty infiltrated his criticism. "He made a capital"—the money he didn't have—"out of his mind." He attacked literature as if it were a piece of property and he played with the property, oblivious of what it stood for. Sean O'Faolain, for whom the *Hound & Horn* was a dropping-in place, remembered Kirstein "bursting out" at Richard one day: "Your critical attitude makes me *sick!*" This attitude, Kirstein thought, went with being an intellectual, for whom the real fact was always at a remove. "Mind is the great cancer."

Bandler had another story to tell. "Dick got along well" in the new job, he said, "it was great fun. . . . In terms of the job, Dick functioned, he did all that was necessary." On the other hand, "very little was necessary, so it was really a superfluous job." Also: "I don't think of Dick as an administrator." But Richard the conscientious administrator got high marks from Firuski. In the winter of 1930 the *Hound & Horn* went national. It left Cambridge and took up new quarters on the East

Side of Manhattan. This was decisive, according to Bandler. "Imagine the echoes of the financial crash . . . and, ah, we had to consider finances . . . and we *were* moving to New York—and there was an absence . . . not in Dick's performance as a business manager . . . but there was an absence of any creative response. . . . So we had to let him go."

Richard thought they let him go because the magazine was merging with the *Symposium*, an uneven hash "of money and intentions." In setting up the merger, Fergusson and Mayor acted as the go-betweens. "The two new gents" on the other side were Philip Wheelwright, then dean of philosophy at N.Y.U., "and a chap named Burnham, also a philosopher." They wanted to hymn John Dewey on his seventieth birthday, and "the composition of money and hagiology was too great to resist." Richard gathered that his own less hearty prose appeared "abstract" to them. Still, he said, his being fired made sense. "With four more or less active editors, enough positive labour can be extracted to get the magazine out without paying me or anyone else to be m.e."

Then what Kirstein called "the fifteen-minute merger" came unstuck. He wrote to Louis Zukofsky: "We had the idea of combining with another magazine, which has since appeared under the title of 'The Symposium.' [But] the negotiations fell through. . . . Our relations during the last few weeks have been most unpleasant." Maybe there was too much weight on the side of the *Hound & Horn*—not the fifty-fifty split everyone had envisaged—or maybe, as James Burnham thought, "the legal and financial advisers in the Kirstein family" exercised a veto. For whatever reason, "The deal had to be called off." It made no difference to Richard. Nobody clamored to have him back again. His job went to Bandler's friend and Harvard classmate, Alan Stroock, who "had aspirations to the good life, like every self-respecting man of that time." The good life, Bandler said, "was associated with art." Stroock could afford it, his father's law firm was his warrant, and when he joined the *Hound & Horn* he worked for no salary. The salary he waived was critical for Richard: it was like the Frost poem where the man chops wood just because it pleases him, and the necessitous tramps dispute his pleasure. The *Hound & Horn* paid its contributors—not much, but enough for writers like Kenneth Patchen and Grant Code to put bread on the table. It paid Richard $2,340 a year. More than ten years went by before he saw that much money again. Losing it, Bandler said, "must have confronted him with a very substantial financial dilemma."

He acknowledged the dilemma in letters to friends, and they were sorry to hear that "the Horny Hound uses you so ill." He was sorry, too, he said, "as I was just beginning to see my way clear to doing something with the magazine, and because I was able to get enough leisure to do my own work without starving or other attenuation." Toward his former associates, he showed his best stoical-literary face. "Lincoln gave me the privilege of telling him," Bandler said. "He took it like a man, but I do recall what he said, because he quoted from Pericles' funeral oration. . . . He showed no effect, except that quotation. And I felt he was hurt to the quick."

The hurt mattered to Richard but doesn't matter anymore and the story of these years, when you add it all up, is by no means unhappy. What matters is the work that got done. The *Hound & Horn* gave Richard his entrée to a greater world, and he made sure that the world would take notice. In the eyes of his contemporaries, what he said on modern poets was "the only criticism of consequence" they had ever seen. "I respect your opinion as I respect the opinion of Eliot," said Kenneth Patchen. Homer Pound, assiduous in reading reviews of his son's poetry, wrote to Richard how "yours appeals to me as about the very best." To John Crowe Ransom, he was "the best man there was, or going to be." Early in the thirties, Yvor Winters saluted him. The essays on poetry and notably on Wallace Stevens—"a masterpiece," Winters called it—constituted "the most solid work of our time." Richard was on to other things then, but the *Hound & Horn* remained his forum for the seven years it lived. This, Kirstein said, was one of the best reasons for the existence of the magazine.

CHAPTER THREE

Good *and* Evil

I N T H E L I F E of Henry Adams, Richard shows his hero oscillating between distrust of power and a willingness to use it. Perhaps, Richard thought, Adams was of two minds, "as all men must be when dealing with good *and* evil in the one lump." This mingled compound presents the marriage he made with Helen Dickson. "Being with you," he told her, "when nothing occurs to make me think our relation impermanent and your love transitory, brings to me all the unity and peace I have need of." The relation proved impermanent and the love, if not transitory, was inseparable from hate. The marriage was real, though, both corrosive and annealing, worth "any labor and any sacrifice," and to say it ended in failure is only to say how it ended.

For Halloween in 1925, Tessa Gilbert gave a party at 12 Ellery Street. Richard was there, a bit down in the mouth. For almost three years he had been in love with her, though he sensed that she hadn't reciprocated his love or not in the way he desired. The heat at which he warmed himself was disseminated in Tessa, the intensity was all peripheral, "a decorative sophistication." Still, after considering "the attenuations and diversions to which the flesh is subject," he decided to pop the question. Would "the dear girl . . . have me?" This was in October. Two weeks went by, and finally Tessa made up her mind. "All heaven's shining flood-gates fell, a negative rejoinder." So it was over between them. Then Tessa began to act "as if she felt she had made a mistake." It was too late, Richard thought, to pick up the pieces, but he didn't know what he would do if she wanted him back again. She had, he acknowledged, "some claim on me." He told his cousin that Tessa agreed with this judgment. She was a great beauty and accepted her due.

For the Halloween party she had got Richard up in a fortuneteller's costume, hanks of black hair descending from a ratty headdress "à la PLO." She sat him in a darkened alcove, to which guests were admitted to have their fortunes told. Helen Dickson was among the guests. She and Tessa were studying with the painter Harold Zimmerman. Her brother Wallace had dropped Helen's name to his partner, but she and Richard hadn't met. Tessa brought them together. That night, she remembered, Richard read Helen's palm for almost an hour, "or so it seemed to me." The attraction was instant and each of them felt it. Before the evening was over, Helen had appropriated Richard—"that's the word," Rob Darrell said—"snapped him right up from under Tessa's nose." A few days later, Richard informed George Anthony that he had severed relations with Tessa. "Meantime," he said, "you will remember Wallace has a sister Helen." Nothing less than a lifetime turned on this offhand remark.

Soon after the party he spent a Sunday evening with Helen. "I cannot say why I should have permitted it, even urged it, to happen," he said. "The fact is, I did; so that now all the peculiar energy I had collected in two and a half years has discovered a new object." He knew he had been reckless, and guilt was nagging at him. It seemed to him that the profoundest error a human being could commit was "to mistake the object and the intensity of its own passion." If you caused "some other person to make that same mistake," you were guilty of the worst breach of human honor. There was another error with which he might be charged, "exquisitely painful at its fullest." Reciting it, he laid open the mistrust of the world, rooted in self-mistrust, that made him hang fire whenever a friend got too close. This was "to believe in and to hope for the permanence of another's passion." He supposed that in the last months he had committed both errors, the breach of honor, too. Tessa had chucked him and then, on his account, "Helen chucked her young man"—Bill Gurney, Wallace's chum. At first he had egged himself on to fall for Helen. Abruptly the real thing confronted him, "realer than I had imagined possible." No going back either: he understood that he was bound. "She has said and done enough to make it impossible . . . for me to leave her." He didn't want to leave her anyway, and though he had bought no rings he said that he and Helen were more than tentatively engaged. Then the skepticism flared again: of course it might all come to nothing. If it did, he determined "to relinquish forever . . . all claims to the female heart." In his character of young rake, he concluded: "I say nothing about the legs."

Helen was less devious and remained so. Over the years, as she and Richard rubbed together, her truth was aggravated. She was, a friend said, "embarrassingly honest" and responded to life "in the most direct and elementary way." She wanted to get married or she wanted to challenge Richard, and she bet him that he didn't have the nerve. It was three months to the day from their first encounter at Tessa's party, and Richard took the dare and went off to City Hall to file his declaration of intentions. He was "fully as well known in Cambridge as . . . [was] Miss Dickson in the Brookline section," and the newspapers were happy to publicize the engagement. Richard was mortified. He was also boxed in, so with a curious inconsequence he returned to City Hall and picked up a marriage license, "lest further questions be asked."

Then he began to panic. He felt himself (in journalese) "not sufficiently well equipped financially to provide his prospective bride with the sort of home she had been accustomed to." When he took the license out, he knew that he didn't mean to use it. So far, his sister said, it was "just for a lark." Being himself and obsessive, he read the fine print and learned that his unused license had to be returned; otherwise he would be breaking the law. So in June, a month for weddings, he mailed it back without comment, "the only one apparently in the history of Cambridge who ever did."

The City Clerk was amused and got hold of the papers; by the afternoon the reporters were on the trail. But "no trace could be found . . . of either Blackmer [sic] or his prospective bride. The details of the alleged shattered romance were bared by a brother of the young man." This was George, a high-school student, all by himself in the house on Irving Street and very much on the spot. The reporter wanted a picture of Helen, Betty said, "which George obligingly brought from Dick's room." The reporter asked a lot of questions, then wrote his story. "Cambridge blueblood jilts fiancée" was the gist. Rob Darrell had met Richard for the first time the night before. "Dick," he said, "was indelibly impressed on my mind the very next day . . . when he departed for Maine with the Dicksons and simultaneously was featured in a front-page story in the *Boston Herald*: Poet returns wedding license." Richard's mother figured in the story, too. It wasn't so, she said, that "the proposed nuptials" had been thwarted by "any family objections." Helen Dickson, no doubt, was as nice as could be, but "young people have a habit of changing their minds." She added her opinion that Helen and Richard wouldn't get married "for five or six years yet." Somehow the reporters located Richard's father. He said the whole thing was " 'news' to him."

Richard was safe in Maine but smarting at what he called "my insufferable flourish in the front page headlines of six Boston papers." He generalized from it in a letter to George Anthony. Love was "mostly a mistake," and required "hypocrisy and concealment of motive." This didn't sound like a bridegroom. But Richard was his parents' son and unfitted for the part by long training. On women he bestowed contempt. He said inspiration was beyond them. "They can never be more than polished mediocrities." Women were the vacuum which Nature abhorred. To fill this vacuum was a chore and one reason for assuming the odious role of a husband. "The husband's obligations are limited, the lover's infinite." If you wanted to be happy, you had better keep your distance. In a sketch for a story or playlet, Richard wrote of his young male and female protagonists: "They know each other very little and therefore enjoy themselves." He expected he wouldn't "shine as a husband," and he was right. What made others weepy set his teeth on edge—getting married, for instance. He thought the ceremony should be held in a phone booth. "Here Comes the Bride" was out, unless played on the jew's-harp or sweet potato. The best he could say, when George Anthony married Marcia, was that marriage was something "we have need of, that we may not waste in our sleep or our hands."

With Helen he was off again, on again. "Is it brakes or gas?" his cousin wanted to know. "What dream of Ste. Theresa prevents you from marrying her?" Richard didn't have an answer and lapsed in melancholy. "I shall be extremely mad," Helen wrote him a year into their courtship, "if you don't cut out the suicidal talk." Maybe the fear that plagued him was "the destruction of the idiosyncratic personal genius." This was George Anthony's high-flown idea. He said impatiently to Richard: You wouldn't "be so much as skinning the knuckles of your own integration by marriage with Helen." It wasn't integration, though, that left him at a stand.

His mother diminished other women for him and made them suspect, too. He needed a woman to take care of him, Francis Fergusson said. The felt need begot resentment. Richard didn't acknowledge this. He took the line—reviewing a life of the stricken poet Cowper—that "plain narrative illustrated by common sense makes a better index to a difficult soul, at least when it is a dead man's soul, than any amount of psychological exploration." In his own case, the plain narrative demands a little glossing.

Allen Tate enjoyed telling how young Richard ate Sunday dinner in Cambridge with his mother, while Helen Dickson sat alone in the parlor. This perhaps was malicious gossip. But "there was always gossip about Dick's . . . attachment to his mother," Malcolm Cowley remembered. "People said that it led him to repress his sexual desires except perhaps once a year, when they would explode in a sadistic fashion."

This was usually after a fight. He was tense with women as they confronted him with a sexual possibility. One of them confronted him and said later to Cowley that "dancing with Dick was like dancing with a steel cable of the Brooklyn Bridge." The tension dropped, however, when a woman was safely married to a friend. There he was "both adorable and sexy."

Toward maternal women, he gravitated easily. Marguerite Dickson, Helen's mother, was that kind of woman, ostensibly passive but with a whim of iron. Friends called her a tabbycat or an old rabbit, but this was only what she looked like. Widowed in her early forties with three children to care for, she met the challenge and then some. She worked for the Boston Municipal League, and after that job folded, for the WPA. She wasn't on relief, though. During the Depression, said her daughter Katharine, "Mother was the only person in the household really earning money." When Richard went to Harrington for the first time, he went to be with Helen but also with Mrs. Dickson. She was writing a book on European history and he came along as her assistant. He wanted to be mothered, Helen Dickson said later, but would never admit it.

So the prospects for marriage weren't so good on his side. On Helen's side, they weren't all that better. Helen, said the painter Kate Foster, was "very vivid and vital and totally the wrong wife for him." Where he dithered, she coped. Anything Helen tackled, she was sure to do well. Whatever the problem—painting or drawing, housework or handicrafts—"no matter how difficult or annoying . . . she'd always stick with it until it was solved." This made her an odd companion to the self-confessed Monster of Sloth. She didn't have much humor and he delighted in the coarser kind. Florence Codman, his first publisher, remembered the sly, amused look in his eyes. "He was that sort of Yankee—more pleased by fun than wit." For Helen, Tessa thought, this betrayed a want of character. "Why are you always laughing?" she asked Tessa reproachfully. Helen had a baleful look like the girl in the fairy tale, Jack Wheelwright used to say. "When she opened her mouth, toads fell out."

Like her mother, she seemed passive. Some friends thought her beautiful, and they summed her up in the incredible hair and the piercing blue eyes. Betty Blackmur remembered the eyes, the low voice, and an image of being soft like a kitten. The gray fur jacket was part of the image, and the Greta Garbo hairdo. Her hatred of pretension was absolute. As Richard in his later years defined the Old Pretender, this hatred grew venomous. She was basically transparent. Her total lack of opacity tormented Richard, a friend decided, and made him act cruelly and perversely to her. "He could not endure the fact of her seamless simplicity; he had to violate and deny it."

Tessa, the lifelong friend and fellow painter and fellow tenant in Richard's psyche, found her socially gauche. To polite conversation, she turned a face that was petulant or sullen. She was extraordinary in some ways, intolerable in others—decidedly plain, especially in her dour moods. This was most of the time, according to Rob Darrell. "At rare times and briefly she could be almost beautiful." One of these times was visibly present to the poet and historian Kenneth Wiggins Porter, who met Helen and Richard at Wheelwright's parties on Beacon Street. Even after forty years, he saw the "beautiful young woman of a dark Irish type." He remembered the hair and the purple gown and how, near the end of the party, a young Harvard instructor who had had enough to drink tried to persuade her to "go dancing" with him some afternoon or evening. He put this proposition while holding a foot in one hand and trying to hop through the loop he had made, and Helen fended him off with great calm and good humor. She gave the impression that there was nothing in the world she would more enjoy doing, "were it possible— which it wasn't."

So Helen wore two faces. Nela Walcott was good at portraits and captured one of the faces. Nela had a psychological grasp of her subjects, Tessa said, and she divined a caged animal in Helen. "This was *exactly* what she was." Helen hated the portrait. "I think I look terrible in it," she said. "I think it's very good," Tessa said.

Helen was instinctively what Richard wanted to be: a natural. Tessa, with less sympathy, called her a primitive. Friends to whom the Blackmurs paid a visit in Nova Scotia found Helen in that setting "a much more vivid person . . . than Dick." Like Kate Foster, they stressed her Algonquin Indian blood and said how she walked barefoot, gripping the earth with her toes. She was insistently tactile, lower case. "Who's sick?" Richard wrote, in his *Scarabs for the Living.* "Who lies awake in sweat?" praying an end to the splitting of the self. "Not you," he answered:

> you see betimes the blackest black is blue;
> where Self recedes in selves, and Day in days.

Viewed harshly, he was literary and Helen was real. "If she lacked the profound general insight into character and history which her husband expressed at his best, she also lacked the ponderous disadvantage of that insight." Richard, giving the character of Marian Adams, meant that she wasn't an intellectual. Her taste was resolute, though, "quick, and shrewd in action; sharp for the ludicrous, unerring for the vain and the sham; exquisitely sensitive of detail." The difference between them was "a matter of emphasis." (Here Richard was comparing Henry Adams and his brother Brooks.) Each was attracted to the other's mode of approach as securing what each one lacked to make "reason divine, or divination reasonable." Helen's real psychic powers impressed him—he thought she might play Georgie Yeats to his Poet—and once during an impromptu séance (inspired of course by the one in *The Magic Mountain*) friends sensed about her a slight but definite feel of electricity: the room was dead silent but there was something in the air. In the morning the neighbors who lived just beneath inquired about all the strange noises in the night.

Helen had a low opinion of the Radcliffe intellectuals with whom Richard enjoyed himself. "Dick," she said scornfully, "likes his women *woolen*." To Richard's volubility, she opposed the Yankee reticence that went with the old farmhouse in Washington County, Maine. But nobody called her shy. Richard noted with mixed feelings "her regular combination of ferocious sincerity and grace." The painter Waldo Peirce put her on a pedestal. He wrote to Richard:

> Tho Washington County's known for vixens
> There aint bin many among the Dicksons.
> Helen's the nearest thing to a saint
> We have outside museum paint.

But she wasn't a saint. With Richard, she was endlessly destructive. He praised an up-to-date composition in quarter tones, and she told him scornfully that playing this music was the perfect way to commit suicide. "Quiet sadness and resignation" seemed for one friend to characterize their relationship, and the characterization rings true. But it didn't preclude episodes and remarks that struck fire. Richard's neighbors in Maine remembered how Helen got on him. "What are you doing?" she burst out one day, apropos of nothing at all. "Just speaking to my trousers," he told her.

Like Richard she suffered colorfully, and like him was erudite in the more distressing symptoms of disease. "Fistular and pustular" was a favorite phrase of hers. Literally and figuratively, she liked to pick at sores. Sometimes at dinner the two of them read together in the big medical tomes they kept in the farmhouse. They took pleasure in the ghastlier stuff, like cancer of the great colon. Being sick they had in common, and Richard in his letters didn't weary of reciting what ailed them. In the spring of 1930 it was impacted teeth. They gave Helen painful earaches and she understood from her dentist that they often caused insanity, too. "Somehow," Richard wrote, this "pleases her, and permits her to say she may murder me in my sleep."

Her teeth and his "monstrous sores" notwithstanding, they decided after five years that they had waited long enough. (Mrs. Blackmur in her hopeful opinion wasn't so far out.) "The dog and I are going to marry," Richard wrote to George and Elizabeth Orrok, "the better to end it all." (One of his mother's pet names for Richard was "doggie," and he fastened this name on his wife.) He took comfort in supposing "that dog doesn't want a 'good husband,'" and he thought that "very likely she and I will get along as well as most." The wedding was set for June 14, 1930. Richard was twenty-six, and except for summers in Maine with Mrs. Dickson and "her two husky lassies," he had lived at home all his life.

They were married in the garden, outside the Dickson house in Belmont. The bridesmaids and the matron of honor wore pale green dotted Swiss dresses and big floppy hats. They carried big bouquets of field daisies. Tessa was a bridesmaid and Helen's sister Katharine, pregnant as a pup, was matron of honor. Murray Borish was there to steer Betty through the line, and so was Rose Drisko, not yet married to Wallace. Lincoln Kirstein was best man at the wedding, which was "a sad one," he said. "A good fat selection of Dickson uncles aunts cousins and chums" attended—this at the insistence of Marguerite Dickson, who thought the presence of family would "sanctify" the marriage—and also, said Richard, "a choice selection of my own surviving relatives, fortunately fewer." Lewis MacKay drove the relatives out from Cambridge. They drank watery punch—it was nonalcoholic, to Richard's dismay. A minister officiated, and that was too bad. The ring bearer showed up late. But finally the thing was done, and Richard and Helen and the Dicksons' two dogs left for Maine in the new Model T that Richard didn't know how they would pay for. He didn't know either how they were going to live "next year or the years after that."

When the honeymoon was over, Richard and Helen came back to Belmont and moved in with Mrs. Dickson and Katharine and Wallace in the big bare house on Waverly Street. The family didn't have much money, and orange crates served for furniture. The vile-smelling dogs had the run of the house. Over this ménage, Mrs. Dickson presided. She was a teacher, and her children's books and her history text for high-school students had brought her, said the papers, "some fame as an author." Life was a game at which she worked energetically, and her daughter and her son-in-law were counters. Helen was her youngest child, and like Richard's mother with her oldest, she held on to this child for dear life. "It was better to bring Richard in than to lose Helen and live alone." Soon after the marriage, Helen confessed to Tessa that she hadn't wanted to marry Richard. She didn't like him very much. What had possessed her, then? She said: "My mother felt that I was taking up too much of his time."

After three years even a rent-free lodging seemed a steep price to pay, and Richard and Helen moved to an apartment on Chambers Street in the West End of Boston. The dilapidated old house had a beautiful winding staircase. The second floor was reserved for the newly married couple, but they weren't alone. Mrs. Dickson moved in with them, and for the next six years they lived together. Richard made what he could from his essays and reviews. "I live entirely on what I write," he told Robert Penn Warren, but this wasn't strictly true. Helen painted murals for the WPA. At night she taught ballroom dancing for her sister Katharine in the studio in Harvard Square. She hated this job. But the money it brought in and the ninety dollars a month she earned from the Federal Arts Project were just enough to keep the wolf from the door.

Her young life with Richard mixed good and evil. It resembled his mother's life in the boarding house on Irving Street—the woman who toiled and the stay-at-home husband. But for Helen as a painter, Tessa said, it was "absolutely marvellous," too, "the first time we were recognized or had any stature in society. You were being paid to produce the pictures which you'd be painting anyway, and somebody wanted them and they were shown and taken places, and you even got supplies. We thought it was the greatest thing that ever happened. We felt *important*. Who ever cared about painters or poets before? 'That's a nice way to pass the time,' people said—like embroidery. Now all of a sudden an artist amounted to something. You painted anything you wanted and you turned it in and it went into government buildings. Different ones went different places." The trouble was, you never saw them again. "One went to a leprosarium in Louisiana, and I thought, oh dear."

Friends assumed that Richard and Helen had worked out an agreement between them. Her part was to cherish "the idiosyncratic personal genius" until it flowered. Then presumably he would take over. By the time he took over, the marriage was a husk, and she lived in bitter remorse for the years she had squandered. She forgot about the good times.

In the thirties money was uppermost because they didn't have it, and they bickered about money, reenacting Richard's mother and father. The refrain ran: "We're poor as rats." Could George Anthony mail them what he owed for Helen's painting, since "we travel on the edge," or could Allen Tate ask Eliot to reprint an essay of Richard's in the *Criterion*: "Only because I'm poor . . . do I dare bring it up." The death of the *Hound & Horn* in 1934 was the end, he said regretfully, "of the only decent pay I've ever had, and used to amount to even as much as fifty cents an hour." Jury duty, a burden for everybody else, was salvation for him, and he said how he hoped to get drawn. He waited in anguish on checks from the *Magazine* and the *Southern Review* and tore his hair when they didn't arrive promptly. "The affair of the check is becoming comic and quotidian," he wrote to one editor. It wasn't comic, however, and it didn't present him in a flattering light.

An amiable request from the Maine Author Collection that he donate his first volume of poems led him to say that, instead of cadging free copies, they "should have no scruples about appropriating moneys for my books." The right word for his behavior was "scriminess," he acknowledged. "The same horrible scruple" which gave virtue to his criticism lent in practical living "only the miser's vice." He was plugging away in these years at Henry Adams, and he knew the sin of envy when he looked at the Adams family and looked at himself. But he said stiffly: "I am glad to preserve my natural underdog's privilege of contempt for the horrid people who have advantages."

He didn't act the part of an underdog. If he got a chunk of money, as from the *Hound & Horn*, he hurried off to Brooks Brothers for a Harris tweed suit. He hit the ceiling, though, when Helen bought two pairs of shoes for two dollars a pair in Filene's Basement. This cost him the friendship of Elizabeth Orrok, who had nothing good to say for Richard after that. But Helen gave as good as she got. Missing Richard one day at the *Hound & Horn* office—he had promised to take her to lunch—she sat down at his desk and wrote her angry complaint, but not on a scratch pad. She dug deep in the drawer for the handmade Italian paper on which he had splurged and of which he was inordinately proud, and she blotted it carelessly, knowing how deep it would cut him.

When the *Hound & Horn* left Cambridge, he didn't have an office to go to anymore. But he clung to his connection with the magazine as it veered among faddish enthusiasms. He wasn't a faddist, only he hadn't made up his mind yet so he listened, reserving judgment, to the Marxists and Agrarians, and to Bandler and the Humanists. Pound and Yvor Winters (a planet to himself and surrounded with satellites) bade for

his attention. They all had something to sell and they saw the *Hound &
Horn* as their pulpit.

Pound proposed that they lie down together, his lion to their lamb,
and Richard responded cautiously, backing away. Then he lost his job
as editor and Pound feasted hugely. But finally, Kirstein said, "In spite
of his lovely poems and his marvellous letters, we couldn't face the at-
tendant coterie of lame duck discoveries he was always capriciously
harboring, and we were relieved to let him be obscene about us in other
'little' magazines."

Yvor Winters was more tenacious and possibly more assured. He also
had his favorite poets, most of whom remain unread, and he knew
beyond argument that "any one of them is a better poet than anyone
else in America this side of Frost and barring Tate and Blackmur." The
Hound & Horn seemed to him chock full of "the most inordinately bad
prose and verse to be found on any news-stand. . . . The stuff is dead as a
salt mackerel and no more nourishing than saw-dust." Kirstein was to
blame. "To print this junk you have passed up work by Howard Baker,
who is a damned fine poet, Rowena Lockett, who belongs in the upper
ten of contemporary writers of short fiction, and Achilles Holt, who is
about as good."

Nonetheless, he was willing to serve the magazine—as he said, poetry
and fiction were a life and death matter with him—and following the
resignation of Bandler and Mayor, he became the chief funnel of talent.
His governing principle, as he expressed it to Richard, was that "a
living writer should be approached with the same cold suspicion as a
dead one." He illustrated copiously: "Pound writes . . . a kind of slipshod elegance." "Burke has all of the vulgar plausibility of a traveling
salesman." Monte Belgion "deserves to be castrated and hung by his
heels." "Yeats is going to do almost as much damage presently as Eliot
has done." The illustrious dead fared better than this, but not a whole
lot better. A friend of Richard's quoted Winters as saying that "in many
instances, Shakespeare didn't know how to write poetry." If you can
criticize God, the friend supposed, "a criticism of all his creatures is
implied."

This rough and tumble gave offense. Tate spoke caustically of Winters the barbarian, tossing off obiter dicta in his Sears Roebuck suits.
"Oughtn't he to be shot loudly at sunrise?" Conrad Aiken inquired.
Richard didn't think so. In the early thirties, Winters stood to him as
the authoritative mentor. His habit was deferential. One critic remarked
his "utter abasement" before Winters' "tissue of bluster." He persisted in
good will, even when Winters showed his teeth. It was tempered by

estimation, however. Winters was a vociferous pedant and something more: "an Irving Babbitt who *really* knows poetry." But though his intellect was powerful, he was the "victim of it as often as its master." Richard felt the weight of focused knowledge and the momentum of a man who knew his own mind. He heard the tone of authority that didn't brook contradiction. All this attracted him: he was still feeling his way. But as with Pound it made him diffident, too. "The tone of authority . . . impedes, or irritates—for it appears in the guise of explicit assertions of fact." So he moved his chair to a distance. He wrote: "Mr. Winters does not apparently find enough authority within his sensibility—in the very tone of experience itself—and is compelled to resort to constructions of the mind outside the data of experience."

That is just right for Winters, the type of the dogmatic personality. It says implicitly how Richard, the type of the empiric, was strong. Also it suggests why the Humanists, like the Marxists and Agrarians, failed to hold his attention except in provisional ways. He was into a diluted form of Christian orthodoxy then, and this dubious affiliation helped to pay his bills. Bandler and the Humanists were cheering him on. But his imagination, both imperious and disabling, precluded more than a token allegiance. When he canvassed a question, he saw it all round and he felt what he saw on his pulses. Reviewing an anthology of American literature, he decided that "the stunting, the lack of virility" in this literature came from "a radical failure in the double knowledge (or awareness) of good *and* evil." The failure was imaginative, an insufficient feeling for the matter at hand. He wrote these words at the end of the thirties. Already at the end of the twenties, however, he was declaring for a comprehensive view, and this unblinkered allegiance predicts his disagreement with the various orthodoxies which defined the *Hound & Horn*. He said how the ideal mind knew a bottomless honesty. This was his mind, "liable to many failures . . . but intelligent to any data in which instructed: a mind of which the very structure is foreign to prejudice in the acquisition of experience"—hence the polite but also pragmatic attending on the peddlers of doctrine—"but which is full of courageous prejudice in assigning meaning and order to that experience." Hence the inevitable rejecting by this provisional man of all fictive order and all meaning that was only assigned.

Humanism, the first of the competing philosophies to which the *Hound & Horn* gave room, was firm on the need for order. Sherry Mangan defined it as "merely moderation carried to excess." But Norman Foerster, a prophet of the movement, said: "The philosophy of Humanism finds its master truth not in men as they are (realism) or in men as worse than they are (naturalism) or in men as they 'wish' to be (romanticism), but in men as they 'ought' to be." Making men conform to what they ought to be was Bernard Bandler's pet project. There was far too much about Humanism in the earlier issues of the *Hound & Horn*, Kirstein said; until the end of the second year, the magazine seemed to him "like a weak echo of *The Criterion*." Then Bandler's influence waned. Bandler had taken his lead from Irving Babbitt, who equated modern times, most notably in art and politics, with "an explosion in a cesspool." Monte Belgion recalled a visit with Bandler to Babbitt's house on Irving Street, and how Babbitt talked of T. S. Eliot, his old Harvard pupil. Over the mantelpiece in Eliot's London flat hung an abstract painting by Wyndham Lewis, Babbitt said. Beholding this painting "he had found positively painful."

Richard was more hospitable, and Babbitt and his "arrogant love of the golden mean" appealed to him, he told Cowley, "like a flock of scabs." One of the things he had learned from Santayana—or, in reading Santayana, learned that he knew already—was that Christian charity and naturalistic insight were closely akin. He had his evangelizing side, though, and the fiction he was writing was strongly tinged with moral bias. Humanism at its highest reach played to this bias. He made gingerly fun in a letter to Wheelwright of "your Anglo-Catholic confrere's notes on Humanism and Religion"—the confrere was Eliot—but he read the notes attentively when they were published in the *Hound & Horn*, and he confessed to Eliot that "a great many people have been struck with a notion of humanism as a substitute for religion—myself especially." Eliot's thoughts on this subject fitted in "amazingly well with what little we have of a 'programme.'" The way things looked to Richard, "no amount of Humanism would be too much."

But he was terrified by Eliot's "sanity" and "lucid assurance." He didn't mind Eliot's being Christian, only he thought "salvation as an occupation ill suits a man of diligent talent." The Humanists had a lot to say about salvation. They invoked man's "higher" nature, but they liked to brood darkly on "the bestial in man." They said an "inner check" was required, though they couldn't express it in rational terms. Babbitt's phrase for this was "vital control," which you exercised to squash "the merely temperamental man with his impressions and emotions and expansive desires." In practice, vital control meant outer control and this meant the hegemony of an aristocratic class. What had Humanism to say, Malcolm Cowley inquired, for "the mill hands of

New Bedford and Gastonia, for the beet-toppers of Colorado, for the men who tighten a single screw in the automobiles that march along Mr. Ford's assembly belt?"

Not much, Richard decided. He put his name to a sardonic letter in the *New Republic*, affecting interest in the writings of the Humanist School of Literary Criticism and wanting to know "of a contemporary work of art either produced by an American Humanist or encouraged or approved by one." The Humanists were certainly short on approval. Mostly a gaggle of angry professors—"the new conservatives of their time," Richard called them years later—they represented, in the extreme form congenial to academies, the natural prejudice of our moral and intellectual half: "either to find our own morals and ideas in literature or to condemn it when they are not there." The amount of literature they condemned was impressive—*Antony and Cleopatra*, for instance, which they excluded from the canon because it dramatized adultery and lust. But Shakespeare pretty generally made them uneasy. "He only mirrored life rather than humanistically transcended it." A good mirror, Richard thought, was worth any amount of transcendence.

Then, in what was virtually a reprise of his critique of Yvor Winters, he came to the core of his disagreement with the pronouncing temper. The principles of Humanism did not arise from individuals—"out of a sensibility, a civilization, a religion, or a generalized experience of any sort—but only from the notions of these." The Humanists could not penetrate, they could not judge, because they existed and moved without data, "without experience of the work in hand." In the appeal to the work in hand—this thing that had no likeness—you recognize essential Blackmur. It was habitual with him, the one string on which he harped. His small body of permanent poetry declares the habit, as does his critical prose until he took to pronouncing. No doubt it was his birthright, a gift beyond elucidating, but also fortified by what he learned, and the process of learning is open to inspection. Though books were crucial to this process, it isn't exhausted in books. The difference is that between the intellectual and the intelligent or apprehensive man, and looms most vividly for Richard in his wakening to Maine.

He came to see that the engrossing questions were not why? or to what purpose? Skirting these questions, not from torpor but in propriety, he limited himself to "the qualitative, devouring What." He set himself to create a language for his sensations and feelings in order that he might better know them. In his notebook he wrote: "What you control only under the form of false names, *you* do not control at all." Control meant taxonomy, not the "vital control" of the Humanists but the preternatural eye. "Gardening is a man's occupation," he told Rob Darrell. This was the summer of 1931, and the tending of small plants was becoming a part of what he called his sensual education. "I have learned the look and feel of some dozen vegetables and something of the worms, bugs, etc., that infest them. For a long time I waked up in the mornings considering the exact texture of the young beet or the early fledged radish or the peculiar flaunting Georgia O'Keefish glory of squash blossoms."

At the same time he was making poems and reading Aiken's poems—the ideal life, as he defined it later: "half reading and half outdoors and half writing poetry; if the Trinity can do it, why not I?" Praising his friend's poetry, he said: "It is not directed by faith, it is qualified by assent to what he feels. It does not run, confronted by life, to the statuary fastness of logic, it resorts to the constant piety of meditation. It is not rigid and right, but amorphous and honest. It is consciousness—a particular agony of knowledge and ignorance—expanding itself." His own expanding consciousness is uppermost here, as developed by the sensual education to which he had submitted.

In the first year of his marriage, when the snow was melting in Massachusetts, he wrote to Aiken: "I hope we shall get down East early enough to see a hundred square miles white with blueberry blossom." He was thinking of the Barrens above Harrington, Maine, and the view south to Tunk Mountain. This view became his study. It wasn't a long view either, as seen by the intellectual from his statuary fastness. Peeping and botanizing was the way to see.

Each spring he and Helen left Boston for Harrington, and for Oak Point on the tidal water. Until the hard frosts of October drove them back to the city, they lived and worked in the clapboard farmhouse Helen's mother had inherited. Wisteria climbed to the roof of the house. A gigantic maple towered over the lilac bush and the birch trees that stood before the windows. The land was hard and the colors were primary, painted as by Rockwell Kent. In the fall, blue herons stood in the tidal pools. In spring the purple finches and purple grosbeaks appeared, and Richard learned that neither was purple. All summer, time frittered and the long shadows made meadow ponds of quiet on the bay. He listened to the calling of crows, not a random discord as he had supposed, but a language of different cries, expressive of love and sadness or a summons to fight or retreat. These discriminations were important.

Beyond the Dickson place, the Paul Fiskes were building on the foundation of the old studio where Tessa and Helen had painted when they were girls. In later years, after Tessa and Phil Horton got married, the Hortons had their own place farther along Oak Point Road—"Disorder and Early Sorrow," Tessa called it—and later still Christine Weston, who made a success at writing stories, built on the turnoff called Willie's Lane. The front doors of the Weston house winched up and gave access to a big verandah overlooking Flat Bay. You could dance straight out of the living room onto the verandah. Dancing suggested the affluent world of Bar Harbor to the south. That was in another country, as Richard liked to say. He and Helen got by without running water. They warmed themselves at the open fire and they read by a kerosene lamp. The amenities were presented by the chemical toilet Richard's bachelor friends had given him for his wedding. Mornings, as the summer waned, were terribly cold. The pump froze, and Richard longed for the comfort of the new house he wanted to build, lined with rock wool against the weather. He tore down a partition between the chimney and the little room where he had his desk, and he installed a new ceiling and new plasterboard walls. On a do-it-yourself basis, progress was slow. What this country needed was servants and retainers, he said.

But he began to be aware how "all the land and the woods were magnificent," and he got angry when friends who came to visit didn't see this. Maine took him two ways. "I shall have nothing to do with farming," he said. "The soft toothpaste of the literary life suits me better." The country people, he told Wheelwright, were all very well, "but like Plato I feel my urban gorge rise from time to time against them and do deeply want the relief of another gorge rising in unison or two part song." He said to Tate, with whom he was arguing the politics of sectionalism, that he would live in Maine all year round "if the agrarian and indeed communistic community of Harrington had only produced half a dozen men after my own heart." But it hadn't, and as the months went by he began to feel the need of conversation.

One friend thought he wanted a salon where people dropped well-turned phrases. This is diminishing. The School of Athens was what he wanted. But he wanted also, with mounting force, to make a virtue of necessity. Perhaps "economic subterfuge"—a poor man's resort to the farmhouse in Maine—might turn out to be "spiritual salvation." What he really wanted was to make over his soul. "Before he came up here, when he lived in that awful house in Cambridge," Tessa said, "he had never once stuck his hand in the earth. He never picked a flower when I knew him. Everything was books. Then in his twenties he found the land and the flowers. He had room to move around in, a year, a garden, the sea. And he jumped into Maine like a fish."

What was good for the natives was scripture for him. They drank unpasteurized milk; so did he, and it gave him bovine tuberculosis. They went to bed with the birds, and it was past midnight when he got to bed—but he was up at dawn to show he was one of them. He ate his dinner at 6:00 p.m. It wouldn't do, when they dropped by at 7:00, if they found him three sheets to the wind. Living on the water, he had to be nautical, so he bought a little rowboat and an outboard motor. "And my God, the way he used it," said Tessa, "it was ghastly." He didn't know the waters at all. He thought he did. Robert Weston was a sailor, so steering the boat fell to him. "Can you read the chart and follow it?" Robert inquired. "Oh yes," Richard said, and he ran them on the rocks. When he went for a dip in the ocean, the cold forced the blood through his ankles. He said, however: "I like the Bay of Fundy to swim in or even the beach at Rockport, but I will come no further south for my swimming than the northerly shores of Cape Cod."

To the perplexity of friends, nautical lingo began to appear in his writing. At first it was mostly parade. He said reading Henry James was like sailing close-hauled or trembling on the tack. Though he had a quick ear for the appropriate jargon, he wasn't a real sailor, Rob Darrell thought, but he "talked and wrote a fine line." What was that, said Dudley Fitts, about Hanging in the Wind's Eye? After a while, Richard was able to tell him. He responded, he said, with equal delight to sailing in clear water and moping along in a fog. He did his share of either. He learned the waters, too. Malcolm Cowley, on rural Connecticut and the yearning of the city dwellers who come for the summer and go away again, gives the sense of Richard's difference. "The ownership of an old house full of Boston rockers and Hitchcock chairs did not endow them with a past. The land . . . was not really theirs; it did not stain their hands or color their thoughts." They wanted to return to the ancestral house, but the door was locked against them. Richard was the rare man who forced the door and discovered a past and made it his own.

On one side, he resembled Cowley's urban intellectuals. "Their real exile was from society itself, from any society to which they could honestly contribute and from which they could draw the strength that lies in shared convictions." Richard lived in exile. But he found a social matrix, both real and mythologized, to which he could affiliate. It nourished his writing and sustained him as a man until, in his late forties, he and Helen broke apart. After that, the pleasant place was denied him. The experience of Maine was permanent, though, his road to Damascus: he became a convert and was saved.

Richard wasn't a country gentleman, but he had "a very great gentle-manliness with the people." Everybody liked him. "He never presumed, he never acted important, he never discussed literary matters." Each week without fail, he and Helen played bingo or spit-in-the-ocean with Ansel and Viola, who lived on Oak Point Road. He was a farmer and a mason; she was famous for her fudge and hard candy. On weekends they went to the movies in Machias, or they went up to Ted Colson's and ate ice cream by the quart. "We all took turns churning—grapenut, peach, raspberry, whatever was in season. And you would have a soup plate and you would eat a dish that big. And then you'd sit around and talk and maybe play a little cards. And that was a visit." Ted had a poetic streak—"limited," Tessa said, "but it was there." On poetry, Richard kept mum.

To one of his new friends he dedicated a poem, but the friend never saw it. This was Horace Hall. "He was usually called 'Hod' and did odd jobs at Harrington, Maine, many of them without a charge." You couldn't pay him for most of what he did. "He came of an ancient family of hare lips and half wits. Otherwise, he was a nobody"—except that he had fought in World War I and died as a result of having been gassed and wounded and generally damaged. "I was very fond of him," Richard said.

When Richard lived in Cambridge, small talk was beneath and beyond him. In speaking, said Jacques Barzun, he chose his words "as if he were going to be sued for slander if he uttered a spontaneous phrase." In Maine he was fluent and free. He learned how prose, the common coin, is sometimes better than poetry, or how the best poetry is prose. Making washers for the stove pump, you could use a piece of harness rein. If you were laying trench wire enclosed in a pipe, you had to pick it in to a depth of five inches. With water pipe, you went much deeper. At first he didn't know this, and when the frost split the pump pipe where it turned its corner to the well, he spent a day digging up the broken elbow. He said laconically how he plumbed the lot together again. In these parts, he told his cousin, the roots reached all the way to China, but the boulders underground were even worse. They didn't always show up when you made preliminary borings. So it was a pressing topic, the way you hoisted boulders out of the ground.

Knowing how to do it, he felt the pride of the initiate. He wrote letters to the city slickers, setting them straight on matters of fact, like this to the editor of the *New Republic*: "Down here in Maine, natives 'work in the woods,' lumberjacks are imported polacks, etc., and woodsmen are good fellows with traps and guns, at home in the woods, and rare." Reviewing a novel that didn't come off, he put his finger on the trouble: "The epistemology is bad; and that is as great a sin for the novelist as for the philosopher." He practiced the epistemology that went with being a country fellow. When a friend was puzzled by a line in Shakespeare where King Lear has to hovel "in short and musty straw," he consulted the *Farmer's Almanac* he was creating in his head. Freshly cut straw was long and flexible, so you used it for bedding. It shredded as it got musty. Short manure was a mixture of manure and broken straw; in long manure the straw was new. This was how you knew things way down East.

"For God's sake," he exploded, when a government agency asked him to criticize a film script on Robert Frost, "do not permit a *pony* to shake any harness bells—a little horse is not a pony, any more than a Morgan is a Shetland." Also: "Milking cows in the open is uncommon in Vermont, especially in the early spring. (Most milk cows are barned at this time of year.)" His superior feeling was that "your script writer has never lived in the country." To the producer he said: better show "your picture to none but the life-long inhabitants of large cities." He had come a long way from Irving Street.

The inhabitants of cities were done to or done for. He became a doer, anyway in aspiration. He watched the men from the electric company stringing wire in the woods, and he admired the easy mastery with which they did their job. "I could wish I might work as well on my own stuff," he said. His own stuff—James, for example, on whom he had been commissioned to write a long essay—showed in a different light. For "the fine cold water," he thanked his editor effusively. "We got five finger-sized holes in a ledge twenty feet down, and in this dryest (locally) of all years have not had less than four feet of water in the bottom. Such are the uses of Henry James and the History of Literature."

Summers, he swung a pickax until his writer's hand grew heavy, and his fingers when he typed made new grammar on the keys. Mostly he was out in the garden with his spade. He couldn't tell chard from Chinese cabbage when he started, but his asparagus bed still bears, and the old plum tree he cultivated. He discovered a joy that he didn't get from books when he came in from the garden, bringing bushels and bushels of peas. Helen was glum; she had to shell them. Around the house he planted Siberian iris and day lilies and yellow lilies. He made the meadow red with poppies and raised them to a great height, and he grew so many harebells that the Pattees, who lived at the end of the point, didn't want for flowers all summer. For every flower in his garden he got the Latin name, and he liked Tessa to challenge him on his Latinity when she and Phil Horton bought the place just up from his. This was taxonomy again.

In a bad summer when the rain didn't come, the garden languished and he fell in spirit. "I do not like things to look so ragged nor to see plants die without blooming," he said, "but that is what I see." A wet spring was worse. It delayed the farming and rotted the plants in the ground. "I worked to exhaustion," he wrote to Wheelwright, "getting my flower seeds planted between rains." The rains got the better of him, and he was condemned to a summer of patchy garden. But, he said, "we have ten million daisies and five million buttercups in our fields on this wet and steaming day."

Every spring he staked out the vegetable garden—twenty-five rows to weed and thin, eleven more to furrow, hoe, paper, and plant—and he began to love poles and even the looks of them. "Your diet here," he told friends who were coming up from town, "must of necessity include green corn, squash, beans, mackerel, leeks, carrot, flounders, parsley, radish, kohlrabi, clams, blackberries, peas, beets, and jellies." Maybe the friends were bored by this litany. It was exactly that, however, and he was saying it over to himself.

Maine meant to Richard the land and God and love of the country. Most of all, it meant the sea. Pleasant Bay and Narraguagus Bay became part of his interior landscape. He sailed the islands and fished the coves, and sometimes in the early mornings when it was still dark—he said in his poetry, "while the ash of dawn was colding through"—he had Ansel drive him to Smith's Cove outside Milbridge and hitched a ride with the lobstermen when they went to sea with their traps. It was open water after you cleared the lighthouse on Hog Island, and they took the long swells at an angle. In dirty weather they listened for the clang of the bell buoy off the rocky place called Ship's Stern. The best fishing was landward of Jordan's Delight, a spit of crumbling mountain that suggested a recumbent statue afloat in the sea. Only the torso was left to the statue; the legs were cut away at the thighs. Below them stretched the meadowland, breaking into rocks. The beach shelved steeply, a litter of broken rocks on which the herring gulls roosted. Sailors gave a lot of sea room to Jordan's Delight, and Richard and his friends didn't land there very often. In his mind he dwelled in the island, however, and he made poetry from what he saw and imagined.

Over the beach the cliff face leaned outward, above the lichen and sea urchins and the washing weed. "O fugitive," Richard wrote, "Crawl, crawl out. . . . And look you down . . . to the easy all uneasing swells." He was apostrophizing himself and saying how this desolate place, where sun warmed the flesh but wind was in the marrow, showed the unity of "good and evil chance."

Sharp striae cut the cliff into the hatchet faces of Mexican idols. The cliff was like the weather and discovered the permutation of things. It was pea green, pale orange, pale brown, gray, silver, yellow, and spotted with the droppings of black cormorants and gulls. At the top and coming right to the edge, a cover of broom flowed in sloping contours, the way a viscous liquid flows. Dragon's blood and violet harebell bloomed in this cover—"a stony garden," Richard called it, "crossed by souring cries." There were no living trees, only a stunted conifer, and just off the island the water dropped to fifty fathom. That was where you set the lobster pots. Far away to starboard the winking light of Petit Manan flared briefly —"Tit Manan" they called it, "lovely though bleak." The bleakness and the loveliness went together.

One perfect day, a dozen friends assembled at Wallace Dickson's in South Addison. They hired a fisherman to take them out on Pleasant Bay. They were going to feast on fish chowder, they thought, and they brought along an iron kettle, and quarts of milk and salt pork and boiled potatoes. But the fish didn't bite, and tempers got short, and—worst indignity of all—they had to buy their catch of "haddick" from a contemptuous native who maneuvered his boat alongside. The rocky beach of Pond Island was coming up fast and they wanted to beach for the picnic right away. Richard said the picnic could wait; first they had to make the circuit of Jordan's Delight. One of the friends looked up skeptically at the excruciating mass of rock and the weathered spikes that used to be trees. Jordan must have been a misanthrope, he thought. Richard was elated, though. He knew how the island was exile and home, and how excruciation redeems.

Wild berries grew everywhere on the islands in the bay. One was called Raspberry Island. Once, in late summer, Richard and Helen rowed out to the islands. Tessa was with them. Ted Colson came along, and they spent the day picking gooseberries until the boat was full. Tessa remembered the sunset. The sky was all saffron yellow, every cloud and the boat and the water. "It was just sailing into the golden bowl. And James's Golden Bowl had a crack in it, you know." This was different. "You felt you were in a magical world, the rolling of the oars dipping into the gold water, and the goldenest sky, and the whole thing was a unit, and we were a unit in it." This was the meaning of Zen, Tessa thought. "We were the center, the core. We were in the core and of it. I'll never forget that ride, coming home with all those gooseberries. And, ah, that must be forty years ago."

Helen wore the trousers in that family, said Kate Foster. She wanted much and she bullied and ragged. This wasn't because she was poor in spirit or vainly anxious after money. "She wants much," her husband thought, "because of the great riches she has, the richness she is." Finding no object, this abundance soured in her. Kate remembered a visit to Harrington in the summer of 1934. "We girls shared the housework between us"—the girls were all painters: Kate and Tessa and Helen, and Emmie Darrell, Rob's wife—"and Dick was the only man about the place." Helen in her role of painter made him proud, and he wished that she might have for her own life the free and willing expenditure of her natural talent. These generous words were his, and no doubt he admired what the talent accomplished. But painting, in his world, was off on the periphery. He chopped wood and grew his vegetables and in the evenings he built a fire. Sorting beans for seed while they sat around the fire, he discoursed on Henry James. The discourse was unrelenting. It was also unvaried. "There might be some games proposed, involving some literary problem or identification of some poem—or they would read poetry aloud." This did nicely for Richard: why not for the rest of them?

Helen by choice and bias was a diffident painter. She went in for muted shades. Her typical palette was like Andrew Wyeth's. She painted water colors of tiny dead birds or tiny wounded creatures, and half hid them in displaced or ill-lighted epicenters. Dead owls, wounded owls, and terrified owls obsessed her. When she got a refrigerator, that was where she kept them—an indelible image for one innocent guest who went to the kitchen for a bottle of beer. After they moved to Princeton, dead cardinals inhabited the refrigerator, too. Her collection of ferocious tomcats supplied them. The cats lay about the house all day in salad bowls. When Helen needed a fresh subject, they went out to hunt.

The farmhouse wasn't big enough or light enough for painting, so Helen and Richard bought a ramshackle barn. Ted Colson took it down and they put it back together in thick woods at the edge of Flat Bay. Richard dug a little pond overlooking the water and ringed it with Japanese iris. They cut out big windows in the loft where Helen painted, and built an outhouse in back. When they were finished, a neighbor left a bouquet of wildflowers on the seat in the outhouse. But they botched the job between them, and the barn began to heave and settle. They hadn't sunk the foundation posts far enough below the frost line, and one day the frost would destroy what they had made.

The area beneath the studio was meant for living quarters. This was so friends from the city could visit. Rob Darrell stayed one summer in "the studio built with Guggenheim money." When Helen went off in the mornings to paint, she didn't want for company. Unlike Richard, she could have done without it. Waldo Peirce wasn't company but a law unto himself, and chaos came to Harrington whenever Waldo came. To Helen's dismay, he brought the twins with him. Also, he always brought beer. The twins shook up the bottles and opened the tops and squirted the beer at the ceiling. Tessa remembered sourly how they wet the bed and how the dye from the flowered mattress bled into the sheets. Waldo was down the road and away before his hostess understood why he'd made up the bed. Boys will be boys, he said, when the twins stole the postage stamps and pasted them one on top of the other. It was another matter, though, when they cut windows in his painting with a razor blade or when, at a drunken party, they set his beard on fire while he snored on the ground.

Richard rose to the he-man in Waldo, who appeared at the door clad in buffalo robes (that was how Helen saw him) and the promise of rum. "Blackmur's Rum" was the title of one of his paintings. Waldo was all for life. He refuted explosively painters in their ivory towers, all the déraciné, decadent painters. They were "deliberately morbid," he said, and he answered by example to "the maggot school" of painting—all that "slick softness without muscle." This was man-to-man stuff, Richard thought. Waldo's painting was like himself—a lot of dash, sometimes slapdash. He painted Richard in a three-quarter pose and the hair came out violent, as if an electric current were running through it. Tessa, to his painter's eye, was all verve and spirits—a gallon of wine and the flashy black boots she had bought from Sears Roebuck. He called his painting the Bootlegger's Bride. Helen in her painting verged on the "deliberately morbid."

Talking with Waldo, you took his meaning on faith. Behind the big beard, he was mashing potatoes. That was how it seemed to Tessa and Helen, the day he barged in on their schoolgirl exhibition in Boston. "Pictures," he shouted (but whether good or bad, they couldn't distinguish)—"names"—"got to get to know yer." He took an advance for the autobiography he was going to write, but never got beyond the title. *Of Sound Mind and Bawdy* was the title, and how could you improve upon that? He wrote wild and ribald letters. They were clamorous with poetry, his own and his translations of Villon and Baudelaire, and only his mother could decipher what he wrote. Richard said that Waldo was "the only healthy and comic genius" he had ever known, and he compared him to Mynheer Peeperkorn in *The Magic Mountain*. Helen didn't venture her opinion. After a visit from Waldo, she went into purdah.

They left the door on the latch when Mrs. Dickson wasn't there, and friends descended on them all summer. "Joe Zilch" was one of the friends. He was Harold Zimmerman, Helen's instructor, and another version of the painter as wild man. In spirit, Joe Zilch was one of *les fauves*. He talked out his paintings, however. He had the habit of getting up at three in the morning and holding a candle beneath his chin, while he studied his face in the mirror. His wife Libby studied Richard. She said that aside from anything else—also in addition to it—he was the best friend she'd ever had. They held hands in public and looked soulfully at one another. Helen didn't remonstrate. She went into herself and counted her losses and measured her hurt. Meanwhile her old teacher was getting ready to paint.

Richard carried on, Helen did too, or perhaps it was all masquerade. Helen flopped on the couch or lay on the floor in postures of martyrdom, and said to anyone within earshot how Richard wouldn't sleep with her. Various friends were anxious to oblige. But it wasn't what Richard called "the debacle upstairs" that turned the marriage bad. This was after the fact. It always is. Already, when Richard married Helen, the crack was in the grain. The trouble lay, he thought, "in the defeat of expectations that ought never to have been assumed as possible." The real trouble was just otherwise, always to look for the worst. Now it confronted him. He had made sure it would. Had he had the wit to know that the worst was coming, he would have readied "the manners now needed." There was truth in this, or an oblique comment on the vulgar back-and-forth to which the marriage had descended. He and Helen, as they wounded each other, were badly deficient in manners. The wisdom of hindsight didn't do much good. "There should be very little satisfaction in knowledge," Richard said, "if it takes you all your life to learn you've been an adolescent fool."

Living together, he and Helen lived apart, and for each the isolation was profound. On a journey to New York in the early thirties, he scribbled these lines for a poem:

> The company of loneliness is most
> What I keep with me ship or train.

Loneliness bored through him, the pin boring the skull, and at last the sense of his own death was ominous. The nothing that he had come to begot a catalogue of woes: "sleep without rest, activity without the peace of termination, emotion without satisfaction, sunshine without glory: a long running down, like the course of radium into lead." He rejoiced gravely that, like the morning star he had no part in his desire. All his friends were gone—this was the old story—and he prayed the God he worshiped to damn them all for the broken piety of friendship. But he was guiltier than they were in his meditated insufficiency—"the inward catastrophe of learned lack"—and he called down curses on himself for his "sin of lack, lack-lustre, and pride." The pride was in desiring more.

Richard looked at his friends and saw how, one by one, their marriages were failing. Dorothy left Wallace Dickson for another man, willfully developing a crush into a passion. Neither was long on ethics, Richard said, and knew his own uncharity, considering the "desperateness" with which we all contend. Still, disgust welled in him and inevitably he brought it home. Trying to reconcile Rose and Ben Drisko, he reflected grimly on his own lapses. When divorce put an end to four of the marriages with which he was most intimate—all this in half a year—he thought how any one of them should have been able to sink tap roots to suck the soil. He said he knew of no marriage that had.

After Emmie went off with the producer Tony Brown, he wrote to Rob Darrell: "there is something that stinks about the way we live, and something excruciating about the kinds of obligations we let ourselves in for." The sense of betrayed obligation possessed him, as if he were living a novel by Henry James. His married friends constituted a paradigm of betrayal. He inspected it minutely and applied it to himself. John Walcott was St. Paul's School. He was handsome, articulate, he embodied propriety. In Boston he and Nela ate dinner at the Ritz. Doing "civilized" things was their passion. But when they paid a visit, you had to have a referee. Nela came from old money and she knew how to spend it. In New York she went to Saks', in Paris to Cartier's. But she couldn't keep her stockings up or keep the liquor from soiling her pretty clothes; altogether, Nela was a dirty swan. Waldo's brother Hayford, when he lived in Paris, liked to watch the swans in the Jardin des Tuileries. There was one dirty swan with bedraggled tail feathers, and all the male swans pursued her. Where was the reason in this? Nela was famous for her cuisine. Her children lived on soda pop and Twinkies. Being forthright meant a lot, and Nela always spoke her mind. She looked you in the eye and said: "Would you like me absolutely to tell you what I think about you?" The day she found Christine Weston's letters to John, she came downstairs in her eggplant chiffon, waving the letters and reading them aloud. She and Christine were great friends, though.

These analogous betrayals spoke to one another, defining for Richard the "calling of husband." He said it was served "with malice and torment and brutal stupidity." Helen meditated on the calling of wife. From the beginning she had had her reservations about the marriage. Her sense of her vocation as artist was strong. Living with Richard drained her energies and dissipated time. Four years after they married, she wanted to put her clothes in a handkerchief, tie it to a stick, and go away. But she didn't. Instead, she picked a quarrel. She was fertile at this. When the carpenters came to help with the renovating, that was an occasion for a quarrel. Digging the well was another. One night she threw the lamp across the studio at Richard. He didn't blink and she bit him in the leg. It wasn't part of his strength but of his weakness, he said, that he put up with the intolerable. The "spreading pattern of toleration" signified the flat response of the enervated man.

When they weren't quarreling, the two of them were dumb. At dinner Helen sat morosely with her elbow on the table, cupping her chin in the palm of her hand. She looked at her plate in silence and Richard looked at his. More than anything else, he had craved the refuge of personal communion. In the one human being who might have offered such a refuge, he had destroyed all hope and had left in her nothing but the bitterness of need and the humiliation of void. He said: "The impotency of my body is only the outward anguished mark of an incapable spirit and a sterile personality."

The penis, after all, was greatly overdone as a motive. What it really represented in the conflict of character was the absence or loss of motive. "The sexuality of life is a very different thing from the ejaculating penis." Relief without emotion was not relief but question-begging. Cold-blooded masturbation was perhaps the worst beggary of all. If you followed this line, "many a marriage must be a poor house." The cold-bloodedness was concealed in the ritual of function. "How many bitter quarrels, how many impossible dissensions, are settled in a good fuck." The agony of one kind of heat was reminiscent of the balm of the other, and brought it on. So "the two-backed beast" was led to think there must be some substance in marriage.

"Man about to leave wife": this was Richard's given for the story he never wrote. The man encountering the woman "feels as he meets her a great cold in his groin and the great warmth of need in her eyes." He knows he can never return as a husband or go forward as a lover. Speaking in his own voice, Richard acknowledged that he had failed as a husband and a lover. What he couldn't expiate, he repented. Forgiveness was out of the question. "Now within a fortnight of 33," he wrote in his notebook: "Let me never more be unready to die." He was unwilling to hasten, as by taking his life. "There is no forelock I would pull." But he said, "I am ready."

The drama of the passing year, as he rehearsed it for himself, was unrelievedly black. Omitting any trace of contention or contrast, he puts our sense of this drama in peril. Perhaps it wasn't drama but only case history. His criticism suggests what is wanting. The jar of good and evil— for example in the life and death of Thomas Becket—where irreparable damage meets intransigent glory, "makes the drama actual." Not happiness but actuality is what we are looking for here. The heartless man pretends that good assimilates evil. His pretension is only that, and differs from asserting that good and evil are endlessly related.

Remount "the stream of composition," said Richard after Henry James, and the relation comes in view between the damaged life and the work the life engendered. The damage of a lifetime cannot be repaired in the act of composition. It can be translated, though. The pressure and stress of that damage are written everywhere in the work. They determine its quality, also its limitation. You can call this determining "the expense of martyrdom in good *and* evil." Only if the life were a mockery of pasted surfaces would one's sense of the relation seem trivial. Art isn't life, as Richard insisted even ferociously, and what he wrote as a critic will stand or fall on its own plane. Nonetheless it seems useful—choosing another trope—to be "a little sensitive to the tap-roots below."

In 1935 Richard clipped from the daily paper the account of a suicide. The man had written to his wife: "I can't say it—that's the trouble. I'm so sorry and so ashamed." This was quotidian stuff. Richard copied it out. Then he wrote again: "I can't say it," and he underscored the words.

In 1935 his first book appeared. He wanted to call it "Craft & Elucidation"—a pompous and cumbersome title to which his publisher objected. She offered him instead "The Double Agent." Florence Codman was the publisher, and Arrow Editions was her personal venture in support of writers whose work she admired. Having read Richard's essays in the *Hound & Horn*, she came up from New York City to meet him. Her abiding impression was of vital self-confidence, not flaunted but intense. She said it was rather like a religious convert's. The mark of the convert is on *The Double Agent*. Twelve essays make the book, and they range for subject from the fiction of Samuel Butler to the poems of Ezra Pound. Sometimes the manner is suasive and urbane, sometimes fevered and polemical. Three of the essays—on E. E. Cummings, D. H. Lawrence, and Hart Crane—are more polemical than critical. The collection isn't haphazard, however. The critic Stanley Edgar Hyman discerned its underlying unity in the ambiguous title: "The double agent is in fact any pair of critical terms"—form and content will do well enough—"and out of their interaction arises a third thing, the poem, the essay, or, in this case, Blackmur's book." Content means the raw material—in James's phrase, "clumsy Life at her stupid work." Form is the issue of the shaping imagination. If you fuse the two successfully, you get a third term. Nowhere does Richard specify this third term. He confronts it, however, on almost every page, and he confronts it almost obsessively in his occasional pieces all through the thirties. It is the reason for being of *The Double Agent*.

"The chaos of private experience" comes first. But it cannot be recognized, much less understood, until it is "ordered in a form external to the consciousness that entertained it in flux." Taking order with the chaos of private experience—that is what Richard is up to.

Reviewing the mostly failed poems of Ernest Walsh, a type of the Revolutionary Simpleton, he had written: "These literary revolutionists persuaded themselves that by a denial of most of the resources of the mind the individual's private experience acquired innate validity." E. E. Cummings enacted this denial. At bottom Richard detested Cummings, and hadn't much to say for Hart Crane or D. H. Lawrence, because their poetry didn't satisfy him. But the bottom is a long way down. Cummings and Crane and Lawrence are possible versions of himself, the offending Adam he struggled to be rid of. Whipping them out was an exercise in self-reproval, more critically in self-regeneration. His tormented life instructed him that no man could be adequate in terms of himself alone. For what he was and what he did, he had to have a form in language both highly traditional and conventional. "The genius of the poet is to make the convention apparently disappear into the use to which he puts it." Cummings and his group—the anticulture or anti-intelligence group—persisted to the contrary. So they lost their chance of escaping from the prison of the private mind. Richard sought this escape with a cunning made sharp by desperation. For the mind which "lacked rational structure sufficient to its burdens, experience was too much." The point is to Lawrence, but also and not less to himself.

In his most affectionate essay, Richard considers the method of Marianne Moore, in whose poetry "life as good *and* evil" is remote—"and everything is done to keep it remote." If this poet, said Kenneth Burke, "were discussing the newest model of automobile, I think she could somehow contrive to suggest an antiquarian's interest." The detachment, which might exasperate, commends itself to Richard; you almost hear him saying that art draws a sanitary cordon around experience—as when, to the charge that his supersubtle fry did not exist in reality, James risked responding that the world would be better if they did. But Richard pulls up short, or rather he finally takes another road. Art for him is analogous to the emperor's golden smithy who breaks and recomposes the turbulence of the sea. Where he is successful, "you achieve experience"—the verb needs pondering—so you "escape, for the moment, the burden of action in reaction." Experience is that body of emotional and sensational fact "which in its natural condition makes life a torment and confusion." If the poet at last takes order with confusion, raising it to a condition where it may be understood, that is because at first he has had the wit and courage to confront it. He cannot deal persuasively in the conflict of character or motive or human purpose and being "except in terms of good and evil, which makes the most actual realm we know."

Stevens, Richard thought, was the great success among modern American poets, and his triumphant success depended largely on "his double adherence to words and experience as existing apart from his private sensibility." You see this triumph in Shakespeare. (Richard, in a letter of 1935 to Allen Tate, is hardly striking off encomia; he is studying salvation.) Shakespeare is the poet of *rational* obsessions, and in him the reality of words is so great "that no other reality, no private obsession however importunate, can crowd it out or do anything but support it." The yield of this total commitment or total displacement is an access of knowledge, even an access of being. Life, which violates the sensibility, impregnates it, too.

Being human, Richard could not escape in his least breath the burden of human experience. These are words he applied to Lawrence. He himself found a way to shift the burden, and that is the indispensable complicating movement without which the drama fails. He discovered or created what he called an external reference. This is variously Maine as it lived in the imagination, or the fiction and poetry he scrutinized in his critical prose, or the vexed business of personal intercourse but written—when he came to write it—at a second remove from the experience involved. In his poetry he addressed his most intimate thoughts. But he addressed a stranger, and he made a common tongue for them both.

CHAPTER FOUR

The Witnessing Art—
Blackmur at Poetry

A T N I N E T E E N, Richard saw himself as the Great Poet. The capital letters are his. He said his role was to annihilate the "sickening 'transition' under which the last centuries have writhed." So far he filled this role "but barely and only remotely." Still he supposed it "worth working for—even a lifetime?" The question is poignant, now that the life has been lived.

He wrote in the diary he kept as a boy: "All these last few days enormous rhythms have swept my chest; rhythms more powerful than those of any poem I can find." He tried to get these rhythms on paper, and throughout one summer he wrote a poem each day. A notebook crammed with this poetry ends with the notation: 230 poems, 52 good. His first Guggenheim application in 1932 records what he called his twelve-year apprenticeship to poetry. "I only want to write a long poem," he said to Allen Tate in his twenties. He was in his thirties when he said to George Anthony, "I have yet to learn to write slowly enough." Then the outpouring slowed to a trickle. "There was a wellspring in me bubbled and even brimmed for so long, so many years, a cold utter boiling, source of all fire, drawn, filtered, purified from upland miles, the second or permanent water-table. This dried up." Afterward his poetry was surface water drawn from runnels and ditches, "fertile but foul, coming in excess but intermittently." He wondered if, in the excess of drought, the bottom ledge might crack or be tapped in a new place, "and the sweet hard water flow again." It didn't flow again.

To his public he recited excuses. He said to one of his Princeton students that he had to go to work to support himself and so stopped writing. Beyond question, lack of money—the wherewithal of writing—beset him. "I'm horribly hard up," he told Harriet Monroe, begging poetry reviews. This was 1926, and the poverty persisted. "I grow poorer with days," he wrote five years later, "and need all the pennies I can garner." Small sums remained miracles. He wasn't Wallace Stevens. In the fifties, Stevens came down to Princeton for a visit. He was severe on Richard (who told the story on himself) for giving up poetry and settling for criticism and teaching. "Stevens, of course, was staying at the Waldorf." The anecdote is amusing but comprehends only part of the truth.

"In some insidious way," said a critic of his last volume, *The Good European* (1947), "death has permeated too deeply into the subconsciousness of this poet, and has killed off, or numbed, the first person singular." The numbing was the cost of the vertigo that attacked him in his childhood and didn't leave off until he died. It menaced his creative power and for long periods drove him on silence. His affliction looked to friends, and to the editors he was always putting off, like run-of-the-mine laziness. He didn't disabuse them; instead, he pleaded the pressure of time. "I worked a few hours the other day on my foulness next to god ballad," he wrote to Rob Darrell shortly after joining the faculty at Princeton, "but there were other foulnesses in the shapes of freshmen and sophomores who trooped in"—and that was that. "Because for so many years I wrote so regularly for *Poetry*," he said to Henry Rago, who was editing that magazine in 1958, "I wish I could let you lure me into doing so again." But he hadn't the time. The life of Henry Adams was going to be his great achievement in prose, and when he died this work remained unfinished. There were plenty of reasons and he offered them endlessly. In his essay on *Madame Bovary*, he spoke to one of these reasons. "Ennui is the ignoble form in which we exercise our instincts for martyrdom: in which we cannot sit still but are aimless in motion, looking for motive." He couldn't find a motive for action, unless the action was to fill the void of silence he dreaded. Always he felt himself "trembling into stone." In 1935 he wrote to Harriet Monroe, for whom he intended "From Jordan's Delight": "It is the only poem I have been able to finish for a long time."

His inspiration flagged but his desire persisted. Robert Penn Warren, who first met him in 1939, remembered chiefly how excited he was at having to read his poetry in public. Poetry, Warren thought, was what he cared about most. Just before he went to Princeton he was writing again after a long hiatus, and was hard put to express "how much of a personal kick" this gave him. Friendly competition with John Brooks Wheelwright spurred him on. "The Ancient Bards were meeting Wednesday at Jack's, and it was so annoying to me that Jack was the only one with fresh poems that amounted to anything, that I set about writing a few myself." Mostly what he wrote doesn't cash as poetry. One of the new poems purports to be "An Image of the United States Senate." His eye and ear must have told him that this poem was inert, but he gave it to John Berryman, who had just been appointed poetry editor of the *Nation*. He said Berryman deserved praise for not having "given up being a writer." Richard added somberly: "most people do give up."

His reputation as a poet remained alive. In the spring of 1941 he was invited to read his "verses to the Cooper Unions." He said he dreaded the event. His letters belie this, however. "You can have no idea," he wrote to the poet Lee Anderson, "how pleasant and reassuring it is to have anyone . . . seem actually to get something out of my verse." He met his own satisfaction in the response of friends. "I think your Churn is excellent," said John Walcott, the friend from Harrington days who died in Italy during the war and whom Richard memorialized in "Three Poems from a Text of Isaiah." In "Missa Vocis," the poem Walcott meant to praise, Richard wrote:

> the mass of new voice
> keeps the great churn going.

In the later poetry, the voice one hears is often shrill or furry with official vexation. Idiom, the condition of vitality, waned, as Richard edged away from the personal themes of his first book to the public and social themes of *The Second World* and *The Good European*. As often for him, "personal" doesn't mean private, but all that transpires—

> the odour of pennyroyal, where your fingers
> frittered and bruised the fresh leaves—

and "public" and "social" all that remains inert.

In 1942 *The Second World* appeared, and Delmore Schwartz wrote to Richard: "It was pleasant to open *Time* this morning and see you described as a remote and excellent poet." But the title poem of Richard's book—maybe the best poem in a slim and uneven collection—had first been published four years earlier in *Twentieth Century Verse*. On a retrospective view, *The Second World* seems a posthumous event. To Delmore, in a letter of 1946, Richard confided his intention of bringing out "another small volume." He said he had "succumbed to vanity." In *The Good European* you meet him in the middle of the journey, trying and mostly failing to find his way back. Reviewers were sympathetic but remarked his unrelenting "dependence upon abstraction," also the "presumption that ideas can carry the burdens of poetry." Early on, he knew this presumption for a heresy. He became a heresiarch in the end.

For the record, he still put his poetry first. "There's no more engrossing work than writing a poem," he told the *Daily Princetonian* in 1951, "especially if you have a hold on it." His hold faltered and he worried minor points in work he had published. "The comma in line 14 of the third sonnet . . . is the cross you will have to bear." A year before he died, his friends Robert Lowell, Richard Wilbur, and William Meredith asked him for a fresh book of poems. "He declined because he said he already had a very generous publisher in Harcourt who would do the book whenever he got ready." He talked a lot about getting it ready. Sean O'Faolain recollected the past and brought it to bear on the present: "One really had to have known the poor and struggling Keats boy of the 20's to feel the vastness of the change." He wondered did Richard's Fanny Brawne see this change "as a betrayal of their first dreams." So Richard's career as a poet ended in sadness. He had prayed he might fall like a meteor, "burnt in its own light." His fall was harder: he guttered and went out. To focus on the end is not to do him justice, though.

Richard claimed for himself a "small crown." Like so many of his friends, he wanted to write poetry. He said he could "rejoice in *having written* some of it." He didn't deceive himself. He made a small body of permanent poems. Among them are the title poem of his first volume, *From Jordan's Delight*, especially the second section, also "October Frost," "Phasellus Ille," "The Second World," "Una Vita Nuova," "Ithyphallics." To make a few achieved poems in a lifetime is immense, like Charles Cotton and Michael Drayton or Lord Herbert or Richard Lovelace. This is the company Blackmur as poet belongs to. So it is too bad or rather derelict that his work has been dropped from anthologies of modern poetry. Time has not had its way with the work; fashion and sloth have conspired to ignore it. Richard in his prosody is a formal poet and goes against the fashion of his time. Also he is unfamiliar, and there is nothing harder than sitting down to poetry you don't know and having it speak to you. That is where the sloth comes in. A generation has passed since he set up in public as a practicing poet. His vital inspiration didn't last long—roughly ten years—and in this he is American, like many of the poets and novelists of whom he wrote in his critical prose.

His early career in poetry is like anybody else's, a record of false starts and misplaced allegiance—

> Memories; blood stains, clotted wounds.
> Shrines; tombs of the slain gods.

You could call him a Romantic, but he didn't read much in the greater Romantics. Blake is an important exception, probably Coleridge, too—the observer, not the prophet. Mostly, he read the epigones. He was strong for Poe and Arthur Symons—he doesn't have to say this, the mark is on the verse—and he responded with nervous enthusiasm to Wilde's "lush, deadly sweet beauty." Swinburne had his allegiance, and he wrote what he thought was like Swinburne:

> So sadly I lie on my pillow of mould
> Dreaming of the days, purple and gold,
> When I was a child, very wicked and wild.

He was an amateur in poetry, for whom the natural bad beat is the anapest.

He didn't get much better for a long time. There is nothing surprising in the badness of his juvenilia until you put it against the quickness with which he came to mastery in prose. It ought to be the other way round.

Partly, Richard got better because he was bookish. One of the good poems begins:

> The comfortable noise long reading makes
> brimming within the inward ear.

He read ten plays of Shakespeare at a clip and he used his reading in "From Jordan's Delight." He took the sonnet form from Shakespeare (not always, but mostly) and made it his own form. His facility in striking off reverberant lines and phrases came from reading the older poets like Webster and Ford. To Harriet Monroe he confessed his debt in two poems to Bishop Henry King, and it is from his study of that great minor maker and his contemporaries of the seventeenth century that he got his fluency in the octosyllabic line. "The first lesson of craft or morals," he wrote in 1937, is "that our means determine, if not our willed purpose, certainly our achieved ends." Characteristically, his means are modest. He isn't a discursive poet, his blank verse is shortwinded, and what he manages best are short lines and the play between, that breath-catching departure from the prosodic norm that is the yield of working in a narrow compass:

> The tough sea island sheep
> towards dawn break up our sleep;
> may they attend likewise
> the death we do this day put off—
> with the faint, fog-cracked cough
> of half surprise.

His achieved ends take strength from circumscribing and circumspection. He is a poet of the apothegm and the epigrammatic couplet:

His whitened knuckles more than mine
showed how death climbs live veins, a vine.

This sounds like Andrew Marvell, and in fact when Richard gets bad it is still generic Marvell, but the political versifier now. The title of an early sonnet, "Since There's No Help," says he has been reading Drayton. The matter and sensibility are out of the nineties, though. Partly this means that Richard is learning his trade. The observation holds for other poems from this period. "Mirage" is one of them—not his best poem by a long shot, but his most celebrated poem. This unrhymed sonnet is old-fashioned literary, like Yeats's "Innisfree" or "Down by the Salley Gardens," and as in those poems the grasp of the fashion is sure:

The wind was in another country, and
the day had gathered to its heart of noon
the sum of silence, heat, and stricken time.
Not a ripple spread. The sea mirrored
perfectly all the nothing in the sky.
We had to walk about to keep our eyes
from seeing nothing, and our hearts from stopping
at nothing. Then most suddenly we saw
horizon on horizon lifting up
out of the sea's edge a shining mountain
sun-yellow and sea-green; against it surf
flung spray and spume into the miles of sky.
Somebody said mirage, and it was gone,
but there I have been living ever since.

Except for Pound and Eliot, American poets in this century didn't much engage Richard in his own practice. A manuscript of his early poems is bound in a jacket that had covered the collected poems of Edwin Arlington Robinson. He heard the elegist in Robinson, "gone where Saturn keeps the years." At eighteen he thought Cummings "pretty high class." So he wasn't all that special in his immature taste. He liked the cinquains of Adelaide Crapsey and in his "Scarabs for the Living" he put them to work with a difference. Stevens is his great discovery among American poets. In the Christmas season of 1924, he and Conrad Aiken found the first edition of *Harmonium* remaindered in Filene's Basement at eleven cents a copy. They bought all there were to buy and sent the books as Christmas cards to their friends. It makes a great story, but there isn't much of Stevens in Richard. Stevens on his mannerist side comes too close for comfort.

The poet Genevieve Taggard gave Richard credit for the best ear since

Emily Dickinson. This praise entails limitation. At eighteen, he said the chief thing the poet wants of his readers "is a good ear and a long training in the production of voice effects." That is a half-truth, but he didn't let go of it. An early letter to his cousin begins, as with an epigraph: "Dans un Palais, soie et or, dans Ecbatane." Poetry—this is what the epigraph means—"is the expression in terms of colour, sound, and rhythm, either of an emotion or of the record of an emotion." The greater poetry is the first. Also he said: "There must be no content to poetry."

Here Richard is following and no doubt vulgarizing Benedetto Croce, whom he got on to early and who functions as a shaping instrument in the elaborating of the New Criticism. This is adolescent Blackmur: "In poetry as in life we should remember always that words in themselves have no meaning, cannot be defined . . . are suggestions, are merely symbols of the emotional vision of man in relation to his environment." So the poet "plays, not with words, but with beautiful . . . sounds." No one would want to tie these effusions to R. P. Blackmur when he came into his force. Who paid more homage to words on their denotative side? But the germ of the self-indulgent stylist is here. In what he called "the wringing of new sound"—the linguistic high jinks which denote the later prose—you recognize the young man for whom sound was more than sense.

His best poems are often euphonious and prone to interior rhyme. They proclaim the rhetorician—a Roman of the decadent period—who nailed rhetoric to the masthead and went down. In the fifties, two of his Princeton students sent him a long critique of his writing. On the poetry they were admiring but caustic, sensing in it "the egotism of the word, which attempts to take power unto itself." Richard likes to make up words and he likes that magical trope which consists of ringing purely lexical changes: "In spending tides, spent winds, and unspent seas." Sometimes the result is unassimilated Hopkins, caught in his unstopped ear: "What wilted waits for water still, what winced." But sometimes chance flowers to choice, as when he puts "the oldest inchoate shapes in words." For the egotism of the word, as his students perceived, was the saving resource of this inchoate and evacuated man. He used to quote Elizabeth Sewall: "Words are the only defense of the mind against being possessed by thought or dream." Out of his deprivation he made "a music of the dry emptiness of the soul caught in reason." Making indifference dance, he carried reason to the side of God.

The mock esthetic he elaborated when he was seventeen predicts his success and ultimate failure. This esthetic is pregnant with despair. Life is an irreducible surd (one of his words), art also. You wrestle with it as you can—"we who have married reason on desperate cause when the heart's cause was lost." But "the gap is absolute" between what we say of a poem and what the poem is, and always you fail to pin down the meaning. Mulling over portentous questions like "What is life?" in an early notebook, Richard sees how no answers are in prospect. Best to conceive life as in relation to other life, not as an abstract entity which theory can rationalize. Already he is a New Critic. "There is, of course, a cause somewhere; but that is a mystery, and I believe it is more pleasant to have a mystery, which is naturally lovely, than to produce a theoretical explanation, which because of its dubiety and needlessness, is not a formal unity and is therefore ugly." His youthful words are banal, but even this early he redeems them: "like the image of a beautiful woman, art is forever remote and intangible, and still perfectly knowable in the beauty of the form."

Art is remote as it supplies no answers. It suffices us, though. It makes a formal unity and is therefore comely. More than thirty years after this, Richard described for friends—he could hardly keep the excitement down —his discovery of his own poetics. The discovery is a resuming in more sophisticated terms of what he had supposed from the beginning. He had been listening to the mathematician John von Neumann at a conference on the Right to Knowledge ("and free beer," said Isidore Rabi). Von Neumann's subject was method in the physical sciences. He defended the thesis that this method was primarily, even utterly, opportunistic. He said it had to satisfy certain criteria of which the layman, who identifies science with truth, is largely unconscious. The criteria he stipulated were five: Rigor, Simplicity, Fruitfulness, Opportunism or Possibility, and the Sense of the Aesthetic Whole. Richard entered von Neumann's terms in his own lecture notes on Dante's great sestina, understanding how this was just the right context. The sestina, manipulating the same rhyme words over and over, is of all poetic forms the most opportunistic and also—in its self-imposed poverty of means—the most simple: "as if simplicity," said Richard to von Neumann, "were itself opportunistic." Don't ask of an idea "that its validity be final." (Richard wrote this at twenty-one.) "Ask nothing of an idea but that it behave." Criticism—and poetry too—is "a good game" when it works, "a delicious solitaire." You "push an idea along from square to square until it topples off the table. The moment of toppling is the moment of validity. Then the mind strenuously resumes its bewilderment."

One of Richard's early students at Princeton was the poet Frederick Morgan, later a founder of the *Hudson Review*. Morgan said he was aware "of a certain fuzziness and lack of clarity" in his teacher's thought, "and of an excessive love of paradox for its own sake." He concluded that "this was not due to any intellectual deficiency, but to what might be called a moral one: a failure of commitment at some profound level." You do not have to accept Morgan's judgment to see where he is coming from. Richard at his deepest level has no purchase point, and this is debilitating. And it is poignant: how much does his lack of formal schooling figure here, not being to the manner born, also his immense and private self-schooling, which raised him above the ruck and left him talking to himself, always arrogant and always unsure? In his skepticism he is like his early hero Pater or an esthetician of the Mauve Decade, but this is inspiriting, too. Remembering James: "Our doubt is our passion and our passion is our task." On the other hand: as his skepticism was absolute, so his resort was to play. "What do you mean," Delmore asked him, " 'a hymn in new whim'? Is this chance flowering to choice again?" He is quoting from "Missa Vocis." Then he says, falling in with this opportunist in language, "Let us ad lib forever." All art on one side is ad-libbing, Blackmur's art more than most.

Nowhere did he come closer to giving his own likeness than in this brief glimpse of Pascal, who displayed "an intense levity in both style of language and deportment of mind: as if the depth of his doubt gave him an orthodoxy, and the force of his *ennui* gave him a security, that permitted the mind to play while it rancored, and even encouraged it to frivolity in all but the most severe rackings of desperation." Levity in Richard, Hugh Kenner supposed, was neither intense nor desperate but only "habitual doodling," undertaken "in the hope that something critically significant will occur." The hope was there, no question, also the play of mind. But it was play for mortal stakes, and anyway no alternative offered.

A poem written in his twenties has these lines:

> You will have seen him sit there reading
> of Stephen Dedaelus and Bloom . . .
> as the words' ghosts ascend the gloom.

"Ghosts" is the word for the infiltrating in Richard's poetry of his acknowledged masters, Pound and Eliot. From the time he was sixteen and for almost ten years after that, he devoured every word he could find of Pound's poetry, "and felt every word either as an appetiser or a meal, and always an invitation to the feast we never quite consume because we never quite sit at the table." He wanted to help "beloved Ezra" in imposing "simplicity upon our generation." He knew no one approaching him for perfection of rhythm. "In England there are poets," he wrote at seventeen.

"In America there is Ezra Pound, Robinson, and Bodenheim." At twenty, he and Pound were corresponding, and he raised a few factual questions about the Cantos. "Beyond these things," he said, "I believe I can account for nearly everything in the work." He wrote out his own version of the plan on which the first twelve Cantos were constructed. Their concreteness absorbed him. Pound had established *"in a poem* not the theory but the created body of the continuity and interdependence of the world." The poem was demanding, though, and Richard said he was aware of only three sufficient readers. Subsequently, he asked Pound if he and two friends, who were hoping to publish pamphlets and small books of prose and poetry, might bring out a number of the Cantos in a limited edition. Presumably the friends were Paul Rowe and George Anthony of the Crucible House, and constituted two-thirds of Pound's discriminating public.

As Richard matured in his own practice, he grew increasingly doubtful of Pound's. His essay of 1933, "Masks of Ezra Pound," was almost finished when he wrote to Morton Zabel: "What I thought of years ago, as long, indeed, as 1920, as a work of appreciation and praise, has become a labor of deprecation and attack far more than I would have thought possible. There remain large nuggets of first-class work, which I am trying to emphasise, and the translations retain their astonishing beauty and virtuosity; but the rest—I intentionally exaggerate—is ruin and obfuscation." He wondered if he had become blind. But he knew no one "who has gone into the Cantos at such length as I have," so could "consult no one with assurance." His conclusion wasn't that the Cantos "need not be read; rather that they must be read in spite of what they are."

The ruin wasn't moral but formal, Richard thought—a matter of composition. His own poetry wants composition, however, and this is the underside of his commitment to modest means. He is a Nominalist among the poets, he doesn't raise his eyes and so misses the Pisgah-sight. Partly he takes strength from this. His intelligence is limited but prehensile. Paraphrasing an early poem, he knows deeply the small things of a life. "Discrete phrases," said Delmore Schwartz, "are the main object of his attention. The way in which they combine is sometimes an afterthought." John Wheelwright said: "the joints of his moods with everyday are thin at times, and one must be alert with utter inner poise to hear or to heed him." So the problem of obscurity is part and parcel of his problem with form. He is a disarticulate writer. He never wrote a whole book and here is a reason why. "The principle of composition"—his subject is "From Jordan's Delight," his correspondent Robert Penn Warren—"is a kind of principle of eclectic, progressive agglutination. The formulae of division have little to do with the inner form." The exercise of the executive imagination (Richard's phrase) depends on formal structure, though. In his failed poetry, he dispenses with it. He is like his later and wary estimate of Pound: he needs a given. His success at sonnets comments on this need.

Ten years before he died, he wrote of Pound: "There is a great deal still to be learned from his practice of poetry and a great deal of liveliness still to be felt in his criticism. I still feel both myself." But mostly what he felt was disabling. In Pound he met himself, the last thing one wants to meet in poetry.

Richard took from Eliot, whom he loved above all other poets of this century, the "jewelled Monstrosities" that suited his own acidulated taste. Also he took the histrionic pose. (Subsequently, Yeats too contributed to this.) He said his early poems were "fragments I have shored against my ruins." When, in his twenties, he deplores the "shroud of sixty years" in which, for poetic reasons, he had got himself up, he sounds like Eliot the old eagle. In 1932, when Richard was twenty-eight, Eliot did a stint of teaching at Harvard. He "limited his class in modern literature to *twelve*." Richard went to hear this latter-day Messiah, and saw from a distance the type of the poet: "mild, serious, nervous, very tall, very white, smiling uncertainly in round cheeks, with smooth-slick parted hair—displayed but undisplaying—altogether, I think, in an agony which he had to make serene." A week later they met for lunch, and Richard "felt in the person the same residual stillness which is the object or punctuation of the poems." From six inches away, Eliot showed more forcefully than the man on the platform: "not only not white but distinctly brown, weathered; not only not embarrassed, but furnished with the weapons for relieving embarrassment. A generous but retreating spirit." The speech came slowly —like the thought, Richard guessed. "Features harshly rather than delicately sensitive . . . probably contorts his face privately. . . . Eyes dark, protected both with and without glasses."

They talked American politics, with which Eliot was minutely acquainted (this was the fall when Roosevelt came to power), and talked about sailing on the Maine coast—the tide rip off Petit Manan, the harbor at Roque Island, the Jonesport people, the thrushes through the fog on Casco Bay. Their meeting put the stamp on Richard's discipleship. His literary heroes were Eliot's heroes—Dante, Montaigne, and Pascal—and they became the subject of the famous course he gave at Princeton. In his life and work he cribbed from the master. "To see beneath both beauty and ugliness; to see the boredom, and the horror, and the glory"—this famous version of the poet's job of work (from Eliot's *Use of Poetry*) recurs almost obsessively in his own critical prose. Eliot incarnated all he wished to be: "Nothing of the defeated the emasculated man: a capable, living, definite body . . . virile. One understands at once the pride with which he calls himself a skipper. Add the poetry to the man and both gain strength." Richard concluded shrewdly: "Unlike James, the social position is secure."

In later years he allowed himself a few modest reservations. He observed how Eliot's notes for *The Waste Land* "ran into frightful bogs of learning," and lamented "the failure to deal well with contemporary poetry, with the novel at all, and the general habit of dealing with all literature on the lines that belong appropriately only to lyric poetry"—a habit that dismayed him in his fellow New Critics. But almost always the poet remained beyond reproach. *Ash Wednesday* was "the nearest to major composition our generation has yet come." *Murder in the Cathedral* ("the largest thing Eliot has done") was "as near major poetry" as Richard wanted to read. No English poetry of the last hundred years was more "profoundly exciting." It stirred him, he told his cousin, "to try to get my own hand in on a few poems."

By and large, the result is pastiche. This isn't surprising. Eliot's poetry played to his fatal enthusiasm for big questions. Richard does best when he answers sparely, the answer being in the detail. In Eliot he met the "wraith of unused skill" that added up to cursoriness in treating conceptual thought. Like Richard, Eliot is primarily a poet of the emotions, "the awful daring of a moment's surrender." Conceptual thought is on his poems like finery. His advice is notoriously to assimilate thinking to feeling. A long poem Richard sent Eliot for the *Criterion* was "too thoughtful," Eliot said. He wrote to Richard in 1926: "the harder you think and the longer you think the better: but in turning thought into poetry it has to be fused into a more definite pattern of immediately apprehensible imagery, imagery which shall have its own validity and be immediately the equivalent of, and indeed identical with, the thought behind it. . . . The more thought that is turned into poetry the better; only it must be, in the final form, *felt* thought."

This is plain to Richard on his critical side. As an editor of the *Hound & Horn*, he returned a batch of the poems to Richard Johns of the magazine *Pagany*. He said they depended on material outside the poems. "Everything merely intellectual," he wrote in his essay on *The Magic Mountain*, "must either be converted into, or deeply allied with, the sensibility." Often in his poetry—in Eliot's, too—this perception goes unhonored and the waste remains and kills. Unlocalized guilt, the accrual of history, lies heavy on the poems. You are expected to take it on faith; no collateral is ventured. To define, Richard said, is "to realise in word and image obdurate things." When these things are intellectual, they tend to remain obdurate. Simple statement suffices. As an intellectual poet Richard only supplicates ideas, but like Eliot can't let them alone. He is mustering his credentials. Perhaps both of them are.

Richard's debt to Yeats is different—not a pose, but a frock or livery he put on and wore until it became him. At first the relation of pupil to master was servile: some of the early poems read like conscious parody. Later the imitation gets more practiced, and you hear Richard's voice above the echoes. Finally there are no echoes, only a lesson learned.

"Our one indubitable major poet," Richard called Yeats in 1935. He never swerved from this view. "That man holds up as none of the others I have tackled do," he wrote to Cleanth Brooks in 1941. Just into his teens, he was intoning the poems to his sister. At eighteen he read the plays. Reflecting on Yeats's poetry, he wrote in his notebook: "The only sound rituals are those which contain excess." When he grasped fully what this meant—not a young man's redacting of one of Blake's apothegms—he became a poet himself. His next sentence reads: "The only sound orders are those which invite as well as withstand disorder." The accommodating man invited disorder in, the agile man compelled it. How Richard mastered these roles, putting on the new man, is the whole story of his achievement in poetry. The experience of Yeats, the great formal practitioner among twentieth-century poets, is decisive for the achievement, on the side of books. Friends who were also poets had their important contribution to make—among them Wheelwright and Sherry Mangan, Horace Gregory, Richard Eberhart, later Delmore Schwartz. They instructed Richard in his craft as they offered a dubious version of the poet; or, in positive ways, when their poetic practice differed sharply from his. There is nothing more illuminating than our assent to an imaginative process, Richard wrote, "whose beginnings shift under us as we look for them and whose ends we must feel as alien."

His assent to Yeats—the objective artist, not the *histrio*—dramatized the need to hide his own dearth and lack of personal force, or you can say his superfluity. For poetry, they mean the same thing. Some of the poems take their rise from experience and yet seem made up from books. Some are extrapolated, and come home as sincere. In "An Elegy for Five" the speaker lies dying; he speaks in a learned rhythm, and convinces you of genuine feeling. Here is a quatrain from "Sea Island Miscellany":

> Once along this coast
> my fathers made their sail

and were with all hands lost,
outweathered in a gale.

Richard is creating his ancestors—he did the same thing in conversation
—and the yield from long looking is to come on second sight and make a
second world, better than the real world because ordered and distanced
and so more nearly true.

In his poetry Richard—like Yeats—made a habitation, and for a few
years it sustained him. He envisioned this habitation when he wrote at
eighteen: "the feelings and ideas which are most my own, which are most
nearly original . . . are, as it were, too *personal*." Reaching for an objective art, he was diffident about writing them down. So far, so good. Then
he shifted his ground a little. "I forget that what I want is my expression:
whatever value it has, is not, to me, the content, but the manner and the
attitude." He is telling us (after Eliot) that value is exhausted in form.

No doubt it is better to say this than to run on about the value of
content, which has no substance for the reader until it is formed. Richard
had a wonderful passage at arms with his friend Eberhart, whose poems
he reviewed in 1938. The review made Eberhart angry: "You erect craft
at the expense of the vital impulses that make a poem. . . . you think of art
only as artifice; you eschew the deeper issues, you skip any relation of
poetry to the times," the familiar guff, like Bill Gorton to Jake Barnes in
Burguete in *The Sun Also Rises*. The short of it is: "Nothing but the
deepest sincerity will do." Richard had written: "I do not charge Mr.
Eberhart with insincerity; it would be nearer home to charge him with
insufficient insincerity—for the best of poetry is Jesuit's trade, once the
end is in view."

That is immaculate criticism. The casuistical temper—taking willful
order with disorder—is the organizing agent of much great poetry—
Donne's, for example. It is only the agent or efficient means, however. In
an essay on the artistry of T. E. Lawrence, Richard saw how "the pang of
conceptual feeling needed a direct base in bodily pain before it could be
forced, by imagination, into emotion." The pain—call it substantial content—antedates considerations of form. Richard's early discrimination is
partial. He didn't come into his force until he pieced it out.

As a young man in Cambridge, Richard was the poet as hero. Poetry
was everything or nothing, not something you did in your closet. To
supply his reading, he went without meals. "He was ravenous for food in
his youth," said Tessa Horton, and she remembered how "after I'd gone

to bed during Richard's nightly visits to 12 Ellery St., my mother used to feed him a really solid meal." George Anthony spoke of this ravenous hunger, and how he never failed attendance at John Marshall's weekly teas. There was always the chance of something to eat. He read the little magazines like *Broom*, the *Double Dealer, Secession,* and kept a file of their addresses. "Bring your *Dials* previous to September," he instructed his cousin. "I have finished October and November." Like Delmore Schwartz, nine years his junior, he was reading Joyce to pieces while his contemporaries were reading *Anthony Adverse*. At seventeen he was submitting his poems to the *Dial*. The editors didn't think these poems successful. He disapproved strongly of the *Dial*'s taste. "I, personally, think them entirely 'successful.' "

His conviction that he was meant for greatness kept him going. But he knew he was a provincial, so looked for correction beyond his own country. He read or tried to read *La Ronda* and *Der Sturm* and *La Nouvelle Revue Française*. He said his French wasn't good enough, but he understood at seventeen that he ought to read his French poets in the original. So he applied himself to Verlaine and Laforgue. Nobody told him what was approved; he made his own hierarchies of value. Rilke wasn't up to Thomas Mann. "But on its own plane," Rilke's *Journal of My Other Self* "stands equally alone." Later he read Baudelaire. At last, he wrote Rob Darrell, "I . . . have him inside me in his own tongue which is the way he should be." He knew no one today could use Baudelaire directly. But he saw how to use him as a "parallel way of feeling—a discipline." Richard the young man was "the only prisoner in a world set free"—quoting from an early poem of his. Through discipline he found his way to freedom.

In his twenty-first year he began corresponding with Harriet Monroe, who played tutor to his still untrammeled, hence unliberated youth. Her death eleven years later brought him, he told Morton Zabel, "a dreadful sense of age, and, worse, of pause." At first, Monroe rejected the poems he sent her for *Poetry*, feeling in them an overstressing of method. In Richard's apprentice work, method means graveclothes. His judgment on an obscure poet of the thirties holds for himself: he is "a vast fascinating register of the mind as sensorium. . . . He has all the irresponsible vitality of the immediate in sensation and of the frantic in perception; all governed, as is usually the case, only by vitiated convention."

Some of the poems were better than this, and some of them were taken. "Alma Venus," after Lucretius, was the first. After a while Richard's presence in *Poetry* was being bid for. Other journals published him, too, like his friend Sherry Mangan's little magazine, *larus*, printed and designed by Mangan and set by hand on his own press in the barn behind the family house in Lynn. Virgil Thomson served *larus* as European editor; he got Gertrude Stein, Robert McAlmon, Mary Butts, and others to contribute. *larus* offered hospitality to obscure poets, too. In the second issue, a poem of Richard's precedes a poem by Hart Crane.

Sherry was a poet of the Pisgah-sight, always raising his eyes from the words on the page. In aspiration he was a genuine poet and wanted to pay homage to the real world. Once at least he did this. The autobiographical story he called "Snow," not published until long after his death, proclaims the poet beneath the skin. Two years before he died, he wrote to Dudley Fitts: "even though revolutionary politics are an honorable occupation, it's poetry I still love best." Loving poetry best, Sherry served it least, however. His biographer said of him: "in his dual devotion to poetry and revolutionary socialism, Sherry Mangan rose above the tragedies that plagued his life and found fulfillment of a special sort." Maybe this was true. Anyway, his dual devotion makes a perfect setoff to Richard as poet and suggests how the poet, as he honors his craft, is primarily the man who bears witness. Richard in the life of Adams gives the pristine sense of the phrase: "One did what one could; which often, for the genuinely political mind"—or, one could say, for the mind beating on poetry—"amounted to no more than acting as witness."

"My influence over Sherry is probably nil," Richard lamented in the early days of their friendship. Sherry possessed a great fund of ardor—this was his working capital—but he dissipated the capital in proselyting for his radical views. If you were a poet, how far did you entertain views? Hopkins, though a Catholic, had no views in his poetry. He kept his spiritual life hidden except as it loomed under the words. "Here is nothing if not feeling," Richard said of the Notebooks, "so concrete, so near the actual, and so free from the falsely vindicating drive of the mere idea." The genuine poet pressed upon his limits, quite aside from the church or state to which he was committed. So he instructed us in the nature of the mature intelligence, which tended always toward the visual.

For Sherry, the mature intelligence was necessarily kinetic. But it wasn't his political bias that disabled him. Horace Gregory shared this bias, and in 1933 Richard inquired into its implications for poetry. He disagreed with Allen Tate, who thought it fatally impairing. Gregory, like Mangan, had only to see his "radical" subjects—this is what Richard was learning to say—"as subjects for poetry and not the ends of politics." The discrimination was critical for Richard's poetry, as the poetry got better. Subject matter was a given: the poet, after all, had a right to his views. Everything turned on the way you fleshed them out. Sherry in his poetry lacked avoirdupois. Mostly he offered the platitude of mere statement—apt and disturbing, but in the end no soap.

He died in 1961, almost unnoticed, and Richard consulted his exemplary failure for the last time. Sherry, he said ruefully, "might have died one day as another." His fellow Trotskyists remember him with gratitude as "our comrade Patrice," the party name he adopted for his clandestine activity. George Anthony said: "To those of us who were not Trotskyists, his life was a sad waste." But the waste is emblematic and makes the life worth recalling.

If you liked him, Sherry was large, jolly, and avuncular, otherwise a big fat Irishman who cultivated a Dublin accent, not having been to Dublin. Under his Socialist politics lived a High Tory left over from the Age of Johnson, also an appreciator of beautiful women, a gourmet, and a drinking man's drinker. "The principal influences on Mangan were Don Juanism and alcohol," George Anthony said. In his cups he paused occasionally, "taking a breath." Eating, he hardly paused. When he went to South America as a correspondent for Time-Life, he applied with such vigor to Argentine beef that his trenchcoat wouldn't hold him any more. This made trouble with the customs officials. "Open your coat, Monsieur, Monsieur," they said. "He did and it was just Sherry, because he ate so many steaks." Reporting World War II from London, he looked like Henry VIII dressed as an American soldier. In his suite at the Dorchester, to which he gravitated as a matter of course, he kept a wardrobe full of beef and John Jameson's whiskey. Later in Italy, when Kate Foster came to see him—they were divorced by then—he anticipated her visit with a list of necessities: a loojah, the iron skillet his gourmandizing required, and patterns of cloth for the suit Greves of Bond Street was going to make him.

His scholarship was passionate and he had the gift of tongues. He dabbled in psychology, he counseled the aspiring young, and the advice he gave other people was always very wise. His sense of humor did him no good. The Germans kicked him out of occupied France when he answered to "Heil Hitler" by shouting, "Wintergreen for President!" He loved dispensing largesse, not least when he didn't have it. Like Micawber, he thought something was sure to turn up. He was right about this, almost until he died. Destitute in Mexico, he wired home for money. His mother sent him one dollar—perhaps she knew her son. Half went for a drink, the rest bought a lottery ticket. Sherry wasn't the sort of whom moral tales are made. He enjoyed his drink, and the ticket won him a hundred dollars.

Rob Darrell found in Sherry "no redeeming qualities," but was awed by "his extraordinary, indeed miraculous feat of quite suddenly metamorphosing from a penniless radical/intellectual/artist into a top *Time* correspondent at some fantastic salary." Then came "as quick and great a Fall." His sister-in-law thought his Irishness the key to Sherry's nature. Conspiracy was the element he lived in. When "that pumpkin hider who became head of *Time*" gave him a list of Trotskyists to investigate—this as the basis for a story on the party—he was delighted to find that two names on the list were pseudonyms for Sherry Mangan. In the secret code he devised for sending Trotskyist messages into Latin America, "Blackmuir [sic] children" signified the Armed Forces. Richard had no children. Maybe Sherry was suggesting that the power of the military was nonexistent, too. But Sherry's little jokes turned to ashes in the end.

Tessa Horton in early days designed a bookplate at his bidding, extolling in Latin the virtue of excess. "Well, he died from excess," Tessa said. This was in Rome, four years before Richard died. Friends buried Sherry in the Protestant Cemetery, near the grave of Keats. "That was his greatest distinction," Tessa said.

In 1927 Richard wrote to George Anthony, "Sherry is a good fellow, a good printer, a good friend and many other good and amazing things." When Richard came to Lynn to visit his cousin, he looked in on Sherry at the Press of the Lone Gull. In Boston they dined together at the Athens-Olympia with Jack Wheelwright and George Anthony and Tessa and Dudley Fitts, or they went to the Ararat, an Armenian restaurant where— this being Prohibition—the inky wine came in coffee cups. "They were a close set," Kate Foster remembered. Richard felt himself "re-sharpened" by Sherry's "points for interest, so different from my own." They were just of an age, but Sherry seemed older. Already his reputation as a poet was established. He published in *Anathema* and the *New Republic*, and in lesser-known magazines with bristling titles like *Front* and *Forge*. As an editor, he chose the worst things Richard sent him. Sherry had no time for nice distinctions. "To Hell with Poesie," he said, intending an appeal to more urgent business. His last poem declares this business—the subject was Beethoven and the bomb:

> If we would still hear music, we
> must also listen to the knell
> tolling for music and for love.
> Will it be only when I see your loved flesh turn
> from red to black, and my already black
> flesh is crackling . . .
> that we shall wonder: did we always
> always in every way, with all our strength,
> fight to prevent this moment.

Fighting to prevent this moment more than evoking it, Sherry was less a poet than a polemicist. Like Jack Wheelwright, he looked to the future. Unlike Wheelwright, who carried his baggage with him into the future, he had no inkling "that in our history is the salvation of our character, and that in our ends are our beginnings"—quoting Richard on Dos Passos. Experience impinged for Sherry as powerfully as for Richard, but when reading him you didn't know this. His engagement with words seemed to depend more upon asserted principle than felt apprehension. "What does not transpire," Richard wrote, "cannot be said to have been experienced." Sherry didn't grasp the problem.

The title of his magazine—*larus*, "the celestial visitor"—denoted a large cosmopolitan gull. Most gulls, Sherry wrote, travel in coveys, "a clamorous crowd all very much alike." Higher in the air he saw a single gull, planing along, flying alone. This gull was "unique in itself." Sherry was unique—"integer vitae, scelerisque purus," Austin Warren called him —also "a swell guy." But he didn't fly alone. "His taking up with the Trotsky faith" was Wheelwright's doing, Virgil Thomson said, "but psychologically determined by his own position as a lapsed Catholic." In the Trotsky faith, Sherry found "exactly those opportunities that he needed for behaving like a Jesuit theologian." But he wasn't a good Jesuit: he lacked the niggling instinct.

Sherry, said Austin Warren, was many different men. Richard's monolithic quality makes you blanch. In the years which produced his best poetry, Richard wrote: "It wears in on me that I have lived a singularly concentrated, thoroughly selfish life." It seems unfair that he should have been the better poet. He wasn't better because he was selfish. Reviewing the poems of Robert Frost, that dreadful curmudgeon, he had this to say: "a poet is in the end, whatever he may be at heart, a maker in words, a true imager, of whatever reality must be brought to bear." You were a poet as you made reality transpire in words; otherwise, as Richard said, no soap.

By the time he was thirty, Richard had earned the right to call himself a poet. Lincoln Kirstein was negotiating with financial backers, hoping to find the money to publish a small volume of his verse. In 1935 the *New Republic* commissioned him to make an anthology of "Eight New England Poets." He was the best of the lot. Wheelwright, whom Richard included in his anthology, thought so. He said that Richard at epigrams was better than Savage Landor, "that supposed unsurpassable master of the epigram." He quoted:

Pride is the thing outside
pride is the itching hide:
the proud man out of doors
goes naked in his sores.
Forgive him that he shrinks inside.

J. V. Cunningham, saluting Richard as among "the foremost 'younger' critics," added his opinion that "your poetry at its best is flawless. I am thinking of the epigrams and 'Phasellus Ille,' in the *Magazine*, and of the 'Sea Miscellany' in the *Hound & Horn*." Yvor Winters agreed, designating Richard one of the five best poets of his generation. He liked the short poems for their "solidity and power." The "bundle of sea-poems" sent him by the *Hound & Horn* was "very beautiful stuff."

The beauty wasn't a function of rigorous form, though achieving this rigor was Richard's settled purpose. Without a form to mold you, you couldn't know where to stop. All you could do was "push on to the corollary and let yourself run down." Sometimes, in his own verse, he let himself run down. Winters was right about him: "He had little gift for structure." Nonetheless he made "extraordinary poems." How did he do this? The answer lies partly in the material—his reconstituted self as determined by his marriage and the saving experience of Maine.

In 1933, reviewing the poems of Horace Gregory, he remarked the difference which shows in a man's writing "when there is imposed upon it the discipline of a subject." Already he himself was making his best poetry, and attesting in it the fact that "a poet seldom gains the discipline which is technical mastery, without the pressure at every point of an adequately disciplined subject." Evidently you needed subjects "to which the medium must be made to conform." Richard knew of no rule expressing this need. By rule of thumb or practice he began to see, however, that "mastery of medium and mastery by substance" go together. Only as you felt your substance as material for poetry did you merit the ribbon of craft.

The failure of Sherry Mangan, whose substance didn't transpire, is vividly present in these remarks. Their particular urgency depends on the success of another poet of the Left, John Brooks Wheelwright. For Wheelwright, discipline was mostly exhausted in content. For Richard, discipline mostly meant form. This equation isn't plenary, though Richard didn't know that. His perceptions in his youthful poetry are like postage stamps on anybody's mail; he doesn't have a locus. Friendship with Wheelwright showed him what was missing.

Wheelwright lived alone with his elderly mother, an invisible but boding presence somewhere upstairs. They lived amid a clutter of Chinese vases and screens in the elegant house at 415 Beacon Street. Here Wheelwright entertained his literary friends. In the early thirties Sherry Mangan was a fixture. Sometimes Kenneth Patchen came by for a drink, or Philip Horton or Delmore Schwartz. Here, said Howard Nemerov, "he introduced me to the dry martini." When you prepared martinis, you kept them on ice for twenty-four hours. This was if you meant them for convincing. On poetry also, Wheelwright asseverated. He was that kind of man—out of the eighteenth century, Horace Gregory thought—but he lightened his pronouncing with iconoclastic wit. Richard expected that the two of them would go on arguing poetry "as long as we both shall live." That is what they did.

They quarreled about meter and how much latitude you might give yourself in freeing up the line. "The poetic mind gets ahead somewhat by counting," Richard said. He stood for control, Wheelwright for what seemed an unconscionable freedom. Sometimes Wheelwright came down on the side of control. "It may disturb you," Richard wrote him ironically, but here and there "your scansion is . . . recogniseably sound." Wheelwright offered all the weapon and penetration you could want, but he wore only the sketchy armor of Don Quixote and went on the uncertain feet of Rosinante. The protective form, "self-willed and full of holes," seemed odd to Richard. If Wheelwright got away with it on parade or in battle, perhaps that was "by the gallantry and force of the ideas." Lacking the protection of form, he left himself open. This wasn't a good, yet constituted part of his charm. How did you reconcile the contradiction?

Wheelwright sinned abundantly, but he presented abundance. The other face of his irregular meter, the dearth of plot, the inconsistency of tone, was "the vigor, innocence and directness of a man who keeps all his interests going at once, a man of variety." If you find him "inchoate, wayward, rebellious, heretical—and you will," Richard said, "do not think it is so carelessly." His direct-eyed shrewdness menaced every orthodox position, his own included, and he relished minute particulars "whether he saw any truth in them or not." So his interests conflicted, but this didn't mean they were confused. Wheelwright's humanity redeemed them from confusion. He was born a Brahmin, and converted to Trotsky. His architect father had designed the building which housed the *Harvard Lampoon*. But the mantle of inherited privilege sat uneasily on the son. Eberhart remembered him coming in late ("by calculation") for poetry readings at Harvard and ponderously taking a seat to the left. "It was always to the left. Was this a symbol?" Like the fur coat and the walking stick, Wheelwright's politics went with him wherever he went. "The main point is not what noise poetry makes," he wrote in his *Political Self-*

Portrait, "but how it makes you think and act—what it makes of you." So his notion of poetry was kinetic, like Sherry Mangan's. Unlike Sherry, he didn't merge salvation in the kingdom on earth. "Always the enemy is the foe at home," he said. The poetry he wrote was tentacular, full of provenance. Content got primacy—this was his half-truth—but he knew that you had to rehearse it. Otherwise it wasted to rote sayings. Just before he died, he was seeing a lot of Kenneth Patchen, an ideologue like himself and a man "compact of talent." But Patchen's new work was "deficient in deliberate sense," Wheelwright wrote to Richard. "I try to tell him that reaction must be combatted by deliberate sense. The dark blood stream is Fascist." Wheelwright didn't consult the blood stream. "Make of the Dictionary your Book of Truth," he said. A line of his reads: "Habit is evil, all habit, even speech." Speech most of all. The proletariat had better make sure not to board the wrong train for Beulah. "It may land you up in Englewood, New Jersey."

In 1936 Wheelwright wanted Richard to hoist the red flag. The Socialist Party was "the only force in the country actively resisting the drift to War and to Fascism." Maybe his friend would "help us out"? Richard was agreeable but unfitted by temper. To the "unregenerate outsider," every orthodoxy seemed heretical at last. But his perception of the Marxist heresy—that we can somehow "escape our limiting humanity"—was qualified in genial ways by the sight of Jack Wheelwright marching with the workers in a May Day parade, wearing his bowler and a full-length raccoon coat. Wheels couldn't escape his humanity and didn't care to.

Allen Tate told how Wheelwright liked to dramatize himself in the role of the New Englander, "putting me, the Southerner, in my place." As his books appeared, he mailed unsolicited copies to Tate. He included the bills. He could do that, not needing the money. Richard was New England, too, but lived across the tracks. This fostered solemnity, his way of authenticating his bona fides. He learned from Wheelwright that solemnity is the last form of the frivolous. After a Tate reading in Eliot House, Wheelwright got his long body under the rug and wormed his way across the room like the serpent in the Garden. At the Yaddo Colony in Saratoga Springs, he appeared in evening dress to the satisfaction of Miss Ames, the redoubtable director. Then she noticed that he wasn't wearing shoes. He was thrown out of Yaddo, and before that out of Harvard, but no one who knew him mistook him for a frivolous man.

As undergraduates, he and his fellow Esthetes drank punch in the offices of the *Harvard Monthly,* or beakers of gin topped with maraschino cherries. Like Dorian Gray they flirted with Catholicism, and they made a cult of decadence. Some had a crucifix on the bedroom wall. All rejoiced in burlesque and spent Saturdays at the Old Howard. But Wheelwright was a poet before he was an Esthete. He sent his poems to the *Monthly,* and when it ceased publishing during World War I, he helped found the Harvard Poetry Society. This was a hoax with a serious purpose. (Serious didn't mean solemn.) The Signet Club at Harvard had a corner on poetry but took a dim view of "simple amusement." Its secretary gave the minutes of its meetings in rhyme. The aim of these meetings was to polish the membership on its "moral and intellectual" side. The Poetry Society declared for simple amusement. Its monthly meetings were binges, John Marshall remembered. Tessa Horton, as a joke, recited at random a group of simple declarative sentences from the grammar they were conning at school: "The otter is a useful animal," etc. The members of the Society looked thoughtful at this and discussed the proposition at length. For one of the meetings Richard showed up late, but not too late "for some excellent Bacardi." Jest and earnest went together. Out of the Society came the Eight Harvard Poets—Wheelwright, Cowley, Dos Passos, and Cummings among them.

Joining poetry circles or putting them together was Wheelwright's avocation. The New England Poetry Club was one reason for being, and he served it from the age of eighteen. (Wearing another hat, he served the Cambridge Poetry Forum in the thirties, and the reading group he called the Bards.) He wrote a history of the club and got his friends to participate. Robert Hillyer was a member, and Foster Damon and Grant Code. They were all friends of Richard's, but Richard stood apart. Twice he declined an invitation to join. Perhaps he was affronted by Wheelwright's endless activity—the dinner-meetings at the Copley-Plaza, the crowded lectures at the Boston Public Library. In 1923, five hundred people were turned away at the door. The subject was Carl Sandburg, a popular poet. This was show business, not poetry as Richard conceived it. The dedicated poet was the undeflected man, and kept free from dust and soil. Or was this the poet manqué?

Wheelwright called Richard down from the tower. That was the role Sherry Mangan might have played. Richard hearkened to Wheelwright. To Sherry he turned a deaf ear. But the likeness between the friends was only superficial, a matter of political persuasion. Sherry was all circumference and summoned to anarchy. Wheelwright, secure in his fixed point, ignored it. He showed how order needed anarchy. The Old Adam in his makeup— not the dram of evil but the necessary leaven of boyishness and wildness —didn't stultify but saved. It guaranteed the order.

In September 1940, while crossing Commonwealth Avenue, Wheelwright was run down by a drunken driver and killed. Richard was grief-stricken, knowing how this poet had spent his short lifetime taking out of the poetry all that was dead, and seeking to immortalize all he left in. "I know; I saw. I mourn his death more than a friend's death; he had so much left to take out, which he knew, and so much more, which he was beginning to know, to put in." After Wheelwright's death, Richard carried his torch. He prepared a selection of the poems for Jay Laughlin and New Directions, and he insisted to his editor at Harcourt that "a good sized book of excellent poetry" lay buried in the unpublished work. Foster Damon had the keeping of most of this work—he was Jack Wheelwright's brother-in-law—and Richard proposed to Malcolm Cowley that they winnow the manuscripts with a view to publication. "It may be," he said to Robert Penn Warren, "that I am hipped on the subject of Wheelwright." He called the poetry defective, but he knew it for extraordinary. It lived "around the corner that most people simply do not turn but ought, sometime, to turn." Around this corner was a perilous freedom. Richard shied from it violently, while supposing that sometime he might turn the corner.

In the late twenties and thirties, he and Wheelwright made a pair, or they made a single self in which Richard's partial self was challenged and completed. The completing didn't mean assimilation. Scrutinizing Richard's first book of poems "syllable by syllable," Wheelwright said how the expense of form was often petrifaction. This was the ancient error on which D. H. Lawrence & Co. had foundered. Bad poetry, Richard thought, was like life itself. The confusion of form dictated "the obfuscation of purpose." But Wheelwright, speaking for the loose and baggy monsters—himself being one of them—tested and purified Richard's allegiance. The change this testing wrought was not the slackening of form but the liberating of content. "The harder the form, the freer the content." That was where Richard came out.

You can say of his early poems what he said of Richard Eberhart—that "he has never so felt a theme as to require his consistent utmost in craft." When he lapsed in gross imitation, that was not for want of craft, or not primarily, but for want of courage. If, however, you let yourself go within the limits of a manageable form, there emerged "the dark accidents of the mind's sufficient grace." This was Richard on Delmore Schwartz, whose first book, *In Dreams Begin Responsibilities*, had appeared like a nova in 1939.

Richard's poems of the thirties were better for Wheelwright's scrutiny, but not as he put off the protective armor of form, rather as he learned how to fill it. His poetry works when the ebullition of felt ex-

perience breaks the surface, and the surface is just sufficiently composed
to show it off.

> O let my heart
> that spurns satieties
> be living hooked from the fresh flood
> but let my soul rehearse
> without benefit or curse
> of a saviour's blood
> its difficult and dangerous art.

He said in 1939 that unity of tone is the best assurance of the affect of
composition. This sounds like a retort on his friendly antagonist. Then he
said—and what follows represents a quantum leap: "Only within an order
can you give disorder room." In his poetry he practiced accommodation,
giving disorder room. He knew or came to know two associated truths,
"that order is imposed on chaos, and that chaos is the substance of order."
The order was real and the chaos was actual; each required the other. He
made the poetry his means to knowledge of the complementary relation
between them.

Richard's major work in poetry during these years was the long poem,
"From Jordan's Delight." His first book of poetry, published by Florence
Codman and Arrow Editions in 1937, takes its title from this poem. The
general scheme of the book "is the endeavor of the self to maintain its
intactness against the weathering by experience." The self is the island.
"The sea represents all the agencies which seek to change and corrode" it.
Philip Blair Rice, reviewing Richard's book soon after its publication, saw
how the corrosive agencies included marriage, importunate friends, the
lure of action, especially political action, "above all death." Rice called
his review "Death on an Island."

Richard lived with death on intimate terms, but the burden of his first
book is survival. The rock that stands above the water presents "the
vestige brought out of turbulence." Or it presents the order that we
achieve—here the metaphor shifts—"only by digesting disorder: the
gravel in each mouthful that we eat." In 1936 Richard wrote to Robert
Penn Warren: "The stable or uttermost place of imagination is the place
where . . . disorder is given room." His tragicomic protagonist in "From
Jordan's Delight," setting out his lobster pots along a breaking ledge
where the undertow or backwash protects them, "finds by the very peril of
his deed the piety of the stable place." Chaos lives at the heart of stability,
and you can put it the other way round. The "fundamental disorder"

declares its connection with "the eddying of order." The poet perceives this connection and makes ecstatic verses. Here is a verse, the last of Richard's "Scarabs for the Living":

> Quiet the self, and silence brims like spring:
> the soaking in of light, the gathering
> of shadow up, after each passing cloud,
> the green life eating into death aloud,
> the hum of seasons; all on beating wing.

Most poets, except the very greatest, when they try the affirmative voice only persuade you of their hardness of heart. Grow old along with me, the best is yet to be, etc. Richard's characteristic voice is not affirmative but acceptive. He knows all things are wholesome until you stiffen to meet them. So he keeps himself quick in the valley of the shadow. "Pone Metum," he begins:

> Be not afraid, if in the great fright,
> for all the ravage and the sack
> and the black frost,
> you find on a moonless night
> yourself intact.

He doesn't blink what he sees and doesn't venture to explain it. He bears witness. "See all we see." His phrase for his poetry is "the witnessing art." It brings him often on misery. The poems themselves, the ones you remember, are equable, though. The violence is in gear, so the whine of protest is absent.

"The quiet in his voice was drenched in strength." This line describes the man, not only the poet. For the poet, the stable place is midlight. Living in this place precludes the chance for certitude. Most truth-resembling poetry is located there, and is remote from the consolations of philosophy. Richard has this figure, in his poem "The Spear": "Salvation is a salmon speared . . . safe from the great safety of the sea." He doesn't want salvation. He is an unbeliever, but "the seriousness of his unbelief rests on a desperate hope" (quoting from his essay on Joyce's *Ulysses*). This hope is "to make an epiphany of the darkness shining in brightness." In one of the sonnets from the sequence called "Judas Priest," he addresses the Communists. He calls them "comrades of a simpler faith." He is more complex as he insists for himself, in his role of poet, on the distinction between action and observation. Shakespeare was "the great exemplar of the piety of persons . . . and shows us especially the desperation both of the quotidian and of the great in human acts merely

by looking at them." As the poet is content to look, he is the Judas who
betrays action, in the sense of remaining aloof.

Like Judas in his poem, Richard made a mirror of his deliberate purpose "where both the horror and the hope stood still." This is the source
of his epiphanies:

> He whom this stillness breeds
> rejoices with a roving eye
> on thistles blown to seed,
> on hills against the sky,
> until in the sun's late haze
> the wild, neap-tidal air goes cold:
> hill and thistle equally old.

In this last of the "Songs at Equinox," slack water meets the wild air. The
order the conjunction makes is eddying or wayward. That is not what
Richard wanted on his legislating side, but it is what he achieved.

A haunting line of his reads: "we walk the earth ahead of all we know."
Richard glosses this line unconsciously in his *Essays in the European
Novel.* He has been discussing in Flaubert the process of the objective
imagination which "comes into existence and drags being after it." The
process is involuntary, it is even subversive of the author's intention, and
suggests why we are satisfied by the great makers of nineteenth-century
fiction. "Each fell on his own reality." Richard in the poetry wants to
dominate disorder but falls on his own reality. What happens in the life is
another and graver story. It isn't domination for which you remember
him, but accommodation.

Richard in his poetry is a desperate man, and it should be evident why
this is so. His poems make an equivalence of exile and home. The dark
and soul's ease are the same. Salt is for wine and the wind is in his
marrow. He thinks hope is fusty; the final excellence is despair. He can't
look on his flesh without loathing. His great sin isn't pride but "the bitter-
sweet sin of gross humility." As a poet he is winter-stoked, and winter
words are his medium. In the first poem from his first volume, he wrote:

> See there upon full sea the still
> Blossoming of Jordan's heath,
> And on the change, all living ill:
> O eddying, bodiless faith.

Many years later, in his last published poem, "Threnos," he used these
lines again for his conclusion: "And on the change, all living ill." Randall
Jarrell saw Richard "sitting in the midst of his own entrails, knitting them

all night into the tapestry which he unknits all day." Sometimes his art "is pure pain, not art at all." When he reins in his desperation, he writes "Phasellus Ille," following Catullus, or he writes "Ithyphallics" on the model, as he imagined it, of a Bacchic hymn. When he throws the reins on the horse's neck, the desperation comes home as merely puerile. His early stuff clamors for an attitude or mask, but to write it off as early is to miss the uneasy shuttling—more hectic, not less, in late Blackmur—between candor and reticence, or between spontaneous truth-telling (which isn't courage but hecticity) and control.

When Richard was twenty-five he wrote to Richard Johns: "I don't see quite why the artist when he is investigating a neurosis should duplicate the form of that neurosis, substituting for the form proper to art what must remain merely a vagary." Any serious writer made the effort to transcend experience "and therefore" to grasp its reality. This is sound doctrine, but so far Richard had it only in his head. The problem of form continued to distract him. It was the angel with which he wrestled—in his criticism, too—and his success in this struggle was only intermittent. He wrestled with the angel because his great temptation was to tear open his shirt front. Underneath, violence was moving.

At sixteen he was filling a notebook with his own poems, interspersed with gnomic sayings from Pater and Petronius, and written out in a more copious hand than he cultivated later on. He has sex on the brain in these poems, he wants to drown deep in a sea of six women:

> Her flesh is fluid cream from hell. . . .
> She calls me to her purple palace;
> I totter, fall and find her solace.

He didn't find solace. His longing, evidently unappeased, is all through his published work. He can't evoke "the final spasm of surrender"; perhaps he didn't often achieve it. He comes across as a passionate man but evasive, always sliding away. For the purposes of poetry the untranslated passion is enervating or nasty, the animal in the thighs provoking "lubricious slime." E. A. Robinson, then a resident at the MacDowell Colony in Peterborough, New Hampshire, was reading this poetry when Richard was twenty-one. (Two years earlier, Richard had got himself to Peterborough for a week's stay.) "Put the soft pedal on the 'guts' stuff," said Robinson. The "'red blood' quality" Richard was pushing at him didn't equate to strength but anxiety.

To manage this anxiety, art's length is required. When Richard fails in his poetry, he doesn't have it. When he succeeds, he thinks a form upon the world and the thought becomes a gesture and a man. Sometimes you feel that he, who didn't feel the lightning strike, is exaggerating the thunderclap. But the lightning is real enough and the poems in which it flickers falsely are "nakedly of and about the human spirit"—a foolish phrase from Oscar Williams, who means to praise Richard for this. The Cavalier poet Lovelace in his best poem craves a nakedness "with her clothes on."

Nakedness is a principal theme in Richard's poetry, also a problem. In a powerful poem from "Sea Island Miscellany," he is afraid that the woman to whom he is clinging will be made "as bare as I am." That is why he holds her closely, so he can't see. He doesn't want "the self coming fully upon itself." He craves company—this was true of the man —but not for its own sake. He used it to persuade himself that he was really there. "Speak now," he says, in the poem called "River-Walk"—

> or we shall hear the bottom of our silence
> echoing.

The clue to take hold of, if you are coming to terms with Richard's achievement, is his search for habiliments to cover his shame, or a still fictive point to contend against the vertigo with which he was tormented. In his successes, he "made of vertigo a music." He disputed his tormented self. The issue of the disputing is an objective art, entailing the sacrifice of self-expression.

In the twenties George Anthony saluted Richard the nonconformist for refusing to murder his most casual ghost. "It is precisely to this characteristic, that should you turn out grand poet I would attribute your arrival." On the contrary, Richard arrived partly as he conformed. Reviewing Foster Damon's poems in *larus*, he wrote that the poet "finds, curiously, that the more he uses the old forms and symbols, while preserving the new context, the more successful he will be." The poems of *From Jordan's Delight* deploy the old forms to assert the new context. The tidal waters and islands of the Maine coast meant for Richard what Aran meant for John Synge. In his love affair with Maine, he shed himself and discovered an identity. This doesn't mean he was untrammeled. He rebelled against himself in a created self. The impinging of felt experience on the verse is obvious and vivid—

> this island has a loom
> Never to be forgotten from the west—

but the experience is most vivid when Richard apprehends it at a remove.

"Jordan's Delight is an island," he wrote to Zabel, "off the mouths of Narraguagus and Pigeon Hill Bays, eastern Maine." This literal place the "poem describes, populates, and identifies," but the identification is only partly verisimilar. There is the real island rock, populated by a simple, bearded fisherman, full of "small-boat intimate pieties." Right up against it is Baudelaire's *Cythère*. The fisherman, rehearsing his piety, speaks or sings rather in Richard's voice. But he employs the refrain of an old ballad as the seed of Richard's refrain. What you see as you approach the island are the flowers and colors of Jordan's Delight—

> Such is the red stonecrop
> The purpling pink sea-pea
> The blue legume with bluest bell
> And blue harebell—

but filtered through the eye of Saint Francis in his *Canticle of the Sun,* and through the ear of Milton in *Lycidas.* In section x, "All Siren's Seine," you meet Richard proclaiming his eddying faith that is part "inevitable denial and earned despair," but "always, I hope, in sensual terms of the sea."

The real sea and "its recurrent overwhelming encroachment" establish, and so let Richard negotiate, what would otherwise be the mere purlieus of thought: "that fundamental disorder and disequilibrium for which any profound conception of order must first of all make room." How shall we know, he inquired later, "what, and in what measure, to accept as living poetry and what to dismiss as merely occasional, or personal, or vain before the possibility?" He answered: look for "the conceiving imagination and for the twist and shape of idiom." Richard's poetry gains assent as it reaches the condition of idiom. He loses himself to find himself, but what he finds is persuasive only as his words verge on flesh.

Toward the end of his life, Richard got a letter from two college students who wanted to know about the genesis of his poem, "Mirage." He said: "You all have your own rights to give my mirage any meaning that suits you." He went on to repudiate the high priori road: "It was not for me an ideal or a way of life or much of anything except a mirage." Many readers of the poem seemed to have thought differently. In fact, "my mirage was an actual mirage on a very hot, quiet day on an island in the Gulf of Maine." No doubt "you might say we felt within a rather dangerous land of the lotus-eaters." But on the whole, the real mirage "made its own meaning." Richard concluded, inconsequently and rightly, "I hope you both can try sailing enough to find out for yourselves."

CHAPTER FIVE

A Failure Worth Making—
The Life of Henry Adams

I N 1929, when Richard was still editor of the *Hound & Horn*, he began "in scattered notes" to write a book on Henry Adams. Half a century passed before this book was published; by then, Richard had been dead fifteen years. The manuscript he left runs to more than six hundred pages, and though it isn't finished it coheres. Richard, if given his say, would likely have disputed publication. The Adams was his own "Greater Torment"—the title of his second novel, also unfinished. Toward the end, he lived with this torment more or less equably. The conviction of failure engenders equability, or at least acceptance, and Sisyphus grows familiar with his stone. Richard said himself: "There is no freedom from a burden so great as thinking it inexorable." He didn't manage to shift the burden, and this brought him on failure. But the failure, though profound, is just short of perfection.

It isn't hard to say why he failed. He was lazy or deficient in character or he lacked the gift for architecture in writing. But the reasons keep multiplying, and the temptation grows to list them at random and let it go at that. Richard's own efforts to explain away his failure are credible only if taken one by one. Taken together, they verge on nonsense—in his phrase, "a little of *hoc est corpus* turned hocus pocus." There is about him a whiff of the early Fathers of the Christian Church (one of his Princeton students saw him as Saint John Chrysostom), imposing on the text which is the life a crazy palimpsest of commentary, and so annulling the chance for clarification. Or perhaps the clarified thing exists on many levels, like the *multiplex intelligentia* of the medieval exegete.

One reason he failed is because his material proved too painful to digest. In the book as written, omissions are conspicuous. When the intractable stuff gets in, it remains undigested—a lump in the stomach. This lump is the warrant of what he made, however. To alter the metaphor, it is the grain that made the pearl. He would not have written at all without feeling the itch to accommodate disorder, not least his own.

The life of Henry Adams was "an incubus not a book." Richard was forty-four when he said this to Allen Tate, and already he had struggled with the incubus for more than half his life. In his twenties he envisaged, as his major activity, "a study of Henry Adams' mind and character." But the struggle with Adams began in boyhood. At seventeen he was reading Henry and his brother Brooks. This was the wretched time when he moved irresolutely between two worlds—a rebellious son to his father, a failure at school with no better career in prospect—and he makes you think of young Adams sitting out the Civil War in London and filling his letters home with precocious ennui. A little later he worked his way through Adams's nine-volume history of the United States during the presidencies of Jefferson and Madison. This was history as art—ironic drama whose flavor was "subrisive" on every page. Adams, he said, was Flaubert before Flaubert. "You may know whom he hates but you cannot tell whom he admires."

Adams, like Flaubert, hid himself from view. Richard resembles him in this. He lived two separate lives:

> one in the world
> Which we must ever seem to treat as real;
> The other in ourselves, behind a veil
> Not to be raised without disturbing both.

The quotation is from Adams, who never raised the veil, Richard said. You could say the same thing of his biographer except that, in writing biography, he came on himself and presented himself. Like Adams, "he had to read his need in another language to understand it as his own."

Richard ended his letter: "I could write a volume on this." He said, however: "I prefer to talk." Despite the lure of talk, omnipresent for him, he set to in earnest, beginning—on his own word—in 1935. Other projects took a back seat to "the enormous amount of work I must do to . . . finish my critical biography." The biography, he wrote to Tate, was "a labour which will consume the next 18 to 20 months." This seems absurd only in retrospect. Though he called himself with reason "the slowest writer in the eastern United States," he was out of the gate and running: in the late thirties and early forties he completed upwards of nine hundred pages. But the labor on which he had embarked was "positively mountainous," both in range of fact and in scope of intention, and no sooner had he started than each began to expand "at a rate that . . . seemed likely to become omnivorous." It wasn't long before he realized that to finish by the

spring of 1938, "as I so blithely hoped," was out of the question. He wasn't
stuck in the least bit, he saw his way through "all well enough." Only there
was more meat in the nut, and some of it harder to get at, than he had
dreamed.

Then he himself began to change and grow. "I almost believe," he said
in 1942, "that my mind is a shade or two larger now than it was"—too
bad, for the time was less suitable for growth than plain harvest. "New
angles and aspects" kept turning up. The book had its own life and
wanted to be "about a thousand pages long." He knew that would never
do, but he kept writing anyway and hoped for the best "in the way of
cuts." The alternative was to break off arbitrarily, he told the poet Jean
Garrigue, "to be aftermath, or . . . corpse growth, or fruitless, seedless
blades." This he wouldn't countenance. So the "Critical Portrait" he intended, as he saw more and thought more, began to threaten its frame.
What he was making was a "personal textbook on domestic politics and
foreign affairs." Personal is the word for what he was doing. He made
passionate sermons on conviction and on the elasticity of institutions, as if
he were writing his own life. In the second summer after coming to Princeton, he finished "a cool hundred new pages on the 1868–76 period plus
the biographies and some aspects of the History," and he worried that
Harcourt would think this elongation "either a trespass or dull." It wasn't
dull—Richard's felt sermons make the best of the book—but by 1943 his
editor smelled a rat or he sensed the dismal future, a litter of broken
promises. So he called for a fresh statement of intention. Richard complied in detail. He said what he had done was to offer "a cross between a
biography and a critical essay," seeking everywhere "an imaginative penetration" of Adams the man—who did not, however, exist in isolation and
whose life was not merely a clangor in a vault. The life of Adams was
exemplary, also replete with meaning. The intent was "to unite him with
the history, political, social, and intellectual, of which he made himself a
mirror." To realize "the man in his habit as he lived" was much—the
sense of imaginative penetration; to come on the times through the man
was even more. Macaulay could do this. He saw life clearly, without
supposing that what he saw—Dr. Johnson, for instance, and the Age of
Johnson—lived only in the eye of the beholder.

What happened next is obscure. Richard's momentum slowed, then
vanished altogether as he confronted intractable problems. Twelve years
went by and he looked once more at his torso of a book and the work he
still projected. He was by then twenty-five years or so into the writing, and
evidently—though he doesn't acknowledge this—he had written all he
could. After the review of 1955, conducted at the instance of still another

Harcourt editor, he put the book away—not exactly a torso, but finished to the degree he thought possible. Why he could do no more makes an essay in psychology—in part distressing, even lurid, in its major thrust heroic.

The trouble that overtook him surprised no one more than Richard himself. In the spring of 1937, he counted his blessings. He had been awarded a Guggenheim Fellowship and two thousand dollars "for a critical interpretation of the life and works of Henry Adams," and he confessed himself "delighted, and freed, by the award." It seemed unlikely that he would get it: five years before, the Foundation had turned him down, and he supposed this second try promised little "except waste time." The time was worth venturing, though. For almost eight years, since losing his editor's job at the *Hound & Horn*, he had bumped from rock to rock, engaged—if you believe him—in "largely disagreeable and entirely useless work." So he hoped and prayed his luck would change, and he trotted out his most persuasive supporters: Lincoln Kirstein; Allen Tate; John Marshall, already a rising power at the Rockefeller Foundation; Cowley at the *New Republic*; Morton Zabel at *Poetry*; Joseph Wood Krutch at the *Nation*. Now that his prayers were answered he could engage, he said to Tate, in work "both reasonably honest and at the proper stretching point of my limitations."

The elation was real, but not the terms in which he couched it. By 1932 he had written more than seventy essays and reviews. Some were distinguished, none of them useless. Much of this was piecework, not a bad thing for an uninventive writer. All of it was managed without recourse to foundations. In these occasional papers, the point of departure was assigned; Richard picked up from there. He was supremely the writer as opportunist, pulling out two rags and sewing them together. That was how he did his best writing. "Our vices father our heroisms," he said, talking of Adams, our "defects predicate scope." The constraints at which he kicked were disagreeable, no question, but had their fruitful side. This was Adams's case. His limitations "produced as well as bounded" his mind and art. Sometimes one's limitations—for Richard the torpor, whipped by the poverty—"do a large part of the work ordinarily attributed to discipline."

In 1932 Richard had sought a fellowship to write critical essays on Emily Dickinson, Yeats, D. H. Lawrence, and Hopkins. He didn't get the fellowship and he wrote the essays. Outlining his "Plans for Study," he said he wanted most of all to feel that he knew how to read and write poetry. To secure that feeling, "no amount of labor" was too much. In the twenties and thirties he labored mightily. Then came official sanction and it obviated labor. This remained notoriously true. Personal obligations enlisted his sense of honor, and he was scrupulous in discharging them. Debts in the abstract were another story, like cheating the telephone company. When he signed a contract, he tended to lose it. In the years at Princeton, work submitted for his judgment found its way to the attic or the bottom drawer of his desk, and was still there when he died. Or he put it before him in so conspicuous a place that, like Poe and his purloined letter, he "the more conspicuously forgot it." Blandly he told how, in mid-December, a ten-thousand-word essay due "at the fifth of January latest" had suddenly come to his attention. He said, "I have not begun it: I had thought of it for spring." Deadlines built up "to the condition of nightmares—both succubus and incubus," and mostly he let them pass. His growing eminence eroded his powers of concentration. As early as the forties, a friend who stayed with him in Maine doubted if he accomplished an hour's work a day. By then, most of the Adams book that he could bring himself to write had been written. So the book, on this reading, was a casualty not of failure but of success.

When he was poor, Richard's staple excuse for not writing was poverty. His work on Adams was going terribly, he wrote in 1939 to Henry Allen Moe at the Guggenheim Foundation, "not on its own account but because I am compelled to do so much outside just to live." In the summer of 1940 he has had to "take on a few more critical jobs" simply to get along. "The result is that the book has again been slowed down." On the one hand, the book suffered as his poverty compelled him "to look for some sort of work." On the other hand, "it is only because I have so far found none that I am able to work steadily on Adams." He didn't spot the inconsequence, but each remark was true. The greater truth will focus on his "natural talent for putting things off when left free to do so."

Money was freedom. The worst thing you could do, if you meant him to deliver, was to offer him money before the work got done. Delmore Schwartz, a friend in power at the *Partisan Review*, understood this. "Finish the book about Adams," Delmore said, "then we will talk turkey. . . . However, as your admirer and disciple since the dead year 1929, I know you too well to give you a lead dime before you write anything." His former student Frederick Morgan, the editor of the *Hudson Review*, didn't know him that well. Morgan found—"unfortunately, I might even say shockingly"—that dealing with Richard was an unrewarding experience. "In money matters he was difficult, unreliable and shifty to a point which might even be termed dishonest." He seemed to feel justified, Morgan complained, "in asking for special treatment not accorded to other writers (such as payment in advance, or . . . payment at a specially high rate)." For a while Morgan "went along with this" out of regard for Richard's work, but "eventually was forced to the conclusion that I wished no further dealings with him."

It wasn't, Richard said, that his only interest was money, but he did "feel that interest like a permanent undercurrent." When it was satisfied he lapsed in torpor, pleading "my usual mixture of guilt and sloth." He had a new title, he wrote to a friend: "The Great Sloth in the Psyche"— but this was his generic title. It filled him with "shame and horror," he said to Philip Rahv. As he got older, he lived more easily with his shame. Perhaps he had no option. His failure to complete the life of Adams derives, on another reading, from a failure of character.

There is plenty of evidence to validate this reading, some of it scandalous. In 1936, on a trip to New York to visit John Berryman, he brought an outline of the Adams book to Harcourt Brace. This got him a contract and a modest advance. He undertook within a year to produce four hundred pages. In the years that followed he changed editors many times, and all of them asked him when the Adams would be done. Fifteen years after the original agreement, Robert Giroux recorded another; it proved a dead letter, like the first. The coming to birth of the Eliot essay he had pledged to Perry Miller's anthology of *Major American Writers* (1962) makes an exercise (he might have said) in salutary maieutics. "Duty bids me remind you that the deadline" has passed: so his editor wrote more than once, being reduced to "the niggling level of the common scold." Apologies were offered and finally the essay emerged. It might as easily have gone the way of the promised book on Henry James, for which cash was also paid in advance.

The story of this book supports the character Richard assigned to himself. He was Felix Krull, he said, and in Mann's equivocal hero, the confidence man, he saw "a marvellous and heightened version" of his own autobiography. The idea for the book was his. He had no business proposing it—his first and pressing obligation was to Harcourt Brace—but two birds in the bush were always better than one in hand. Against the early poverty, he never left off building his defenses. Even in the famous years when nobody would have challenged his credit, he carried a bankroll fat enough to choke a horse. He didn't need it and he knew this. Only it made him feel better, he said. When he traveled abroad it had to be first-class and weighted down with steamer trunks, like a relict of the Gilded Age. He didn't need all that panoply either, except as it constituted the visible sign of grace. His deepest commitment was to writing, but not to one book at a time. Books were like trading ships, at sea and at hazard. So this provident writer hedged his investment, unwilling to risk what he had in one bottom. In the fifties, when his Harcourt editor asked wearily about the Adams, he countered with the offer of another unwritten book—his *Primer of Ignorance*, which he didn't finish either but from which he hoped to wring an advance.

He drew a blank on that one. With Henry James he was luckier, and in 1940 he signed a contract with New Directions. A month after signing, he said he needed more money for personal expenses. This need was both real and obsessive. He got the money and his interest waned. Final copy, however, was due "by the first of October at the very last." Richard wrote to Jay Laughlin: "I have every firm hope of getting the script to you on that date." The date went by unnoticed and the correspondence turned bitter. Laughlin wanted his money back. Richard, agreeing that the fault was mostly his, thought it too bad that "the situation between us should have led to letters and postcards of the character yours have taken on." He regretted that the postcards were open to any casual reader. Also he regretted that he couldn't return the money.

Eight years later, when Laughlin wondered if he might make "my annual request for information about the James' book," Richard answered insouciantly: "Be of good cheer, as Cato might have said to those trying to get into Purgatory; you have only another lifetime to wait." For Laughlin the James volume was always "on my mind, though with no violent notions of immediacy." Richard said it was on his own mind "only now and then." Twenty years after the book was first mooted, he worked his publisher for another advance. Maybe Laughlin admired Richard's sleight of hand. As late as 1964, he was still professing himself "ever eager." Richard's death a month later brought the long charade to a close.

To point the moral is mostly odious and almost always insufficient. Richard wrote, however, in the life of Adams: "The development of new ability to react seems to depend often on an increase in hardship." When the screws were tightened, "the accident of insight" followed. This lucky accident showed you how to discern and seize the challenge of survival. The award of a Guggenheim for 1937 put an end to the years of hardship and so took the pressure off the screws. In 1938–39 the award was renewed, and Richard exulted. "A second straight year should see the book done." The following year he began his long residence at Princeton. He was home free, and the Adams went unfinished.

From the beginning, his book-in-progress took the eye of a larger public than he generally attracted. Lincoln Kirstein in the thirties put the word around that Richard was at work on the Definitive Biography, and editors wrote to ask for serial chapters. Bernard Berenson at I Tatti was delighted with the news; he volunteered his correspondence. Friends were encouraging and none had an inkling of what lay ahead. "How goes Henry Adams?" Florence Codman, Richard's publisher at Arrow Editions, inquired in 1936. Morton Zabel, a year later, raised the same question, and Allen Tate the year after that. There were dozens of such letters and Richard kept them all. Perhaps he had a taste for self-mortification. The most painful of these inquiries came in a letter from Helen, his wife. She was staying on in Maine, he was teaching in Princeton. Their marriage was a ruin and the two of them were wise to keep apart as they could. Together or apart, they bedeviled each other. Toward Richard's work Helen affected indifference. He was the intellectual, a word meant in reproof, and indifference was the other face of her disdain. Sometimes the black bile in her spilled over, though. He cared most for his poetry, so she took to declaiming it. A friend remembered how her voice dripped with malice and contempt as she spat out the line: "Wind was not . . . flat was!" The Adams was another chance for getting at him and she took it. She knew that the writing was giving him fits, and she wrote to ask if the publishers had "set any more dates" for completing the book, "or have they decided that date setting is a waste of time?"

Time wasted and Richard began to make promises. His first deadline was the fall of 1936. This he shifted to "early next winter." But the winter came round and then another winter and he said: "More time is needed." In 1939 he was sure to finish by fall, which he amended subsequently to spring. The deadline kept receding—to 1940, then 1941, "or at least by Christmas." In 1942 he said that "the book should be finished by summer." When it wasn't, he wrote to Harcourt: "I do not possibly see how I could not have it done by the first of the year."

To one promissory note he added a contingent phrase: "unless Princeton University swallows me up entirely." Invoking Princeton became a standard resort. Even before he got there, Richard predicted that the university was going to "impede" his progress—a self-fulfilling prophecy. His "new kind of life in a strange place" wasn't easy. His teaching job consumed him, even on a half-time schedule. Still he said that Harcourt might "count on me" by spring. A month later, however, the English Department was "so packing . . . him with work" that he couldn't feel sure any longer.

Princeton learned what Harcourt knew, that the Adams was always doing, never done. Year-end reports from the Chairman to the Dean, recommending Richard for a raise in salary, invariably present the book as "awaiting its turn." But the stars or whatever were inauspicious. First poverty hobbled him, "the absolute necessity of making bread and butter." When he stopped being poor his health, always precarious, made for rough going. In 1938 the "whole winter was torn up by an emergency case of appendicitis." Since the mid-thirties he had suffered from sinus trouble, and with loving detail he wrote how his skull was full of "rotten tissue and bone." Back he went to the hospital. "They tell me," said Christine Weston, his novelist friend, "that your nose has suffered an operation usually associated . . . with the noses of unfaithful wives in the East." He wasn't amused and it wasn't a laughing matter. "I've been punk," he wrote to Rob Darrell at the end of the thirties, but this was his normal condition. It wasn't wholly uncongenial. An ulcerated tooth "left enough pus to furnish the beginnings of an infection in my face and jaw." The tooth came out but his tonsils flared up. After that it was psoriasis, a nervous disorder brought on by the sinus operations, then arsenic poisoning brought on by the treatment for psoriasis. His eyes had always given trouble (one reason he alleged for not going to Harvard), and this trouble recurred. So he excused himself by pleading bad eyesight, or later a bad heart or bad liver. To these problems he assimilated the outbreak of war, a personal affront. "If the Germans will not kindly collapse," Richard wrote, "there'll be another long interruption, I suppose, and with justification." The military were sure to get him, and even if they didn't he supposed that his book would not be published in wartime. That was why he had gone to Princeton in the first place. "You can see that all this made a difference to my plans; for I had counted at least a little on the proceeds of the book; so when a job was suddenly offered me . . . I felt I had to take it." His measured semicolons suggest that rhetoric was filling in for the truth. And yet all he said was true.

On and on he went, making plausible excuses but looking to the brighter side, too. Though he wrote in the forties that the book "pokes along," he reported enthusiastically that it would "really be finished this spring," or maybe—this to John Berryman—by late fall or early winter. "Seriously! Omega!" His editor Lambert Davis, growing "a bit frantic," allowed himself a sly remark. Time seemed to be playing "some Adams tricks," he said. "What about it?" Richard answered promptly: "I can ABSOLUTELY have the finished script in to you by"—but the date doesn't matter. Princeton, as often, kept him too busy; four months later he wrote: "My sense of humiliation has touched near bottom."

For the first time, his assurance was beginning to falter. "It may be by nip and tuck I shall finish after all"—increasingly, this was the tone he adopted. But he continued to submit new material, and by 1946 what he had written added up to "about 900 pages typed." He knew he would have to whittle it down, but rejoiced that the end was "actually in sight." Six years after this, he was still having "last minute difficulties." To his new editor Robert Giroux, who hadn't heard it all before, he said that the Adams was "nearing birth." He said the same thing to the ever-patient Mrs. Thoron, the niece of Henry Adams. The help she gave him was indispensable, beginning in 1935, but he complained that she was always looking over his shoulder. That "reticent and unwilling race, the surviving relatives and friends of Henry Adams," supplied another reason for not getting forward. In the summer of 1955 he had a burst of fresh energy, and was "now resolved," he told John Crowe Ransom, to finish up. But though he worked like an anchorite—that is what he said—the result was not all he had hoped for. So the great work became "my poor Adams book," always on the verge but "never nearer than the verge."

Richard had—or thought he had—one more chance to shift the burden. For 1961–62 his friend David Daiches arranged his appointment as Pitt Professor at Cambridge University. Historians had held this appointment before him, but never a literary person. So Richard became, as Cambridge honored its forms, Professor of American History and Institutions. The title defined him in his last years; a fish out of water, not a scrupulous critic but a seer. His lectures at Cambridge, Daiches supposed, should "look at America through its literature rather than through its law or political history." He had other ideas, however, and he told C. P. Snow how he intended to deal "with the nature of the New Empire in politics, and . . . in morals." He was "deeply involved," Daiches said, "in his own particular research into and reflections on aspects of modern literature and history." This involvement did him no good with the Cambridge students, who stayed away in droves. For the subject of his public lectures, he suggested Henry Adams. Perhaps lecturing on Adams "might furnish the motive for finishing my enormous work on him." He added: "If you want Henry James as well I am sure that also can be arranged. (I have also an unfinished book on Henry James.)"

Did he believe in his heart that he would ever finish either? He said he did in so many words, but the tone in which he said this makes a setoff to the words. "If I wait long enough," he wrote, "I shall find that my friends between them will have done all the preparation for those two long books that I myself began so many years ago." The preparation was like waiting for the Beast in the Jungle. It never came in view, and the hopes he cherished of bringing it to bay were, as he admitted, only "vague hopes" after all. In the spring of 1961 he was "just getting to the verge of returning to my own book on Adams"—with uncustomary candor he confessed that he hadn't touched it "for twelve years or longer"—and thought he would use "the opportunity of lecturing on him at Cambridge University next year as a means of getting ahead" with the book. When he sailed for England on the *Queen Elizabeth* in September—first-class, as always—he had only a hundred pages to go, and his editor at Harcourt, the last of many, cheered "the good news that your year . . . abroad may well produce the final chapter." Before leaving, he had a photostat of the manuscript prepared and he carried it with him, supposing that "I shall at last finish." There was the usual contingency: he said he would finish "if everything goes well."

It didn't go well. "The year at Cambridge was mixed"—his own verdict when it was over. He was already a sick man when he got there—circulatory problems made it hard for him to walk—and his rooms in Christ College were up a flight of stairs and freezing in the English winter. At one point he fled to Athens to get a little sun and a little conversation—even worse than the abominable climate were the clenched faces of his colleagues. Leslie Fiedler had lectured for Richard in Princeton and he was spending the year in Greece. They talked about the Adams book—"he was clearly never going to finish," Leslie said—and about his unpublished novel, the two making a felt association for Richard. In the pleasant afternoons, he went for long walks with the Fiedlers' little girl. She remembered with perplexity the nice man who thought he was climbing a hill when there wasn't any hill. "He really seemed weak and failing and more open than he had ever been before."

When Kate Foster, his old friend from the twenties and thirties, met him for dinner in London, she saw the sickness and the gloom. She thought Richard was feeling the final break with Helen—by then their divorce was ancient history, but Helen just recently had married again—and she said how his reputation didn't travel well. Christ's had elected him a Professorial Fellow and he was tickled to dine beneath the portrait of Milton, the Lady of Christ's, and to break out the port that had been laid down in 1814 to celebrate the defeat of Old Boney. But what he professed came across as mere mystification. "Incomprehensible," said Graham Hough to his students. "You can imitate . . . Mr. Blackmur, simply by refusing to express yourself clearly." That was John Wain's opinion. Richard to his English colleagues was less confused than perverse (they gave him that much), "deliberately *refusing* to reduce his meaning to simple terms." At High Table the dons got on him. "A bit exotic for your taste, I should have thought," said the Master. This was the night they served swan. Richard said, "It tastes rather like peacock." He was always good at gamesmanship, but keeping the side up told on his nerves. At Oxford for a sherry party given in his honor by two former students at Princeton, he consulted his fingernails while Hugo Dyson and C. S. Lewis, acting out their English best or worst, engaged in the usual persiflage between initiates of a club to which, they made it clear, he would never gain admission.

Then his lectures flopped badly, and this confirmed him in the sense of not belonging. He "was always a difficult lecturer, pursuing his own thoughts with great subtlety," Daiches said. Though he "really wanted to lecture on Adams," this provincial writer was "not quite the sort of thing to appeal to Cambridge students." Three public lectures were slated, and Richard let it be known that they would wind up the book. Advance publicity seemed to assure a good crowd. But he gave the first lecture to an empty house. He had to feel, he said (harping on the old string), that the audience at Cambridge had consciously rejected him. On advice, he dropped Adams and switched to Henry James. So the last chance went by "for the completion of his Adams under his hand." Richard's editor said this. His good-natured idea was to palliate failure. The last chance is a fiction, however. It had vanished long before, or perhaps had never offered.

In his achieved poetry and in the criticism of poetry, too, Richard mostly ends with an ellipsis. The manner is putative, an ugly word he liked. This speaks to his honesty or you can say his myopia. He wrote of Adams, incidentally of himself: "He was not only sufficiently liberated, he was deprived. He knew something was missing that had to do with the sense of unity and the sense of purpose." Richard, like Adams, discounted the possibility of knowing; the mind was a watery mirror at best. "When we call man a rational animal," he said, "we mean that reason is his great myth." He deprecated in Conrad the refusal or incapacity to flesh out the truth, but truth was opaque for him—most of all truth in character —"veiled like an Eastern bride." How a poem made its meaning—or a man and a woman: Adams and Marian Adams, at a guess Richard and Helen—was "intractable to any description." Struggling to see Adams plain, he conceded "the essential impenetrability of words, the bottomlessness of knowledge." The concession makes for hard going, if your business is with discursive prose.

An early essay of Richard's, "The Failure of Henry Adams" (1931), suggests "that for a man relentlessly honest, there is no failure like success." Richard in his own work denied himself success, and in the process he made a great book. Paradox is of the essence in telling this story, mystery also, as different conclusions are potential. Adams was for Richard the type of human greatness—that was what he said to the Guggenheim Foundation—and fulfilled the type in his conviction of failure. The failure was, however, not the ruin but the making of the story. Like high tragedy, it communicated a sense of propriety—the end being predicable of the beginning—and so "buttressed the greatness of his work." Adams enacted Yeats's prescription: he chose "for his life's work of all things difficult the most nearly impossible." Then, deliberately, he "pushed his problems to the point where their solution *became* impossible." This was the expense of greatness—meaning, first, the using up of one's talents in the life and art; meaning also the cost in personal failure as the problems one confronted and hoped to resolve drove one on silence at last.

So failure was "the expense of greatness." Richard's second critical book, published by Florence Codman and Arrow Editions in 1940, glosses this phrase in thirteen related essays, the essay on Adams being the centerpiece. Richard quoted T. E. Lawrence, with whom he led off: "There could be no honour in a sure success, but much might be wrested from a sure defeat." The great mind confesses defeat as it is "compelled to measure its knowledge in terms of its ignorance." The circumscribed mind wins a paltry success by not perceiving the littleness of what it knows. Or it indulges in the dereliction of poetic duty, which Richard makes synonymous with "fidelity to the actual." To enjoin this fidelity and to say where and just how it is wanting—for instance, in the poems of Hardy and Dickinson as they ran toward dead convention or the rehearsal of formula—is the major business of the book. Dereliction is when the writer balks at letting things "declare their own significance." The writer whose commitment goes to the unvarnished truth tries insistently to apprehend the whole—though all of us, quoting Richard in his essay on Eliot, "are defeated almost to the degree that we try." The commitment—he calls it "the burden of understanding"—is perilous, however, and matched only by the burden of ignorance. Passing between the two exacts loss of faith, "seen in critical practice as the constantly increasing incredibility of *any* given intellectual bridge-work." For the life of Adams, what this means or portends is failure.

The elliptical thing wrested by the biographer from his sure defeat is diminished necessarily, insofar as it is elliptical. Its peculiar character—the pathos that informs it, the doggedness, the "almost intolerable reticence" (Richard's phrase for Adams)—turns, however, on its incompleteness. For the man and his book, the decorous figure is the broken arc. Saying more meant seeing farther, and Richard saw as far as he could. Ideas of Order were partly notions or guesses or abstractions of hope. He makes the equivalence, reflecting on the poems of Wallace Stevens, and he honors it in the biography. How do you order the facts of a life unless by imposition, threading beads on a string? The greatest writers —you can number them on the fingers of one hand—cope with this question more adroitly. To the writer whose sensibility or intelligence is inferior, the question hardly arises. Samuel Butler, for example—on whom Richard had written in *The Double Agent* and whom he intended as a foil to Adams—"was a Mencken of other days" who, knowing only a little, "never suspected the measure of his ignorance. Adams' sense of his ignorance was the stalwart sill he stood on: it kept him going and brought him a failure worth making." The ignorance which Adams, Richard also, acknowledged was cousin to humility and not negative but positive, "the final form of contradictory knowledge." But all knowledge, the kind that matters, is contradictory. Necessarily, the pursuit of knowledge leaves the great mind at a stand.

This failure is our own in prospect—that is how Richard puts it, but he is adjuring himself. Never nail your meaning down too closely, he used to say, "for in time another is sure to spring the nails." It isn't for nothing that Montaigne was the most congenial of all his masters. In the life of Adams, Richard wrote: "Montaigne is the great master of ironic wisdom, of wisdom which by the poetry of its manners suggests another version of itself in the very act of finishing or polishing off its present expression." The generosity of these manners as he displayed them entails, for Richard, not an easygoing irenicism but something like despair. Maybe that is too lugubrious. In the Eliot essay, agreeing that ultimate truth is inaccessible, he goes on to say that there is still every reason to enjoy ourselves, "with hands thrown up but without alarm." Anyway he understands, after Montaigne, that the skeptical intelligence, if only it is rich enough, works its own bafflement. "In reconciling two points of view into one it manages to imply the possibility of a third and quite unadjusted point of view." If you look long enough, order opens on chaos. Looking long and not blinking— that is the great writer's commitment and the expense of his greatness. "When you look into the abyss the abyss rises within you."

In Adams, "who never liked shutting his eyes or denying an evident fact," Richard presents the model of his own character, also his predicament. He is the man looking into the abyss. "One tends very largely as a critic, I suppose, or at least in one's best work, to paint either one's own portrait or the portrait one would like to fill out." That is Yvor Winters, commenting on the Adams essay of 1936—where, however, "the portrait is still a little in advance of you." What it lacked (as Richard put it years later) was "the smile upon the Sphinx," a visible attesting of "the

anonymity of all the meaning we know and cannot grasp, of all the suffering wonder in us that is never satisfied, and, too, of all the need in us that
ends in peace without emptiness, and, finally, in emptiness without terror." The failure of the hero who discovers this final emptiness is "the
result of the most arduous labour of which the whole imagination is
capable." It is not an incidental failure but integral to all aspiring worth
the name. The hero investigates all the varieties of knowledge to the point
where they add to ignorance. Then he has no more to say. So perhaps
Richard himself.

Here the paradox consists in the duplicity of language. "Thought asks
too much and words tell too much; because to ask anything is to ask
everything"—the great perception of Scholastic philosophy—"and to say
anything is to ask more." The rationalizing temper doesn't see the problem or thinks that to raise it is merely perverse. It believes in the chance of
nailing down the truth, so constituting the city of God on earth. Yeats,
another failed hero who exemplifies the expense of greatness, was partly
disabled by finding himself in a rationalistic society. This society was
"deliberately incomplete, because progressive," but supposed that completeness—the plenary view—lay just around the corner. Against it Richard, following Adams in *Mont-Saint-Michel and Chartres*, appealed to the
psychology of the Christian Middle Ages. The older psychology—not
dour but only skeptical, insisting on our incorrigible ignorance—was led
"to the notion, the very presiding, all-swallowing notion of Failure." But
the failure is triumph as, in the process of declaring itself, "it snares all
that can be snared of what we know." The ignorance of the hero is
scarcely deprivation, except in last things. It is "the final name we give to
our plunder from experience at that raised level where it is again its own
meaning."

The partial accumulating of fact and its penumbra ("our plunder from
experience") could have, as it was partial, no formal end in view—no
bound of the waste, no city of God. This precluded the writing of conventional biography. Richard saw the difficulty very early, though not its
dimensions, and his first précis of 1936 rejects the writing of what he
called straight biography in favor of "an essay in rational imagination."
The great and predominant interest, he asserted to his publisher, would be
that of Adams's mind: "what he represented and made and *was* as a mind
and sensibility, rather than what he provisionally and accidentally was as
a mere man. The mere man is for us only colour and setting. The book we
want is a critical and interpretative portrait with just so much straight

biographical material as to rouse and maintain the interest of those other-wise dull, enough given to suggest and imply the abundance of what is not and really cannot be given."

In 1943, and again in 1955, he modified his original scheme, hoping to come on or compose the unity of Adams as "an extreme articulate type of American intelligence." In the middle of the night he must have known this hope for chimerical, unity or wholeness being only "the ideal which stands in place of the actual." But he desired it deeply, and when he wrote of Adams he aimed at its achievement. "A new home in the wilderness" was his phrase for what he desired. At first he proposed to examine the type in twenty-four chapters, divided in five general groups. The structure he hit on finally is very different, but only in superficial ways. Subsequent versions of his early proposal are essentially cosmetic and intended to mask his own growing desperation. As a writer he wanted form, and he thought that by tinkering he might conceal the absence of the wanted thing. Friends and colleagues equated this absence with an imperfect grasp of technique. Richard couldn't manage a total book, said Willard Thorp, his chairman at Princeton. The labor of marshaling scholarship bemused him. Bernard Bandler, his associate on the *Hound & Horn*, thought he would have problems doing anything sustained or on a large scale. No *Paradise Lost* for him. But these are trivial rationalizations. Henry writing to Brooks Adams comes a little nearer the mark. Commenting on his brother's deficiency as a writer ("you need above all else, Form"), Henry recognized the same lack in himself. "There has always been my own gallows! All my life I have labored and sweated to get Form and always I have failed, because the difficulties become enormously increased with every enlargement of detail." That is partly the problem his biographer confronted. But the problem isn't exhausted in Richard's refusal to accept the tidy truth that falsifies.

His meditated scheme was both linear and causal. His psychology as it deepened gave this scheme the lie. In a letter to William Arrowsmith he deplored a review "which said that all my previous statements make a progress and a unity, which astonished me more than it pleased me." He couldn't say: "Respice finem"—where the end is there in the beginning. He said instead: "In our ends are our beginnings." He meant in approved fashion to begin at the beginning, but he never wrote the first chapter of the book—the birth of his hero, the years of childhood in which the child is seen as father to the man. Partly, as he said, Adams in the *Education* had been over the ground before him. For Richard, however, all that etiology was factitious. He wasn't a fumbler in matters of technique. His vision of things was atomistic. In the life of Adams, he wrote, "each moment—each chapter" would make an emphasis, and that is what he gives us: not catena exactly, but a series of splendid moments. Like James in *The Spoils of Poynton* or Conrad in *Victory*, he missed the one thread that tied his story together. Perhaps it wasn't there. James and Conrad at the end of their novels lit a fire to get clear of the business. He wasn't put to this expedient: his hero died.

In the fifth and final group of chapters which formed the original plan for the book, he was going to demonstrate the unity of Adams and his ultimate value. But all assertions of unity were suspect; only multiplicity was real. "All one's life one had struggled for unity," Adams wrote in the *Education*. But "the greater the unity and the momentum, the worse became the complexity and the friction. . . . The older the mind, the older its complexities, and the further it looks, the more it sees, until even the stars resolve themselves into multiples." At twenty-one, Richard thought that life was an experiment "in the attainment of at least a picture of unity in motion." The experiment, as he pursued it, didn't prove out. In his Guggenheim application of 1936 he said he knew "there was an extraordinary unity in Adams." In the same breath he said that in "the real world" you stumbled on failure as you resorted "to any ideal of order, of light, of unity." So from the beginning he was riding two horses.

Like Melville, one of the whipping boys in whom he castigated himself, he was, in his attitude toward all conventions of the mind, a through-and-through skeptic. The more he wrote and the deeper he dived, the more persuaded he became of the everlasting elusiveness of truth. In *The Expense of Greatness* he quoted Melville's *Pierre*: "Like knavish cards, the leaves of all great books were covertly packed." Perhaps in his biography he was only packing one set more. In a letter to Lambert Davis at Harcourt, he said "it would be pleasant if the book itself were so manipulable" as the straightforward account he supplied. That was how the letter began. Then came the account and then the doubtful conclusion: "Maybe this won't do."

The "universal lurking insincerity" at which Melville stood aghast was to Richard "just the most fascinating aspect of the face of dramatic truth." He thought the conviction of it should liberate the artist's honesty as he dealt with his material. For Melville, this insight brought him on dishonesty: feeling our condemned state as unreprievable, he denied his inmost feeling by utilizing conventions of character and form in which he didn't believe. Richard in the biography has no truck with vitiated convention. If his honesty is liberated, however, that is only partly a good. The medium makes the difference, not dramatic but matter-of-fact. Answers in a novel have no need to pass the equivocal, Richard said, "which is the realm of felt value." He was writing biography and didn't have the answers.

The life of Adams as he left it is conceived in three books, which make a trinity. This was the only tolerable form of unity, he said. He didn't say why and doesn't have to. For the writer who misses the sense of organic form, number is available, the simulacrum of form. You start with a doublet, and if you are lucky it breeds. Richard in his first critical book, *The Double Agent*, had this kind of luck; now he looked for it again. "War and peace need a third phase," he said, "as liquid and ice need vapor to fill out and judge the concept of water, as God the Father and God the Son need the Holy Ghost, or hell and heaven need purgatory, or act and place need time. The doublet *needs* what it makes." What he needed was a coda to fill out and judge the unity of Adams, his "American Archetype." It ought to afford "clues to Adams," he said, and he thought he might write it in terms of "the trichotomy . . . Adams as entertainer, as exile, and as high priest." (Shift the sequence of the first two terms and the trichotomy works for Richard, too.)

He reserved his coda for the end of the third book—"Richard's Prison Song," he called it: the story of Adams's last years. Disease and darkness made the major part of this story, lit now and then by Adams's discovery of medieval music, "the ultimate art" to his biographer, "incredibly the least committed to any prejudice or experience except itself." After all, the greatest art was circular and resolved nothing but the formal problems it posed. Climbing by your art, you got no higher in the end than where you began. In his concluding pages Richard is Adams, the prisoner of age, living in "an inner incalculable remoteness," a man who could not open freely, who hated direct questions, especially from strangers but even from friends, and froze on them in response. "The ice protected him."

Richard's account of his hero's old age was completed by 1938. He grappled with it early because in his dyspepsia he found it agreeable, or perhaps more nearly true than the assurance of young manhood before "the passion that united the ambition flowers and falls apart." This shows in the dark eloquence of his prose. "Hic Jacet Homunculus Scriptor": Adams's self-composed epitaph was, proleptically, his own. "Here lies a little man who was a writer." For himself if not for Adams, the littleness was incontestable, and what it mounted up to remained obscure. The end didn't crown the whole. You recognized the end only as it was "time to go." Adams "was down to the bare point," Richard wrote. "The universe had not only abandoned him but also seemed about to abandon itself. Where was the stoic discipline for that?" The story finishes here, with the death of the hero on Maundy Thursday, 1918. The promised coda never got written.

The first book, which should have begun *ab ovo*, begins in the middle of things. In the early chapters attention goes to National Politics, in the concluding chapters to Foreign Policy at the turn of the century and after. "The Burial of My Grandfather's Doctrine" is the title of one of these chapters and functions as a working title for all of them. The grandfather was John Quincy Adams. His doctrine was integrity, an atavistic doctrine in the new age of McKinley and Theodore Roosevelt. Richard, not less than J. Q. Adams, is the hero of these pages, "an eighteenth-century man with moral principles enriched by the experiment of a rational imagination." The imagination was rational as it led him to anticipate the ruin of every good thing. But he didn't wring his hands. He quoted often and with evident application to himself the line from Horace which contemporaries applied to the old President: *"impavidum ferient ruinae."* Whatever the event—"the felt stain of catastrophe in one's own twentieth-century life" —he undertook that the ruins should strike him undismayed. Like Adams he found in stoicism "his sole personal protection against a collapsing world." This was true for the grandson as well. "All his life, stoicism had been . . . an obsession: a boy's pride, a man's will, a prison and a refuge, an incentive and an aggravation." But Henry Adams spoke for Richard when he called the faith that sustained him "a stupid resource." He said it was "the only one," though.

In rough manuscript notes that turned up almost fifteen years after Richard's death, this occurs: "Stoicism is moral suicide: necessary to the weak and young." The only positive structure was skepticism, our means of descending "the long ladder of doubt." So the biographer, like his subject, is not hopeful, only staunch. As he inspects the darkening scene, his own sense of integrity is outraged but never invaded, his own skeptical apprehension of life is to the front. Here he is, the man in his habit, commenting on Jefferson's misguided disdain for institutions, which "are to society as original sin to the individual—the birth-sign of radical imperfection"; or on the Constitution of the United States, a "dubious and provisional and daring" experiment, the fruit of conviction which is only, "it may be . . . the experiment of great men," as faith is the experiment of our Lord. These are pretty wan sayings, and if taken to heart they make the act of writing, or resolution in writing, problematic. In *The Expense of Greatness*, Richard defined conviction as the "inward mastery of the outward materials of experience." The definition crops up again in the life of Adams, where individuals master fate as they have this conviction. Clearly the idea intrigued him—writing to a friend, he said it "made my cateyes climb." Given his psychology, it is probably inevitable that the inward mastery on which resolution depends should show the stigma of radical imperfection.

Richard wasn't Toynbee, taking Toynbee as the type of the regisseurial intelligence. His strength and mastery are not imperial but provincial. If he makes a good moralist, that is because he is coming from felt experience. "The further he went into history, the more his sense of the actual in his own time and place prospered." His delineating of the past comes alive as the past is insistently palpable, not much violated, as he liked to say, by ideas. Unlike Brooks Adams, he knows nothing of the law that governs for civilization and decay. The past is assimilated to the present, and "there" turns out to be "here"; this line from Wallace Stevens speaks obliquely to Richard's conception of the nature and scope—it is also limitation—of the critic's job of work. Seeing and telling are parochial. First things first: not foreign policy but Adams's friendship with John Hay, the Secretary of State. That is the major plot. The subplot, "taken half as citation from the record and half as the expressed vehicle of friendship," is Adams's attempt to influence Hay's conduct of foreign affairs. With the subplot "we must now continue," Richard writes, after a long excursus which is the real burden of the story. But in the end "we will come back to the friendship, just as history herself, no matter how long the projected view, in the end comes out in the individual imagination who feels her. The story is everything, when found."

Assimilating past and present, Richard means the past to bear on the present. History describes a continuum, or perhaps a dreary round. From American statecraft after the Civil War, he draws a political maxim and applies it "to the condition of 1942." Jefferson, who left his unresolved problems to the next generation, makes him think of FDR. The posturing of Adams's contemporaries, as they occupy the seats of power, suggests "a moral for all outsiders—all of us who represent nothing but the conscience of the world of affairs, all of us condemned to watch those who, as they think, hold power, overwhelmed by it in its very seat." This sounds like the didactic writer of the fifties and early sixties. But Richard had a long way to go before he got there. In *The Lion and the Honeycomb* he takes hold of your lapels. To break his hold isn't difficult, though. In the life of Adams he is saved from the debility that goes with polemicizing, because his mode of address is *ad hoc* and *ad hominem*. This is the fortunate side of his distaste for abstraction. It isn't Everyman but Adams who wears the sound money blinders "of his time and ours." Richard meant to create in Adams "the portrait of a type." He said, however, "the type is an Individual." Aaron Burr, like Huey Long, presents the anarchist at heart, and John Randolph of Roanoke, the anarchist on principle. Each is depicted, like Adams, as "that kind of individual who ends by producing types." But Burr and Randolph and Adams are only types as, first of all, they are themselves.

The life of Adams verges on a tract for the times to the degree that the types keep recurring. "The arena of power which aggravates them to action" is discovered "today" in Royal Oak or Dearborn—in the radio priest Father Coughlin, in Henry Ford. This shuttling back and forth is by intention heuristic, to use another of Richard's words. Seeing how the muddled reading of American policy under Grant "has been characteristic in our history at least from Jackson's time to the immediate present," he wants to do something about it. Modern historiographers, for whom partisanship is the cardinal sin, will give him low marks for this. The partisanship argues trouble for the future. So far, however, Richard's involvement is only here and there, and the artist or, say, the annalist takes precedence over the pedagogue and the reformer. "The story is everything, when found." The story makes a moral "rather than a historical critique, and being moral it will fasten on men's manners and on the principles, or policies, which the manners were meant to exhibit, or to replace when they did not exist." There is plenty of judgmental thinking in Richard's book, not much "political science." Like the historian Tacitus, whom he admired, or the chroniclers Froissart and Bede, other favorites of his, he doesn't venture to instruct us in techniques for survival. Mostly he contents himself or exacerbates himself "by giving a close account of what did actually survive."

The account is validated by what he called "a good deal of arduous, ardent, and fairly systematic reading in literature, philosophy, and American history." Like all the great critics, he was a deep scholar. This isn't said enough. Matter of fact is the element he works in. But fact is not the engrossing thing, nor is it diplomatic history that Richard is writing. He disclaims the attempt, and so outflanks more recent scholarship. Though he ended his labor a generation ago, his work remains unimpaired in its essentials. No more than Macaulay—or Adams himself—is he open to revision where he lives. The writing, though often eloquent, is more direct and unmannered than patented Blackmur, but as full of implication. Here is an example, on the old age of Adams: "The fine faces of the old, when they have not fallen away or grown dismayed, represent everything in life that can be finished." The biography, not finished but not attenuated either, lives in this phrase.

Richard saw his early essay of 1936, "Three Emphases on Henry Adams," as containing the finished book "in petto," but he didn't mean it for exemplary. "The essay is tight, condensed, indicative, almost a blueprint." It has only the momentum of intention. That is patented Blackmur. The book makes a contrast—powerfully declarative in temper, unafraid of obiter dicta, discursive in style (a decorous style for the matter), patient of explanation, "comparatively looser, expansive, illustrative." It possesses the momentum of mass. Only once as a writer did Richard achieve this.

Book II in nine chapters, "The Virgin and the Dynamo," is the center of the trinity he designed. It makes the most sustained piece of writing in the book, and as it builds in mass it gathers momentum. In the account of Adams's progress from early days at Harvard College almost until the end, Richard's wayward progress looms visibly. The telling quickens with the imaginative sympathy of a fellow traveler who also lived on "Knife's Edge," the parlous place where Richard located his hero. Each was an avatar, "the incarnation of deity in human form." The world sought to exclude the renewed experience of the atavistic man, "for it is such experience that re-opens all human problems in full challenge and fascination." What course could Adams sail next, he inquired in the *Education*. "He had tried so many, and society had barred them all!" Having no alternative, each man lived in exile. Each in his restless curiosity "was directed and misdirected by two New England characteristics: conscientiousness and skepticism." Adams in consequence, T. S. Eliot said, "could believe in nothing." Richard could believe in nothing either. To Jack Wheelwright, he plumed himself on possessing "a really ardent speculative intelligence." This went with New England. As he was conscientious he let his intelligence play freely, and what it touched it dissolved. There was no use for Adams in the crooked and supine administration of Grant: nor in his time for Richard, the self-anointed "conscience of the world of affairs." Adams was luckier than Richard: his exile persisted and brought him on the writing of *Mont-Saint-Michel and Chartres*.

In "The Virgin and the Dynamo" Richard celebrates this book and conspires successfully to make a rival creation. Evidently, even painfully, the vanished world of the High Middle Ages engaged Adams in his deepest place. "Himself lacking faith, he so ached with the want of it that he possessed himself imaginatively of man's reach when faith was live." Out of the living faith emerged a "vital, shaking balance" where both imagination and reason—each of them, to this skeptical intelligence, resting on an act of faith—composed "a single, and felt—if perilous—equilibrium." Enduring, it made possible man's highest reach. Then it broke, and the Middle Ages declined.

The perilous equilibrium has its analogue in what Richard called in the poetry his "eddying and bodiless faith." This faith allowed him to accommodate briefly "all known disorder and . . . to fit in new disorders as they were felt." The Middle Ages, on a cursory view, were not greatly accommodating. Twelfth-century society argued for stability and the immanence of law. But as it was vital, it had to make room for "whatever was irregular, exceptional, outlawed." It made room in the representative figure of the Mother, "who raised to divinity above law the inconsistencies of human needs by shedding favor on them all." The problem was historical but personal, too: how to keep the organism from flying apart while admitting the irregular virtues of "flexibility and variousness" which distinguished, for Richard, the quick and the dead.

He never canvassed this problem in terms of himself. He dramatized it and that was better, in his account of the Virgin of Chartres, "the one divinity that made tolerable the burden of justice and law." It is the fate of imaginative writers, Richard thought, "that their lives fall gradually into the patterns of their works and are finally lost there." If this doesn't happen often it happens here, and offers the sole excuse of exegesis and biography: "that by those means we sometimes ourselves best pursue the patterns into the works." To come on himself, Richard needed a fiction or point of departure. Adams and the Middle Ages gave him what he needed. When he celebrated the medieval achievement, he wrote of the best of himself. "The dramatic form is meant for purification," he said. Bringing his innermost self to the form, he experienced an emotion. This gives the writing its rare tone of exhilarated feeling, not bettered by him and hardly equaled elsewhere. Always he deprecated the personal voice, and was never more personal than in seeking to encapsulate the lesson of the past "that balance is better than control, that responsibility is better than rule, that risk is better than security, and that stability is death."

Richard didn't welcome disorder but sought to coerce it, having something in him of which to be afraid. He wasn't a fool. But he wasn't a coward, and didn't blink its corrosive presence. He said, however—and this is his one most comprehensive truth—that "disorder is merely the order you have not yet discerned." He met this truth in the medieval exaltation of the Virgin and Mother, who stood for all that was not unity: "and this was the whole human race." (An exaltation so great could only have a tragic fall.) The new mind, Richard's mind, on meeting the ancient aspect is confirmed in what it knows, and the result is spiritual autobiography.

What Richard knew, in particular what he knew of his native insufficiency, has not been honored much in modern times. That is part of the autobiography, too. Modern man announces the unity of things to the degree that his purview, just that, is narrow. This is the theme Richard sounds in *The Expense of Greatness*—when, for example, he censures Eliot's attempt to impose his Idea of a Christian Society: knowing as he does that "ignorance is ubiquitous," it is surprising that he should attribute "a relation other than imaginative to his authority." It is the cost of the imposition that concerns him here. Why, he inquires, did Catholic Christianity after the Middle Ages subordinate the Virgin to the personal realm, while the Protestants drove her out altogether? Put more sharply: why did man, at the very moment he got most help from the Woman, assume for himself an omnicompetence "exactly equal to that very omnipotence of God from which the Virgin had been created to protect him?" An adequate answer, Richard said, will gather together "almost all that is questionable in our own society," while showing us "an image of the peril of what loss in which we stand."

The book he wrote shows this image, not least in its character of personal testament. Richard used to describe his politics as Conservative Christian Anarchist, and in the life of Adams he explains what this means. The point of view behind Adams's mythical party "is conservative because it holds hard to what survives in man's mind, Christian because it feels it must encompass in a single piety even the most contradictory of the values which survive, and anarchic because both all the values and every act of encompassment are products of an order of forces that are beyond the scope of the mind to control and that are perhaps alien and ultimately destructive to it." Richard took the full measure of this alien and inimical order of forces, and in the end it defeated him. Until the end, however, he continued to cultivate his garden with all the more intensity, just because the crop was not in view.

So the tragedy of Richard's imaginative effort comes in its obdurate pride. This resembles the tragedy of a man's life. In *The Expense of Greatness*, Richard pronounced on the effort and the life. The triumph of both, an equivocal triumph, "is to represent the actuality of failure."

Failure doesn't mean unfinished. The expense of greatness is failure, vindicated partly as it is actualized. When Blackmur the mere Homunculus Scriptor is deficient in the labor of actualizing, the book he made, smarting almost with a sense of its own integrity, brings in its revenges upon him. The evaded thing—what he didn't or couldn't render or, in his own words, what "really cannot be given"—crowds and overflows the margin. He knew very well the loss he stood in peril of. His image for this loss is the banished woman created, as he said, to protect the deific man from his assumption of omnicompetence. But he is mute on the woman insofar as she touches him. For Adams, she was Marian Adams. Richard, who made the identification, wrote of her personal letters in *The Expense of Greatness*, and he wrote how they showed a winning sense of humor absent in her husband. When the humor failed, Marian Adams killed herself.

In the middle chapters of the first book, Richard told the story of Adams's return from the narcosis that engulfed him after his wife's suicide in 1885. The suicide was for Adams the inconsolable thing, the one event, said James, which "had everything that could make it bitter to poor Henry." Twelve years later, the bereaved man looked back: "When one has eaten one's dinner, one is bored with having to sit at table. Do you know that I am sixty in six weeks, and that I was only forty-seven when I finished my dinner?" This personal reference is rare. For Adams in the *Education*, Marian Adams—Clover was the familiar name he gave her— might never have lived. The pain of her loss and his complicity in it were unbearable, so he shut them from view. Guilt was his inheritance, Richard believed, "that sense of general guilt, which . . . sensitive and imaginative people of all sorts do feel as a result of our terrible failures to be what we are not." In the death of his wife, Adams's "unassignable guilt" found a focus—not the woman and her loss or not explicitly, but the woman at a remove—for Richard symbolized in the figure of the Virgin and in Saint-Gaudens' monument to Marian Adams in the cemetery at Rock Creek Park. Each was a penitential creation. The suicide for which the penance was enjoined "obsessed the latter end of Adams' life." So much his biographer knew. But Richard, edging closer, was more and less than a biographer. As he wrote, he became his own guilty subject.

In 1943 Delmore Schwartz proposed that he and Richard write a play together—he said, unfortunately, "for the fun of it." Delmore set the scene: "an evening in Cambridge in the eighties in which the brothers James try to elicit through innumerable dodges and subterfuges the reason why Henry Adams' wife killed herself." They ask Adams "many devious questions in their beautiful styles" and he deliberately leads them on, partly to tease them, "somewhat to punish himself." At a key point, "a veritable Jamesian moment," the ghost of Marian Adams appears "and the whole thing ends in immense ambiguity which Edmund Wilson will proceed to destroy, explaining that it is all sex." The ambiguity which gathered for Richard about the suicide of Adams's wife haunted him until he died. He helped to create it. In "the dark figure" at Rock Creek his wife Helen was incarnate and the figure became, as for Adams, "the whole object and only source of his own reaction." You have the constant sense that their relation was "as if afloat, like some island of the south, in a great warm sea that made, for every conceivable chance, a margin, an outer sphere of general emotion; and the effect of the occurrence of anything in particular was to make the sea submerge the island, the margin flood the text." That is James in Richard's favorite novel, *The Wings of the Dove*. In the novel, Kate Croy says to Densher: "I engage myself to you forever." So they pledge eternal vows and seal their rich compact, the woman taking the lead. In such matters, as she says, men know almost nothing but what women show them, hence the abysmal need of the man for the woman. Whatever the need, the compact didn't hold. It didn't hold either for Adams and his wife, any more than for Richard and Helen.

Richard had the facts of the suicide before him and they are clear enough, like the facts which purport to explain his own failure. Marian Adams, having lost her father, lapsed in depression, so took her own life. There is, however, her last note, which—until Richard saw it—no one other than her nieces had ever seen. Henry Adams, she wrote, was such a man as "God might envy." Of herself in this relation, she said only: "If I had one single point of character or goodness I would stand on that and grow back to life." But the point was unavailable or unavailing. So Clover went upstairs to rest, took the potassium cyanide from her photographic chemicals, and died.

Richard knew that he had to confront the suicide or leave his work unfinished. But Helen or the ghost of Helen stood before him, warning him off. He was the paragon who "bears and hopes and despairs"—Clover's characterization of Henry Adams—and Helen the woman whose life he could not save. He didn't drive her to suicide—she lived eleven years longer than he did. If he tormented her, on a hostile reading destroyed her, he took as much pain as he gave. So Helen wasn't Marian Adams. But the stain of guilt, deserved or not, discolors his journals—guilt for the irremediable thing he had done, a killing or cankering. Unluckily for him, the pole about which it collected was not the living woman—with her he could have coped—but the dead woman who represented her. Partly this is inference, rising from fact. Richard, in fact, could not confront the suicide. "I think that I *have*," he said, when he had barely begun to write, "in everything but the finishing touches." This was not so, or the touches—not flourishes but the essential strokes—were never applied. In his Guggenheim proposal only a few months later, he promised to assess the notions or root ideas which governed Adams in his life and work. Among these notions, important enough to need a chapter to itself, was the centrality of friendship and the social life. "It is in this chapter," he wrote, "that I shall have to deal with Adams' marriage, and with the enervating, re-creating shock of his wife's death, apparently by suicide."

He dealt abundantly with Adams the enervated man, and he dealt superbly with the revival of the creative instinct. Like Adams, he left the marriage and the suicide alone.

In 1943 he committed himself "to deal with the married years and with the old age . . . since Adams omitted the first from his book and had written it before the second began." He writes as if he had discharged this commitment: "You could say I repaired the omissions in Adams and added to his story." What he added, however—"Richard's Prison Song" —tells less than the omissions he could never bring himself to repair. In the context of his hero's withdrawal, he wrote: "Men are not so much marked by experience as by the precautions they take against it, and by the devices to which they resort to reduce the experience they could not help having to tolerable form." Taking breath, he made this apothegm: "Thus our deepest knowledge is that which we reject in order to live."

He intended in the year at Cambridge to go back to the life of Adams, but he hedged his intention when he thought of Adams's wife. "One of the things that I have left unfinished, though I shall probably not take it up in any lecture, is my chapter on the end of Marian Adams—not that I expect more material than I already have, but I want tact to combine with force." More than tact and force were wanting. "You have in a sense identified yourself with Henry Adams," a discerning correspondent wrote him as early as 1937. This was "no doubt one of the most auspicious states in which to write biography." The correspondent, Mrs. Elva dePue Matthews, a novelist whose writing Richard criticized for pay, had ventured a year before to give him her own hostile reading of Adams. Now she saw too late for whom Adams was standing in, and regretted that she should have been "so loudmouthed." The identification she proposed was more and worse than filling out your own portrait, and as she drew nearer it didn't show as auspicious. The "guilt, or sin, or penance to perform"— Richard's words—that drove the failed husband worked like the mines of sulphur in his biographer. Mrs. Matthews said how the poison he could not help ingesting "contaminates the whole system."

Guilt contaminated Adams, until time at last had its way with the guilt. In the end, it renewed him and begot the great work of old age. A year before his wife's death, he published his second novel, *Esther*. The heroine from whom the book takes its title is modeled on Clover Adams. "To admit the public to it would be almost unendurable to me," Adams said. It was written in "heart's blood," published under a pseudonym, and neither advertised nor offered for review. These circumstances suggested to Richard "an act of exorcism or objective suppression, as if Adams could not get rid of an inner burden except by printing it up and throwing it away, as one drives a pin into the wax image of the person whom one wishes to destroy." Richard's own case is similar and different. The suppression is similar but absolute for him. He didn't print his story but let it fester, and in the end the guilt he harbored was enervating, not renewing. "One loses what one is," he wrote of Adams, the posthumous man. "Despair comes when hope is seen to be vain without any lessening of the intensity with which it is felt." So far, his own case. He addressed it in his poetry: "My heart's hope is my soul's despair." Here he and Adams diverge. For Adams, at last "the sense of fate descends upon the sense of hope, and a new hope is born."

Richard ascribed the guilt that obsessed his hero to "that vertiginous feeling of falling short which besets us in our personal relations as well as in our ambitions." Then, as if he were catechizing himself, he said again: "It is the guilt of what we are not, and cannot ascertain, rather than the guilt of what we are. . . . No power of reason or law or ordinary understanding, only the miracle of imagination or understanding by faith could absolve that guilt." The context is his revision, in 1945, of a paragraph from the biography that had given offense to Adams's niece. Concluding the revision, he quoted Adams: "Even penitence was an impertinence." Mrs. Thoron annotated this letter and sent it back. She wrote in the margin: "Do you want to twang the *guilt* string four times in one short paragraph?" Evidently he had no choice.

On a visit to Hanover, New Hampshire, in the fifties, he traveled through heavy rain to Cornish and "gave two bemused hours to the Saint-Gaudens studio." After the visit he wrote to Mrs. Thoron: "There is a little head there from the Rock Creek figure which gave me back again the full feeling of the figure itself, and crowded me with the feeling of all that lies behind my poor book." What lies behind is personal and the matter of biography. As the subject of the biography is more than a cartoon, the occulted thing remains mysterious, though, like the Rock Creek figure of which Carl Becker wrote:

The eyes are half closed, in reverie rather than sleep. The figure seems not to convey the sense either of life or death, of joy or sorrow, of hope or despair. It has lived but life is done; it has experienced all things, but is now oblivious of all; it has questioned, but questions no more. The casual visitor will perhaps approach the figure, looking for a symbol, a name, a date—some revelation. There is none. . . . What does he make of it—this level spot, these shrubs, this figure that speaks and yet is silent? Nothing—or what he will.

Richard, looking for an answer, tried harder than this. In six pages of meditation found after his death—never published, and never sent to his publisher with the rest of the Adams material as he wrote it—he went back in mind to the grave of Clover Adams. "Adams at Rock Creek looked at himself": that is how the meditation begins; but the portrait Richard draws of the "trembling of the self into stone"—a line remembered from the poetry—is his own most faithful portrait. Richard is the dreamer lost from his dream, the man pursued and driven and drawn, the small man—Homunculus Scriptor—cut away. The force of life declares itself in death. Awaiting his own death, that is what Richard discovers. "Death was the perfection of waywardness; gave it order and end and a kind of limitation that amounted to unity." So the unity we seek to achieve all our lives is recognizable only in that anonymous state when we return to undifferentiated matter.

By Adams's direction, the monument he made bore no name and no inscription. "It was the monument, the expression, and the aspiration" of that anonymity, evacuated of meaning, which "one's ordinary living self" could hardly bear to acknowledge. "It is the anonymity of all the meaning we know and cannot grasp . . . it is the face upon chaos: the rejoicing in the abyss." Only understand the meaning of "the smile upon the Sphinx" and "life as it is lived—life as one lives it oneself—becomes radically impossible." For the living man who has looked into the abyss, this smile was "intolerable to contemplate." In his anguish, he reacted from the point of view of life. But the point of view was irrelevant, Richard wrote— "like one's own, before the coming experience itself. The deepest insights sink in quicksand once they reveal themselves to have their final source in the extremity of personal need."

His own need was overmastering, and he saw how it could never be met. "The soul is committed to so much that it does not know; and our best snobbery, confronted with the instance, is but reminded the more, with a pang, of its own ignorance." Speculating on the springs of sensibility and matter, he could gather only the truth of recurrence. "We see the water rise and lift and stir the particles of bright sand; then see the sand settle and the wet disappear; and as we know each instance to be eternal, we know also that the process is recurrent: and know most that these qualities of eternity and recurrence together make up the only meaning the process shows."

Seeing so much, you saw everything: "You saw *what it was*, created out of chaos, that comes again to chaos. Beyond that there was nothing to see, because beyond that the human imagination could not go, except that by sheer multiplication you could see it again and again until your eyes tired and the vertigo in which vision ends set in." The vertigo or fear of falling which had racked him from his earliest boyhood—and emptied him, too, giving to torpor the appearance of peace—he defined here as "the feeling of chaos itself." To ignominy as well as consciousness, this feeling puts an end. "It brings peace therefore to aspiration as well as to the sensibility which aspired." This was the peace permitted him.

He agreed that his own sensibility was primitive, and what is primitive, he said, is nearest to chaos. His saving grace, though he doesn't claim it for himself, was to make the primitive actual. "It takes great imagination, which is the greatest form of human courage, to envisage the actual in the primitive, to unite, in the single eye, the chaos which comes before with the blacker, because more actual, chaos that comes after." In "the awful pride of human passion," he affirmed that unity and he met and accepted the full horror of all it denied. His unfinished book registers the passion, and as it is unfinished, the expense. Almost as great as the great believers, he said, "are those who know the horror where belief ends; for it is only through them that we know what it is we believe, and lose, and must needs believe again."

CHAPTER SIX

Diabolus in the Scale—
Blackmur at Fiction

THE MIND OF Henry Adams, his biographer thought, had constructed itself primarily for a public and political life. This life failed to nourish, or a hostile society withheld the nourishment it might have offered. So Adams turned toward a new life "which should be predominantly imaginative and prophetic." Richard went the other way. Like Adams he wrote two novels, also short stories and plays. They don't disgrace him, and no one except his biographer need read them. In his mistaken sense, he was born to write fiction. But this superb critic was short on creative talent, so he followed a blind alley for years. He belittled his real talent and at last he put it in jeopardy by joining the academy "after twelve years of abstinence from jobs." He had failed at the one thing that mattered, so why shouldn't he throw in his hand?

Had he succeeded at fiction, he would have disappeared in the work. But everything he made declares the maker. One early story tells of the hero's first job, with Western Union, and how on the first day he rides to work on the streetcar wearing his brand-new uniform and supposing that all eyes, especially a girl's eyes, are looking at him in derision. The imaginary shame is more than he can bear, so he gets off the car, sneaks home to his room, and never wears the uniform again. Years later, Richard recited the outline of his story to a friend. He didn't present it as autobiographical—he didn't have to. "It is often in his relative failures," he said, "that an artist's drive is most clearly felt." His reference was to Henry James, "in whose purest successes there is the sense of the self-born, self-driven, and self-complete." Missing this kind of autonomy, he lets you see more clearly into the forces that drove him as a writer of fiction.

He had begun writing fiction while still in his teens and thought he had the makings of a novelist and playwright. At twenty-six he wrote to Rob Darrell: "You will be surprised to hear I work a little on a novel." This was *King Pandar*, the title designating but also defining his ambiguous hero, Henry King. At a guess, the hero's name conflates the names of Henry Adams and his closest friend, Clarence King. These were elective affinities for Richard, and he wished he might throw himself into the work and do it for day wages. The writing got most of his time, though, and explained "the paucity of new material" for magazines like *Pagany*. By 1932 a first draft was ready for Scribner's. This publisher blew hot and cold. *King Pandar* wasn't "really a novel," one reader thought; it didn't go anywhere. Richard's hero, the Boston lawyer Henry King, is out for fame and fortune but lives mostly in the mind. Anticipating Richard a little but not much, he has come to the middle of the journey, and sexual fantasies are dancing in his head. A pretty girl attracts him: she is young enough to be his daughter, and mostly that is how he treats her. Inside him, however, lurks "a crazy, delighted buffoon." This other self makes trouble for the "concentrated, busy man" he tries to appear "in the eyes of those to whom he was a personage." So King is a house divided. Looking in the mirror, he comes upon himself and quizzes himself, engendering what the reader for Scribner's politely called "metaphysical perceptions." Maybe they meant that Richard was "by temperament and gifts a poet or an essayist rather than a novelist." In any case, it was no to *King Pandar*.

The disgruntled author had an "excellent money losing novel" on his hands, and he knuckled down to the labor of revising. For him, this was always uncongenial. Richard wrote slowly but didn't blot a line. In his autograph copy, where words crowd on words in that niggardly script of his, changes are few and far between. "Are you getting on with the novel?" Kenneth Patchen inquired. Evidently the answer was no, and Richard said how "the work of finishing seems one of supererogation." But he had promised himself to write a thousand words a day, and for once he kept the promise. Within a year, the novel like himself was "in abeyance and servitude"—his self-slighting way of announcing that he had finished after all. "Our novels appear to have been finally peristalted at almost the same minute." This was Conrad Aiken, also no slouch at putting himself down. Sherry Mangan, back from a week in Maine "largely spent in the company of that artificially aged dodo, our old friend Dick Blackmur," reported to Jack Wheelwright on the experience. The critical utterances of the old friend continued, he said, "to give me a pain; but—would you believe it?—he has written a quite good novel, which so impressed me that I am trying to get Boni to publish it."

Nothing came of Sherry's good offices or of subsequent appeals to fifteen other publishers. "The novel is well written—and overwritten"— that was the consensus. In despair, Richard turned to Arrow Editions, where Florence Codman was a friend in power. "She came down to Maine and she had blonde hair and a very light skin and a kind of oatmeal jacket on, and she was all done in beige and white, a blonde woman with blonde fingernails." That was how Tessa Horton recalled her. Florence Codman "was very bright and a very nice woman and she thought Richard was simply marvellous." Nonetheless, she agreed with all the others. Partly the trouble was personal: it is a ticklish question to say where Richard begins and his hero leaves off. Each sees "a cold face" in the mirror, "an outsider's face." King, stripping off his undershirt as he dresses for bed, "did not wish to appear ridiculous, even to himself, and for years no stress of emotion had permitted him to appear covered above while naked below." Sitting beside the young girl he desires on a drive to the water for a swim, King looks at his dingy legs with dismay. "He was naked, he who needed always the drapery of forms and purposes." Perhaps, someone suggests, they might make a trip out to Roque Island (the scene has shifted to Maine), where the loony scion of a rich family is kept away from the world. He barks like a dog, and this is hypothetically amusing. King doesn't want to see him, however. "Often I have felt that I might lift up my own head and bay the moon." Madness is "always among our possibilities. . . . Anything might happen—to any of us."

Richard got angry when his literary agent surmised that "the book was based on personal experience." But he is his own hero, and in the title he impeaches himself. "King Pandar forever," he wrote at twenty-one. The context was Tessa's rejection of his offer of marriage. She wanted it both ways, however, and was seeking "to preserve in me the peculiar character of a passionate uncle." He didn't care for this but acknowledged that the "bulls-eye yawned, hideous, and I couldn't see it for smoke." On a harsh view—Richard's own—his surrogate-hero was the essential pandar, "the uncle of uncles, at once archetype and apotheosis of all the pedagogic uncles that ever were." The pussyfooting style tells you what he is. He partakes of Henry Adams, the doyen to his adoring nieces ("an avuncular relationship," as Richard described it, "which in the last thirty two years of his life was quite the closest Adams ever had"), also of Lambert Strether, a catalyst to others but inviolate himself. The role of pretended uncle was "the perfect profession, the perfect ardour for me," King Pandar says ironically. It permits him to enjoy his vicarious pleasures without putting himself on the line. To hope for more and better was a game for old men "who no longer have the strength of despair." So "never hope."

That is how the novel ends—"in abeyance and servitude." There was hope for Richard as a novelist, though. So much of what he had written seemed good to Florence Codman that she felt "another and better novel

. . . [must be] in the offing." She was right. Even before winding up *King Pandar*, Richard had started *The Greater Torment*. An excellent title, Murray Borish wrote to say: "the comparative arouses interest." Richard found it in *Ash Wednesday*, where the greater torment is love satisfied, and he meant it to signalize the bad taste that goes with fruition. Surfeit or rather emptiness is his point of departure, surfeit being the father of much fasting. The way he presents his given is hopeful but makes you quiver. "What will a man do if he *mistakenly* thinks his marriage is terminated or evacuated as by enema?"

This melancholy tale of a collapsing marriage is firmer in style, deeper and surer in perception than its predecessor. These were Florence Codman's words. But she doubted if Richard's characters had enough spunk to help themselves. From Peter Holm, the Beacon Hill physiologist, and Eleanor, his frustrated wife, "driven at once by the need of escape and the sentiment of irreparable loss," what could come? Or what could Richard do "to lighten the leaden weight" that oppressed them? His overt "concern with death" had wrecked *King Pandar*, she told him. Now again he was coming straight from the shoulder, with a hero so pared down as "to indicate the theme and nothing but the theme." Criticizing the conclusion of the novel as Richard projected it, his correspondent fell on a slip of the pen: how could the thin-blooded hero "make his mental and emotional adjustment to Helen?" In a journal entry, Richard laid bare his radical involvement in the fortunes of the hero, who "turns away because of the inadequate fire in his own bowels." This was sufficiently barefaced, just what he reprehended in fiction. He saw the problem, however, and attempted to address it by presenting his story from the point of view of four different centers of awareness, hoping in this way to find "an objective consciousness." This was how he proposed to save the novel from himself. Dramatize the thesis, he wrote to Rob Darrell, and "the morals won't count, only the drama."

That was easier said than done. Richard acknowledged that his novel required "an enormous amount of work yet," and he kept "plugging to plug the holes" or to flesh out the bare bones of his cautionary tale. He didn't succeed. His novel-in-progress strongly reminded one reader of John O'Hara, "though it is more civilized, more intelligent, and much less vivid." He began to wonder if he shouldn't break off and begin another and more "popular" book. Florence Codman didn't think so. "What are you writing novels for?" she inquired. "Personally I don't see you, with your special interest and talents, getting to the pulp stage." This was understatement, but Richard took the point. He said he would carry on, and his friend was "most tremendously glad." But the three books he planned, constituting "a novel of Crime, Punishment, and Penance," never got beyond the first. No ending was predicable of his story of love lost between a man and woman for whom no meaningful reprieve is in the offing. He would have disputed this. "Things can never again be the same between them"—Richard in his synopsis is echoing *The Wings of the Dove*—but that is "all to the good." He is saying that life is good because it resembles the peace of the grave.

For Richard the novel was "the most independent, most elastic, most prodigious of literary forms." Twice failing with the form, he experienced catastrophe. On the face of it, he put his failure behind him. "Relations never end," he wrote, "but the artist must make them appear to do so." At Princeton he told a favored student how he once wrote a novel "about a professor," which Scribner's rejected. "After he became famous Scribner's tried to get it back, but Dick decided to keep it buried." His hero Adams had no such compunctions or fantasies. The two novels he wrote "best clarify themselves" as substitutes for something better. In the biography Richard looked at them piecemeal. The middle chapters of the first book are devoted to his critique, and are narrower in focus than the end and the beginning. Potentially the gain is in greater intensity, but this gain isn't realized. Adams, the author of *Democracy* and *Esther*, brings Richard, the dejected novelist, on himself.

In his dejection he shifted allegiance and turned toward a life of engagement. Not entirely, of course. "No man turns wholly," Richard said of Adams and his turning toward a life of art, "for no one wishes entirely to be saved from himself." He continued to see himself, even in the Princeton years, as a maker of fiction, and he continued to promote his fiction with friends like Delmore Schwartz and John Walcott. Happiness was when they signified their approval. "Of course," he wrote to Jay Laughlin at New Directions, "if you should decide you wanted my novel . . ." The ellipsis says he is holding his breath. A Princeton colleague recalled his "fierce desire"—it hadn't waned in middle age—to achieve publication for this much-loved work of his twenties and thirties. Teaching crowded him hard and perhaps in the end it destroyed him as an artist— though gain and loss went together for Richard—but he still set up as what he called the creative writer, meaning "the writer who tries to be creative under the peculiar but pressing distractions" of the classroom. As 1941 began, he devoted the first week of the new year to the first nine pages of a new novel. (He meant to call it *The Queen of Tarts*.) "The exhilaration was genuine," he wrote to George Anthony, and he kept as his own "best prospect" the chance of completing the whole thing within a year. But this chance, like the green light which flickered for Gatsby, was already behind him.

Could he ever have grasped it? John Hall Wheelock, a poet and professional reader for Scribner's, read his first novel and admired much of it "profoundly." Pay more heed to structure, Wheelock advised him, and "you could write a novel . . . of great distinction." Had he stuck to his guns—this was what Helen said in their first years at Princeton—and still cultivated the "urge to work . . . in spite of the snowball of the students' visits," he might have found that "seeing eye" which opens on the life of things. He didn't linger long enough to find it, and not lingering he lost his momentum. "The maxim, if you want it, is this: Writing alone increases authority in an author." Keep writing, he counseled the students in his classroom, "and you will find suddenly that your words and the pattern that runs among them have an organic life of their own." Organic life was the wished-for end but it doesn't often materialize in the fiction. It was, Richard thought, "the [very] decay of my character Henry King" that sharpened awareness of his moral dilemma. This dilemma was the seat of life. "'But I am not able to render it," Richard said. Elsewhere, in reference to fiction that wasn't achieved, he wrote: "the values asserted are far ahead of the values rendered." He is his own best critic, the shoemaker whose children go without shoes.

Sometimes in his fiction "organic life" peers through the lattice. His old curmudgeons and disagreeable women manage the persuasiveness that goes with a surfeit of bile. But these are incidental successes. Mostly, said Florence Codman, character as he conceived it lacks "tolerable proportion." Christine Weston, who lived near him summers in the big house overlooking Flat Bay, was a novelist herself and took strength from his critical precepts but not from his practice. She told Richard how his "people never really attract one another, they don't dazzle, nor seduce, nor persuade." The hero of *King Pandar* came across to her as "a most sinisterly prize-prig." Was that Richard's intention? His women were sinister, too. Otherwise they were wraithlike, a fault and a definition. Maybe he ought to call his novel "The Bitch, the Pandar, and the Holy Ghost." Normal folk, on his uncharitable reading, are nothing—strange, when you think of his love affair with Maine. (The physiologist-hero of *The Greater Torment* is "tainted by that which was not of the intelligence.") In the play he wrote about Lindbergh, he described ordinary people as "meaty with the life that occupies without glorifying time." Not glorifying time, they aren't meaty either.

Richard knew you could make credible fiction without character. His own example for this kind of fiction was Santayana's *Last Puritan* where, as he put it, "characters are not well drawn in their externals, are thin in their blood, and are wholly inadequate in the expression of the stock personal emotions." Santayana rejoiced, however, in the seeing eye that Helen craved for Richard, and it brought him, Richard said, on "an incomplete but profound imaginative insight." In Richard's fiction, imaginative insight is missing. This comments on the weakness of his strength. He is strong in articulating orders of being. The essay on James's Prefaces offers a superb example. Taxonomy, his old gift, enables him here, and is fortified by what he called the rational imagination. Sometimes, however, his asserted orders seem less real than imaginary, and the exercise of reason merely petulant or shrill. For instance: "There is an element in every sensibility for which the periphery of things is often enough." But to stop there, like Hemingway in his *Green Hills of Africa*, is self-deluding. "Let us say rashly, omitting all the rest, that when the only principle of control is peripheral, then, at the center . . . private and uncontrolled, unrealized emotions will creep in." This creeping in is scary. That is what the hectic prose seems to say. Instead of the confusion life exhibits, we want a rational art which improves and orders life "with the conscious illusion of form."

But Blackmur the storyteller is best on the periphery. The controlling principle he discovers at the center of things is felt as illusion and sponsored by personal need. In the life of Adams, omitting this discovery, he achieves a failure worth making. In the fiction he proclaims it, and the result isn't form but sclerosis. The decade that had passed since the writing of *King Pandar* ought to "show all the fruit" of the "unsure and uneven living" that lay behind him, Helen thought. But the showing was contingent. He needed, she told him, to revisit the past and anticipate the future "with an eye which is not going to get pleasure from things only if they arrange themselves in a preconceived pattern." Courting this pleasure, and so evoking this pattern, was his fatal possibility. Helen feared "you have lived a little bit that way."

The preconceived pattern lies heavy on the early stories, where the staple stuff is "desolation and the sense of a hidden, utter dreariness." Ideas that seemed propitious found their way into his journals: the anatomizing of his own misery, for instance (he was going to call this one "Physique de Désespoir"), or, as title and theme for a book of short stories, "Diabolus in the Scale"—a term from music, Richard said, denoting "the long travail of mine undisguise." Diabolus was the devil with whom the composer struggled. Pound invoked this struggle and its aftermath in *Mauberley*, where his failed esthete cultivates "the obscure reveries of the inward gaze." Nothing happens and stone dogs bite the empty air.

Richard in his projected title is remembering Pound, but not to adorn the tale. His point is to the amalgam of disparate qualities which is the achieved work of art. Order trembles on disorder, and the opposite is true. If the artist is successful, he brings the devil to heel. But the turbulence that marks the struggle or the whiff of brimstone remains in the work. This residual thing redeems the work from marmoreal coldness.

Over thirty of Richard's stories or sketches for stories survive. Editors didn't clamor to see them. To some he attached the inevitable rejection slips. Mencken's *American Mercury* wasn't high on what he wrote, and he said how he had little use for Mencken. His New York agent Brandt & Brandt didn't offer much encouragement either. Richard the discriminating critic, reviewing the failed poetry and prose of other writers, could tell you abundantly why this was so. Three things were wrong: "emotional language in excess of its impetus; a stock response to a stock situation; or a stock response to a unique situation." If he got published, that was thanks to the benevolence, not always the acumen, of the little magazines. Richard Johns at *Pagany* liked his fiction enough to solicit a story. Sherry Mangan admired it, too, and when Richard was twenty-three, *larus* published "The Cut," a dreary imitation in Eliot's worst manner, la la etc., a young man who has seen better days.

Sherry didn't regret this young man's effusion—it met his own deplorable taste. Richard the critic gave him nightmares, however, and provoked him to doggerel verse:

> I heard "Apage, sus!" and "Go back, sir!"
> and saw Winters and Tate and Blackmur;
> three old eagles (or crows) on a gate,
> sat Winters and Blackmur and Tate;
> all a-whittling fine critical splinters,
> were Blackmur and Tate and Winters.

The criticism, Sherry thought, was only scholastic flummery, but Blackmur at fiction was writing from himself. Characteristically, this gets it backward: the criticism stands on its own feet; mostly the fiction totters unless supported by biographical interest. Walter Pater appears at the window, also the ghost of Oscar. Each is prominent in the journals, and each in occulted ways is perhaps a lifelong presence for Richard. Here he is, the strayed reveler out of the Mauve Decade (from a story called "In Joachim's Smile"): "I would not have you think me morbid. Morbid is a child's word, a pedagogical word; it has to do with people who find evil in the heart of God rather than in the ill-stretched senses of man. I have been something of a student of evil in the senses. . . ."

The good stories are the Maine stories and date from the years just after Richard's marriage, when he and Helen were living in Belmont. The sentimentality at which he smiled in his reviews proved in his own case responsive to treatment. Assuming always that "something real exists," the writer need only learn how to manage it "without deceiving himself or anybody else." Richard learned to do this. *Désespoir* in the abstract takes second place to the annals of men and women. When they get together they don't have much fun, but at least they get together. The integrity of these stories rises from their provenance and is generally exhausted there. As in the achieved poetry, the experience of Maine makes the difference. Richard isn't strong on incident. He is strong and laconic, though, on matter of fact. Country speech is verisimilar—except when he stumbles on preconceived patterns, the stock response to the unique situation; his eye for detail is always true when it pauses. The writing is not often livened by imagination, but feel for the land and piety before it set him clear. Clamming on the tidal flats for three dollars a day is almost the whole business of one story, and almost enough to make a story. Quoting from "Conflagration," where the fire is physical and spiritual too: "Being weatherwise was his experience of the wisdom of God."

This sense of the verity of things strengthened as Richard went forward. *King Pandar* impressed John Hall Wheelock "because of its very definite roots in an almost factual realism." Precision was Florence Codman's word. She singled out the morning swim, the picnic, a dinner party the hero gives for his friends. The setting is variously Boston and the coast of Maine, and Richard knows either, you suppose, like the back of his hand —Frank Locke's on Winter Place, the Athens-Olympia, the fishing grounds off Oak Point, the islands in the bay and beyond: Flat Island, Petit Manan, Mark Island "like a busted derby." Henry King makes a believable lawyer. His creator is at home with the idiom and machinery of legal business and corporate business. In *The Greater Torment*, he plunges into medical lore. The hermetic professions, what they used to call the "mysteries," get his fascinated attention. This was a reason for praising the fiction of James Gould Cozzens. Like Cozzens, Richard knows whereof his professionals speak.

But language was both his glory and his nemesis. Sometimes the good ear defers to the inner ear, and "the Jacobean patter"—his own phrase— puts the story in peril. "It was if"—when a Yankee farmer heard himself speak—"he heard the denunciation of some intimate profound betrayal." What the reader hears is Professor Santayana of Harvard or that Henry James who functions as catechumen to his own priestly instructor. "I have a particular rot in me, I know, of Santayana and Henry James," Richard said. The rot glows with a particular phosphorescence. You know whom you are reading when you read Blackmur's prose. Lawyer King, addressing his legal factotum, finds that the boy "grew more and more nominally his audience." King, like Professor Blackmur, is inclined to forget his audience or to use it as a sounding board. "He ventured rhetoric for his soul's salvation." The story, in the meantime, must shift for itself. Rhetoric is ventured, but not communion with others. It isn't surprising that the hero comes up empty-handed in the end. This doesn't distress him. "His eloquence . . . the purity of his thought, was the one thing he kept fastidiously his own."

When King leaves off speaking with the tongues of angels, he is said to speak "with resolute vulgarity." There isn't enough resolute vulgarity in *King Pandar*. Peter Holm, the physiologist, isn't much convicted of it either. His wife supposes that he doesn't know what plain speaking means. With him it's all velleities, proper to a man who broods much, like Richard Blackmur, on "the inexpugnable deceit that went with the use of words." Holm is a man at sixes and sevens. "There was within him . . . a jarring, a shredding, a positive metallic grinding of anticipating nerves; and at once an awful sick lowering, a falling apart, an impendency of the physically inchoate." Evidently, even fiction doesn't suffice to keep this writer in check. He needs the absolute discipline that goes with close analysis of poetry or prose. His style, bitten by poetry in the pejorative sense, longs to be freed from reason.

Saint James (as Delmore called him) participates in this crucified style, but its origin for Richard lies deeper than books. The interacting of men and women is almost always the violating of either. What Richard thought about life is depressing and possibly just, but the fiction isn't concerned enough to supply the ground for what he thought. A joyless party in *The Greater Torment* is "big, like a pregnant woman, with the ripening crime of the life to come." This simile made Florence Codman sit up sharp, and she wanted to know how the novel begot it. You have to go outside for an answer. Frustration and betrayal are simply in the cards, so the mutual trespass seems to Richard foreordained. When Henry King was young and could have had his Gertrude, "ecstasy had been undone by . . . fear." The woman lies down beside him, he hears her guttural cry—and he sends her away. "Nothing had happened." Like the life of the author, the novel describes a broken arc. Though the aging hero (he is only pushing forty) gets a second chance, it comes to nothing, too. That was just as well for Gertrude, who "would have touched the muddy bottom of disappointment." Spending the night with his mistress, King feels how "her strangeness, sleeping beside him, was intolerable." Clara the mistress is attractive and disgusting. These qualities are not opposed but complementary.

Though Richard's characters in his second novel live on intimate terms with "the haunting, maddening consciousness of sex," it isn't the torment of unsatisfied love that gives them the horrors. "The horror of intimacy" (Richard's phrase) is what they are fleeing. "Their sterility, their impotency is terrifying," Florence Codman thought. When the hero, "with all the good will in the world," provides his wife with a lover, she found "no good will in the deed, only a mean sort of indulgence." To her question, "What vocation do . . . [Holm] and Eleanor discover together?" the implicit answer must be none. "They exist in a limbo of sexual desire which is fiercely accurate and in its segregation horrible." Characters in Richard's fiction move together, never meeting, in a delicate dusk, or they confront each other from the opposite sides of a chasm. Talking comes hard to them (but not soliloquizing), and even in love they "think only in the profound terms of their own dishonesty." This is a problem, and Richard does his best to resolve it. He tries for concrete being in his imprisoned characters through violence of word or deed. As a motto for the second book of *The Greater Torment*, he had in mind the lines from Gide he used to say over to himself as a boy:

> L'humilité ouvre les portes du paradis;
> L'humiliation, celles de l'enfer.

He doesn't scant humiliation and the hell on which it opens. One publisher who turned him down remarked and resented "the vicarious hot stuff in Blackmur's writing on the women." King Pandar, who does duty for the author, betrayed "an essentially childish sexuality . . . the kind Boston boys have when they're on a tear in New York."

The given in this fiction is apt to be melodramatic. Richard, having no recourse, perceives everyday business in radically sensational ways. A young woman loses her virginity to a drummer, and so loses her man. An unscrupulous lawyer compromises a lawsuit involving the corrupt directors of a big corporation, one of whom has married the woman he loved and sired the daughter he covets. The lawyer is Henry King. He loses the girl but wins a judgeship, attesting the serendipity of things. In *The Greater Torment* "disasters ensue and pyramid": the suicide of the drug-addict psychiatrist Eugene, who loves the wife; the commitment to an asylum of Florence, a hysteric who loves the husband; the incarceration of Horace, a Communist, also a lover manqué, for rioting against the established order; and, on the fourth day, the funeral of Eugene. These events "are not events merely, they are shocks administered" to the protagonists and represent life *"borne in"* upon them. "Only through the blows of the switch," says Addie Bundren in Faulkner's novel, "could my blood and their blood flow as one stream."

Richard had what he called a prehensile imagination, "able to grasp sensitively, intimately, in the sense of closely, like the monkey's tail on the branch, or the fingers on the ladder rung when the foot slips." Applying this quality to the imagination, he defined it as "the quality of being in direct, absolute and undifferentiated contact with the substance of interest." That is not a negligible possession. Ideas tempt him, however, and "the full picture" (his phrase) crowds lower-case things to the wall. Florence Codman, commenting on Eliot's *Family Reunion*, writes as if Richard's work were before her. She thought the play "an amazing piece of Nature Morte" and went on to say why. "I believe the chief fault lies in Eliot *listening* to himself . . . not only to sounds but to ideas and their movements at the expense of *seeing* as a dramatist sees action, character, and the voices." Coincident with his discovery of Maine, a chief source of detail for the fiction, Richard was discovering Virginia Woolf. "I suggest that you include in your 'serious' reading *To the Lighthouse*," he wrote to Elliot Paul. "There are so many small things seen, so many brief sentiments achieved that the words and the sense of their living objects quicken like a flight of birds across a low sky of the mind." As appreciation, this could hardly be bettered. Then comes the tempering. "There is something *just a little* morbid, just a little timorous in the soul under Mrs. Woolf's writing." Richard means that Virginia Woolf is satisfied to stick with "small things seen." That hits off nicely his own limitation, but he doesn't live with it equably.

In his poetry when it doesn't work, and most of the time in his fiction, Richard hastens from the periphery to the center. His master Henry James exhibits this impatience, too. Morals to him were a primary consideration "because he could not envisage them as *only* secondary." The world didn't show enough in the way of gratuities, either as refuge or point of departure. (Richard in the mid-forties had committed to Robert Spiller at the University of Pennsylvania twelve thousand words on James for the *Literary History of the United States*, and he wrote to Allen Tate how the labor of meeting this commitment had buried him "up to my neck." The result was worth the labor: ruminating on James, he encountered himself.) "He never went back into the whole force of love, only into so much of it as could be conceived morally." So while he aimed at the full picture, he "had to resort successively to the lesser forms of the allegory, the fable, the ghost-story." He did best when, toward the end of his life, he made a cross between the drama and the fairy tale. This is what you get in

Richard's fiction. The language which vivifies or petrifies the fiction is often convoluted, because the matter of everyday is too thin to detain him for long (he is an allegorist), or because that matter is like a tangled thicket through which he looks for the truth and doesn't find it (he is one of the sons of Pater for whom the matter of everyday remains on the level of merest sensation). Honesty denied the pattern he was looking for. He might have accepted this—he did in the life of Adams—and come down on the side of unblinkered perception. But that meant abject surrender to "the barbarousness, the irrationality, the formlessness" of life. He wouldn't have it, his own fevered life was in question, and he inveighed relentlessly against "the corruption of the novel as the chief form of rational art." Thomas Wolfe was anathema because he declined to give "perspective and direction" to his art. John O'Hara's famous first novel, *Appointment in Samarra*, had to be bad because "its crucial gesture is inexplicable." He is right, of course, but he makes the point so obsessively in his essays and reviews of the thirties and forties that rightness verges on hysteria.

The allegiance to Henry James plays into this hysteria, or you can say that Richard was James without the spendthrift talent and that his misplaced allegiance was to his worser self. James shows "the hall-mark of the home-made mind," and it drove him partly to makeshifts. "All his life long, without ever exactly acknowledging it," he had "to make substitutes pass for the real thing he knew must be there but could never grasp." You feel the pertinence of all this to Richard, not least in his transparent pretending, comic, poignant, and stylish by turns. "It was the eloquence and passion with which he made the substitutes pass, not the act of substitution, that gave his writing stature and even a kind of contingent reality."

The act of substitution is most vivid for Richard in the canonizing of form, the indispensable resort of this desperate man who identified reality with the random spinning of particles. For fiction, perhaps for life, "form, we might say, is the only sanity—the only principle of balanced response," and to declare it is "the minimum of your rational responsibility." Form was the warder which held chaos at art's length, the great good thing by which alone you apprehended reality, then brought it to heel. For the making of this doctrine, more precisely this hopeful incantation, James was the *fons et origo*—one might say the Sacred Fount. Richard said he learned from James of "that central adversity of the human condition which rises from the 'otherness' of every individual from every other individual." But he didn't have to go to the master to learn this.

The names of the acts which you and I perform together are common,

Helen Palmer, Richard's mother, at eighteen

George Edward Blackmur, Richard's father, in his thirties

Helen Palmer, Richard's mother (top row, third from left),
with her family in the 1890s

Richard with his younger brother, Ted,
in Cambridge in 1911

Richard
at 52 Irving Street,
Cambridge,
in 1914

Richard in the late 1920s

Helen Dickson, Richard's wife,
in the early 1930s

Murray Borish in the 1920s

George Anthony Palmer, Richard's cousin,
in the 1920s

Helen and Richard on their wedding day,
June 14, 1930

Richard in Maine in 1938

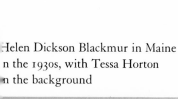

Helen Dickson Blackmur in Maine
in the 1930s, with Tessa Horton
in the background

Tessa Horton in 1930

Tessa Horton in the early 1940

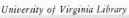

John Brooks Wheelwright
in 1939

Richard in Egypt in 1953

Richard in Japan in 1956

Richard at home, in Princeton, in the early 1960s

he wrote in his youthful journal, "the acts themselves being private and impregnable." As we are incorrigibly separate, the stigma of our reality, failure to connect becomes the norm. Documenting this failure is Richard's strong suit. In the short fiction he makes a cult of impotence. That is one way to read the unfinished life of Adams. The reading holds also for the novels and plays.

Like James in the middle years when full success eluded him, Richard struggled in his fiction "to tap the force that is under or overwhelmingly within life." He struggled with Diabolus and the struggle wore him down. Like James, he turned to the drama for relief. The parallels hold uncannily. "Exiled and alienated"—this is Richard on James—"he tried his hand some half dozen times at what he hoped would be the popular well-made play." Edmund Wilson encouraged Richard and put him on to Harold Clurman at the Theatre Guild. Clurman made a severe critic but was stimulated, too, and offered to read future scripts. Craving even "a simple assurance of being"—his own judgment on himself—how could Richard set up for a playwright? He answered the question partly by begging it. The six plays he left, mostly unfinished, don't look hard or often at the man in his habit as he lived. A summary comment of his on *The Spoils of Poynton* states his own case as a playwright. "The thing reads like a well-made novel trying to be a well-made play about manners with the men and women left out; but with the distinction that rather a cynical fable is about to be unfolded in an atmosphere of sheer brutal brilliance: moral humiliation without moral compassion."

Humiliation—remembering the passage from Gide—opens the gates of hell, a tenebrous place where characters exist as if behind scrim. Richard calls them He and She or Old Man and Young Man, supposing that the drama of Expressionism will acquit him. Emulating the doubtful practice of late Strindberg, whom he was reading at eighteen, he peoples his stage with whey-faced abstractions like Brother to the Corpse and Married Sister to the Corpse. He possessed less sense of theater than sense of propriety, and so ensured the disaffection of the audience he didn't have by keeping the Corpse itself in the wings. The Mask of A and Mask of J are more persuasive, he thinks, than common-garden persons called Avis and Joseph, and maybe—given his shrinking from life in the buff—he was right. His male and female protagonists drive you back on Cox and Box. A longer version of the play in which they figure concludes: "Avis goes out, falling, and Joseph goes out, stumbling." This is meant to be comic. The ground note is invincibly serious, though—"that oldest, saddest music of the world."

Most of what he wrote for the stage is damp with strenuous purpose. Style is like rhinestones in the five-and-dime. (Conrad Aiken had commended Wallace Stevens's verse plays as a model.) "While your style," said Harold Clurman, "does save the play from the drabness of base realism, it also robs the play of reality." The blank verse, a flaccid version of the old Shakespearian rag, the sardonic stuff, and all that insistence on telling the truth, ought to denote the intellectual as amateur who has wandered into the theater and wants to use it as his pulpit. But this isn't so. Not to blink the pulpit thumper and the devotee of Bernard Shaw. When the plays work, however—and sometimes they do—it isn't for intellectual reasons. "You try to be intellectual about something which does not affect you intellectually at all but which is interesting precisely because one feels you are emotionally involved in it." That was Clurman's judgment, and the script he was reading bears him out.

"Follow the Leader" was the title Richard chose for this impudent and jauntily attractive play. "An old man, aware that his son wishes to get rid of him, determines to triumph over his son by taking away from him his only pride and love—his family." That is Richard's Argument. Sift it a little and you feel how he is turning the tables on George Edward, his own much-hated father. Richard the critic comes down hard on his authors when they fail to steer clear of autobiography. Anyway, he thinks they should hide themselves among the stuff. He isn't at pains to do this himself. His idea of concealment is to give you a mirror image of the truth: left is right and dorsal is ventral. An army colonel—like Lucky Lindy—becomes a navy commander. Look twice at the faithless son and degenerate husband and you recognize George Edward, who gives the lead to his harum-scarum family. In bed or out, he can't make ends meet. So he turns pandar and lays down his wife for his friend. Richard is the friend, the young man who desired his father's wife Helen to make him immortal with a kiss. Exercising a writer's privilege, he participates emotionally in the role of the go-between, too. The dramatic mode was attractive because it allowed him to play many parts in one person. He plays the broker-husband who holds the door and the lover who enters. He is also, to quote him, "the fellow behind the scenes who is responsible for everything that shows and sounds, from the first gesture to the last cadence." Plays, in this respect, had it all over real life.

He embodied the role of the godlike director partly in his Shavian hero, who brings the bad tidings to the inhabitants of Heartbreak House—or the boarding house on Irving Street. Captain Shotover functions as the model for the ancient who fixes you with his bony finger. Like the pandar and cuckold, he walked up and down in Richard's imagination. (A later obsession was Bloom in *Ulysses*, his eye to the keyhole while his wife is being topped.) *Heartbreak House* was the play he chose when asked to give a guest lecture at Princeton. In his lecture he arraigned all the petty tyranny and the feckless behavior under which he had groaned as a boy— the skipper drunk on the bridge, the ship heading for the rocks. Shaw's defeated people cultivated only "the illusion of occupation." Having "reminiscence in the mind, vestige of old habit in the body, and surd of old need at heart" (that was how Richard spoke from the podium), they did their pathetic best "to make their actual lives something to get on with." With their inevitable failure, this speaker was on intimate terms. "Navigation!" he rumbled in his old lion's voice, and the students moved back in their chairs. "Learn it and live, or leave it and be damned!"

His catechistic side didn't win him a hearing in the theater. The play, he said to Aiken, had the bad luck "it no doubt deserved." The producer Jed Harris, gossip told him, was "occasionally a fool," so Richard tried for an audience there. The results were the same, though. "Better luck with the next," Aiken wrote from England in 1931. In his next play, "a mad nasty thing about Lindbergh," he joined hands with Lincoln Kirstein. This meant that each of them systematically wrecked what the other had done—"though I do most of the writing and he most of the wrecking." Richard thought they could "make it nasty enough so that we stand a good chance of being bought off"—an odd way to put it, as if plays were synonymous with making a nuisance. He took heart from the scandalous success of "the recent play about Sacco and Vanzetti," executed the same summer Lindbergh had flown the Atlantic. This play—presumably *Gods of the Lightning* (1928)—had been "bought off almost immediately." The Boston censor declined to issue a license—"anarchistic and treasonable" were the words he used—so the play was banned in Boston. You couldn't ask for a livelier sendoff. Perhaps, Richard thought, he had it in him, like Maxwell Anderson and his collaborator, to cut a figure in the eye of the crowd. "It's a swell subject anyway," he said.

What he did was to thumb his nose at the crowd, and hardly anybody noticed. Months later, the four-act play he and Kirstein called "Hero" was still "resting in the lap of some damned fool or other in New York." Not even a yelp was forthcoming, and from Kirstein "only doubts and worries and then complete silence." The silence was general and it persisted. With the failure of "Hero," much emotional capital went down the drain. In Commander Fraser, the tormented protagonist who plucks defeat from the jaws of success, Richard drew himself on his dark side. His amiable young man who becomes a haunted celebrity by flying nonstop to Buenos Aires —this was Richard hiding his tracks—is the familiar figure he kept in the closet or under the bed, the hero for whom failure is the bloom on the rose. The equivalence is bad enough, insupportable when the playwright or novelist enjoins it. (Henry James is the cardinal case.) "You've made a success," a worshipful young woman says to King Pandar. He answers: "Some of us would rather make a failure."

Roy Fraser in the play makes a horrendous failure and so gratifies the puppet master up there in the flies. As he does this, the audience heads for the exit, which was part of the desired effect. If his audience didn't know it, Richard wanted them to know that love satisfied is the Greater Torment. All ambition is hollow and the best joke is when you achieve it. This is what the hero discovers. So he runs away—like T. E. Lawrence, who never tasted his triumph but what he spat it up, or perhaps like Private Meek in Shaw's popular success of 1931, *Too True to Be Good.* This whimsical version of Lawrence in exile carries with him the suggestion of "an imprescriptible joke." That is how it is with Richard's hero, except that the joke is on him. He can't elude his private demons, no more can his creator. Lawrence, fleeing the demons, dies on his motorbike. Commander Fraser, standing in for Richard, is a suicide, too. He kills his better Genius.

"Almost everyone I know," Richard wrote in his journal, "is a fugitive (or would be) from the life society compels him to lead." The flight is in the heart (drama being its projection), which "to live at all must desire the impossible." The blighting of this desire engaged him as a poet, and he brought out what must have been his favorite quotation: "My heart's hope is my soul's despair." Heart's hope was "the intermittent, the recurring" sensation "of understanding and friendship and ease, the satisfaction of a skilled life, the labour of use, the glory of feeling, an atmosphere of light, the exhilaration of calm," and the conviction that somehow these desired things might prevail. Hope lay most of all in supposing you might enjoy "the luxury of an order which is not a privation, but the very composition of fullness." The soul knew better than to entertain this hope, and that was the final knowledge Richard's aviator-hero confronted. Running from the crowd, he runs down his childhood friend. The friend represents the buried self who casts a cold eye on the public man for whom the satisfaction of a skilled life has all gone into specious applause. He is also the social conscience which nags at the hero on his best or eleemosynary side, enjoining the labor of use. These roles are clean contradictory. Richard in his bedevilment makes room for them both.

It wasn't surprising that the artist seemed to his biographer (James to Richard) both "a hero or a traitor to his proper heroic role—and should seem so to the artist himself." The disfranchised monk is the emblem for the artist. He "finds himself with such a high value that he cannot assent to society as it is but has a great craving to assent to it as it ought to have been." The playwright and his protagonist come together here. Richard is the artist who betrays his art, and the selfish dropout from society whose dedication to his art constitutes betrayal, too. Either way he is damned—a congenial situation—so he performs on himself an act of ritual murder. Never mind what the world thinks, his self-lacerating hero tells an inquisitive reporter, the death of the friend was no accident. The confession destroys him, but in equivocal ways it sets him free. The adoring crowd finds him out and instant fame converts to villainy. A new image succeeds, however. "If they can't have a hero . . . they'll have a traitor." The hero is likened to Benedict Arnold. "He betrayed his country. . . . So have you."

Here the play ends, and with it Richard's career as a playwright. Nowhere is he on record as summing it up. A tentative summary is indicated, though. What he wrote for the theater begins where all art begins, in the foul rag and boneshop of the heart. He needed a ladder to get out of there, and mostly he didn't have it. This makes for bad plays and fruitful annotations. In the plays he is dramatizing the struggle he assigned to Henry James, "between the mutilating conventions of society and the integrity of the individual." His own ambiguous success was still before him as he wrote, but already he adumbrates, in the half-cracked figures he imagined for the stage, the self-designated failure who lost his nerve and rejected his talent. You do not have to concur in this judgment, only to see that it was his.

In his own view he is Benedict Arnold, the archetypal traitor. He protested too much; nonetheless, he was right. He didn't render to Caesar the things that were Caesar's. This was a crime, and in his public career he made expiation. You cannot write "of the standard in your bones without self-immolation," he said in the life of Adams, "nor is it possible to do more than point to and piously adulate the base upon which you stand—especially when the standard and the base are irreconcilable." As he entered middle age, the academy was the new base on which he chose to stand. The thing in his bones—anyway, one cherished thing— was implacably other. So he set up the terms of the problem drama which occupied the rest of his life.

Francis Fergusson, the friend from the old days on the *Hound & Horn*, thought Richard was losing his critical talent even before he got to Princeton, and perhaps this is true. But middle age, if it meant for him the eroding of youthful promise, meant also a fresh access of being. He began to spend his talent with a difference. *The Expense of Greatness*, his second critical book, shows the difference. Winding up the book, he has this to say: "The priest requires the church. . . . The lawyer requires the courts. . . . The doctor requires the hospital. . . . Serious writers are no different; for them it would seem today that the university is the only available institution, whether in the offing or at hand cannot certainly be said, except by the university itself." His last sentence reads: "I think at hand." Maybe a fateful pause ought to ensue here.

In his youth, as "an isolated personality dwelling quite entirely within myself," he was emphatic in asserting "how little I, personally, have to do with this or any other world." His isolation was morbid—and nourished the sinews of his art. He called it horrible but beneficial too, and he said to his cousin how he filled his loneliness with the creation of poetry and fiction. Accepting his loneliness, he practiced what other men preached. This was the religion of art. Like James, he preferred art to nature. The "symbols or fables" to which Adams, the man of action, grudgingly applied, quickened for him with a life of their own. His mind constructed itself primarily for a life of art. Only art could supply "all that life cannot do for itself, give it . . . the intelligence and meaning and completeness of form." Merton Densher in *The Wings of the Dove* suffered as James suffered, Richard wrote at eighteen, "and was defeated in more ways than one—including those in which, to our minds, James won." The victory was artistic as when, taking "a hint from clumsy, stupid life," you made of it "the beautiful intelligent instance." It is because such sentiments rose out of him like prayers that for Richard art was enough.

But his religion, Malcolm Cowley told him, "led to futility for the people who practiced it—to loneliness and hypochrondria for the men of genius like Joyce, and to suicide or insanity for the little fellows like Harry Crosby and Scofield Thayer." Death, Crosby thought, was the hand that opened the door to our cage. So he shot himself (as nature imitates art, in the Hotel des Artistes), first painting his toenails and tatooing the soles of his feet with a pagan sun symbol and the Christian cross. Except holiness, he wrote in his diary, "art is the only clean thing on earth." Poetry had saints, Jack Wheelwright said later, but Crosby wasn't one of them and his death was his best poem.

Scofield Thayer, with whom Richard had corresponded in the early twenties when Thayer was editing the *Dial*, spoke scornfully, like Crosby, of "that alien thing, the American public." In his tastes and sensibilities he embodied the esthete, "slender of build, swift of movement, always strikingly pale, with coal-black hair, black eyes veiled and flashing." The way his lips curled reminded a friend of Lord Byron. Like Richard he traced his lineage back to Santayana, and announced that art was the only way to national health. His self-appointed role in clearing the way was to astonish the stupid, bewilder the clever, and "whip the *crème de la crème* from the milk-pails of the Elysian Fields." This, he said, was what the *Dial* was up to. The American public took him at his word. He sank in depression and the *Dial* sank with him. A few months after it died, Harry Crosby killed himself—a fortuitous connection, but it makes a coherence.

Maybe Crosby and Thayer were only weeds or wildflowers and couldn't survive the heat of the day. But even Joyce, the high priest of the religion of art, had paid the price in bread and laughter for his priesthood. He had achieved genius, Cowley agreed, "but there was something about the genius as cold as the touch at parting of his long, smooth, cold, wet-marble fingers." After all, the hermetic life brought you on misery. Cowley said to Richard, "That path I think is closed." There were "many paths still open," however.

To Richard, debating which way to go, it seemed clear that you had either to abandon all hope of prestige, like Joyce or Melville before him, or become an entertainer like Twain. One of the most distinguished poets of his acquaintance had "never in thirty odd years of writing earned more than three thousand in a year." A distinguished novelist he knew was only able to live with the aid of a Guggenheim, and applied subsequently to teach freshman composition at Harvard. Of Richard's three most distinguished painter friends—Ben Shahn and Waldo Peirce are two of them— "one has private means but has never sold more than enough to pay his overhead as a painter, one lived—or starved—on about six dollars a week, and the third told me that he had not paid an income tax for six years."

But it wasn't poverty alone that made him take thought. Success was perilous, too. "Our saddest stories," said his friend, the poet Winfield Scott, "are biographies of 20th Century American writers." He pointed to Thomas Wolfe, Hart Crane, Vachel Lindsay, Fitzgerald, O'Neill, Sinclair Lewis, Edna Millay, and Hemingway's story "when we know it." To say what had gone wrong, you needed "a combination of psychologist, sociologist, literary historian and critic, as well as an expert in alcoholism." Richard had no answers, only questions. He asked himself why so many "eager young talents" had turned "abortive and sterile," or why, if they "succeeded in keeping their talent alive into middle age [they] either reduced their standards, fell silent, became eccentric, or went abroad." Perhaps the writer carried with him the seeds of his own destruction. Years before, coming for the first time on the idea of hubris, he had written of that insolence of spirit which possesses men of the world who turn away from the world. "Hubris is a happy quality for the gods, but for men fatal; yet man goes but a little way in the ideal world before being possessed by it—and in the end overwhelmed by it, or on account of it; for it is one of the characters of such greatness—of all greatness maybe—that it is the most easily destroyed."

His faithful disciple John Berryman instructed him how this was so. Berryman had followed Richard's lead ever since discovering "the merits of this prophet" in back numbers of the *Hound & Horn*. Like Crosby, he had nothing to say to the man in the street. Unlike Crosby he was a genuine poet, and his quality aggravated his remoteness and despair. "Unfortunately," he wrote, "everything good in the end is highbrow." Deploring this truth, he refused to let it go. The Book Review editor of the *New York Times* ought to aim, he said, at "the instruction, serious entertainment and elevation" of his audience, "rather than a flaccid catering to it." This wasn't meant for a joke. But the popular boys, as he called them, laughed him out of countenance, and like Scofield Thayer he lapsed in depression. "There is no one at all he won't blow up with," Delmore Schwartz wrote to Richard. He didn't "mean to be personal," only—as he said himself in one of his poems—he was "half mad with hope . . . in love with life," not least as it might be. This love affair drove him on shipwreck.

The problem for the serious writer, Richard said, was to steer successfully between that rock which was the audience—always it wanted less than the writer could provide—and the rock of institutions "which wanted commitments of him he could not make." So the problem, recalling *Heartbreak House*, was navigation. There was another way to put this. Within the sensibility of every artist, he wrote in his journal, license and discipline maintain an uneasy but vital equilibrium. License provokes to full response, discipline looks insistently to bring this response within bounds. So discipline meant the creating of form. Richard understood how form becomes a carapace—always he kept before him the example of Gilbert Osmond in James's *Portrait of a Lady*—and how the emotionally stunted man used his intelligence "predominantly to prevent the full response." To achieve this response, you had to reject "the partial choice of the defensive intelligence." He knew in his marrow how steep a price you paid for the rejection: "The experience of it issues in vertigo." But no alternative offered for the man who stood for life against death. To himself, he wrote: "I will keep my vertigo."

In a different context he envisaged a state of war "between the forces of intelligence and the forces of violence, and he saw how, in this internecine war, "if either side kills itself the other is murdered." Survival needed a balance of forces. "A better word for balance would be *homeostasis*" (he is remembering a favorite text of his young manhood, W. B. Cannon's

Wisdom of the Body), defined as "the critical maintenance of precarious bodily states." For more than half his life, this critical maintenance persisted. He got older, however, and one side of him poached on the other. He wondered if "contemporary artists in any probable society [could] permit themselves the pride, or the waste, as the case may be, of the total role of artist?" As the forties began, a negative answer seemed indicated. The New Critical mode, his one greatest achievement, showed as illusory now. "It is plain," he wrote, "that we never do in fact understand literature solely by literary means."

The self-doubt in which he lingered was powerfully fueled when *The Expense of Greatness* received a "savage and mendacious" review in the *New Republic*. The reviewer—"a man I had supposed a friend"—was Harry Levin, a young Harvard professor and a pioneering student of Joyce. Levin, who sneered at Richard for his critical myopia—"Mr. Blackmur has a dictionary," etc.—was "blind," said Delmore Schwartz, "to the grandest and plainest virtues of Joyce." Not understanding what Joyce was doing, he begged the important questions "with inexhaustible ingenuity and foolishness." Delmore was an adept for whom Joyce presented life in all its fabulous vitality, and donnish appreciators who fingered his sacred book like a piece of Limoges provoked him to sardonic amusement. Proposing a masquerade party in honor of Henry James, he suggested that Levin appear as Gilbert Osmond.

But Levin was blind also to Richard's integrity, as in asserting to Edmund Wilson that influence had been used to prevent publication of the review. "Wilson did not of course believe that," and wanted Richard to compose a formal reply. This he wouldn't do. Levin was welcome to his opinion, "even, if he likes, in smart-alec language." The gratuitous malice wounded him, however. Levin, he wrote to Jay Laughlin, appears to have distorted his view of me out of all possible sense of friendship, or, as it seems to me, probity." There was the imputation that Richard, in the essay on T. E. Lawrence, had never read Lawrence's *The Mint*. But Levin knew, Richard said, "from conversations with me," that this wasn't so. He knew also that to quote from the book was forbidden. Richard felt at a loss to explain the attack, which seemed "to have been quite deliberate." George Anthony had an explanation. He saw Richard's lack of method, also his lack of formal degrees, as a gauntlet thrown down before the academic critic. Richard, said Rob Darrell, liked to compose with his feet up on a sofa, "thinking for long intervals before he wrote by hand a sentence or two." Meanwhile "my typewriter was going at full speed." How the honors divided between them was, however, a sobering experience for Rob. This negligent performance (that was what it looked like) had produced *The Expense of Greatness*. What did that say to Harry Levin, whose Teutonic work habits were a source of amused speculation?

But Richard wasn't heartened by this comparison between them. "He really felt the knife," George Anthony said, and he wrote in the same anguished letter to his cousin how "the game of literature is mostly shit; the shit of deliberate misunderstanding, the shit of ill-will, the shit of patronage, and the worst shit of intellectual snobbery." Hemingway was just then the fashionable target, and Richard grimaced at the spite and envy and "tear the man down shit" he heard whenever he encountered a literary gent. "There is a doctor in NY (Park Avenue) who does literary people, he is going to do Hemingway; he is also Stark Young's doctor." This was the author of *So Red the Rose*. Young positively got an erection, Richard said, "in anticipation of hearing that Hemingway is actually impotent."

When he looked at himself, his revulsion grew higher. Closing in on forty, he felt increasingly alone. His marriage to Helen still had years to run, but he knew it for a failure. The "horror of positive boredom" weighed upon him, and he regretted in himself "the inability to act or feel with satisfaction." This regret bred others. Old friends were falling away. Lewis MacKay was dead. Paul Rowe, like Murray Borish, "is beyond us," Richard wrote to George Anthony, "these being two of my continuing regrets and griefs." Among the friends of the thirties, Delmore had showed more promise than any. But his marriage, like Richard's, was heading for the rocks, and his career, begun so brilliantly, seemed to hang in the balance. Living alone in Cambridge in the house on Ellery Street, he wrote plaintively to Richard how the ghosts of friends dead and living came to visit him at night. They were Richard's friends, too.

Tessa and Elizabeth, when they were girls, had lived just down the block in the old house littered with mementoes of their father, the composer. Henry Gilbert had been dead for twelve years. "Here many a time," Delmore remembered, "Tessa ate [and drank] with inimitable zest," and here she won her famous wager, sitting bare-bottomed for five minutes, maybe more, on the cake of ice they had ordered in for the drinks. On the ice, you could see the smooth print of her bottom. "Here we saw for the last time in this difficult and beautiful life Harry Zimmerman and Jack Wheelwright." Zimmerman—Joe Zilch, who taught Helen and Tessa— had died of brain disease at the beginning of the forties. A drunken driver did for Wheelwright in the same year. More regrets and griefs. Wheelwright lived, said Matthew Josephson, "moved about, wrote, and pursued his fantasies with an air of freedom and independence that you do not often find in men." His friends had supposed he would be holding forth forever.

"Here the stairway must be entitled Nella Falls," Delmore thought, remembering Nela Walcott and her broken tail feathers and her elegant parties. Who could forget the parties? Nela hinted over cocktails at the dinner to come, but the cocktails dragged on and the soufflé rose and fell or she forgot to take the food from the freezer. You could eat what Nela served with a teaspoon. She might have had her pick of all the men, when she was young. But Nela married John Walcott, and they went at each other like Kilkenny cats. This didn't say they weren't happy. John wrote novels, like Richard, but somehow for him things never got started and when he died his dreadful, inconsequent death, getting out of the car to change a tire in the rain, his youthful promise died with him, and John Walcott was another ghost.

Some men lived to write their own obsequies, and perhaps this was worse. Delmore didn't put it that way in his letter; he spoke of the others who lived. "Here Haskett wooed Libby fast as light." She was Richard's old flame and Harry Zimmerman's widow, and he was Haskett Derby from the fancy Salem family—"the kind of guy," Tessa said, "who'd sit down on a cow chip and laugh his head off at the fool thing he'd done and the fool that he was." Tessa brought them together, as she had brought Richard and Helen together. "I thought I'd accomplished something wonderful," she said. "But he complained about her, that she drank too much, and she complained about him, that he was always visiting his mother," and that was the end of their marriage.

The poet Win Scott made a bad marriage, too, but failure seemed the element he lived in. He proposed this conclusion himself. "In speech, in love," he asked rhetorically, "in what have I not failed." When Richard knew him first, he liked to talk about the bomb he had packed in the mail. Handle with care! he was saying. That was only poetry, though, and the bomb turned out a damp squib in the end. "Here," said Delmore, "Winfield Scott was much drunker than anyone I have ever seen." Drinking was one problem and impotence another, but neither got at the heart of Win Scott's dilemma. Like Delmore, whose age he was, this friend waited hopelessly on the American Dream. He loved New England and her poets, and in his own poetry he sought to do them justice. But "thirty wakes me," he wrote, "and what have I done?"

Delmore at thirty had the world at his feet. But license gained on discipline, and an acute observer could see how the shifting balance assured the destruction of both. Censorious or compassionate friends laid the destructive process to alcohol or nembutal. Richard made a better diagnostician. He said how "almost anything would do to start a poem" for Delmore, and almost anything "would serve to end what had been casually begun." In his own notorious difficulty as a writer, constrained and verging on impotence, he felt the difference between them, and from the difference he drew a moral. Delmore's apparent freedom was licentious. Even the early and prodigious success, *In Dreams Begin Responsibilities*, showed how this facile writer "had too little difficulty with his subject matter ever to find out either the strength or the impasse . . . which lay within it." Delmore wrote in *Genesis*, where the falling off begins:

> Playing with emotion is playing with water,
> a looseness quintessential which corrupts.

So he defined his peculiar corruption. Sometimes discipline corrupts more efficiently than looseness, and this was the corruption which beckoned for Richard.

From the years of vagabondage he knew how "the activity of the artist is full of guile" and how, preying on society in the service of his art, "he is held an outlander, an outsider, indeed the alien himself." He took pride in what he knew, and rehearsed Eliot's dictum that "anyone who has ever been visited by the Muse is thenceforth haunted." But the high tone he adopted made enemies. Hostile readers like Granville Hicks and Louis Zukofsky said he was betraying a trust. He met the accusation head on: "And so I was and am and shall. Trusts imposed on me merely by sincerity and passion ought to be betrayed just so soon as the way is found: in the hope, no doubt, that one or more may be found that cannot be betrayed. I have my own trust to keep." So he accepted, perhaps with a touch of vainglory, "the prison of the independent mind."

But the man who said *Non serviam* was guilty also of "the heresy of the independent mind." The more he wrote, Richard acknowledged, the greater the heresy became. Envy informed it, an insistence on the bewilderment behind all coherent thought, concurrently "the wish to destroy: to be oneself, in the midst of thought, dead." He was the grandson of that Reverend Palmer who went out upon the roads in the service of society, and defiant pride in him was tempered by shame. As Delmore enfranchised his outlandish self, Richard in the forties called it in question. "In the midst of the licentious exploration stares, stands, shines the star of discipline." This star grew brighter.

At thirty-five, Richard said he "almost" wanted "to pass beyond my scope and see what I can do with a piece—political or religious, certainly moral in its plexus,—about the sensibility of this age." Five years later he said to John Marshall that a report he had written for the Rockefeller Foundation "wants to be more evangelical than I myself want it to be." What he wanted was ambiguous, also what he got. Recalling his mother's father and grandfather, he confessed that "some devil of clerical ancestry thrives in the hollows of my bones." He feared this devil and cherished it, too.

The clerical devil got its chance when Richard went to Princeton. For a long time, he denied it a hearing. He said to Zabel at *Poetry* that teaching was "intolerable," at best "a crippling sort of work." But sustenance "of the money-colour" was always on his mind, and when Horace Gregory took a job at Sarah Lawrence, he allowed himself second thoughts. Teaching, Gregory insisted, wasn't all that bad—though he confessed that if he were "in your place (without children, without immediate and pressing responsibilities)," he would keep on the outside himself. "The only great loss is loss of time and there is a vague hope that somehow one is actually talking to a generation better than one's own." This hope spoke to Richard where he lived. Also, like Gregory, he was sick of his own generation, flabby expatriates or delighted swimmers in the destructive element who confused sex with Bohemianism, then with metaphysics, the machine age, and Marx. So he undertook "a deliberate and extensive campaign after the Sarah Lawrence Job and the Lesser Hell of life in New York." His campaign misfired, though—"thank God for that," said Genevieve Taggard, a disgruntled member of the English faculty at Sarah Lawrence—and he decided after all that he was better off on his own. Three years later, when his benevolent friend Moe at the Guggenheim Foundation put his name in for a job at Pomona College, he said he was grateful but "primarily a writer." It was "worth some expense of security, etc., to maintain that primary character."

On the other hand Ivor Richards, a "peripatetic pedagogue," had come to terms with the academy and not forfeited his character. I. A. Richards looked like a pedagogue and belied what he looked like. His hair was peculiar and you thought it should be long where it was shaggy-short. From behind you mistook him for a half-plucked black hen, but a gingerly hen who "gives the appearance that he is somebody else about whom he must be very careful." This wasn't from self-importance. He liked to joke, he liked to drink, and no carapace covered Ivor Richards. One pet subject was lobster fishing, another was the diabolism of Aleister Crowley. Serious subjects like love or the soul, the bane of the merely defensive intelligence, popped into his everyday speech. "Then all of a sudden he will want to read a poem." He didn't caress it either, like a piece of Limoges.

He seemed, Richard said, "to get more out of poetry, like it more, and demand more of it, than anybody I ever met." Poetry was always on the verge with him. Richard thought of this friend when he put the looming question: "Can contemporary artists deliberately ally themselves with existing institutions . . . ?"

Other friends had entered the academy, too. Foster Damon had gone to Brown and Allen Tate to Princeton. Francis Fergusson was teaching at Bennington College, and Richard wondered if a place might be found for him there. An opening in modern poetry and fiction stimulated him to go up for an interview, but the professors wanted him to talk about beauty and truth and he got on his high horse and Helen got on hers—she was there to be inspected by the faculty wives—and that was that. He said he had no intention anyway of holding down a regular job, and when Frank Morley, his editor at Harcourt, pushed him at Princeton, he agreed to go along only out of "the necessity to get the minimum living." Then in June 1940 the offer from Princeton actually came through, and in fear and eagerness he took it. The pay was $2,200—raised $700 at Allen Tate's insistence—and this meant three squares a day. "Being paid will save my skin," Richard wrote to Jay Laughlin. Tate was Richard's passport to the academic world. He had joined the Princeton faculty only the year before to direct a new program in Creative Arts. This job demanded more than Allen had expected, and soon he was casting about for an assistant. Philip Horton was his first choice, but Philip had promised to teach English A for Theodore Morrison at Harvard. He suggested his impecunious friend Richard Blackmur. So the thing was done. Tomorrow, however, Richard was sure to move on.

"The whole thing is an adventure for me," he wrote to Tate, and he looked forward to "using a different talent, or an old talent in a different way." He had hardly got settled in his new home when a letter arrived from Austin Warren. Austin was Dr. Warren, a Princeton Ph.D., and didn't approve of Richard the self-educated man. He wrote kindly, however: "Few appointments can have given such universal satisfaction to those who wish American letters well as yours." He concluded: "I hope that you will enjoy teaching—and that you won't too much enjoy it." There was plenty of enjoyment in the years to come. On a negative view, it dramatizes for Richard "the treason of the intellectuals." But everything depends on point of view. For example: coming down from his ivory tower, said a skeptical critic, Richard engaged "in a work of public persuasion, evangelical, almost apocalyptic." This engagement explains the rediverting, or you can say the drying up, of his talent. The apocalyptic strain by which you know him in age doesn't eventuate in prophecy. His last books are fuliginous, much smoke mingling with a little fire. In the end he stood before his public like a humor character whose bias ran all one way, not funny but indurated: R. P. Blackmur the Great Man or Old Pretender.

This reading of the last years comprehends a piece of the truth. A few months before he died, Richard wrote to a former student: "In dreams we lose our responsibilities." So much for Delmore and the hegemony of license. But the waning of license put period to his own art as well. In his brief efflorescence as good poet and absolute critic he calls to mind his slightly older contemporaries, Hemingway, Faulkner, and Fitzgerald—"extraordinary persons," Cowley wrote of them, "but they lacked the capacity for renewed growth after middle age." Having done their best work early, "they had no second careers."

Richard resembles these writers of the Lost Generation but differs from them profoundly, and in the difference resides his identity. His second career is like a second life. The "total role of artist" was too much or too little. But to the friends who loved him, not least to his admiring students —there weren't a whole lot of them, he wasn't Mr. Chips, but there were enough—he came to represent a hero of our time who struggled with the devil and gave the devil his due. He did this until he died. Only what engaged him wasn't fiction any longer, but life.

CHAPTER SEVEN

The Pedagogue of Sensibility

A S LONG AS the weather permitted in the fall, and long after
Richard had gone back to Princeton, Helen stayed on in Maine. He was
just beginning his second year of teaching when she wrote to ask, satiri-
cally, what had become of his girls. She said he could hardly "keep up a
discreet silence forever." Maybe Richard had nothing to tell her. Helen's
innuendoes tickled his vanity, though. Like an adolescent he was sprout-
ing fresh hairs, and she wondered what they symbolized: "the rise of some
new era in your development perhaps—the hairy ape that has hitherto
been hiding under a bushel." Helen liked the hairy ape but not the Princeton professor. About the professor she said in utter desperation: "He just
talks and talks and talks." She kept after Richard to throw up his new job
"and all jobs for good" and come down to Harrington for nine months of
the year. He said he didn't "dare take the risk."

Access to Princeton gave him greater freedom than he had ever known.
The passionate grasp at reality that had enlivened his young manhood was
reduced at last, he said, to "nails in the palm or even fingers in air." Like
the great authors he most admired, like Aristotle or Dante or Shakespeare
or Joyce, he needed an institution to see through corruption darkly. (His
own greatness breathes in the ambiguous way he put it.) Princeton gave
him what he needed. He knew that the institution might smother as often
as it inspired. Knowing this, perhaps he knew that Princeton restricted his
freedom. Einstein, the most celebrated resident of Princeton in 1940,
thought that the people who defined society there enjoyed "even less
freedom than their counterparts in Europe." But they seemed "unaware of
this restriction since their way of life tends to inhibit personality development from childhood."

The inhibiting impressed the poor man with his poverty. This became a
moral event. On the affluent man, it worked in subtler ways. Edmund

Wilson, '16, reflecting on the death of his classmate John Peale Bishop and his near-classmate Scott Fitzgerald, concluded that "Princeton did not serve them very well." His wife Mary McCarthy (she "has had considerable opportunity to observe the men from the various colleges," Wilson said) thought that "Princeton didn't give them quite moral principle enough to be writers." What it gave was "too much respect for money and country house social prestige." Wilson saw "both Scott and John" as having fallen "victim to this."

On the face of it, Richard made an unlikely victim. Nursing his martini on the terrace of the Princeton Inn and watching the ducks on the impossible green of the golf course, he didn't feel like a millionaire among the millionaires; he felt like the Underground Man. From his first days in Princeton, however, you can see how this feeling blurs and changes in him. Alienation described him, but only on one side. It didn't preclude the need for acceptance. "He liked Princeton too much," said Mike Keeley, who helped Richard out in the Creative Writing Program. "Most people who come to Princeton like it too much." Richard was only two years or so into his new career when he told Delmore proudly that he had a fair chance of being kept on. The "academic assurances" by which he set store meant little to his friend, and Delmore implored him not to "permit yourself to be defeated by your handsome minor successes." That was New York City speaking, however.

From the perspective of Princeton, Richard's successes didn't figure as minor. Princeton, as they said, was the Best Old Place of All, not just the same as other places, indifferent to the business they transacted, and remote—unlike Yale and Harvard—from the life of the pullulating cities. "The college town stood apart from the metropolis and was content to keep its distance," said Richard's friend Robert Fitzgerald. "Of what is sometimes meant by intellectual life—the Bohemianism of the cities and the shiver of the advanced in art and thought—of this Princeton seemed curious but not envious." Young wives in Princeton, when they went shopping, wore tennis clothes and riding clothes. They wore ribbons in their hair. The older women were hard-faced but handsome, and as a rule more impressive than the men. Though Princeton was a man's town, the women made the better soldiers. Princeton men were ruddy-tanned and well set up like Tom Buchanan, the greatest end who ever came out of New Haven (a surrogate for Princeton). They smoked pipes and wore tweeds, not always of the newest but always of the best. "It doesn't matter what you wear here," said Richard's colleague Ted Hubler, "so long as it was good once." Eavesdropping on these couples, as at the movies in Palmer Square, you found you knew everybody of whom they were speaking.

Only a few dozen people lived in Princeton, or so it seemed, and they all went to the same parties.

In the closed community to which Richard came, right and wrong were calibrated precisely. Your antecedents were right or wrong, and how you reached for the check or let the other fellow do it, the way you furled your umbrella. A rebellious undergraduate in Fitzgerald's first novel, decrying the "snobbishness of this corner of the world," makes up his mind to go elsewhere. He can't do it, though, anyway not in spirit. "Wherever you go now," the hero assures him, "you'll always unconsciously apply these standards of 'having it' or 'lacking it.'" For better or worse the malcontent has been stamped: he is a Princeton man.

The world outside constituted an extension of the little world of Princeton, like Steinberg's map of America seen from the point of view of New York, and the greater world was calibrated, too. Chicago you approved "for a certain verve that transcended its loud accent." However, Chicago was a Yale town. In Baltimore, on the other hand, Princeton was at home. Baltimore was Southern. Princeton was and still is partly Southern. This indigenous character appealed to the self-made aristocrat in Richard. But the snob and great panjandrum was a democrat too, and it irked him that the hotels, "both of which, through a holding company, the University owns," discriminated systematically against Indians, Burmese, "and such like." When "a very distinguished man whom the Rockefellers were sending here for a week . . . a Mr. Bose" who had come to town principally to see him, was turned away by the Princeton Inn and the Nassau Tavern because of his color, Richard wrote angrily to the State Department. "Mr. Bose did not stay a week. He stayed one hour with me and returned to New York quite legitimately outraged, as I myself also was."

Mr. Bose and such like would fare better today. But history, as Richard discovered, dies hard. The honor roll in Nassau Hall, on which were inscribed the names of young men of the College who fell in the Civil War *pro patria mori*, divided almost equally between North and South. Southern gentlemen coming north to the College of New Jersey brought their body servants with them. The descendants of these manumitted slaves formed a distinct community around Witherspoon Street, below campus. They identified with Princeton and tended to look askance at the black population of Trenton. Not that Princeton had been hospitable to them. In his tenure as President of Princeton, Woodrow Wilson, a lover of man in the mass, excluded the black man from his solicitude. So did his successors until the other day. Only with World War II and the arrival on campus of naval officer candidates did the color bar begin to go down. After the war three former black cadets applied successfully for regular admission—the first of their race to do so. "Not so," said Willard Thorp, Chairman of the English Department in Richard's time. "There was a Negro here in the days of President Witherspoon." This went back awhile. "Studied with the President. Lived in his house. Fellow from North Carolina named Chavez. Same name as the chap who grows grapes."

Richard the rare bird was like this fellow Chavez. This made him an object of invidious compassion. A faculty wife he knew liked to tell how the Princeton alumnus who lived down the street had asked about her husband's class—not the class he taught, but with which he had graduated from Princeton. "Oliver didn't go to Princeton," Richard's friend said. "I'm sorry," the alumnus said. Getting admitted to Princeton was a process almost Byzantine in its complexities, and the career didn't always belong to the talents. Until the 1920s, admissions was the purview of the Old Boys. You rang up Professor X, who took it from there. Then Radcliffe Heermance—of "our" Department, said Willard Thorp—initiated in formal ways the scrutinizing of credentials. The definition of the latter remained mysterious. The director put great stock in the personal photograph. "Would I wish to room with this young man?" he asked himself. If the answer were negative, the application fell from sight. Howie Stepp, who served as assistant to Heermance, remembered a recruiting trip beyond the Hudson River. Elated at having found an outstanding high-school prospect—a Merit scholar, a debater, large, prepossessing, and captain of the football team—Howie reported back to the chief. "Splendid!" said Heermance. "What is his name?" "Sienkiewicz," Howie said. "What a pity," the director said.

Likely as not, Richard's colleagues were graduates of Princeton. At the annual Pee-rade in the first days of summer, they put on funny costumes and the whole town wore the air of a college reunion. These festive occasions were reserved to the initiate. Town and gown rejoiced in this, as in the annual Bicker or fraternity rush which determined admission to the eating clubs on Prospect Street. All thirteen clubs were good, but some were better than others. Princeton undergraduates knew what it meant to be tapped by Ivy, "detached and breathlessly aristocratic," or Cottage, "an impressive mélange of brilliant adventurers and well-dressed philanderers," or Tiger Inn, "broad-shouldered and athletic." If you were the type of the noncommittal man, you got elected as a sophomore to one of these ranking clubs. After that, said Fitzgerald, you were sewed up in a bag for the rest of your college career, with luck for the rest of your life. Not everyone was lucky, otherwise the club had no reason for being. Edmund Wilson was distressed when Arthur Mizener acknowledged "his permanently gnawing chagrin at not having made the right kind of club."

Richard also detested all forms of discrimination that were not discriminations in talent. He was, however, an outsider at Princeton, and what he thought didn't signify. This rankled. Early letters dwell gloomily on his unhappiness. He felt like a transient set down in a hotel, and more than once he complained of "Princeton's flat and windless lands." Princeton was "lazy and good-looking and aristocratic," rather like a spring day. Harvard by contrast seemed sort of indoors. Fitzgerald made this contrast tell for Princeton. To Richard, however, the move from New England was like another fall of man. In the newly acquired beach wagon which he didn't drive himself—he had hallucinations of things appearing in the road and coming at him head on—he sat morosely next to Helen at the wheel. They drove south on U.S. 1 through the most poisonous landscape in America—past Brother Moscato's dump and the evil-smelling refineries outside Elizabeth and the red rust of suburbia that ran all the way to Norfolk. Just before they got to the Princeton traffic circle, they could see on their right hand the spires of the university dominated by Cleveland Tower—Goon Castle, the undergraduates called it. The disjunction seemed meditated, like a work of art—first the industrial wasteland, then this chimerical thing.

For Richard's student Frederick Buechner, the chimera loomed visibly. Buechner's heroine in the novel, *A Long Day's Dying*, has a rendezvous in Princeton. She is going to meet Professor Whitewall (né Blackmur). Leaving the highway she takes a smaller road that leads down a hill, across a bridge, then up another hill to the college town a few miles away. "As she crossed the bridge a break in the trees revealed a glimpse of pseudo-gothic towers flat against the bright sky." Greeting these towers, you think (as you are meant to) of Oxford and Cambridge, also of Disney World where the façades are made of plywood and where, if you are tall enough, your eye travels beyond the sight line. The "rich illusion"—Fitzgerald's phrase—cast an uncanny spell. Buechner wrote about it from the skeptical side. Never in their lives, his classmates were told, would they have it so good again. It was hard for them to credit this, even harder to suppose that the great writers they read in class had a vision of blackness beyond the "lovely, green place out here." They were victims of disease and didn't know it—"the lovely, giddy, green disease of this . . . sweet and dangerous hospital that nobody wants to leave—ever."

Fitzgerald had his different view of Princeton, also partial. "Far down the shadowy line of University Place," his undergraduate hero saw a white-clad phalanx breaking the gloom. Young men who form a ghostly procession—they have walked arm in arm through the deep blue nights with Aaron Burr and Light-Horse Harry Lee—are marching rhythmically up the street in their white shirts and white trousers. Their arms are linked, their heads are thrown back, and they are singing:

> Going back—going back,
> Going—back—to—Nas—sau—Hall,
> Going back—going back,
> To the Best—Old—Place—of—All.

At the end of the novel, Amory Blaine—he has left Princeton long since, but found nothing half so good in the world outside the invisible walls—is going back himself. His story recapitulates the sojourn in the desert of the Chosen People.

Richard wasn't going back, and on pain of death he couldn't sing the college songs. Einstein's "quaint and ceremonious village" seemed an improbable oasis to him. He might have dropped in on Princeton from another planet. That was what his urbane colleagues supposed. So he vexed them by playing the role of "small-town feller." He told them how, if you meant to grow strawberries, you had to prepare a sandy soil. (He got angry when they tried to tell him.) At the pretension of his colleagues, he poked merciless fun. To Allen Tate he said how it pleased him to measure their minds with an inch rule. The downstairs apartment on Linden Lane, north of Nassau Street, which Tate had hunted up for him, set his teeth on edge. Chambers Street in Boston was a palace to this. Nights he lay awake listening to the violent sexual antics of the mathematician who lived upstairs. He worked off his irritation by scandalizing friends with accounts of his own sexual antics.

Even in his own place he was never less than lonely, and when Conrad Aiken wrote to urge "a little beano with such as K. Burke," he jumped at the chance. Burke had mellowed personally and matured intellectually "since I last saw him," Richard said. The amiable quarrel they kept going between them dated back to the days "when all the Jersey cows were blue," and Richard the young man was feeding on "the cyanotic blue" of Santayana. They were united, said Burke, by a genuine bond, having "worked out educational routines for ourselves, largely sans the direct aid of schools." Now, as their academic careers were getting started, each was stigmatized by "the same bar sinister." Richard's students were alert to this distinguishing mark. If he thought it degrading, that wasn't what they thought. But they feared for "poor Blackmur" when the Princeton Bicentennial celebration came round "and all the faculty were to march in their academic robes with their gold tassels and their different colored hoods." So they got him a black robe and sewed it "all over with those frilled-out paper sleeves you put on the ends of lamb chops." Not everybody thought this amusing. "As could be expected," said one of the students, Richard offended his senior colleagues by coming on without benefit of formal credentials. The offense bit more deeply because "he knew ten times as much as all of them put together." Malcolm Cowley resembled him to Kenneth Burke and Ramon Guthrie "among leading academics of the post World War I period who never went to college or dropped out of college." All three, Cowley said, "had more learning, were sounder scholars, than any of their rival Ph.D.'s."

Burke, unlike Richard, wore this learning easily. "He has the most agile and resourceful mind I ever met in conversation," Richard reported. It was Kenneth's agreeable notion "that he and I should spend our lives controverting each other in public." But Burke was holed up in the mountains of north Jersey and Richard lacked the wherewithal to travel. He said he wished to Christ people didn't live so far apart. "But they do." The problem, as Aiken put it, was "how to combine earnings with a Good Life (beano plus)." It didn't appear tractable to Richard. His earnings were piddling—this remained true for all the years he lived in Princeton—and his Scotch soul revolted at the expense. "I have never paid so much for mere living," he complained to Jay Laughlin, nor "gotten so little out of it as here."

Mostly, his colleagues gave him a wide berth. Students said how Willard Thorp "in his ornate tweeds" turned a dead eye on Richard and how Larry Thompson, the biographer of Frost, tried to carry a white flag between them. But his horse kept getting stuck as he went back and forth, and altogether it wasn't an auspicious beginning. Meeting with the colleagues, Richard pulled a long face. (Helen's was longer.) Sam Howell had met the Blackmurs at parties in Cambridge when he was a young instructor at Harvard, and he said to Charlotte how nice it would be to have the two of them over for dinner. But this, Sam discovered, was one couple on whom you practiced all your social wiles in vain. Richard and Helen didn't have a word to spare, and talk around the table dwindled, then died, and it was hard to say who was happier when the front door closed behind them.

The older men in the department thought Richard's presence at Princeton absurd, and were horrified to discover "a Blackmur cult" springing up around them. They warned their students to keep away, saying with truth how the supremely well-educated man was in many things illiterate (but not, said Mike Keeley, "in the things that really counted"). To Robert K. Root, Richard walking on Cannon Green below his windows in Nassau Hall seemed a desecration. Friends were alarmed when this eminent Chaucer scholar, having moved from Department Chairman to Dean of the Faculty, did his best to expel the offending presence. In the end, poetic justice was vindicated, though, and Root died a scholar's death at the MLA convention, falling into the potted palms in the lobby of his hotel.

The cold shoulder the mandarins turned on the new arrival wasn't meant personally. They turned it on all mavericks of whatever persuasion —on anyone, said Keeley, "who was a writer rather than a scholar." For Robert Fitzgerald, Princeton "was the cross-rip between the life of the imagination and the life of scholarship." These people who set up for critics "think they can tell us how to teach literature; but we know how to teach literature," one of Princeton's elder professors had said. This angry discrimination induced paranoia in Richard, and the paranoia grew as he himself grew in eminence and—outwardly—in poise. When in later years a young and admiring colleague asked to sit in on his graduate seminar in Dante, Montaigne, and Pascal, Richard peppered the room with impossibly learned questions. What business did he have with these three pearls of Romania? The answer was implicit in the way he paraded his knowledge of Romance language and history. He "had it in mind," his embarrassed auditor decided, "that I was a spy sent over . . . to document his philological inadequacies." So Richard honed his credentials fine and then finer.

"The Princeton people hated him"—that was Irving Howe's sense. But Princeton wasn't a monolith and Richard wasn't an ingratiating man. Group activities revolted him, and when he taught summers at the Cummington School he said how, "like most group things," they "betrayed the abyss." With the young writers-in-embryo who came to Cummington hoping to hear him, he showed something less than the patience of Job. "I fear I hurt the feelings of some of the less talented infants," he said. Colleagues walked warily when Richard was by. When he had enough to drink, he fixed you with an eye more glittering than twinkling. Early days in Princeton, before the professorial image took hold, he became the hairy ape. Eileen Simpson remembered how, one New Year's Eve, he stripped to the waist and danced with a chair, and how a colleague's wife felt herself threatened with bodily harm when he held the chair over her head. He didn't mean any harm. His idea of fun—recalling a favorite expression of his—was getting four seas over your water lines. To his colleagues, it seemed a doubtful idea.

He had his friends in town and in other departments, however—Borgerhoff in Romance Languages and Harold Stein in Politics, the composer Edward Cone—and he passed endless hours drinking coffee in the Balt or the library lunch room and gossiping with cronies like Mike Oates and Frisco Godolphin. Delmore was still a friend, and Richard nailed him

whenever Delmore was "passing this way." They argued Socialist politics
and they drank old fashioneds well into the night, getting to that state
"which afflicts me," Richard said, "of rhyming ad lib." The trouble was that
neither could remember what rhymed. For a while Scott Buchanan and
Stringfellow Barr—they had founded an experimental college in An-
napolis—were glad to keep Richard company. There weren't many academics about whom Winkie Barr would have said the same—a nice
reverting on the outsider of Richard's own contempt for the academy.
Sundays he went canoeing with John and Eileen Berryman, or Stow Persons the historian, and Dorothy Persons who ran the library at the Institute for Advanced Study. One Easter weekend he and Helen and the
Persons drove south to the Blue Ridge and over the Skyline Drive in
Virginia. Stow Persons remembered how Richard brushed his teeth with
Myers's Rum on Easter Sunday, then finished off the bottle.

With these friends he fumed in private. In public he conveyed his eager
sense of professional obligation. He wrote Heep-ish letters to the Department Chairman. Sometimes he redeemed them. One handwritten letter
being hopelessly blotted, he said how in his haste he had spilled a glass of
milk. Some of his colleagues "were just acute enough to know" that he
was putting them on. "His very existence on the same campus" challenged
their existence. He was the artist as teacher whose force of mind converted to action and attracted or compelled other action. Words were a form
of such action, he said, and the man of letters had that form in his charge.
What did this say to the pedagogue whose business was vending inert information?

"Old bald heads" was Richard's derisory phrase (after Yeats) for the
scholars in whose company he found himself at Princeton. In the early
years, he hid himself from them. The Creative Arts Program, "quite separate from the English department," was a privileged sanctuary. Christian
Gauss—he was Dean of the College and had conducted the interview
which brought Richard to Princeton—had established the program to
dramatize his own personal commitment to the arts. He wanted, said Richard later in a deeply felt tribute to this friend, "to put the creation of arts
and letters officially on the same footing as the study of their history."
This made him an eccentric figure in the academic community a half
century ago. His reading of the literature of his time epitomized the Old
Guard against whom the moderns had had to rebel—the "sewage" of
Aldous Huxley, that kind of thing. Gauss was aware, however, that he
represented "not a doctrine of life but the condition of living," and his
understanding of the human condition took rise from awareness of his

own hidden excesses. "He had the remote warm weariness of long intimacy with the incurable unseemliness of human beings." Richard's sentence does duty for them both, and that is often true of the character of either man as given by friends. "He was a semi-outsider, he had the imagination to see and the warmth to care about the way a young man of literary inclinations but outside the academy felt. . . . No one else in Princeton," Irving Howe wrote of Richard, "showed any such feeling."

Richard saluted in the Dean his modesty and compassion, also his certainty in decision. You have the feeling that his own incertitude plays into his admiration for the energetic man. Gauss was what he wanted to be. But certainty in Gauss was tempered, it was fortified too, as it rested on insights other than its own. The Dean, like Richard, felt the force from behind, and he stood like Richard for all that was anonymous and random. He could afford to be wrong on the mere facts, Richard said, because he kept himself responsive to the life that engendered them. The uncommon man disagreed with historians who cried up the past as the key to the present. "Only out of our own experience," he wrote, "can we understand the meaning of our own lives and the lives of others." Not books but experience was the key to the meaning of history. "Caesar's life has no more examples for us than our own." Richard said this, after Montaigne.

Dean Gauss presented the outsider in Princeton, and the walls had come tumbling down before him. His native place was far away in the German community of Ann Arbor, Michigan: "sweet Auburn," he called it, "the loveliest city of all the plain—indeed of all the world." No one from the old West Side of Ann Arbor went to college in his younger days just after the Civil War—not one of his youthful playmates, he said. "None of my three brothers ever considered that it was a possibility open to him." Christian Gauss was the rare bird. Gauss the elder sold groceries, and candy for a nickel to the neighborhood boys, and he ran a saloon in the yellow house on the corner of Liberty Street—*die Freiheitstrasse*, as they knew it then. The family lived upstairs above the store. Fred Wahr remembered how the neighbors were pleased with the wisdom of hindsight when Woodrow Wilson invited the young man to Princeton. He married a very dignified wife, this early friend said—a lady, and not from Ann Arbor.

So Christian Gauss in his beginnings, as in the startling success that disputed his beginnings, makes you think of Richard Blackmur. But he differed from Richard, being cut from a single piece of cloth. He didn't put on airs, and he wasn't a malcontent either. Coming to the fabled place, he took it in stride. College campuses, Princeton's included, were nothing special to him. "It was not the number of years men had spent on their formal education that made them interesting . . . but the degree to which they had retained and developed their powers of initiative." He disliked what he called "zucche senza sale," and he said how these saltless pumpkins multiplied as you got closer to the Atlantic seaboard. In the young men he admitted as friends, Gauss looked for the savor. Edmund Wilson and Scott Fitzgerald were two of the friends, Richard was another. Gauss, estimating Richard, saw a version of himself, the talented man from the wrong side of the tracks, and he made up his mind that for once the career should belong to the talents.

For his protégé, the Creative Arts Program seemed the right niche. With the help of a grant from the Carnegie Corporation, Gauss had got the program started in the fall of 1939. Like Richard, he had the ear of the foundations. His frequent appeals for help were eleemosynary, though. He wanted money for Nabokov, or to fund a professorship at Princeton for Hermann Broch ("one of the gentlest and finest souls I know"). Admiring Edmund Wilson, he meant to do him a kindness, and Wilson was his first choice to direct the CAP. But the English Department jibbed at the appointment—Wilson was too contentious, or he liked to drink, or else the contentious man had a scunner against Princeton. That was Allen Tate's opinion. In any case, it was Allen who got the job. That, he said, was how the cuckoo found its way into the nest. Richard was the cuckoo.

Allen and Richard had begun corresponding in 1929, and Allen in the thirties had boosted Richard for his Guggenheim grants. A phrase of Donald Davidson's—he was Paean General for all the Fugitives—says how they joined hands. They were "Still Rebels, Still Yankees," each passionately loyal to a cause irretrievably lost. Tate's cause was Southern, but "there is a New England, too," Richard reminded him, "with the ruin of unused or deprived possibility in her bowels." Sometimes loyalty in Tate was endearing, sometimes it gave scandal. When he talked about Gettysburg and how the rebel charge broke against the bayonets of Stannard's Vermont brigade, tears filled his eyes. This was endearing. Tate on his native grounds was a bigot, however. Homosexuality brought him to a boil—as when Allen Ginsberg came to lecture at Vanderbilt—and he made it an emblem for what was wrong with modern times. (Robert Frost was the same.) Stokeley Carmichael, a demagogue, came to Vanderbilt, too. He touched off a ruckus in the black community, and this, Tate supposed, was the end of the world. "The negro race," he said, "is an inferior race." But he wrote in "The Swimmers," one of the permanent American poems, an absolute account of a lynching remembered from his boyhood in Kentucky. What was controversial in Tate, Richard said, was often a matter of temperament or temper. "There is a strength to his language superior to any ideas that may be detached from it."

Tate's Fugitive politics, said his friend Tom Mabry, had "no spiritual significance for the majority of people, whose social and economic inheritance grows increasingly urban." But what was a Fugitive, Tate wanted to know, and he answered: "quite simply a Poet: the Wanderer, or even the Wandering Jew, the Outcast, the man who carries the secret wisdom around the world." In his essay on *Ulysses*, Richard said how the Jew is Everyman the outsider and how, "in each of us, in the exiled part, sits a Jew." Richard was a Fugitive. But neither gave a damn for the *poète maudit*. Each studied punctilio. Aware that manners made the man, Richard wasn't enough aware how sometimes they were simple evasion. Tate when he was young had the best manners of any man Malcolm Cowley ever knew. Cowley thought he used politeness in defensive ways, however, and sometimes as an aggressive weapon against the stranger. He brandished this weapon in his polemical wars. He has kept up a running battle "this quarter century," Richard said, and might have been speaking of himself.

In the thirties, Allen and Richard celebrated each other at a distance. Richard wrote in praise of Tate's *Reactionary Essays*, and Tate doubted "if any writer of any sort, at any time in literary history," had ever received so perfect a review. On Richard's achievement, he went up and down. Some of the poems he called worthless pastiche, some he esteemed handsomely. *From Jordan's Delight* was the best American poetry of the decade. About Richard himself, he had no reservations. "I can't tell you how much I admire you," he wrote. "It is good to be living in the same age." Richard stood to Allen like acolyte to master, the way Delmore stood to him. Allen's mind attracted him powerfully as a type, "because it integrates its insights at the level of experience." But this early judgment was partly fallacious. The least New Critical among the New Critics, and paradoxically the most academic, Allen all his life was bemused by ideas. Later Richard saw how he delighted in "the power of received philosophy." His "use of *dogma*" needed for completeness Richard's "powers of *elucidation*." In fairness, you could put it the other way round.

They talked the matter out at Princeton. They thought very differently on fundamentals, Richard said, Tate "being always instinctively on the side of the absolutist angels, I still lost on the provisional side. It is in this sense that he discounts my 'philosophy.'" Richard held that his philosophy "is whatever it is"—like Eliot's remark that the only unity in Shakespeare was in the sum of his works. "I may change, or grow, or blow up," he said. In the meantime he was satisfied merely to "variegate about a cumulatively sedimenting norm." This didn't satisfy Tate. "Like many admirable minds," he is "absolutely scared and footloose (headloose)," Richard said, "if, for a moment even, he feels himself without the support of something that will do for a philosophy." Richard himself "almost" preferred the quicksands.

They hadn't met until the fall of 1938, when Richard's friend from early days, the poet Ted Spencer, invited Allen to lecture at Harvard. Jack Wheelwright was in the audience—until he died, he was the catalyst for Richard and had introduced Matty Josephson, later Lincoln Kirstein, now Allen Tate. Robert Lowell was there, too—Caligula Lowell, Richard called him, the Emperor of Ice Cream. After the lecture Wheelwright brought Richard up to the platform.

So Tate and Blackmur were face to face, an agreeable way to be for the two years they spent together at Princeton. When school was in session, Richard from his next-door office could hear Allen quoting him through the open door. They spent summers together too, teaching at the Cummington School in Massachusetts, where in the early forties Allen persuaded Richard to join him. Then comes the dreary denouement. Richard at Princeton made a cunning politician. He "connived," was the way Allen put it. Richard said he expected to depend on Tate "for orders and aids." But he had to dispose of his rivals, Allen said, and the deference was only a blind. Given his lack of academic credentials, he had to claw his way to the top. When Jacques Barzun in a book review called Allen a Fascist, Richard went to Gauss in defense of his friend. "Allen isn't *really* a Fascist," he said. This malicious anecdote strengthened with time. Later Tate had Richard saying: "Allen isn't a Nazi, just a Nazi sympathizer." Sequentially or not, and after three years at Princeton, Tate found himself out of a job.

Between Allen and Richard there was never a formal occasion of war, and what happened in Princeton—whatever did happen—is mostly the embittered and so distorted creation of memory, not a tissue of lies but rather encrustation on fact. Richard said to Tate: "Violence is always inexplicable; it is the gap between words; between actions." Willard Thorp saw Richard as pushing Tate out: "He wanted the job for himself." Malcolm Cowley was aware that "Allen bore a grudge for a time; he supposed that Dick had undercut him." The day the Japanese attacked Pearl Harbor, Richard wrote to George Anthony: "Gauss inclines to want someone else to replace Allen and to let me stay providing that is agreeable to the new man and to me." Donald Stauffer, who took the chair in the English Department when he came back from the war, supported this account. Tate was unreliable, Stauffer said to Francis Fergusson, so Gauss turned against him and Richard fell heir to the job. Francis thought this was probably the short of it. "The creative writing program under Allen Tate had not been successful," an officer of the Rockefeller Foundation was told. His confidant was the President of Princeton, Harold Dodds, who expressed "complete satisfaction" that Tate was out and Richard was in.

The changing of the guard went without incident. For more than a decade, Allen and Richard continued to send friendly letters back and forth. Richard wrote how more students than ever before had crowded into the program. But Tate was on to other things. John Ransom had asked him to put together a special issue of the *Kenyon Review*, and he wanted Richard to contribute an essay on Baudelaire. They worried about the war. Allen was too old for military service, but should Richard be drafted he might be sent for training to one of the Southern camps, Forrest or Oglethorpe. That would put him, Tate said, within visiting distance of Monteagle, the mountain community in western Tennessee where Allen and Andrew Lytle had established a permanent base. They didn't meet in Monteagle but kept together, in Richard's phrase, on the longest slopes of the mind. They swapped opinions on poetry, and Richard gave his opinion that Tate wrote better poetry than he did—"of another and more valuable (more deeply useful, referential) magnitude." That was what nineteen years of reading had told him. He concluded his letter: "In this something less than human world I am all the more faithfully Yours and Caroline's."

But Tate's anger was building, or ill-meaning friends conspired to build it. He had plenty of anger. At Minnesota in the fifties, he began to elaborate stories. He "was an inveterate gossip, occasionally with malice," said one of his students, "also capable of being dishonest." His stories mixed true and false. He said how Richard neglected Helen and pushed her at other men, Edmund Wilson and Slater Brown being two of the men, or how Richard told the world that he had brought Allen to Princeton. When Allen wanted a fellowship from the Institute for Advanced Study, Richard was there to block him. Or Richard spoke slightingly to the Rockefeller Foundation of Allen's effort to finance a reunion of the Fugitives in 1956. Friends who might have known this didn't know it, however. Allen in his later years "tended to turn a baleful eye on most everybody," one of them said. "Ah, the Villa Serbelloni!" Allen said of the Rockefeller estate on Lake Como, where Richard's friend John Marshall presided as director. "How I hoped to be invited there! Guess who told Marshall not to invite me?" It went on like this for twenty-five years.

In 1959 "Dick made partial amends." He wrote an essay "for my 60th birthday," Allen said. This was "San Giovanni in Venere," Saint John the ascetic tangled in the arms of Venus, Tate the ideologue secure in his beliefs, at the same time absurdly and triumphantly outside them. In this ultimate tribute, Richard paid his respects to "the different temperament of Tate—more active, more engaged, more cavalier" than his own. Tate was mollified a little. He offered to introduce Richard's collected poetry in 1965. But his rancor ran deep. As for his fellow New Critic, "I ended up disliking him," he said. His taste was deep, too, and this required, Richard said, "the love at the bottom of his contentiousness." Necessarily, one jostled the other.

Tate's great men in modern letters were Eliot and Ransom. When he lay dying, their photographs hung on the wall of his bedroom. "My two masters," he said. In this context, he summed up his long career and his long and equivocal friendship with Richard. About Richard, he said: "He was our best American critic." What did these critics have in common? Richard replied, in his eulogy of Tate: an ancestry in art for art, belief in the independence or absolute sovereignty of poetry, a skeptical view of rationality as it pretended to embody and discriminate skills, and last and most, "a tendency to make the analyzable features of the forms and techniques of poetry both the means of access to poetry and somehow the equivalent of its content."

This defines the New Criticism, which Tate and Blackmur created between them and which they applied with a difference. The two of them as critic, Ransom said in the thirties, "would make the best in the world." They never made this composite critic but, their difference notwithstanding, they ate the same bread. There is the letter old Henry Adams wrote to Henry James, after the death of Will James: "We all began together, and our lives have made more or less of a unity, which is, so far as I can see, about the only unity that American society in our time had to show."

In the early forties, the power to make or break that Tate ascribed to Richard was still remote in time. He began to gather power, or it dropped in his lap, with the departure of George Stewart, Tate's successor as Resident Fellow. The "new overlord" wrote fact books and was "quite a decent chap personally," in Richard's opinion. Tate called him dismissively a "stud writer." Whatever he was, all those would-be poets and novelists got under his skin and he left the program after only one year. Richard supposed that he would soon be following Tate and Stewart out of town. The Carnegie money was almost all gone, and anyway Creative Arts seemed a pointless luxury in wartime. For a while Allen's friend Henry Church lent support. Church was the heir to the Arm and Hammer fortune, and descended from the man who invented bicarbonate of soda. He was also a patron of the little magazines. In Princeton, where he had settled in 1939—"because I was there," Allen said—he subsidized the arts with his Mesures Fund. This was only a stopgap, however, and by 1943 Richard's head was on the block.

The English Department might have met his salary by giving him a full-time appointment. At this suggestion, Dean Root turned all colors. There was, however, "a scheme afoot," Richard wrote to George Anthony, "to make me a Lecturer in Humanities (which would give me a good deal of liberty on top of a small amount of drudgery teaching)." The scheme depended for success on the fund-raising prowess of Richard's friend, Mike Oates. He was Professor Whitney Oates of the Classics Department, and later (so the story went) he made Robert Goheen the President of Princeton. In 1943 he put his prowess on the line. He got the attention of a wealthy donor and secured Richard's fourth year in Princeton. "Two thirds free time and one third teaching or committee work," the new Hodder Fellow exulted. He supposed he would get a lot done, "beginning now."

But his country was at war, and though he called himself "old, and otherwise disqualified for military service," he said it became him to serve. "As I share the peace, I must share the war of my society." His sister Betty believed him "a definite pacifist." He wasn't a pacific man, though. The sickness ravaging Europe was "a mere modification of the heart's action," he said. This sounds distressingly like his friend John Berryman, who makes you feel in certain poems of the forties that World War II was a fly in his ointment. But Richard in the forties wasn't projecting his ego on the world. He was saying (like Henry Adams in 1914) that war held no surprises for him. To "the horror of human weather across the water" he brought his own horror. The man who couldn't help standing out from the crowd wanted a uniform badly.

A month after Pearl Harbor, Waldo Peirce inquired: "Wot are you doing for yer kink and country?" Richard answered in the spring by applying for a commission in the Marine Corps. But a mild heart condition kept him out of the Marines, and an ancient and oversize tuberculosis scar he hadn't been aware of denied him an active commission in the Army. (He didn't want the Navy, he told Robert Penn Warren, even if the Navy would have him—there were too many admirals already.) Perhaps he might take "the secret weapon job in Maryland," he wrote cryptically to George Anthony, or go "travelling round the world" with the Quartermaster Corps. But these possible sponsors had other ideas.

So he tossed on the "unfeathered bed of uncertainty," and then one day he went out and bought special underwear to keep himself warm and signed up for sky-watching in Princeton. The underwear was expensive and Helen gloomed at that, but Richard loved spotting airplanes, Tessa Horton said. Why was this? "He loved duties." The phrase tells of the man more than volumes. At night he stood watch "and he talked about the stars and the planes that came over," and during the day he taught public speaking to the engineers and dealt with what was left of the Creative Writing Program. He didn't estimate highly his chance of beating the draft, and as the war went on he kept expecting the ax to fall. But being drafted was preferable to being "swept off into some Washingtonian other-other land" like Phil Horton and John Walcott, and if General Hershey didn't call him, he said he might enlist in the ranks.

This was fantasy. A medical report from his insurance company added high blood pressure to his other ailments. About his migraine headaches he didn't have to be told. Filling out a questionnaire for the Alumni Association in 1942, he said he was thirty-eight, classified 3-A, without degrees, without military experience, without membership in any professional or scientific society. Also he wasn't an alumnus. Maybe, he said, he would "end up in a factory."

It was Helen who went to work in the factory. Her job was inspecting the hydraulic tubes they used for braking operations in the new torpedo planes. Until her body rebelled and she had to cut back, she did this for fifty-four hours a week, getting home from Trenton at past two in the morning. In her spare time she painted at Nela Walcott's; John had been posted to Italy with Intelligence, and Nela and the children were living the war out in Princeton. But to Helen's austere sense, spare time was a reproach, so when Tate wrote to invite them for a visit, Richard had to say that "Helen's conscience won't let herself off." Sleeplessness afflicted her but she had never been so buoyant or so full of conversation, and friends like Delmore yearned to hear her stories of the industrial life. "She stays up talking as long as mud, and when she gets up in the morning goes on where she left off"—about her work or her fellow workers, or the visual effects her painter's eye was always sizing up in the factory.

Helen had joined the union and carried a card and this was impressive, but what impressed Richard most was "the air of authority and ability which she wears." Also, he said, she looked good in overalls. He looked at himself and the contrast was painful. Hoping "to be either in or out" of service, he felt "much depressed at finding myself still in an uncertain and anomalous situation." The uncertainty persisted. This didn't mean giving up, though. He kept on communicating—with his students, not least with himself. Like that Adams whom he called the pedagogue of sensibility, he was the teacher as artist and he knew how the good teacher wakens to his own lesson. The "prime charm of wakefulness" was his peculiar charm. "He had his long wakening, through an endless varying crisis, and at almost intolerable expense." He liked Princeton too much or he liked it too little, he tormented himself, perhaps he sullied himself. But the yield was worth the expense.

"I have never before done any teaching," Richard wrote in 1940, "and the experience is engrossing in all senses." This was putting it mildly. At Princeton time fled before him and he had to beg off when asked for a book review, having time to look at nothing "that was not shoved under my nose." He saw no reason at first why he couldn't combine teaching and writing, and he even aimed "to produce a book every two years, using," he said bravely, "about half my time." It wasn't long, however, before he was saying how he was "disappointed at the short steps I take." The Creative Writing Program which earned him his keep was conceived "at an almost luxurious high level," but that didn't mean featherbedding. He learned from experience that massaging the egos of thirty-six freshmen and sophomores, the normal complement he and Tate split between them, "pretty much exhausts as much energy and time as the regular work of a professor."

His students had one faculty in common. This was a "putative" perception, "the product of deciduous conventions with the leaves off." The "good pedagogue" whittled away at these conventions by promoting an interest in detail. If he succeeded, concern with detail begot concern for general principles. He failed more than he succeeded. "Engineered inertia" was Richard's phrase for the adolescent mind. "What I have seen of his writing," he said of one student, "is mere scatter-minded violence, like the pimples and splotches on his face." No need to press hard, though: "he has his own bellows." Richard in the academy wasn't an affable, pipe-smoking kind of man.

By and large he kept these journal comments to himself. Criticizing poems and stories, he let the students suppose that he and they "were immersed in the ocean of these things as friends and equals." On his evangelizing side he believed this and it made him, said Tate, "a remarkable teacher." In one student's opinion, English majors who graduated from Princeton before World War II were hopelessly antediluvian. Only those who had sat at the feet of the master and knew "his work and presence" were saved. "Merely his presence" made the difference. "He simply is this campus," said a young poet who wasn't an acolyte and saw him with the warts on. Students whose names he never knew came up to a mark they wouldn't have dreamed to set for themselves. He held them to the mark, demanding of them "the most unrelenting and exciting kind of conscience." He did this by pretending that "we were as intelligent as he. You knew you weren't, but he made you want to be."

One quality all great teachers have in common—selflessness (never mind that great teachers are mostly vain as peacocks). They don't put themselves forward but dedicate themselves to bringing the other fellow on. To the students he brought on, Richard became the final censor—"the imaginary audience I had to please as I wrote my fiction," said a novelist-pupil. Twenty years later, "the habit of imagining his approval" was still ingrained in the poet Bruce Berlind. ("Days when I so much as saw him *felt* different from days when I did not.") Mostly you had to take his approval on faith. The garrulous man was stingy with praise, and the downright critic was as neutral as litmus paper. This doesn't mean he was bland. He had his fierce opinions, but he never got between you and the book you were reading. "He challenged you but never stood in your way." It wasn't his business to make the students over in his image and likeness. This was what happened, however.

"Where do you come from?" one of his young poets imagined people asking. The indicated answer was Omaha or New York City, etc. He heard himself answer: "I come from R. P. Blackmur." His letters to the Slavic scholar Sidney Monas went through the war with Monas like things you wrote in your phylactery, until they were lost in a POW camp. "This was the spell he cast," said the poet Theodore Holmes. He accepted Monas "as a citizen of the only realm to which I cared to belong—the country of letters." Perhaps he was "more generous with his patents of citizenship to that exclusive country" than Monas would have been in his place. A young novelist Richard had in tow remembered how "he always took what I and the rest of us wrote as seriously . . . as he took Joyce or Yeats." This remained true even when the writing was "more than a little terrible." The music critic Peter Rosenwald, who wrote for Richard "embarrassingly bad short stories and plays," would never have ventured to look beyond himself, "had it not been for Blackmur's belief in one of his less inspired students." But belief isn't just the right word.

"There are too many boys," Richard told the poet Jean Garrigue, "all grasping, because all, they think, drowning. They will most of them have been wrong, but who could count [on] that?" Not counting on that, he spooned out his life in great dollops to "the little boys here," spending on them, Tate thought, too much time altogether. Though he put in long hours, he had little patience with the office-bound mentality of the academic world, and he understood that long hours didn't promise results and rewards. Praise from this teacher—"my first and best," said Franklin Reeve—constituted the ultimate challenge. When Richard praised a poem he had written, Reeve met the challenge by saying how the poem could hardly be worth much, since twenty minutes or so was all the time it had taken. "How old was I, he asked. Eighteen, I said. It took you eighteen years, he said." The austere man was a soft touch. The odd undergraduate who left off a batch of poems could always count on bending his ear. Sometimes he got his own back. He said to Mike Keeley, "Well, Keats at seventeen wrote worse than you do." It wasn't his business either to winnow the chaff from the wheat.

In the forties a student poll ranked his course in Creative Writing among the most popular in the college. That left him gaping. He wasn't aware how he captured the minds of his students, and not just the best of them. A dozen years into his Princeton career, he still had no inkling of what they said about him. In this he differs from his hero Adams, who was sure that his own effort was going to have a posthumous effect. Richard was sure of nothing, unless his unworthiness. Even so he is like that Adams whom he resembled to a spring, haunting those "who once drank of it before it sank and the sand dried."

Meditating on the death of Saint Augustine, an early biographer said: "Yet I think that those who gained most from him were those who had been able actually to see and hear him." That is how it was with Richard. His prose and poetry remain—a considerable testimony, but not all-in-all sufficient. What is wanting is the testimony of "those who had some contact with the quality of his life among men."

Early students recalled their teacher, his pale oak-colored hair high and fluffy on his head, always looking as if he'd just washed it, the inevitable cigarette held carelessly between the third and fourth fingers—a mannerism they tried to imitate. Abruptly young Richard, seen through eyes even younger than his, had become a character. This character was elusive, blending immiscible things—a type of the Stagyrite or encyclopedic man, but endlessly provisional in applying what he knew, a type of the esthete but finally moral in his estheticism, a "virile and uninhibited" presence but "distant, disciplined, learned," jealous of himself but a mentor to many who were never in the formal sense his students. "Only a fairly good teacher" was his colleague Tex Kaufmann's opinion— but this was in formal situations. "You needed more to 'over-hear' him than to listen in the normal academic lecture-frame. He *showed* us how to 'be' a critic; he created a sense of personal possibility."

The style he made for himself or fell into was mostly monologue; he didn't teach at all in the ordinary sense, but carried on "an unceasing experiment" in expression. This was self-expression but no one complained, since Richard had something in him to express. "His talk smoldered even when it didn't catch fire," and when he talked he enveloped you in the sound of his voice "with its soft, dark rhythms and its . . . strange and difficult Maine accent." You felt you shouldn't reply, unless you could match "the muted and attenuated logic of his monologues." Richard didn't encourage overt dialogue, said one student, "though perhaps he tried."

For the poet Louis Coxe, the most remarkable thing about him was the way his mind "gathered itself together and moved, tentatively at first, then gathering momentum proceeded to surround, embrace and define the possibilities *there*, in the poem." Sometimes he soared high into the intense inane, as when he told his class in Poetics how the rise in the price of bread during the late Roman decadence went with a decline in metrical proficiency. He gave as his example the "poor verses" of Venantius Fortunatus. Maybe he had read them. When he said these things, the students looked the other way or they kept their eye on the length of ash that tipped the Pall Mall between his fingers. But even when he faked, said Leslie Fiedler, "he did it with style."

Coming into class and finding the word "lycanthropy" written on the blackboard, he made this his point of departure for the hour's business. It wasn't all faking. He had it in him to bay the moon. Remarking how Richard talked sense and much nonsense together, Fiedler sometimes thought that he invented the famous Blackmur style "to keep himself from knowing when he was talking one and when he was talking the other." Frederick Morgan, a founder of the *Hudson Review* (for which Richard shamelessly took credit, Morgan said), thought him particularly good with writers of his own time like Stevens, Eliot, and Thomas Mann. Morgan much preferred Tate, though, missing in Richard "a unified and powerful critical methodology." This will be matter for praise or blame, depending on how you value the importance of a unified methodology.

The encyclopedic man had the mind of a pack rat. Throwing nothing away, he found it hard to retrieve the bits of broken pottery and string he shored against his ruin. Writers who weren't always students of his sent him their poetry, with a self-addressed envelope thoughtfully enclosed. Would he be good enough to comment? The answer was yes, if only he remembered. He left behind him a substantial pile of self-addressed envelopes. But helpless inquiries from students, often vast in scope, met him at his best or most indulgent. Generally they wanted to know What is truth? and he hoped that his rejoinders "will not have wasted your time," and even looked forward "to seeing your study when you have produced it." For friends on the way up, like A. Alvarez, William Arrowsmith, and the poet Frederic Prokosch, he worked hard at opening doors. This was generous of him, and flattered his sense of being a maker and shaker. On Robert Lowell's application for a Guggenheim grant, he was glad to bestow "my blessing." Recommending George Steiner to the Institute for Advanced Study, he said how this protégé "comes very near being the only man so far appointed . . . in the field of literature." Predecessors-at-a-remove included T. S. Eliot, Francis Fergusson, Kenneth Burke, "and myself." Richard supposed that this wasn't "bad company for Mr. Steiner."

Vanity took second place to disinterest, however, and he tried to see to it that all his friends, good, bad, and middling, tasted the wages of their virtue. He was a poor judge of talent and didn't much discriminate among them. "To be a friend of yours," said Delmore Schwartz, "is to deprive oneself of the full benefit of your criticism." Perhaps, said Leon Edel, he felt special "sympathy for the 'underdog,'" being himself "an outsider in academe." Edel the outsider benefited from this. Lacking a "stepping stone into academe," he might never have got going after the war. "Dick gave me a leg-up," he said, "and I have always been grateful for that." Others benefited, too. He pushed Irving Howe for a professorship at Brandeis, and it was only thanks to him that W. S. Merwin, "a hopeless student" who dedicated a volume of his poetry to Richard, wasn't kicked out of graduate school.

Edel was perplexed, however, when the underdog "didn't behave as if he was" one. In the struggling years at Princeton, he dressed to the eyes. Rogers Peet was his tailor, as "by appointment." Tagging along on a visit to this gentleman's tailor and "faced by a choice between two fine suits," Delmore bought both of them. This he called "a Blackmurian choice." The expense of greatness, said the novelist Wright Morris, saluting his friend's essay on Henry Adams, "included a fine pile of small fry bills." This negligent sentence sums up pretty well the life and work of R. P. Blackmur.

A lot of him was play. "When he laughed, his whole face laughed, the eyes especially." Often he was bawdy, sometimes scatological. To a student who was leaving for Turkey, he offered this piece of advice: "Never have sexual congress with Near Eastern melons. I'm told they put the foreskin in jeopardy." He liked to make his friends squirm with talk of the "piss hard on" that vexed him when he woke in the morning. This went inconsequently with an air of total commitment to the mind. "Every gesture, every thought, every inflection of his voice . . . was dedicated to the high seriousness with which he regarded its processes and preoccupations." The right nuance for him counted more than straight talk. Also, he didn't like straight talk. He surrounded what he meant "with a nimbus of uncaught and uncatchable meaning, rather than let any possible nuance escape." This wasn't to the good, said one disapproving critic, and it wasn't an act. "It is deeper than that; it is really, at a profound level of sincerity, a dislike of too overt statement, of a subject-matter that jumps too blithely from one skull into another; it is our modern *odi profanum vulgus.*" There is something to this hostile critique.

"To 'sharpen the ear' was a basic goal in his teaching," and he quickened in Dan Seltzer his lifelong interest in theater when he spoke on the syntax of living dramatic speech. To his students he offered "self-confidence and cheer," but he wasn't Robert Browning jumping up from the table with his mouth full of food and telling how God's in his heaven. When an aspiring writer came by the office to see him, he began: "You want me to say that you're a great poet." What he said was that poetry is onerous business, striking a second heat on the anvil, and that it's working at the poetry, not being the poet, that matters.

"Awe for RPB" went with being his student. "You stood in awe of . . . his precision, his daring, and his mysteries." This was Geoffrey Wolff, who wrote the life of Harry Crosby where the means were mysterious and the ends were pathetically plain. "Even today," when the poet William Meredith summoned up the ghostly presence of his dead friend, he felt "like a little, or perhaps retarded, boy." One student's phrase was "worship at a distance." W. S. Merwin revered him from this distance. "We all stood in awe of him, colleagues too," said Frederick Buechner. Nobody dared call him Dick to his face. "Even John Berryman, his partner in creative writing, never went further than Richard." This standing in awe was painful, however. Richard preferred irreverent banter. If you pulled his leg, at least this suggested that you took him for real. "You could only press him so far, though," and there were times when he bristled—like the time, Keeley said, when "I accused him of putting his hand up my wife's dress. He took very serious umbrage at that, he was a Maine gentleman and would never do such a thing, even though I had caught him in the act."

Being a gentleman was something you worked at. That didn't argue hypocrisy, since Richard took a dim view of man in the natural condition. But he wrote in his notebook: "I cannot play only those roles which exclude the role of myself." He didn't like being selected, as by nose, ear, and hair, and he lamented that neither the regard nor the disregard shown him "applies to that in me which would respond." Lionized by the students, he had to play the lion. He got his revenge by talking in a whisper, leaving his audience "hanging over the table for the crucial words that were often softer than the rest." He didn't deign to repeat them. But the sybilline role he adopted bred insecurity. His pose depended for success on its dramatic effects. So the audience he pretended to despise sat in judgment upon him, and what it judged was aloof from the matter.

Colleagues gossiped about his intransigence and fierceness, "as if (being in Princeton) he were Clyde Beatty," training tigers. That was one image. "Sailor and monk" was another. Or he was like "the priest in relation to his flock," and the flock waited on his words with "religious intensity." Bullying wasn't beneath him, nor evasion, nor striking off allusions you couldn't grasp and weren't supposed to. One gnomic performance began with the refrain: "Heartbreak House, Headlong Hall." The ostensible reference was to the play by Bernard Shaw. But there was, Richard said, "something in this that smacks of Thomas Love Peacock." He proceeded to illustrate, compounding confusion. Maybe Bernard Shaw was everyone's business. Not everyone was reading Peacock, but that made no matter to him.

The lessons he preached were "altogether terrible." You hung by your talent as by your fingernails. But you didn't take yourself to heart. Instead you practiced "the seriousness of frivolity." Poetry was a game. Piecing out this definition, Richard made a great phrase—"A game is a refuge precisely because it is a purview: a privation of intelligence." If you meant the game for real play, you had to play with real things: "Genuine extravagance was of real wealth, and real wealth had to be earned." Sometimes, not often, his students took him to task for "these [frightening] demands which you casually set up before us." Despite the negligent air, he wanted to create "artist-saints and poet-prophets." If you didn't have the genes for this, he kicked you "contemptuously into oblivion." He was by temper a man of the Yellow Nineties, and in his teaching and writing he aborted connectives. Exposition at least was beneath him. To explain, said Tristan Tzara, is the amusement of numbskulls. Richard defines the pedagogue or expository man, but resembles this high priest of Dada. You almost heard him saying (except that he shunned declarative statement): "I am by principle against manifestoes, as I am also against principles."

Ask him where he stood and he looked bleakly down his mustache. Views were for the Philistines. He gave "no sign of compromise" with the hunters after meaning (if you are bored with the latter, you will love him for this), and sometimes it was "terrifying to realize that he was demanding a response to literature far beyond that of which one felt capable." He "expected us all to outdo Shakespeare," his students complained, and occasionally he brought them "down into tears because they did not." The expectation was wry, of course—his way of wringing the most from his material. But he was as pitiless with himself, calling his own work "detritus."

This side of him his students glimpsed only remotely. The arrogant man was humble, his humility shading to self-abasement. "Not: be yourself," he adjured himself. The everlasting imperative for survival was to be a little less than yourself. "Give room, give room." He said he could think of "no person or group in the least interested in any effort of my whole being," and he said he knew no one who wanted "anything I could create." But in the dust, he exuded assurance. "I am Sir Oracle," he seemed to say when he lectured. Lecturing tormented him, though. He dreaded "the idea of speaking to a crowd," feeling, he told John Berryman, "unsuited to the honour," and when he performed in public stage fright took hold of him, his voice disappeared, and he stood on the platform "in an altogether ungracious dishabille." Listening to himself or listening to the Holy Ghost at his ear, it wasn't surprising that he lacked a sense of his audience. He was proud and wanted pride, and one student who loved him wondered at the uneasy mix of self-consciousness and "marvellous arrogance," and the belief you couldn't shake that "he was a lousy lecturer."

Allen Tate had been over this road before him and did his best to offer support. "I did not ask Mr. Blackmur, who had had no previous teaching experience, to conduct a class in his first year as Associate; his work was wholly in private conferences with the Sophomores." This was the kind of teaching Allen liked best. It allowed you to defeat the system, all that histrionic posturing beloved of "the mere literati"—Billy Phelps at Yale, Buzzer Hall at Princeton—who leaned over backward "till the skull bangs the floor." It took him awhile, but Richard got the knack of "the armchair method" and there, said Allen, his success was "most gratifying." He wanted to declaim, however, the evangelical side of him wrestling with his fear. "What good is a man," he said, "if he can't get up and talk on his feet?" Delmore called him "your Senatorship," and in fact he saw himself as Senator from Maine—even, said Eileen Simpson, as President of Princeton. If only he could learn how to lecture, he said wistfully to Cleanth Brooks, "I should greatly look forward to talking about the *language* of poetry; it's so never talked about."

He learned how to lecture, but in an alien tongue. Unwilling to condescend—unable by temperament—he brought the students up to his level. They didn't always know what he was talking about, but even the least of them knew himself in the presence of a mind turning over. This can't be said too emphatically. He liked to torture the truth or perhaps could do no other—he was R. P. Honeycomb, said his student Frederick

Crews: the type of the wooly-minded critic. He was also the type of man thinking. In the fifties he lectured at Douglass College, Rutgers, and his student-host, regretting how "our background was inadequate in almost all cases," wrote to thank him nonetheless "for the level of your speech." What pleased the audience most and evoked the most response was "your abstinence from levelling down."

Robert Hollander, his colleague and later his panegyrist in two or three memorable poems, thought him on the public platform "the most invigorating teacher of literature I have ever encountered." There was the lecture he gave on Dante's great sestina, "Al poco giorno." You felt that he himself had come to the short day and the great sweep of shadow. "The lecture gasped, tottered, and finally settled ruinously into total silence. He stood there, I thought debating whether or not to chuck it all up, leave the room (with twenty minutes still to run before the bell), perhaps even leave the earth (which he was soon enough to do)." Then, amidst the growing discomfort of the students and Bob Hollander's growing panic, "he began to recite the forty-two end words of that sestina, one after another, in English, and without another intervening word." Hollander felt that everybody there, "for the first and last time," understood how a poem came together. "His voice, as his mind found the solution to what he wanted to say," moved out in firmer volume, repeating the words, "and filled us all, and clearly himself, with the sense of mystery and triumph that characterizes not only great art but also its spectators, when they are momentarily united in elevated attention." He was, said Hollander, "the chain of our needles."

Some of Richard's friends supposed that, for him, lecturing was a game he trifled at. He catered to this impression. He liked to say that he never lectured from more than three notes. "And the three notes were three words, always prepared over martinis at L'Hiere's," the French restaurant in Princeton where he held court for two hours in the middle of the day. "He would sit there," said Mike Keeley, "pull out his little paper, and write down a word or phrase, then another, and then a third." The words were no good unless they were Delphic. "And that was all the structure he wanted, the beginning, the middle, and the end. The rest of it was talk in between." If you thought the talk improvised, this was what he wanted you to think. He was pretending and not pretending. Improvisation was of the essence of this morbidly fastidious man, and that is one reason to trust him. How can you know a thing, he said, until you have put it down "to see what will happen to it in a new medium and what it will attract to itself." What you know finally is not what you stipulate "but what comes otherwise to be there—what was dragged into being by the agency of the language used and by the symbol made." Lou Coxe could still see him "pushing the blot of ink around till something came—then off on one of those flights of controlled and articulate fancy."

The other side of this he mostly kept hidden. His notes for teaching are fanatically detailed. There, nothing is left to chance and "talk in between" is estimated to the last semicolon. The "impenetrable but fascinating mumble-from-notes" that one student remembered hearing speaks of many things, but not the trifler.

The man who never got out of high school stood for rigor in the classroom and held views on education that might have mortified his liberal colleagues. This was if they took thought. He wanted the students to study technical subjects that required the guidance of a teacher, or subjects aloof from their immediate comprehension. Why bother with classes in contemporary literature, when you could work all that up on your own? His students were outraged, Northrop Frye remembered, when he "made them read such people as Smollett." He held to this line in spite of the famous seminars he gave on the great modern novels. He was large and might have quoted: "Do I contradict myself? Very well then, I contradict myself."

At faculty meetings he hawked "a sort of prospectus" for a seven-year course, four years on "the ulterior techniques of the imagination," three years more on "the symbolic imagination itself." Students might enter or leave the course at any time. If they entered, he undertook to make them dance. But he wasn't a drillmaster, perhaps recalling the masters who had seized his own youth and purged his own fire. The department thought twice before it penalized a student for lateness or other delinquency. This was sure to elicit "the Blackmur moral speech," as they called it. "We are not a hospital for the cure of the morality of the young. We are not here to judge our fellow human beings in terms that are not academic." Etc. Richard was saying that he could never vote to penalize anyone, being a natural delinquent himself. This meant in practice that everybody passed. With one shrinking student he determined to keep his mouth shut. "I don't think he has the type of personality or structure to sustain or support my kind of structure. There seems no balanced anarchy in him." With another he feared that "I may have trespassed on his sensibility a little; which is sin." He promised himself not to tamper with the students' lives, knowing how "they trust me too much."

Frederick Morgan saw him breaking this promise. "In his relationships with his students, Blackmur was friendly and sympathetic. He liked to get involved with them and with their problems." But if he offered helpful counsel, there was "in his involvement with us" an element that Morgan found suspect, "a desire to live vicariously through us and to manipulate our lives. He was not always discreet, and was not above playing one of us off against another." Maybe Richard was guilty of these desires and lapses —he had his feline side. He responded almost in personal ways to the story a friend told him about Henry James, who went to a funeral where he had no business and sat as close as he could get to the grieving family. "Where emotion is," said James, "there am I."

For other students, however, he typified the emotionless man. Philip Quigg, subsequently editor of *Foreign Affairs*, thought him "extraordinarily laconic." Whatever you got out of his course in Creative Writing was "by osmosis." If he wasn't a cat he was an elephant, and blind men were exploring his flanks.

This he would have called a fair account of perception. To himself he seemed partly a fraud. In his notebook he wrote how some of his student poets "make out to see in me an unassailable integrity," where in fact what they saw was "only an accidental facade of features and overt style." This façade, Richard thought, "would be most useful to me were I to keep on teaching, since boys cannot bear 'very much' reality." Outside the classroom, his austere manner was an obstacle, though, and he said to himself how it "gets in my way and shortens my audience." Nervous of the audience, he sat a bit apart in social situations, detached but observant, his enigmatic smile like a metonym of the physical person. He had only one manner, for parties or the public forum, and in the golden mouth profundities mingled with rodomontade. Free-and-easy was beyond him. That wasn't because he was looking down his nose or his mustache. The formality in which he dressed himself was part and parcel of the fear. Also it had its own integrity. He was his English father's son, and formal because he was formal.

The course he gave on Dante, Montaigne, and Pascal focused attention on the "order or organization" of these three principal types of Western imagination. Dante personified official order for him, and he appealed to it constantly. Catholicism was always out there, a possibility on the edges of his mind. In Montaigne, who nourished him all his life, he saw "a deep relaxation of that order"—still fortified, though, by "a sense of the organization things have in themselves." He put Montaigne below Dante, the order he declared being only "provisional." Montaigne is, however, the chief of all Richard's authors—his students remembered gratefully how "you . . . [were always] rubbing our noses into him"—and what is Richard himself if not the embodiment of the provisional man? So order and its relaxing tugged him two ways.

Then came Pascal, and Richard threw up his hands—but not in dismay.

Pascal is the excruciation of order, "pushing always toward the destructive pang of conscience." To come to terms with his intransigent ego, you needed "a sense of the intolerableness of even the most necessary order." Recognizing this sense in himself, sometimes rejoicing in it, Richard is Pascal, at whose highest pitch order becomes a great disorder. The merely fastidious man, always hurrying, Richard said, "to take part in practical charades," never estimates this problem of disorder in order. Richard was fastidious but not merely anything. Dreading the chthonic underground, he learned to confront it. "The more we extend the field of the predictable the nearer we come to the unpredictable," he said. He craved acquaintance with the unpredictable. In his poetry he wrote: "My house lies open to the weather." That wasn't simple statement, but a victory achieved. He sought in the classroom to discover what he called the modus vivendi. In this mysterious place between god and the devil, the values of the intellect spring. He likened them to "poppies in the Italian wheatfield or anemones in the Lebanon." There speaks the Old Pretender who has been around the world. But the point is to his honoring of incidental things.

CHAPTER EIGHT

A Lion in the Path

SATURDAY NIGHTS were Richard's "at home" nights, and the friends were still there when Helen got home in her overalls and carrying her lunch pail. Looking over the scene, she let them feel how she despised it. Wasn't there a war on? and they sat around talking. Like Yeats's hysterical women, she was sick of poets who were always gay. John Berryman was one of the poets. He was only twenty-nine in 1943 and already had failed miserably in fifty different ways. Art sustained him, however, and he preferred it to life. "What day of mere living," he asked himself rhetorically, "presents so rich and complicated an experience?" Since his undergraduate time at Columbia, he had counted himself among Richard's "most devoted admirers," and when Harvard let him go his friend Delmore wondered hopefully if Richard might do something about this. Marriage to Eileen had much improved John, he said, "and he is really a good teacher." Employers by the bucketful discounted Delmore's opinion and Berryman himself had ceased hoping for anything, "only not to disgrace myself or to be disgraced," when Richard came through with an instructorship at Princeton. This event proved decisive for both.

It was "simple as fingers," said Richard offhandedly. He lobbied "the villains of the piece," as he called them—Willard Thorp and Gordon Hall Gerould, the Chairman—and the lobbying turned out successful. In his fourth year at Princeton, the supplicating outsider had become the power broker and dispenser of favors. Richard found this new role to his liking, and he played it often in the years to come—with William Meredith, Richard Eberhart, Randall Jarrell, and a host of others. By 1946 he was close to the seats of power where Tate had been before him, and he got Harold Dodds to let him hire Berryman as his Associate in Creative Writing. "You might do worse," Delmore wrote, than import "one of the children of Israel from Cambridge," and when he went to Europe in 1952 that is what he did. He hired Delmore to run the Program, with Saul

Bellow as spear carrier and Tommy Riggs assisting them both. Sherry Mangan, the sometime friend, hearing of "the canonization of Dickie Blackmur," said morosely: "I have always predicted he'd be a dreary success." Sherry was on the way down.

John Berryman at Princeton was the token of success, the first of Richard's many protégés, and the relation between them has its emblematic side. Berryman, like Richard, composed an anthology of foibles and ailments. His eyes were bad, his nerves were worse, and he suffered from epilepsy. Like Richard also he didn't mind a drink, and David Daiches remembered how, when the three of them were teaching summer school at the University of Vermont, John—full of insolence and a deal of Planter's Punch—climbed to the roof of the Sugar House Hotel and had to be pulled down by the irate proprietor. He was the wild man Helen favored in Richard, and his wildness flourished rankly as he got older. Where Richard on the surface was phlegmatic New England, John's demons were all up front. His voice, when he hectored you, had "the quality of string on a tightly tied package when you pluck it." Hyperenthusiasms made him a hot friend, Robert Lowell said, also wearing to friends; Delmore, who was one of his dearest, said that "no one had John's loyalty, but you liked him to live in another city." One city to him looked as bad as the next, though. He taught briefly in Detroit at Wayne State University and this was a stupid place. (Harvard, he said, was only less stupid but twice as pretentious.) Princeton seemed "academic, suburban, parasitic." He hated his teaching and called it "heavy and unrewarding." He found his students agreeable but unspeakably ignorant. The program was a hodgepodge "from which they learn almost nothing." Richard got him an apartment and he hated it, too, and groused bitterly like Richard before him. The Resident Fellow was on the way up, and in 1943 he quit his dusty digs for a pleasant house on Princeton Avenue. For the new boy, however, the merest hole-in-the-wall was sufficient. Self-pity consumed him, and self-hatred when he took his own measure. "My talent lost, like my hair, sex crumbling like my scalp. Disappointment and horror. And the collapse of will: self-distrust, contempt, sloth, and paralysis. Everything begun . . . everything abandoned. Every day I wish to die." It all reads like Richard, communing with himself.

When Berryman's initial appointment at Princeton collapsed in a matter of months, he contemplated fasting to death. He didn't follow through on this; he continued to live in Princeton for the next ten years, and Richard, growing into importance, became his mentor. "My critical practice has attached itself to no school," Berryman said later, but "in its inception" Richard's practice was decisive. He was "your Educated Person," and "his intelligence and moderation and wisdom, displayed endlessly in charming and spacious conversation," were a source of daily surprise. Helen said, however, how Richard had gone cerebral, and turned into the man who didn't do things anymore but talked about them endlessly. These perceptions depend on each other.

Richard was Berryman's Henry in *The Dream Songs* before Berryman was Henry, "a white American in early middleage . . . who has suffered an irreversible loss and talks about himself sometimes in the first person." Third person was more like it. What was wrong with Henry? "They took away his crotch," Berryman said, but surely this was after the fact. Anyway "he had the job"—this was Richard giving the character of Orpheus, incidentally his own character—of "re-creating the motive of which he had been deprived." *A Primer of Ignorance*, his last book of essays and vitally different from the work of younger days, says how he coped with the job. Frederick Buechner, who studied with Richard and also with Berryman, decided in italics that Richard was *sounder*—a grave charge, if true. Richard hadn't yet told forty years but "seemed an old gull drying his wise wings in the sun, Berryman a sandpiper skittering along the edge of the tide." Florence Codman, when she paid the old gull a single visit in Princeton, found his hair gone white and his belly growing stout. "The old simple give-and-take" which Christine Weston remembered from Harrington days was shading to high-and-mighty now. This was partly a pose, partly a refuge, and partly the man in the grain. Oliver Wendell Holmes, meeting his friend Henry Adams by chance, thought him delightful. "But when I called at his house and he was posing to himself as the old cardinal he would turn everything to dust and ashes." That was how it was with him at home.

In *The Freedom of the Poet*, Berryman defined his craft: "Love of the stuff and of rhythm, the need to invent, a passion for getting things right, the wish to leave one's language in better shape than one found it." Poetry, he said, "is a terminal activity, taking place out near the ends of things." Richard was more laconic, and on his New Critical side averse to general statement. "Anybody can have ideas," he said. Delmore called him a "patriot of the actual." The radio, reporting life at a remove, was "the great instrumentality of the unactual" and made the *Times* seem absolutely impinging. In his first year at Princeton, after much general talk about the poetry one of his students had submitted, he got down to brass tacks. He wrote in his notebook: "The abstractions of metre and phrasing seemed earthy and reassuring like a sunrise." This reassurance waned.

Once Helen, her defenses down, evoked a picture of Richard the young man. He was the type of the Romantic poet, and in bitter reverie she recalled his poetic soul. Later Sean O'Faolain marveled at Richard's "transmogrification" from a Keats to a Jeffrey. John Berryman "struck some of us," Bruce Berlind said, "in something of the same way that Byron must have struck his contemporaries: as the walking archetype of the brilliant, erratic, guilt-laden poet." Beneath all the posturing, though, "he was somehow the real thing." This doesn't suggest that Richard was specious. Dying young goes with being a Romantic poet, and unlike his friend Berryman Richard survived. He wrote in these years: "There is a disorder vital to the individual which is fatal to society. And the other way round is also true." In his survival gain trenches on loss "and the other way round." He knew how "we survive ourselves in alien forms, and that no one would murder us sooner than our own children." Their love turns to hate as the familiar focus of our instincts begins to change. But a man's style or mode of perceiving "should have as many breakthroughs as possible," Richard said, the center of an aspiration being not in its consistency but in its transformations.

In the twenties most writers lived by their wits but now in the forties, said the *Partisan Review,* "many make their living by teaching in universities." What did Blackmur the newly minted academic think of this? Richard wrote out his answer "from the point of view of the old free-lancing risk those of my age grew up with as natural." He said the writer in the university faced different temptations, "to do more teaching—to make more money—and the other temptation, to lead more than two kinds of social life." The last was the poignant temptation for him. By social life, he didn't mean tea parties or cocktail parties. His point was to life in society as opposed to Romantic isolation, the near-starving poet who thumbed his nose at society. "The artist is inimical to *any* society," he wrote at eighteen, and can be "disciple to no tradition but that of isolation." He had lived in his garret for a long time, however, and this youthful bravado struck him as jejune. You didn't pay your bills when you lived a life of isolation. Besides, he wanted to get in the swim.

Comparing Henry and Brooks Adams who are his own two selves, the contemplative man and the polemicist, Richard said how they enacted the difference between the artist and the lawyer. "The second excites you to a verdict where the first persuades you of a substance." Richard in the academy sought to translate this substance to action. But the side of him that clamored for action was cast down by the side that discountenanced action. He was like the men of *Heartbreak House,* a force without an object, prey to restless lassitude but lacking an aim. Like his version of Proust, he thought of himself as anti-intellectual. This was partly strategic: he wanted to keep free from the petrified intellect and the hide-bound point of view. "He maintained intelligence at the pitch where it refuses action; he preferred transmutations to action, the shifting of the phases of the heart to the phases of the reason." His deepest appeal was to the deep viscous memory, and of this the heart and reason were only two decimations. Feeling so in his bones, he made war on himself when the public man took the head of the table. The fascination of his later years consists in the enacting of this internecine war.

Already the life of Adams hints at his growing dissatisfaction with chronicling the events of the past. Like that errant John Hay who took the path Henry Adams might have taken, he engages "to invent a *modus vivendi* for every dispute." Picking up where Adams left off, he speaks in his own voice, bringing the past to bear on the present. He does this prescriptively, too. Why did American foreign policy fail and how can we remedy the failure? Give him a hearing and he is eager to say. Like Adams, he corrects the present by looking to the future. Criticism becomes "man's means of finding the incentive of trying again." You can see how the drift is more and more to ideas and how the impulse is becoming what he would have called heuristic. His fiction is a casualty of this drift and this impulse.

So is his "myopically precise-close up New Criticism." (Sean O'Faolain is describing it.) Subjective, obscure, and not involved enough with "the conditions of society"—that was what middle age told him. "The burden of criticism in our time"—an ominous phrase—was "to make bridges between the society and the arts." *Time* Magazine took appreciative notice. It was matter for pride that Richard and his friends who had made the New Criticism were "internal free-lancers," but this pride was alloyed with disquiet. The New Critics were "without adequate relation to the society of which they expressed the substance more and more as an *aesthetic* experience." Their partial expression was disabling, Richard said, not least for himself, and he spoke with mounting intensity of "the elite of writers in America" who stood aloof from "the forces which shape or deform our culture." The intensity comes home as shrillness, and the preferring of the abstract entity to the man in his habit signals the change from absolute critic to inferior metaphysician.

In his notes on Irving Babbitt—they make one of the persuasive essays in *The Lion and the Honeycomb* (1955), and there aren't so many essays in this collection that persuade—Richard said how literature might illustrate the history of ideas or exemplify patterns of life. You were to remember, though, that "the ideas are merely primary"—a nice way to put it—and the patterns merely prior to the literature itself. The last essay in the collection takes a different tack. In the criticism of literature, Richard insisted, philosophy was "not only possible but necessary." Only a dozen years separate these two citations, but the change they dramatize is immense.

Even in middle age the dry cough of age afflicted this writer, and you can see how in his mind "understanding replaces rather than crowns experience." Though he said, beginning his "Anni Mirabiles" lectures, that it was always a help to speak from a text, he dispensed with the text or used it—and so demeaned it—only to point a moral. Good-natured editors on the fringes of literature who envisaged "a true *Geistesbewegung* able to act in history and come to the aid of men in our apocalyptic epoch" got inside his guard. He should have blanched at their prose, but he was flattered when they numbered him among the "spiritual and intellectual leaders of our time," and he agreed to participate in a joint enterprise designating "the limitations of the procedural obsessions that afflict the modern mind." When his guard was up he called mere intellect the mere manners of the mind, and said how the man who makes himself all intellect or all opinion is all manners and no man. In his writing of the forties and later, he came close to approximating this mannered man, and often what he made was organ grinding, little more. Good sense was a casualty of the exclusive appeal to reason.

At the Vermont Summer School, when he taught there for Jack Aldridge in the early fifties, he wanted to tell his students "how morals get into literature" and he spun a portentous lecture on the subject, taking "as my private title between the Numen and the Moha." A generation later, Aldridge retained "a very clear recollection of the stunned reception accorded" this lecture, given to an audience not simply of students but of literary ladies and assorted townsfolk whose ears were tuned by the lucid periods of John P. Marquand and Dorothy Canfield Fisher. Through the Numen and the Moha, Richard sailed "in full majesty and obliviousness." This took some doing. The erstwhile New Critic remarked how criticism cries in the dark, "crowding its darkness into the blaze of noon." But his crying, if inchoate—the style of the pneumatic prophet who has got the gift of tongues—has become purposive now, "in the interests of beautiful reason." If you prefer the heuristic mode, you will applaud the change from tacitean annalist to unacknowledged legislator of the world, and perhaps there is a case to be made for late Blackmur the meliorist and progressive. Also you can say that the change was inevitable for this man whose isolation chilled him to the bone.

Richard looking in from the outside is like those alienated characters whose alienation he had hard words for in the fiction of Ford Madox

Ford. "They are ourselves beside ourselves the wrong way." What was the right way? Here is an implicit answer, from another essay of the forties: "It is society that is immortal, not the positions from which we look at it." The role of hero in the modern age was usurped, Richard said, by "the impotent, the defective, the psychotic, or by the artist himself." (You see from this why Faulkner left him at a loss and how, step by step, his criticism of modern fiction is jeopardized by his criticism of life.) The rebellion presented by these modern heroes was necessarily inadequate, "neither divine madness nor diabolic," for the struggle with Diabolus signified no more than private hysteria unless your life and work attested "the actual momentum of society." Otherwise all your ardors were only "struggle in flight." Maybe joining the academy involved the chance of losing "the real delight in imaginative risk." This chance was worth taking, however. After all, said Richard, society persists, and "somebody someday will see what the commitments of our society really are."

From the vantage point of Princeton, he set himself to see. His mode of seeing was imperial, also contingent. He turned a negligent eye on projects that developed "specificity in an area of knowledge." His preference, he said, was "to generalise an area of knowledge." The Integration of Knowledge or the Anthropology of Leading Ideas got his fascinated attention, and he sought to bring his own ideas "out of the clouds and into Princeton." He made a slogan: this was "a time to tamper rather than tamp." You weren't to value knowledge for its own sweet sake, but insofar as it led to "the solution of human ills" or presented "the means of manipulating society." This apostle of praxis aimed "to apply that knowledge in action and judgment." The "one indubitable enterprise proper to the mind" coped with knowledge "by so criticising its variety as to discover its use and its unity." As he went up on his social-scientific balloon ascension, ballasted with facts and figures, he didn't rise into the perspicuous air of truth but "into his own stratosphere of ellipsis, abstraction, and impossible style." The role to which he aspired was that of social engineer, a critic nearly anonymous. This role eluded him. Instead he became a magnificent crank. In terms of what he became, not much got accomplished—or not in a practical way. The journey he made sticks in the memory, however.

At the Institute for Advanced Study, where he went in 1944, Richard began to view with alarm. He expressed this alarm by sitting on committees. He attended the MLA. When Henri Peyre gave a paper in Baltimore in the late forties, Richard took the part of respondent. The discussion went as follows:

RPB. You like the word "sharp" in English. I think your French word is better.

HP. Yes.

RPB. And I'd like to adopt it over in English. "Volupté" seems to be a very fine word; move ahead with it!

HP. Yes!

RPB. It's what came into my mind.

HP. Thank you. It's extremely interesting.

At a gaseous conference on American Thought, he explained to such as Granville Hicks that we hadn't tried enough to understand, "if not control," what the intelligence had created. "St. Augustine would put it that we have preferred to submit to the created thing rather than to master—or understand—the creator." This sentiment makes every kind of sense. The tone—or tilt or twist—is emasculating, though, that of a leader writer in the *Times*. It must have curled Hicks's hair. He was the panegyrist of the Great Tradition who had characterized the "impassioned quibbling" of the New Critics as a game to no purpose, the game not being purposive. Now here was Richard evidently agreeing with him. Agitated by the encroaching sea of political parochialism, Richard looked away from particulars, reaching instead for "the general relation of the particular." James's figure in the carpet absorbed him. He wasn't reading James, though. To John Marshall, he said: "I read nothing but Toynbee in the late evenings now."

Marshall and friends had got him into the Institute in the School of Economics when his tenure as Hodder Fellow expired. Years later, going on about his war work—it had to do, he said, with "international fiscal and monetary policy"—Richard paid homage to these friends, "the most extraordinary men I ever expect or hope to meet." Walter Stewart, the economist and a permanent member of the Institute, functioned also as a Rockefeller trustee. Stewart and the President of Princeton were thick as thieves, Marshall said. Lucius P. Wilmerding belonged to the Institute, in the School of Economics. In the city he belonged to the Century Club. So did Harold Dodds. Richard Blackmur, the man who banked on rejection, never lacked for powerful supporters. They stood by him, too. He was the outsider, a maverick, a sport, and gravitated naturally to men like Walter Stewart, a former investment banker and Case Pomeroy partner who admired the conservative cast of his work on Henry Adams.

In the mid-forties Richard's foothold in Princeton was still precarious, however. He couldn't count on the Institute for more than a year, and inevitably life in limbo took its toll. "I suppose my affairs prosper," he wrote wanly to George Anthony, but he wished his mind prospered as well. Tate had got him the offer of the Poetry Chair at the Library of Congress and he thought he might go to Washington in 1945, or possibly to Bennington College. But his sinecure at the Institute allowed him to get "down to the close stone" on his writing—"for the first time in years," he was able to work without interruption. Stewart, estimating the "high quality" of what he had done, found himself "inventing ways which would justify us extending his membership for another year."

He set the web of the Old Boy Network quivering. "To all appearances there was no mechanism. Yet behind the scenes in constant and vigorous action" moved an elaborate organization of the whole Princeton world"—a graceful redundancy. That was Professor Osgood in his bicentennial history of the university. From the center of the mechanism, Stewart wrote to David H. Stevens, the Director of the Rockefeller Foundation: "What is the best use to be made of a year of free time of a person like Richard Blackmur?" From the periphery, the answer came back: "Permit Blackmur to continue studies in literary criticism." John Marshall dispatched the necessary funds. Richard said Marshall would have made an excellent butler. This wasn't meant as a sneer. Marshall was a friend of long standing, also a friend in power. At the Rockefeller Foundation he had become Associate Director. An American Maecenas whose accent was old Eastern seaboard like Nelson Rockefeller's before he aspired to the common touch, he thought Richard "an endlessly tappable fount of wisdom" and served him up, said Alfred Kazin, for breakfast, lunch, and dinner.

David Stevens drank from the fount of wisdom, too. Twice at least the Director invited Richard to ask for a grant. "Good matters of this sort with you," Stevens thought, "should not be neglected or postponed too long." Richard fell in with this thinking. Never having been to Europe and considering Europe "the reward of all good Americans," he advised the Foundation how it might finance his trip. Walter Stewart, he wrote, "seemed to think there was no question." There wasn't any question. Richard's presence in Europe, Marshall observed, would offer "an opportunity for him to become acquainted with European writers and writing." Richard made a first trip in 1952, almost a Grand Tour, and it took him fourteen months. Going over, he danced nightly with his "true girl," a widow contessa named Vera Ragazza. Her name, he suggested, "must be a late form (for those of full figure) of anima semplicetta." He had set up as a linguist for the journey abroad, playing records in Italian every day before he left, and Stanley Edgar Hyman in a critique of the early fifties saluted his apparent fluency in Greek, Latin, Italian, and French. Hyman had to concede his "admitted unfamiliarity with German." To Leslie Fiedler, however, it was equally apparent that Richard "did not *really* understand any language other than English." This didn't preclude a deal of talking.

In Bologna, where he found a home away from home, he met the young poet Alfredo Rizzardi, and later he applauded Rizzardi's "elegant undertaking in rendering me into what I sometimes like to believe is my rightful language." He figured as "Maestro" to the students who translated his essays and poems, and he engaged them in debate on the finer points of Italian grammar. Keeping abreast, he read every day in *Corriere della Sera,* an acceptable surrogate for the *New York Times.* (In France it was *Le Monde,* in Switzerland *Die Zeitung,* which cultivated, he said, "rather a higher level than the T. L. S.") Back home in Princeton, he formed the habit of pausing before Zinder's on Nassau Street to read the Italian papers to friends. At a state dinner given by the University of Bologna, he insisted that Fiedler bespeak him in Italian to the professor of Hungarian literature, who knew about as much Italian as he did. "Tell the gentleman," Richard said, "that poetry is a black light." He "got me drunk enough," his translator said, "so that I was willing and able" to do this.

Traveling in Italy, Richard took the part of the Good European, "a fragmented Italian with strong Tyrolean features and a feather in my spirit." Three days in the Dolomites did that. "The mountains made me," he said, "Venetsia [*sic*] disfecemi." The love affair with Italy into which he threw himself was part rodomontade, but it never staled nor was it diminished by a "sense of the loss of mystery." His Bolognese translator presented him as living "in questi giorni in Italia," and for his better self this became a permanent abode. "As for me," he asserted, "I am an Italian," and he thought it would have to be "mere infatuation" if anyone liked Italy more than he did. Above Cortina he saw again how things were formed out of their own chaos, and seeing that, he saw order, but of a parochial kind, and how the order was beauty "whether of the clouds or of the grapes or monks pissing on the roadside." This strongly recurring sense in him of disorder swapping back and forth with order, or of order as the emanation of disorder, qualifies the nattering about institutions which pops and fizzles in the later work. For example, from "Ara Coeli and Campidoglio": "The odor of cat-piss in box hedges remains with me: as if the box were getting back at the formality with which it had been trimmed." Like the love affair with Maine a generation before, the experience of Italy altered what he was. It put a feather in his spirit and later it allowed him to slough the leader writer in the *Times.* "As the fellow said: In the mountains, there you feel free."

Not every encounter pleased. Venice was "the night-vase of humanity." But it had its indispensable uses "in the absence of plumbing and restraint." Mostly he was willing to take things as they were. He drank negronis in Harry's Bar, and like all the other tourists he looked around expectantly "to see if Hemingway was there." He was his own cicerone and pointed out the beggar women "with babies like detached goiters," and the heavy legs of the girls that hung "like rotten pears off the pillions of the motorcycles." He wouldn't have made much of a tour guide. On Elba for a week, history seizing his imagination, he ruminated on the greatness of Napoleon, like himself the type of the exile and outsider "who had all the greatness possible without virtue." Opera spoke to him too, and he followed the season from Bologna to Salzburg. At the Salzburg Seminar, on which he reported to his sponsors at the Foundation, he took over one day for Harry Levin. With some of the students he made a great hit, others he puzzled, "but was notably successful," said his friend and fellow seminarian Ed Cone, "at the Bierstube in the evenings." Levin as often was honing his ax, and when the session wound down and "we were all giving little speeches at the final dinner," he said how "Blackmur spent an afternoon explaining literature to the students, and I spent the rest of the summer explaining Blackmur."

To Marshall's reiterated suggestion that "I might want to go to Ankara or Istanbul," he returned an affirmative answer, having taken the suggestion "into my mind for a week or two." Following the sun, he journeyed to Egypt, Lebanon, and Turkey. In Beirut, Marshall said, the Arab students were wowed by his lectures on Henry James. He wanted to spend Christmas, he told his sister Betty, on the banks of the Nile. Princeton and his classes were expecting him, though, and he sailed home from Genoa in the late summer of 1953. He got home almost two thousand dollars in debt. Mike Keeley was flabbergasted "when he told me what he needed to travel abroad." Edward F. ("Chet") D'Arms, Marshall's associate at the Foundation, speculated on his needs and made a testy memorandum. Richard had stayed at the Frankfurterhof in Frankfurt and the Vierjahreszeiten in Munich, he said, and these were the most expensive hotels in either city. For D'Arms, on the other hand, a small pension was good enough and a room without bath. Why wasn't this good enough for Richard? "Perhaps in the future, in cases such as Blackmur's," the Foundation "should try to suggest less expensive hotels and restaurants."

The suggestion did no good. Not being to the manner born, Richard in middle age set out to make amends. Three years after returning to Princeton he was off on another hegira, "to return I know not when." In Naples, wanting to hear the opera at San Carlo, he was alarmed to discover that "my Smoking is in the trunk and the trunk is in the Dogana's." You couldn't go to the opera unless you wore your "Smoking." In Zagreb he announced a "communal relationship" with that city and proposed to end his days there, the claims of the workaday life notwithstanding. Leaving his sumptuous hotel in Berlin, he sauntered along to Kampenski's on the Kudamm, and over long lunches made himself acquainted with half the wines on the wine list. He did the same in Rome, idling away his sunny afternoons at Nido's on the via Borgognona. "Only the idle virtues earn the sun." That was what he was saying, and the Rockefellers and their ethic were far away in New York City. One lovely city ran into another. "I have heard him . . . do a superb job," he wrote, recommending Fiedler to the Fulbright Commission, "in Parma, or it may have been Modena." He became a connoisseur of art and volunteered to lend out of his own collection photographs of Caravaggio "which Alinari took for me." You could see the fratelli Alinari behind their tripods in Florence, or was it at Rome?

To Europe and the Middle East, his familiar stamping grounds, he added Japan, where he engaged to lecture on "The American Critic in Action." In 1959 his Japanese lectures made a loose-limbed book. *New Criticism in the United States,* he called it, but the criticism wasn't new and the New Critical mode, to this activist professor, was already dead as the dodo. En route to Tokyo he stopped off at New Delhi, wanting to inspect the Taj Mahal. He rode on an elephant. He ran out of money, and the Rockefellers were constrained to add another thousand dollars to his stipend. He expected, said a friend, to be patronized, and was. For the record, he denied his favored connection. Sometimes he tipped his hand. He wrote in 1951, apropos of his two-week session at the University of Vermont: "I gave my Rockefeller friends a good account of the whole thing yesterday and found good ears." When Cyril Connolly, writing in the *London Times,* made fun of "privileged Mr. Blackmur" and "the world of subsidy" in which he lived, Richard said he knew the secret of Connolly's pique. "He is convinced that I have both hands in the Rockefeller pockets. I wish it were true." It was certainly true that he considered the Foundation his personal fief. "I shall be seeing the Rockefellers"—that was how he used to put it—"and shall want to bring up your name."

The Rockefellers were concrete but spelled abstraction for Richard. Under their aegis he wrote "papers"—the word is his and conjures up the functionary in striped pants or the denizen of a think tank—on "the cultural situation of the writer in this country," or the "Economy of the American Writer," or the "American Literary Expatriate." These generic figures dwell like Richard in "the deep-riven swindling chasm between perfection of life and perfection of work." Even in this chasm, the stresses of society operated visibly. You could see them, so do something about them. That made the Rockefellers, always faithful to their Protestant bias, sit up straight. They paid heed when Richard told them in his reports how "the special problem of the humanities in our generation" was to struggle against "the new illiteracy and the new intellectual proletariat." In the offices at the Foundation, "Blackmur items" circulated freely. He reported on the tariff as it affected book production, or on the USIS or else on "Advertising as a Technique in Psychological Warfare." "We should ponder and discuss," said Chet D'Arms. Marshall, having read Richard's essay, "Towards a Modus Vivendi," wrote in the margin: "I quite agree with D'Arms." Thirty offprints of this essay went for distribution to the Middle East. Richard ought to go with them, Marshall suggested, to promote "a sense of community in the intellectual enterprise."

The Middle East, where he dazzled the poor Syrian wogs (Saul Bellow's phrase), was for the future. For the present, he hiked out every morning the three miles to the Institute, a pleasant cluster of Georgian buildings at the edge of a wilderness throbbing with birds. He stayed at his desk until six in the evening and played to himself the role of philosopher-king. Interruptions were welcome only when "associated with Treasury people whether American or English or League of Nations." Every so often he ventured a question "to prove that I am here . . . but hardly ever why." Why was he at the Institute and what was the good of his subsidized life, separated from the world "beyond any measure I have yet taken," at the same time involved with the world and its business up to his elbows? He was forging his identity as prophet and seer. The rest of his life declares this identity.

The English political philosopher Walter Bagehot gave him a point of departure. Reading Bagehot, who had looked with a direct eye at "what was actually going on" in the political society of the 1860s, Richard saw how he himself might fashion "a layman's policy in politics and culture." The policy was to be catholic. He wanted "to look at a culture as a whole" or to look at many cultures with an eye to their underlying sameness. He was saying how the leaves are many but the root is one. America and Europe were Rome and Greece "all over again." But a two-point bearing wasn't sufficient. You needed three points to determine position and project a course, and Richard wanted a vantage of the Middle East as his triangulating point. Also, he wanted to go to the Middle East.

He understood that his proposed policy was only academic unless he could bring it out of the clouds. With his left hand he was working on Adams and American foreign policy in the 1890s. Describing with disgust "actual practice in . . . [Adams's] day and our own," he said how "the work of intelligence is all to do over again: to speak again, and still, in a fresh voice." This was the voice he cultivated, but not in a vacuum. He insisted that his convictions be dressed, however briefly, in the authority of power. "The author is he who has the task . . . to employ that power." This author had moved a long way from his impotent and isolated beginnings. But even in his beginnings, zealotry bears a part. He wrote as a young man, when attacked by the Communists for want of moral feeling: "I have been trying to keep moral feeling down all my life." Now he abandoned the effort.

An idea obsessed him, he wrote to Walter Stewart, "which if not platonic is yet probably visionary." He wanted to create a "Layman's Quarterly" in Princeton as his personal organ for making a better world. This wasn't a new idea either. "I know it's just throwing dust in your eyes, or mine," he had written to Jay Laughlin at the end of the thirties, "but what this country really needs"—more and more he allowed himself this kind of phrasing—"is a magazine . . . [promoting] salvation; penance; contrition." Though he didn't "particularly propose" himself as editor-in-chief, it seemed clear that he was willing to serve. He had never got over the demise of the *Hound & Horn*, and a cryptic and mournful passage in *A Primer of Ignorance* speaks of 1934 as a time of deprivation for him. This was the year the magazine folded. Ten years later, in an enormous report for the Rockefeller Foundation on "American Literary and Critical Magazines," he surveyed the field with a view to resuscitating "the word I had lost"—not the *Hound & Horn*, it was dead beyond recall, but some better version of it in the present.

For his model he took the *North American Review*, knowing how Adams had been editor there. For fifty years, Adams said, this famous periodical had served as "the stage coach which carried literary Bostonians to such distinction as they had achieved." Its province was not only artistic but social and political, and Richard wanted his quarterly to go under the same name because it "reflects our intended reach." With the beginning of World War II, the *North American Review* had ceased to exist. But John Pell the historian—he had lived over the Dunster House Book Shop when Richard was clerking for Firuski—still held the copyright. Thinking this a "propitious time" to resume publication, he agreed to make way for Richard and associates. Stewart and Wilmerding were among the associates, also Christian Gauss. New friends and supporters included Julian Boyd, the editor of the Jefferson Papers, and Edward Mead Earle, Wilmerding's colleague in the School of Economics. All of them understood that the great days of the *North American Review* were a half century in the past. "But if we say merely that the experiment has never been tried since"—this was Richard, concluding his Rockefeller report—"we have the only answer appropriate to make: an incentive to try, and see."

His report was descriptive and made "an argument of policy." The slick-paper magazines hardly merited notice, except for invidious contrast. "Where the slicks invite slacking, a critical journal would invite hauling close, and closer." The alphabet journals, appealing to scholarship meanly construed, were beneath notice, too. So were most of the miscellanies, satisfied with the *faux bon* or middling good. "PMLA and *Yale Review* are examples. The one fortifies the encased mind; the other dilutes the inert mind." A magazine, in any case, was only a miscellany and aimed at entertaining its readers rather than advocating views. Scofield Thayer and Sibley Watson had done the best you could do with this kind of magazine. They had unified the *Dial* through literary taste, standards, and principles, and the taste was unexceptionable, the principles, too, but "the miscellany obviates its own standards." What was wanted among periodicals today— there went the phrase again—was a critical quarterly with a strong bias and dealing with "the arts, the sciences, politics, philosophy, and religion, as they impinge upon the lay mind at its best." If you wanted to know the purpose of this quarterly, Richard answered without hesitation: "Changing the minds of its readers."

Nothing human was alien, and the review should consider "all aspects of human affairs." Its bias, said Wilmerding, should reflect the conservative side but only in the sense that Jeremiah was conservative "when he urged the people 'to make a stand upon the ancient way.'" Richard in the first of his "Anni Mirabiles" lectures explained what this meant. "The true anarchy of spirit should always show . . . a tory flavor," he thought. "It is the artist above all who *realizes* that revolutions—however fresh, violent and destructive, however aspiring, or groping, or contagious—have *already* taken place." Revolution, like murder, was the emblem of failure, only "the usury of dead institutions." These remarks call in question the efficacy in last things of all contractual change. Richard in the full tide of enthusiasm wasn't calling in question, however. Partly his enthusiasm was whistling in the dark. His notebooks for these years reveal the desperate man. To keep the desperation down required "every ruse of God and the imagination." So he became a public man—by his own definition, "all but an emptiness." He wanted "to prevent private laceration from showing," and this was one of his ruses.

On his public side, he drew inspiriting conclusions. A review that really meant business might be effective out of all proportion to the number of subscribers. He pointed to the "influence and attractive power" of the little magazines he most admired. Eliot's *Criterion*, never seeming "to have made any attempt upon anything but a minimum audience," raised "fundamental questions of the whole Western Culture." The questions persisted. The original *Dial* under Emerson and Margaret Fuller had never counted more than three hundred subscribers. In a far bigger country, *Poetry* counted only three thousand. But the *Dial* in its successive avatars, especially the last, was unforgettably itself, "the leading international journal of the arts and letters printed in English," and *Poetry* made the reputations of 95 percent of those American poets who first began to publish in the years of renascence after 1912. What he and Kirstein and Bandler had done he knew on his pulses, and he knew and estimated for the Foundation the successes of Rahv and Phillips and Delmore Schwartz at the *Partisan Review*. Of all the journals he surveyed, this was the most energetic and urban: but "urban without urbanity, vulgar without cheapness, intense without fanaticism, widely aware with no pretence of omniscience or panacea." His friends Brooks and Warren at the *Southern Review* had planted the banner of the New Criticism south of the Mason-Dixon line. They had created a forum for the poetry of Randall Jarrell. Richard said they made a difference, in his own life too; it could never be possible "to work for better or more generous editors." So he built his case for the Layman's Quarterly he intended to publish.

But he had a long memory, also a filing cabinet stuffed with facts and figures, and when Eudora Welty—"a charming girl"—came to town full of her own project for starting a little magazine, mutual friends referred her to Richard, who "knew more about the subject than anybody in the world." Among other things, he knew that the *Hound & Horn* had lost between six and eight thousand a year, and that the *Southern Review* sold more copies in Tokyo than Atlanta, and more in Massachusetts than Georgia, Alabama, Mississippi, and Florida combined. In the Sahara of the Bozart, it lived not because anybody read it but as "a part of Huey Long's effort to make his state shine before the world." No wonder this magazine had foundered. Maybe that was the fate of all the little magazines, failing "some sort of endowment or patronage." He didn't mean the sort of patronage the Kingfish provided, and he didn't see how mere money was tangential to the heart of the matter.

His own venture looked doubtful, that is what his letters said, but he couldn't resist the impulse to stand like a prophet upon the ancient way. "Habbakuk was alive again, and it seemed right that he should be." He began to gather statistics and beat the bushes for funds. But money wasn't the critical problem. Direction was the problem and there were too many directors, each with his own point of view. Sessions that attempted to formulate policy lasted well into the night. Wilmerding hammered out an editorial platform. Discussion ensued, and he threw it in the wastebasket. Julian Boyd had a try and "followed Lucius' precedent." Richard, being neither fish nor flesh, saw the merit in every position while declining to opt for any one to the exclusion of any other. "The brethren had better decide on a programme before they go any further." This was H. L. Mencken's opinion. He had made a great success with the *American Mercury* and was also, as he said, "the oldest and wisest man now extant on earth." He agreed that a magnificent chance existed "for a really independent and intelligent magazine," and he was flattered to suppose that "the new *North American Review* will be a sort of *American Mercury* addressed to a smaller audience." But when he came up from Baltimore to offer advice in the spring of 1946, he heard the conflict of voices and said succinctly: "Tell the boys to forget it."

The sine qua non was unity of purpose, "one of the great creations of the mind," Richard said ironically. Putting on his singing robes, he defined it as "the chimera looming in the rancorous fog of wanhope." As things turned out, this wasn't a bad definition. "All attempts to set up magazines devoted to free discussion have failed," Mencken told the boys. Nothing looked feebler than a magazine of opinion which admitted all shades of opinion. Catholicity was Richard's great vice or virtue, however. He was more and less than catholic, almost Laodicean. Doubt jostling conviction menaced his public role. This contention described him from the beginning. In his adolescent years he had sneered at Christianity. Later he changed his mind or perhaps his mind deepened. He wondered if he had been fair in his critique of Eliot's orthodox polemic, *After Strange Gods,* and he asked himself if it were not "true that the religious bias . . . is alone capable of leading, or pushing, us away from the abyss we have within. A long fall without the sanction of tragedy; that is life without religion."

But he couldn't believe. Religion figured for him as a portmanteau term, comprehending every system of belief social, political, or esthetic. Reflecting on the Christian faith of Eliot and Hopkins and the magical faith of Yeats, he conceded with deep distress his own need for emotional order. He had to concede also "the ill-satisfaction of that need" through church or magic or political persuasion or social engineering. He sought to articulate a faith for himself, and his career as public man makes a vivid gloss on this undertaking. But no formal conviction was in the cards for him. Convictions were to span the wastes "in which only, for the most part, we have time to live; the waste of the world and the waste within us." Times without number he quoted Montaigne: "I will suspend judgment." This motto was "the beacon and horn and bell in the great fog of his doubt," with which he felt his clothes permanently damp and clinging. It made a bad motto for the *North American Review*. Richard the evangelist, who hoped like Jeremiah to find "the straight and right way, and so to walk in it," must have known in his heart that the straight and right way was a fiction.

His phrase for what happened next is "the shock of new will on old purpose." Where he had made a failure, others might succeed. But it wasn't his failure in the present that drove him. Wanting to dispel "the legend of early doom," he made himself the shield and buckler of the little magazines. He was remembering the early thirties and "the word I had lost." Looking for money, he went hat in hand to the Guggenheim Foundation, where his old patron Henry Allen Moe was now a familiar friend, not to say a retainer. "Dear Moe," his importunate letters began. He distinguished for the Rockefellers the magazines they ought to cherish —as they said at the Foundation, the ones which represented "the cutting edge of literary advance." He trimmed and sharpened his Rockefeller report and sent it to the *Sewanee Review*. "The Economy of the American Writer" (1946) made a tract for the times and "raised the editorial ire of *Harper's*"—to Richard's satisfaction. He said this highbrow magazine was no better than the slicks in truckling to "the standards of the new illiteracy." He himself disclaimed solutions but insisted on the urgency of his diagnosis. Someone had better listen to him—that was the gist. He concluded his essay: "All's Alexandrian else."

In the fifties his crusade was still going full blast, and in *The Lion and the Honeycomb* he showed American culture shooting Niagara. "Despite the growth of population and education," maybe because of it, the audience of committed readers had continued to dwindle. "Three thousand copies an issue for the literary journals"—not just coincidentally the circulation of the *Hound & Horn*—seemed the most you could expect, yesterday or today. This hardly added up to self-support. But "in the market of the arts," as Richard put it, money was the indispensable "agent for freedom and for the maintenance of standards." Charity was welling in him, also good hope. "I have been asked to put a bee in your bonnet," he wrote to John Marshall in the early forties. The *Kenyon Review*, where his friend Ransom presided, would surely go under "unless some foundation" stepped forward. But it "should live, and deserves support." So he fired off his shot in the dark and "if there was a target hit, good." He hit the target, and the *Kenyon Review* got the grant that allowed it to continue. In the course of things more money was called for, and he made fresh representations. He thought it "in no way indiscreet" of him to say that the prospects looked good for renewal. "I will pray for you," he wrote to Ransom. He did better than that. Soon the *Sewanee* and the *Partisan Review* were clamoring for help, and when the *Hudson* began to publish in 1948, it wanted help, too. Literally, the word got abroad. What could Richard say about the "possibilities of procuring from the Rockefeller Foundation financial aid for Swiss publishers"? It was his fault and his pleasure that he was asked to say: he had hinted at these possibilities himself.

He worked hard at exploiting them. Writers around the country received letters from him, asking "your best opinion as to what literary magazines now being published in the United States are of the most use to literature." This wasn't a polite *causerie*. When he gave the word his word was taken up, the Foundation supposing that action was "in order" along the lines he suggested. He explained how the earlier years of the century had produced what they called at Rockefeller Center "a veritable rash" of little magazines. Though the officers knew that "not all the aspirants merited publication," there being among them "crackpots, posturing bohemians, half-baked aesthetes, and other riffraff," Richard told them how the chaff included pure wheat. With Cowley and Trilling he constituted a troika to advise the Foundation on spending its money. Ideas were mooted and translated into action—for a School of Letters at Kenyon College (Richard forgetting how he felt about such things at the Cummington School), or for a program of Literary Fellowships. In bringing these schemes down to earth, the anti-academic thought first of all of the academic world since, as he said, it was "for the university to preserve the standard of intention and perhaps of final judgment" in the arts.

This prosecuting of good works—the record fills reams of paper in the Rockefeller Archives, beginning in 1941—was intended to address "the problems and opportunities of the writer in America." To Richard the young man, Allen Tate had insisted that these problems "were not only insoluble but really ought to be insoluble forever." Otherwise you lost the tensions which gave a culture its vitality. In political terms, Richard called this sentiment defeatist. But he thought it "a sound sentiment for the artist to make use of in relation to his view of his material." In this view, problems were something you wrestled with in the material, and opportunities were how you resolved them.

From one of his literary correspondents, Richard got what he called a "hoitsy-toitsy" reply. To Wallace Stevens, "the objects in the attic of life" had never seemed dearer than when he saw Richard & Co. approaching them with their pots of gilding. "I have a horror of the sort of thing that is done for money," Stevens said. "It has nothing whatever to do with what means anything to me nor, I believe, to you." This reproof to the promoter of causes was written on the stationery of the Hartford Accident and Indemnity Company. Stevens didn't see that as telling against him, and a subsequent letter says why. If you believed that "the great corrupting force in literary activity in this country is that its object is to make money," what were you to do? "There is only one answer." The writer, as he faced "the point of honor," had to "support himself in some other way" than by writing. There was an alternative, but Stevens declined to entertain it. This was to indulge "that form of publishing (or being published) in which it is possible to make money."

But money, which never stuck to Richard's fingers, wasn't the essential point, and Stevens—like Richard in his report to the Rockefellers—skewed the proper emphasis a little. The essential point lay in the difference between public and private, writing in the world's eye and doing the world's business, or saying, like the poet, how fluttering things have just this quality of shade. Tocqueville, whom Richard put to use in his "Economy of the American Writer," thought those nations or peoples accomplished most in the here and now whose eyes were fixed on the hereafter. Stevens, in his set-to with Richard, was indifferent ostensibly to the here and now. He was the type of the Alexandrian poet, and in his own words he stuck stiffly to the type. While Edmund Wilson "adds a good deal more to the *New Yorker* than the *New Yorker* adds to him, still," Stevens said, "the Wilson of the *New Yorker* is not the man that made Wilson famous." Richard is the type of the Alexandrian poet who has lost his way or found a better way. He answers to either description. Robert Lowell wrote later, in a poem "for Richard Blackmur":

> His logic lacerates his vision, vision turns
> his logic to zealotry.

There is the word *corvée* which Richard got from Adams, meaning a tax or forced labor or, in modern French, a bore. Richard, like Adams, "felt the burden in all three senses." He agreed that "public service should be a *corvée*: a disagreeable necessity." Perhaps he didn't find it disagreeable enough. Yet in the letter he wrote to Stewart proposing a Layman's Quarterly, his tone is disinterested. Relying on God's mind was not sufficient, he thought. The secular mind had to assume the burden "of controlling what God certainly did not make." The context is the dropping of the bomb on Hiroshima. "Chaos," Richard said, "is the condition which makes aspiration necessary." As his life and work suggest, there were different modes of dealing with chaos.

In 1945 Richard sent a "statement of intentions" to David Stevens at the Rockefeller Foundation. He intended "either a series of essays or a small book on the desirability of a policy aimed at a mixed (deliberately varied) polity, economy, and culture." This project had "always carried in my mind the title, A Primer of Ignorance," he said. But until now there hadn't been "a book to go with it." Nine years passed, and his Primer was still the "new book I have been thinking up recently." He signed a contract to write it in 1956, but confessed a year later that, "as usual," he hadn't done "what I said that I would do." He died without finishing, and Joseph Frank put together what he had written, piecing it out with essays in modern fiction and poetry and earlier essays on Adams and James. So this last book, like other books of his, presents "fragments of an unfinished ruin."

But *A Primer of Ignorance* is only formally Richard's last book. He said to Marshall how it had been germinating at least as long ago as student days in Cambridge. The young esthete wasn't altogether shut away from the world or indifferent to wordly concerns, and his proposed polity is both old and new as it makes an exercise in "saltatory heuristics." You might pronounce the "primer" either way, he said—"yours as well as mine and everyone's who will read"—but however you pronounce it, thinking of *McGuffey's Reader* or Roosevelt priming the pump, the book is a primer *for* something, as Richard put it in the fifties. *The Lion and the Honeycomb* is this kind of book too, written In the Hope of Straightening Things Out. The source of each book, or the quiddity of either, lies in Richard's reports to the Rockefeller Foundation. The rubric for each of them, as he wrote to Marshall, is "thought becoming action." Granville Hicks was right and wrong about Richard. His economy was mixed, and he was in one man a sciolist and an evangel.

In most of his books Richard cheated a little, drawing on the past to fortify the present and, not incidentally, to eke out the book. The best work in *The Lion and the Honeycomb* is from the past: considerations of Adams, T. E. Lawrence, Henry James. One later essay convinces and James provides the subject. Matter of fact redeems this essay, not the same thing as marshaling facts to support a particular purpose. "I do not like art which solves technical problems for anything but itself." Richard said this in *A Primer of Ignorance,* where art addresses many problems not strictly artistic. In *The Lion and the Honeycomb*, the aperçus by which you know him are meant for efficient, as when he seeks to enumerate and implicitly to engender "the virtues of the complete scholar-critic." He thought he was Saintsbury, but was too wakeful for that and lacked the charm of a major belletrist.   More than half the seventeen essays in the book succumb, in his phrase, to "the platitude of statement." In these essays, even in the literary essays, he is feeling for the substrate or underlying form. This is work for the aged. Aristotle, the connoisseur of surfaces, was his hero from old days. The new hero, if not Plato, is platonic.

Titles had always given him fits. *The Lion and the Honeycomb* (after Yeats and Judges 14: 5–18) counts among his best, though he didn't think so himself. The title he gave his introductory essay—"Towards a Modus Vivendi"—was, as he wrote to his editor at Harcourt, "*almost* a better title for the book." As a subtitle, he offered "Essays in Institutions." That was where "all the evils in man's life come from," Richard had Montaigne saying. He added himself, "but there would be worse evils without them." Everything in his book was "about the institutions which surround and impinge upon literature, and which connect, or fail to connect, Letters and Society." (He was the critic who in early days had got rid of the ligatures; and the word "about" was his particular abhorrence.)

The corruption of institutions is the weakness of men, he wrote in the life of Adams, and he saw the process as continuing: "the weakness of institutions is the corruption of men." He attempted to redress the weakness of institutions. Resentment rose in him, or you can say civic virtue. In an apothegm he caught the good and bad of this: "Resentment is the primitive form of responsibility." In his character of responsible man, he let other commitments slide and gave first place to "my portrait of the American animal." The portrait was meant for kinetic. He "inquired in a dozen countries," including New Zealand, about the reading habits of a postliterate world. Arthur Sulzberger at the *Times* was his source for statistics regarding that newspaper's "rough geographic distribution." For Richard, grace abounded in the columns of the *Times*. The Educational Testing Service, down the road from Princeton, caught his roving eye. "It is here to stay," he told Phil Horton at the *Reporter* magazine, "but we must make sure that it does as nearly as possible what we want them to do rather than have them do merely what they can do." Why did it fall to him to make sure? The answer lay in his sense of *noblesse oblige*, fueled by personal resentment. He belonged as by right or fiat to the governing class, but the real power was the money power, and "the general unintelligence, which is infinite," turned a deaf ear when he lifted his voice. Here is his self-portrait, from *A Primer of Ignorance*: "None of the politics of his society has any use for him and none of them will publicly put up with his support." Denied the chance to cut a public figure, he became the lion in the American path, "looking about to see whom he may devour."

Richard knew that he spoke for the party of the dead—he called it, after Adams, the Conservative Christian Anarchist Party—and in a chapter on Eccentricity he intended to write, he said that he would show how the members of this party, if reabsorbed by society, were lost as friends and poisoned as intelligences. He didn't draw the moral for himself. Instead he accepted the wooden nutmeg of reform. In the earlier book, he said how it was with "The Politics of Human Power." In the later book, he offered to diagnose "Pathologies of Culture," and this was the heart of the book. As society was "plastic and buoyant," it ought to take the pressure of his fingers. Delmore called this plasticity the mark of "deathly sickness," and went on to express a fundamental difference "between your senatorship and my belief in critichood." The institutions which Richard granted to be bad but expected to correct "cannot be corrected," he said. The Conservative Christian Anarchist believed this, but not the man of good hope. His intention in proposing "A Burden for Critics" was, "to say the least of it, evangelical." Prosecuting this intention, he chased what he called a "Disconsolate Chimera."

As he concluded *The Lion and the Honeycomb*, he looked at Walter Lippmann and passed judgment on himself. "There is too much Arnold (and perhaps too much Irving Babbitt) in Lippmann, too much of the Northern Renaissance, too little of the wildness of the Greeks and the Italians. The will of God is certainly not Jacobinical; neither is it strident and single." Richard the Jacobin loved his new employment, though. He wrote to Marshall: "I cannot remember ever having been more serious in intent and I never felt wider things opening before me." The inveterate Blackmur-watcher Sherry Mangan likened him to Matthew Arnold, and said that his "sesquipedalian jargon" would constitute a case history for post-Socialist historians. Anyway, the comparison to Arnold is right. Richard, like Eliot, often quarreling with "that half-hero," was fascinated by his effort to enlist literature in the service of religion and society. What did you do when "the tower of the true city" was falling?

His own attempt at an answer is the symbolic imagination, as patented in the essay on Babbitt. "The purpose for which Mr. Blackmur has invented his symbolic imagination," said Joseph Frank, is to achieve "the secular equivalent of a religious imagination that has become moribund." Even in the "Anni Mirabiles" lectures which stand as the first section in *A Primer of Ignorance*, he presents literature as "making a kind of irregular metaphysics with both the tools left over from old institutions"—the

Church being one—"and the tools of the new sciences such as anthropology, psychology and sociology." Perhaps all four lectures might "constitute a proof of Matthew Arnold's proposed pudding about poetry as a substitute for religion."

He never found the substitute for which he was looking, and a generation later his forays into sociology and politics seem, on their intentional side, a little dusty. "Eschew a line of study," he wrote in his reflections on Toynbee, "in which the work done dies together with the worker." This work is journalism. A lot of late Blackmur is high-toned journalism, and you feel as you read it how a great critic is losing his way. But there is more than a scantling of permanent stuff mixed with the abundance of chaff, and its interest is not exclusively literary. This sets it apart from the permanence of early Blackmur. What sort of criticism surrounded "the explosion of great works of literature which took place in or about the year 1922," the period of "Anni Mirabiles"? Richard answered: "What we value in the bulk of it, and in the bulk sifted out and generalized, has very much the same sources as the literature itself." Criticism of this kind, to which he turned in the late forties and after, is not so much enabling as autonomous. The humble exegete has acquired the habit of pronouncing, and often his pronouncements are surds. Like Rimbaud, he reserved all rights of translation. "He has found himself speaking a private language and has grown proud of it." In lesser writers, this habit disgusts. Late Blackmur makes you suppose that the habit is indigenous, also becoming. When he held forth, said his friend Richard Eberhart, "one thought of Dr. Johnson in London, although Blackmur was slight of build and incidentally, had I think the smallest mouth I had seen on a man." Eberhart wondered at "the great, large words that came out" of this mouth, "sometimes for hours at a time." The manner (not "mere manners") with which he dressed them is in the end the compelling thing with him, not the "ideas" nor exegesis, however acute. This means that late Blackmur is more fun, if less "useful," than Blackmur the New Critic.

At forty-six, surveying the up and down of things "these three hundred and fifty years," he comes home to you as older than God. Immensely patient of himself, he says—assuming your interest—how in Berlin he turned to "Sir Walter" for his bedtime reading. In London after the ballet he runs on about his dinner, and who should be mindful of this? "As I remember, it was a Greek dinner with egg-lemon soup, vine leaves, and resinous wine at the Akropolis restaurant, surely all appropriate to the subject." At his country hotel in the Île-de-France, his hosts bring unbidden a bottle of Margaux 1925. They know him and his tastes, as the lord of Penshurst knew Ben Jonson. His friend Eugène the gardener imitates for his pleasure the cries of animals and birds. *Co-co-ricò*, he cries, imitating the cock, and there supervenes a flash of lightning and a damp gust bringing rain and the image of the Chapel Perilous, and "I thought," Richard says, "of the cows in the outskirts of Palermo." This manner may amuse or deject you, but you cannot imitate it except in him. By turns whimsical and poignant, it rises from the contention in this divided or, say, capacious man between the wordly philosopher and the devotee of the Pisgah-sight. "Plato, I take it, would lead us out of the wilderness. Aristotle would make us at home there."

Richard on his Platonic side was like that Hawthorne who, because society did not feed him enough, "had therefore to create a society in his imagination." He had no place to sit in, "neither an ivory cellar nor an ivory attic nor any flight of stairs between." Growing up in the inhospitable decade that followed World War I, he felt himself alienated from a society "increasingly less aesthetically-minded—less interested in the vivid apprehension of the values of the individual." As he said, his days were passed among enemies. He bided his time and got his revenge, becoming the lion in the path. "It is when you have lost, or think you are about to lose, the objective recognition of your values, that you assert them most violently and in their most extreme form—as every unrequited lover knows." Responding to the sense of loss, you might become an anchorite, a suicide, go into your shell, or set up in a new business. There were plenty of examples in his own time for each of these alternatives. But whatever response you made, the governing principle was to be "as conspicuous as possible about it."

Richard made a response for everyone to see. Mass culture having knocked together a world of papier-mâché, he declined to live there. Instead he attempted valiantly "to create a new kingdom of man: an independent, individual morality against the society that made it necessary." This, he said, was the glory of Joyce in *Ulysses* and *Finnegans Wake*. It is his own glory, and his late prose is his better habitation. Like the men of Lacedaemon in Thucydides' phrase, "coming from a city no more being, and putting ourselves in danger for a city hopeless ever to be again," he undertook our salvation, in part to save himself. The balloon ascension that carried him into the intense inane isn't inevitably or altogether comic. "Now," says Mann's hero, the young Felix Krull—he was Richard's alter ego—"Now you look plain and unpromising, but one day you will rise to the upper world magnificently adorned, to take your place at feasts, at weddings, to send your corks popping to the ceilings of private dining-rooms and evoke intoxication, irresponsibility, and desire in the hearts of men."

His better habitation makes a coherence, but isn't open to rational inspection. In the essays that made him famous, and after that for the rest of his life, Richard took the side of reason, and in his late essays he still wants to extricate us from "The Great Grasp of Unreason." Paradoxically, however, he is doing at the end exactly what he reprehends the Expressionists for doing: re-creating reality in rivalry with his own wishes. Even in the sociopolitical essays of *The Lion and the Honeycomb*, perhaps most of all in these essays where the appeal goes insistently to reason, his incentive (the word he uses) is to put reason outdoors. He liked to quote Maritain —"Art bitten by Poetry longs to be freed from Reason"—and he suggested that to think of these longings and the passion that attends their release is to understand "how great-spirited men have made great works by heroizing the longing to be freed from reason." There was a swarm of bees and honey in the carcass of the lion, and from strength much sweetness came forth.

Perhaps our mass society afforded no role for this lion to play, only "that of coquette." This was Adams's dilemma, living between his two worlds. But if the role sullied, should the intelligence flee to its great pyramid and "play no role at all?" In *A Primer of Ignorance* Richard gave his answer: "The writer's role is to play whatever role he can put himself into from emperor to clown." He tried on both these roles and, for both, "play of spirit" was the great desideratum. "There is no play in it," he wrote, reviewing a tiresome piece of special pleading. "It is evangelical, as so many of our countrymen are when dealing with the grave matters of the mind." His negative judgment carries more force, it being the judgment of a part-time evangel. He was never more in earnest than in the lectures he gave for the Library of Congress in 1956, but when the Government Printing Office got his title wrong, he was willing to go with the printer— "Annie Mirabells" did nicely for grave matters of the mind.

In *The Lion and the Honeycomb* the evangel is to the front, and partly retrieved by the feather in his spirit. Sometimes the feather is flaunted unawares, Richard not always knowing when he was emperor and when he was clown. "*Moha* means cow. . . . the cow that is in all of us, as Dante observes in his Purgatory." For humanity degraded, it is "the best name I know." This seems unlikely. The dark rabbi had his occulted reasons, however. "*Moha* is a Sanscrit word I got from a physicist (one time a poet) who in turn got it," etc. The physicist was "Oppie"—Richard's friend Oppenheimer, a poet in the days of the *Hound & Horn*, and later director of the Institute for Advanced Study. The improbable association of these two great *fakirs*—Oppie in his tragic mask and flowing cape and Van Gogh hat, and Richard the artist-hero struggling in marmalade— extends beyond the words on the page and becomes a mythological event. The mythology is public where the style is hermetic, involved with and emblematic of the history of the times. Finding in a friend's essay the word "reticulate," Richard insisted, "You got that word from me." Then he made material his vision of a line of giants, stretching back to the past and transmitting the flame: "I got the word from Oppie, and Oppie tells me he had it from Will James."

Say that his glory was he had such friends—like President Lowell of Harvard and Justice Frankfurter of the Supreme Court (with whom, you understood, he had almost succeeded in bringing off the acquittal of Sacco and Vanzetti). For younger friends he reconstructed his first years at Princeton, when Dodds and Gauss and Luther Eisenhart, the Graduate Dean, all sought his counsel, all being protagonists of a better time. To these fabulous years he opposed the immediate present in which the bu- reaucrats now regnant courted him no more, they dimly perceiving how he dwarfed them. In the North Country where he might have been senator—a conviction he protected by retaining his citizenship in the state of Maine—he was the trusted confidant of laconic farmers and fishermen. You saw him tying flies in his Connemara Cloth. The early Negro min- strels whom he remembered "as a black-faced reverberation in my own boyhood, especially in Waterville, Maine," swept the way for "history." That was "in the summer of 1912—where I also heard William Jennings Bryan."

This talent for personalizing the proximate past and locating himself at the center was his special talent, and he is spendthrift of it everywhere in his late essays. He hopes "T. S. Eliot would agree with me if I say . . ." but what he has to say isn't uppermost in the construction. The cursory manner is part of his bag of tricks, and intended to denote the man who has forgotten more than most of us have learned—"as Jung says some- where," etc. He suspects that Chaucer was learned. Then "there is Dante; there is Vergil; probably Sophocles; and of course the Indians and the Japanese." The reticent manner is tactical too, a way to aggrandize this hypothetically reticent writer. The achievement of Burke and Ransom and Tate, "my colleagues of twenty years," inclines him to say only a little. After all, "I speak of friends." In private, however, he drew a long bow, and Burke and Ransom and Tate became his sacred band. But the stories he elaborated bore a creative relation to truth.

It was like this with the ideal society he built in his head, "della vera città almen la torre" (the words he put before *The Lion and the Honey-comb*). This society or "polity" was not a fiction precisely but tangential to experience, "the embrace of shadows which may yet become real." When he got to Rome, he saw a city where "everything may be explored, and especially the Cities of Man's Making." But the tower stood less visibly than it had for Dante the pilgrim, dreaming his dream of polity. He said how the city had become a spreading stain, and he made up his mind to write a polemic against the monster polemic that assured its destruction. Journeying on to France, this latter-day pilgrim went again to Montaigne, looking for fragments to shore against his ruin. The technique of fragmentation was "the form for survival in treacherous times," and the unity he commended in his papers for the Institute showed as diversity when all was said. In Montaigne, a city of the mind, he found once again "the word I had lost since 1934: Epecho: I will not budge, I will suspend judgment." Never mind that for him, as for the great Pyrrhonist, the true tower was falling. He made himself elastic even to the thinning point, and his "most of arrogance" consisted in hoping for "that conflagration of thought and emphatic fact which we call miracle."

Too many hopes were impious, though, and too many despairs "a mere chattering of teeth and decorum." Not hoping much nor despairing either, he doubted creatively, knowing how "there are times when one doubts not to find the truth but in order to dissipate it till it appears in new form." When his heart or head recoiled in horror from the roles he played, sensing how they were withershins to the bitter realities which almost brought him to despair, he added partial creations of his own. Sometimes they "affect the original ones by becoming part of them for all aftertime." That is what happens in *A Primer of Ignorance*. "All the culture of present and past news rises and inhabits me"—Montaigne and Toynbee, styles of ballet in London and Zurich, Ara Coeli and Campidoglio, Hildebrand's failed Christian republic, the St. Bartholomew's Day Massacre, Thucydides on the Sicilian War—"all in which I live and move and have my being. I am a green study."

Once, late at night, Richard quoted the miraculous sentence with which Doughty begins his *Travels in Arabia Deserta*: "A new voice hailed me of an old friend, when first returned from the Peninsula, I paced again in the long street of Damascus which is called Straight; and suddenly taking me wonderingly by the hand 'Tell me (said he), since thou art here again in the peace and assurance of Ullah, and whilst we walk, as in the former years, toward the new blossoming orchards, full of the sweet spring as the garden of God, what moved thee, or how couldst thou take such journeys into the fanatic Arabia?'" Let this sentence stand as epigraph to Richard's account of his travels. He had it by heart for most of his life—it figures, for instance, in the essay on T. E. Lawrence which opens *The Expense of Greatness*. " 'What moved thee, or how couldst thou take such journeys into the fanatic Arabia?' " To answer this question, Richard set out on his travels. But he knew the answer before he left home. On a Cambridge Public Library slip, he had scribbled as a boy another quotation from Doughty: "Here is a dead land, whence, if he die not, he shall bring home nothing but a perpetual weariness in his bones."

Like Lawrence, he might have called his last book A Triumph, and so it was, but of the imagination, and concluding in an emotion ambiguous and not to be borne. To feel this emotion, you needn't make a journey to the ends of the earth. In the second of his "Anni Mirabiles" lectures Richard quoted *Ulysses*, a passage everyone knows: "We walk through ourselves, meeting robbers, ghosts, giants, old men, young men, wives, widows, brothers-in-love. But always meeting ourselves." That is how it was with Richard abroad, who knew it all proleptically in his expatriated soul. He brought with him on his travels the essential part of what he left behind, and in his writing he said what this was. Like Napoleon in exile, he had fought fifty battles and learned nothing he did not know at the beginning.

At the very end of his second trip to Europe, he looked all over Rome for a copy of Piranesi's print of the contrasting flights of stairs that lead up to the church of Santa Maria Ara Coeli—steps pointing to "a discontinuous process and not at all to the substantial anarchy of administrative order"—and down from the Roman Campidoglio, "a waterfall forever flowing." One flight gave on the unfinished Christian church, another fell away from the unfinished pagan state, and sitting across the piazza, like Adams and Gibbon before him, he summoned his own confusion "which is almost like a liberation since it comes as the beat of history." The print he wanted eluded him, though. But when he got back to Boston, he found and purchased an excellent copy of the second edition. It had hung for seventy years in the house of a maiden lady, across the street from the boarding house on Irving Street where he had lived as a boy.

CHAPTER NINE

Through the Ashes
of His Chance

AT AN ACADEMIC CONCLAVE in the late forties, "peculiar little oddments like R. P. Blackmur" offended Louise Bogan in her poet's soul, and it pleased her to hear that Richard was "on the way out at Princeton." His colleagues or some of them had put the word around. He confounded them, though. Wanting a permanent place in the academy, he used every weapon he could lay hands on. Stories circulated about "his unscrupulousness and dirty academic politics." Leslie Fiedler was fed on these stories by Francis Fergusson and Robert Fitzgerald, when the three of them taught with Richard at the Indiana School of Letters. "Without the proper credentials," Richard at Princeton "had to fight for his life." He wasn't "above using brass knuckles when he had to, or sacrificing a friend to save himself." He wasn't above flattery either, and one critic said how his judgment was vitiated by "an excess of charity" toward colleagues who occupied the seats of power. Saul Bellow in his novel *Humboldt's Gift* preserves a fossilized caricature of the rough and subtle politician. "To become professor without even a BA . . . it speaks for itself." This is one version of Blackmur on the rise.

The outsider was resourceful but not self-engendered, nor did he pull himself up by his bootstraps. Friends gave him a leg up, and if he didn't always speak his thanks, that was because he tasted the ashes of success. In 1946 he made his way back to the English Department where Donald Stauffer, newly returned from the war, presided as Chairman. An aspiring critic of modern letters who looks like the Marine he was in the photograph that hangs in McCosh 22, Stauffer had the wit to recognize the genuine article in Richard. He became the friend in power to whom Richard on his political side responded like the needle to the pole. Walter Stewart was that kind of friend, equally at home in the board room, the Institute, and the university. He and Richard got together every day at 5:00 p.m. in the famous white-tiled Balt on Nassau Street. In 1945 Stewart had arranged a meeting with the President and the Dean of the College. He wanted to know "what their plans were with reference to Blackmur." Gauss conferred with Dodds, then he wrote to Richard pledging to reappoint him as Resident Fellow "after the defeat of Germany." You get the sense that he was taking these matters up one by one.

On the threshold of success, Richard looked at himself and estimated his prospects. Being himself, he didn't like what he saw. In 1945 he wrote in his journal: "What is there in me—for me—to please? I stink in my own nostrils." He dreamed of self-strangulation. The conviction of his unworthiness, long germinating, was "now quite matured." On going to bed or at waking it came "back and up, like nausea or the sense of filth." Also it broke through sleep, or attacked him in the middle of a page of reading. When it appeared, he said, "I can do nothing." Struggling to hide his unworthy self from the world, he offered himself "in superficial exchanges, as if I were good coin." The pretense, it seemed to him, was revolting. Cy Black, his Princeton colleague, remembered the day he sat in the fireplace and covered his head with ashes. No need to say what he was saying.

Because his body betrayed him, he despised his body and prayed God: "Give me the strength and courage to contemplate this heart, this flesh without disgust." Because his heart was closing, he thought himself monstrous. He was the man—quoting from an early poem—who had "married reason on desperate cause when the heart's cause was lost." He married reason, but the partnership turned out equivocal and the impassioned form his words took symbolized his personal division. He understood how his culture—all that edifice of words—was on one side deeply sadistic, and two of his students, cruel as only the young can be, imputed to him "the guilt of the egotism of the word." Elevating the status of language, he hid the world as immediately experienced by an ersatz world of his own devising. Or you can say that he made this world golden. In the winter of 1950 he dreamed of "an intense struggle, in a place of high illumination, to break a knot of coiled live things." The things were not snakes but human beings contorted like snakes and muscular like the mind—"like Dante's mind in Dante's Italian." When the knot came undone, "it was a *word* which, at supreme effort, burst out of an unknown language into the known." The function of this word was "to make everything plain."

A passionate need for security prompted this dream (Richard said so himself) and others like it in the forties and early fifties. Self-knowledge didn't mean self-acceptance, however. Sometimes, in contempt of himself, he took the anti-intellectual side. "In his New England regular fellow phase/pose," he came up to Meyer Schapiro. "You New York intellectuals, you're too ratiocinate, too intellectualistic," he said. Schapiro replied: "Mr. Blackmur, when you use your mind, you don't use it up." Most of the time his mind did heavy duty, its office being to erect a moat defensive against the self. He knew what he was doing and he said he knew what ailed him. "But I cannot cure the ail because I know its source was in health."

Health made him capable of passion, and the passion brimming in him found no release. His marriage was dying and his poetry and fiction, like the man who had created them, belonged to the past. A fever sent him to bed, and the complicated design of the wallpaper in his bedroom turned into a novel with interweaving plots and characters of surpassing interest. Maybe this novel would have made his chef d'oeuvre but, getting better, he said he had forgotten it all. He was embroidering Coleridge on the writing of "Kubla Khan," and the ground note for both of them was failure. Quoting from his *Essays in the European Novel*, an emergent work in these years: "He had walked a bridge over the chasm of life and now the bridge was broken." The middle-aged man who survived in the present was hardly recognizable. Only in ecstasy could you recognize the true self. However, "ecstacy happens in response." Looking to the future, Richard envisaged a "pre-mortem interlude" in which the ghost he had become might abandon itself to its vices. He wrote in his notebook: "The days or years that remain after this date I consider as posthumous." The date was January 14, 1946—he still had almost twenty years to go. This is another version of Blackmur on the rise.

His reappointment in Creative Writing took care of the next two years. Melancholy didn't cancel ambition in him, and he turned them to account. With Stauffer's backing, he won promotion to Associate Professor. The title sounded good but meant little beyond hopes and aspirations. Three years down the road loomed a final review. How does a man respond, living under the gun, and what does this do to him in his deepest place? Richard in his late forties was the sum total of his miserable childhood and lonely adolescence. Add to this the long years as a near-starving free lance. When he came to Princeton, a single year was all he could look for. A decade went by and he was still hanging on, but only at the pleasure of the powers that be; every ensuing year was filled with trepidation for the future. The parlous life makes the indurated man, if he is lucky. Richard was this man, but not tempered as by fire. Just underneath the indurated exterior, he was all quick. Hoping, he called hope "the sole, the immaculately conceiving parent of despair." Friends thought him bored, Mohammed waiting for the mountain, when it was his vertigo that made him sit still. Verging on despair, he busied himself with "practical charades": who's in, who's out? etc. That was inconsequent but he was human, and so made little of contradictions and disjunctions.

His Chairman supported him and that augured success. So did Ged Bentley, an outsider like himself. Having come to the department from the University of Chicago, Bentley didn't suppose that Princeton was the axletree on which the world turned. This made him suspect. But he was a prodigious scholar, and if his colleagues didn't like him they left him alone. In later years and possibly for the wrong reasons, Richard earned this grudging tolerance. That was for the future, though, and for the present his chances looked dim. One influential colleague who passed for Mr. Chips —a man with skin like the pages in old library books—stood strong for the academic side. Richard called him the Brazilian masturbator. When he walked along Nassau Street he jigged and jagged. Blackmur would go up only over this colleague's dead body. Approximately, that is what happened.

In the years after the war only four persons in the Princeton department held the rank of full professor, and in those four all power resided. It wasn't in the cards that they should agree on which of their protégés to favor. So there was deadlock. Then the President of Princeton intervened in Richard's behalf. Harold Willis Dodds was a political scientist who resembled a wise old heron. For almost fifteen years he had served as a trustee of the Rockefeller Foundation, and his intimate friends were Richard's friends, too. He didn't find Richard an easy man to know, and said he couldn't understand what the famous critic was driving at. In 1942, when Richard gave a public lecture sponsored by Church's Mesures Fund, Dodds attended conscientiously but came away befuddled. He understood that the department was divided, however, the aged against the young people on the make. Usually he found himself on the side of the young people. It was that way in the spring of 1951. Every appointment to a professorship at Princeton had to carry his personal recommendation. Finally he let it be known that he was for Blackmur. The recalcitrant full professors were summoned before the Committee of Three, the adjudicating body which oversees all promotions at Princeton. The professors were instructed in the writing on the wall. They understood they had no option, so they traded. Professor X went up, pulling Richard along with him. "Richard Blackmur had one great triumph," said Virgil Thomson years later. "He was made a full professor at Princeton."

Heart's desire, when Richard finally achieved it, came too late to make him happy. The happiness he found—the unhappiness, too—was remote from public honor and public dejection. He still wanted "desperately to know what constitutes the Sacred Fount, what there may be, in maturity, that a man and woman can draw on together." This knowledge eluded him. At a guess, he couldn't entertain it. The passionate man was deeply evasive, and perhaps his mother and his wife wore his sword Philippan. In Japan, where he enjoyed a feast of sensibility, what stuck most in his mind was being bathed naked by a geisha girl. He dwelt on this experience to his friend Jay Martin, the biographer of Conrad Aiken. "Both exciting and embarrassing, both adult and infantile, both innocent and sensual," it must have revived in him, Martin supposed, "crucial erotic memories (unconscious, of course) of being bathed or handled by a mother as an infant." This epiphany offers a key to his nature, and suggests how the child was father to the man.

As he rose in position, he found himself increasingly alone. When one of his students who had fallen in love asked him naively if it would last, he wondered what to say. Maybe "that the essence of whatever happens is eternal," etc. To himself he said, however, that "the body of man does not desire the eternity of essence but the immortality of flesh." He had his Platonic side but he wasn't a Platonist and didn't want "the pattern of the honey of generation." He wanted "the substance that caused the honey to flow." That was what he wanted, but not what he got and evidently not what he gave.

"Look at me," Helen said to one of his students. "Would you say that I'm a handsome woman? Would you say that I'm an ugly woman? What do I look like to you?" The student, abashed, made his dutiful answer. "I *am* beautiful," Helen said. "And I feel that I've been cheated. I'm not old. I'm still attractive to men." She set out to prove this. Far away in Bolivia, Sherry Mangan rejoiced in the rumor that Helen had "gone off with the somewhat livelier Slater Brown." He was "Bill Brown of Greenwich Village and Webster, Massachusetts" (Malcolm Cowley is describing him in *Exile's Return*), "the Columbia boy who had been imprisoned with Cummings in the enormous room." In Princeton, where he lived with Allen Tate and Caroline Gordon, he and Helen carried on a long affair. To Helen he presented an early version of Richard before Richard entered his Matthew Arnold phase. Sometimes he sounds like Blackmur the critic as *roi fainéant*. "Art is the superfluous," was one of his sayings. Tessa Horton called him a charmer. She said he was totally unreliable, though. Watching Helen fix dinner, he put his proposition. "If you ran away with me, you wouldn't have to peel potatoes." But Helen said: "I might not have any potatoes to peel."

She didn't run away with Slater Brown, she stayed on in Princeton and turned life upside down for herself and for Richard. Being around the two of them was "like an Ingmar Bergman film." They should have split apart —their marriage was a torment and had been for years—but they clung together desperately, needing each other and not knowing how to satisfy the need. Living at close quarters exacerbated the difference between them. Richard loved money and Helen despised it. He loved the outward signs of power where she was all inward. He saw himself as an aristocrat or Renaissance prince, and let you know what he saw. He wanted a "proper" house; it had to contain two copies of the *New York Times*, one for the inevitable guest. Betraying these ambitions, paltry, ludicrous, or poignant, he left himself open and Helen rushed against him with "her best tiger rodomontade." When T. S. Eliot came to town and Richard asked him for dinner, she said brusquely, "Let him bring his own chop." Selfish, without affection, abyssal in his "ignorance of what affection is"—these were her phrases for Richard and maybe they were just. But justice was intolerable, "whether rough or fine," Richard said, and made life a mere convention of discourse. He called his personal inadequacy "unforgiveable sin," and defined this sin as "the condition of so living that one's strongest expressions gain no response and one's strongest responses are either dodged or contemned or dreaded." Even "in the guise of least friend," he knew rejection. Being so charged and so rejected left "little alive of value, and that little the ache of loss and sickness at heart." Richard wrote this to himself and concluded: "There is no escape."

He and Helen had plenty to yoke them together but no buffer to keep a civilized distance between them. In their case, two was a crowd. Manners disappeared before their overwhelming need, and life together became impossible. Congratulating his editor on the birth of a son, Richard said there wasn't any congratulation "I should like to receive myself more than that." He died childless, however. This was by choice. In early days he and Helen had lacked the money to raise a family, or her health was precarious, or else the marriage looked doubtful from the beginning. "Few of those people in their 'crowd' had children." In principle, the two of them were sorry. To the poet John Holmes, Richard regretted that he had no "children to communicate about." He made up for this by playing the role of surrogate parent. A godless man but god-fearing, he stood as godfather to the children of friends, like John Hartle and Adam Alvarez. They found him properly foolish and allowed him to climb down off his high horse. He sent them whimsical post cards, the kind he wouldn't send their parents. At a fly-by-night carnival he let himself be persuaded to ride on the Tilt-a-Whirl and sat unflappable and pleased as the forces dragged him different ways.

The avuncular man specialized in little girls "not above the age of eight," thinking that age "the best of all." Sex didn't obtrude on the undemanding hours he spent in their company, and that was all right with him. There was never with him, said his young friend Joan Jurow, "the slightest sexual vibration," and she observed "an Alice in Wonderland quality" in their encounters. Kindly, gentle, and amused, this "rather childlike person" operated quite comfortably on "a 12 or 13-year old level." Operating on this level, the bristling and defensive adult who saw an enemy behind every bush could let his defenses fall. "Human and tender" were the words that described him. Jennifer Pattee, who lived on Oak Point, was all protruding teeth and adipose tissue. Seeing herself in the mirror, she fell to weeping. "But," Richard said, "you're very beautiful," and this ugly duckling never forgot.

He wanted children of his own, but the best he could muster was "a collection of semi-nieces, being the daughters of various friends." His emptiness beset him like hunger. He said his stock of human need ("my chief riches," he called it bitterly, the legacy he willed to his heirs) was "greater than any satisfactions that have come my way." The need wasn't abstract, "but for this man and this woman." Supplicating the holy trinity of "affection, friendship, love," he waited in "passionate misery" for the helpmate who might accept "the unbearable burden of love." But the objects of his affection were like Rilke's version of the Prodigal Son who ran away because he couldn't bear the burden. He was the No-man, Charles Bovary, "bearing all burdens—bearing most, and best, of all" the burden that his wife had been unable to bear his love. (You see how his essays on the European novel play into his life, and the other way round.) The platitudes of marriage remained real for him. Helen found his reality either platitudes or lies. "He had not enough force to win reality; she had too much to accept what offered, too little to make it over." It was the fault of fatality and Richard measured the fault.

Helen never read these bleak reflections of his, but she echoed them uncannily and applied them to herself in a long letter she wrote to Richard from the house on Princeton Avenue, just before their marriage dissolved. Richard had once so much desired her that death, he used to say, would be more welcome than the other loss, and now she knew herself "no longer really necessary" to him. She said how her love had become a burden from which he dodged away. Could he not understand the emptiness this brought her, "to have been so much to you once and now so little?" Tessa, years ago, had been like that to him "for that brief period which so happily turned into something more comfortable for you both." Perhaps this placid ending was what he desired for Helen and himself, "an agreeable old-friendish intimacy." It didn't meet her wishes and appalled her sense of justice. Like Isabella in the play, she cried out for justice. Richard said, however, in his essay on Tolstoy: "What is beyond remedy is beyond judgment: is its own justice." Helen never got that far.

Her love for Richard had grown with time, she said; his had slowly settled. "And nothing in my whole life has ever hurt me quite so much." She exhumed his old letters and quoted him against himself, or against himself as she perceived him. She said this wasn't from spite. Perhaps she was seeking a clue to the mystery. " 'What it all comes down to is that I prefer being with you to anything, that I like what you do and say, that your beauty influences me like great art—only [more] intensely, personally, that my actions and thoughts have more meaning when I can refer them to you, that the sight and touch of you thrills me, that you satisfy when you wish every dream and instinct.' " He had told her that without her he found himself at loose ends and vacant and she had believed him, taking his words for truth though "perhaps they were just lovely sounds." The thought of this drove her half crazy. She granted herself "distorted and queer and a trial and a nuisance," and she saw how "frightful violence and turmoil," rising in her, enveloped them both. That wasn't her fault, though. Whose fault was it then? She left him in no doubt of the answer.

The hardest part was knowing complete happiness and then having it fail. Richard had "not had to know that." But Helen didn't know what Richard knew. She pictured him meeting constantly with his highfalutin friends, one of them a woman, "a gay fluttering fool," and this, she was sure, gave to his days a superficial brightness. This brightness made his "frivolity" a rainbow, and she contrasted it bitterly with her own dullness. He fostered the sense in her of watching the game he played from outside. Who will leave the gay game, she asked him rhetorically, "for the unhilarious person who looks in the window"? He remained her one resource—"my other person," she called him—and she lived alone except for him. The Thursday nights he spent on campus conducting his Gauss Seminars "I spend just missing you completely waiting for time to go by so the night will be gone and another day shall bring another night, and I shall see you." Always alone, time and hours piling up on her, she felt like a squirrel on a treadmill, but "I cannot stop loving you now." He had done the one thing she dreaded, "the thing that ends most loves, the easiest thing to do in all this world"—he had got used to her. "And I because I have a different sense to living have kept the foolish colors before my face, have done what I once thought impossible for me—I have found you always new and let myself be saturated with you."

So Helen looked forward to a death in life, as Richard had looked forward to his posthumous life. But her death, she said, would come another way and be easier and harder. "It will be living not dying. Being choked and smothered and crushed by someone else's weight and arms. When it is yours I only want. This frightful emptiness I feel will be filled by another's passion. Maybe I can be so burned I will not think of you at all." She ended her letter: "You cannot know how much I have lived with you in my heart. I hoped I would in yours."

This was the last letter she ever wrote him, anyway the last letter he kept. In 1951 she filed for divorce. Not knowing the story of Richard and Helen, you might suppose from her letter that he had left her. But he would "never have left her," said one of their friends, and he himself said emphatically that he didn't want the divorce. All the blame fell to him, though, and he didn't decline to accept it. He took to guilt like cream and she kept him in supply. About what had happened, he would never say a word. He kept mum when John Berryman tried to quiz him head-on. Gossip was beneath him and "only the kindest things" occurred to him to say. "I wish only the very best for that woman." That was the line he took. In the fifties he continued to send her his books, and he longed for news of her whereabouts and doings. "If you have any news, good or bad," he wrote George Anthony, "I should like to hear it, for I know nothing."

After the divorce and with the kind of gross unlikelihood that only life attests, the two of them lived together, execrating each other but unable to pull apart and unwilling—perhaps from simple inertia—to parcel out the household goods and look for separate apartments. Eventually Helen moved to rural Hopewell on the edges of Princeton. She had her eternal cats and they needed space to roam in. "Helen has named her new kitten Blackstone!" wrote Delmore, amused and a little incredulous, to Richard who was on his first trip abroad. "She appears to be more accustomed than she was last winter to the trials and misunderstandings of a former wife." All her life she had put Richard down as cerebral, but when he returned from leave she began to attend his lectures. What brought her into campus? "The hope of attracting young men," Tessa said. Mike Keeley said, however: "She was as obsessed as I was with the man." She was human like Richard, and had her inconsequent side.

George Cope, called Dee or D, was Richard's student, "a very good friend" to one mutual friend, "a *nasty* man" to another. He and Helen became lovers. They went to Harrington to live in the old farmhouse which Mrs. Dickson had willed to her daughter. Helen invited Richard to visit them there—another monstrous improbability that no fiction could hope to address. Did she see him as Bloom, looking through the keyhole?

From the day of the divorce, however, the good place in Maine was lost to Richard irretrievably, and he lived in felt exile the last fifteen years of his life.

Dee Cope served as principal of the local high school. He and Helen got married and were happy for awhile, but in time he divorced her and married again. Her animosity toward Richard grew high as she got older. It warmed her to say, "I gave that man twenty years." She didn't see or didn't say, unless to herself, how he had given her the same. When she heard that he was dead, "she burst into tears and said she was sorry he had known so little *joy*." But she wouldn't honor his wish that he be buried in Maine overlooking the tidal water, and after he was dead she sued his estate, wanting the money from his insurance. Helen died of cancer in 1976, two weeks before George Anthony Palmer and eleven years after Richard. Through the years she had saved all his personal correspondence, and just before she died she destroyed it.

Richard in the fifties made shift to get through his "pre-mortem interlude." It wasn't all dust and ashes. His twice-weekly lectures on the European novel enjoyed "a huge succes d'estime," and he gave them on his own time, working off a felt need. Sitting behind a table in Whig-Clio or the Poetry Room in Firestone and partly hidden by a cloud of cigarette smoke, he addressed the chosen few, most of them women. His appointed authors were Thomas Mann, Joyce and Flaubert, Tolstoy and Dostoevsky. In Dostoevsky he found an alter ego, and reading him at night made his "sleep deeper if not sounder." He put *The Brothers Karamazov* among the ten books that had influenced him most. "Dusty the Drifter" was going to provide him with the stuff of a major work, his "most 'important' book," except for the life of Adams. The book was already there in his voluminous notes; the only problem was "to boil them down and then sugar off." More than once he said how the book was nearly finished. But like the plan he announced "to do a separate book on Joyce," his plans for Dostoevsky reduced in the end to a handful of essays and the inspired seminars he gave at Princeton in the late forties and early fifties. More "fragments of an unfinished ruin," and it isn't hard to see why.

Dwelling on this author's blacknesses, Richard spoke of his own inmost place. Dostoevsky, he said, was haunted by "the power of the 'Other' thing, the other self, the dark side of the self, the substance and drive of that secret world in us which the devil creates." Partly the formal thing he created in his essays was intended to master the devil, and some of his urgent sentences had for Delmore "the force and lightning of great proverbs." His startled auditors got the sense that he was talking to himself. He improvised his talk from the heart of the text, speaking without pause or pausing only to turn the pages of his spiral notebook. This unmeditated performance—that was how it seemed—heightened their feeling of being in touch with the good and true of the mind, and they leaned forward in their chairs as Richard, with a word, removed the structure of his novels and laid the ends bare. At his best—and "he was never better" —he presented a hybrid of Socrates and Coleridge. His "Tuesday night explorations" constituted a rite of passage, and one colleague thought how tenacious he was and how presumptuously intimate, as he wooed and summoned and flattered the text. "Softly stubborn, often muzzy and distracted, at times obsessed, evasive *and* alert, intellectually inefficient, lonely and passively dependent on the involuntary fascination of others, he coalesced into a presence that almost literally cast a spell."

Friends considered that Richard achieved "his supreme moment" in these lectures on the novel, and the fact that no one took them down seemed as much a calamity to the young poet W. S. Merwin as the burning of the library of Alexandria. But the lectures weren't lost altogether. They appeared in petrified form first in the little magazines and then, the year before he died, as his *Eleven Essays in the European Novel*. It was the European novel he was writing about, however, and his reach exceeded his grasp. This didn't deter the pansophical man, and he didn't say no when a former student of his moved to put him on the board of a literary journal in Russian. Already in the thirties Yvor Winters had reproved him for venturing "remarks about the subtler qualities of Propertius." He had little Latin and less Greek, but he was R. P. Blackmur and had the Holy Ghost at his ear. To validate his remarks he did what he could, and in his lecture notes for the course in Poetics he called the "hymn in the throat," he wrestled with Latin pronunciation. He knew French well enough to read Maritain in French, and his essay on Flaubert shows him attempting to get inside the living tongue. The fall of the Tower of Babel seemed a fortunate fall to him, and this eccentric reading quickened his interest in linguistics. He understood how different language traditions entailed different perceptions of reality. This meant that translation entailed falsification. So the word was sacrosanct. All of New Criticism reduces to these formulations. Understanding so much, he let his criticism depend on translation.

He made mistakes, and learned colleagues were glad to point them out. These mistakes weren't decisive. But by not reading his authors in the original, he forfeited linguistic purity, and that was decisive. He said better than he knew how the theme his novelists were dealing with didn't matter, "for the theme, whatever it is, disappears into the texture." In his essays he disengaged the theme from the texture, and the novel became a vehicle for political disquisition or for making prose poems. "At any rate," said this poet—he has been discussing *The Brothers Karamazov*—"let us think of the 'Book of Alyosha' as set to the music of the novel we do not have as well as to that of the novel we do have." In a notebook filled with jottings on his European novels, Richard quoted Isaiah: "Woe unto them that seek deep to hide their counsel from the Lord, and their words are in the dark, and they say, Who seeth us? and who knoweth us?" He wondered would "the work say of him that made it, He made me not? or shall the thing framed say of him that framed it, He had no understanding?" You would hardly say that he kept his counsel hidden. Sometimes, however, he worked in the dark, and sometimes his maker's hand compelled the potter's clay.

Self-indulgence in Richard, or call it the artistic instinct, aroused the hostility of exegetes more humble than he was. They said he engaged in verbal jugglery or deliberate obfuscation, and they called him a charlatan. He wasn't a charlatan, but his critics weren't wholly off the mark. Like any writer worth the name, he played the opportunist, pushing the blots of ink around until something came. What Johnson said of himself, he might have said, too: he could write at need the life of a broomstick. But his inveterate skepticism hardened with age or grew more flamboyant. His last years or late period pit the saving opportunist against the absolute skeptic. When he succeeds in this contention, he makes permanent prose. On his skeptical side he inquires idly, however: What is truth? and doesn't stay for an answer. As the question becomes imperious, also disheartening, the New Critic goes out the window.

In the forging of the *Eleven Essays*, his disappearance is imminent. Richard said to his audience: "But Mitya had holes in his socks." Then came an expository passage. After this, the rose rabbi resumed his incantation. In the absence of connectives, you had to listen hard. Like a modern poet or a modern philosopher, like Yeats or Wittgenstein, he preferred the free-standing paragraph or the gnomic refrain. "As he kept coming back to it, it began to give coherence and clarity to his remarks." The coherence and clarity were like that of an Expressionist painting, however. "One of the most extraordinary intellectual experiences of my life," said Richard's colleague Dudley Johnson. Extraordinary is the word for his seminars on the novel, but though intellect participated in the experience, it wasn't an intellectual experience.

The notorious difficulty of his prose from the beginning—"Academic Swahili," Louise Bogan called it—turns partly on his disbelief in the counsels of rationality, anyway as they offer to speak to last things. Thought wasn't a life raft, only a beacon, like Portia's little candle in a darkening world, and "to confuse the functions is tragic." Words didn't image reality for Richard, and in one of his youthful stories he makes a character speak "with that assured tone which indicates that a word may be its own best antonym." Often, said his friend I. A. Richards, "he left me guessing around the possible meanings of his utterances rather than catching them." This wasn't his fault exactly and he wasn't playing a game. "Sometimes it takes repeated readings of his sentences to understand their meaning. And what's worse," said an in-house reader of the Adams manuscript, "I don't think Blackmur can write in any other way. His essays are like this. His mind works through concentric circles of qualification."

When an ingenuous editor asked him for "an article of interest to younger children," he said how his boyhood reading of Schopenhauer had disabled him ever since from writing anything "for children under 18." This piece of whimsicality didn't obscure his own distressed perception "of my naturally and . . . irretrievably polysyllabic mind." He didn't conceive the world in "simple declarative sentences," and to write a book "in words of one syllable"—what they wanted him to do on Henry James, he said indignantly—frightened him off his feed. "I'm not that sort of animal," he wrote to Jay Laughlin. He was right to be frightened off and his skittishness made him a better critic. He knew himself twisted by the "defects and virtues" peculiar to him as a man, but he hoped "by the grace of God" to do his writer's job "as well as I can in my own lights and darknesses." He wanted to communicate and he wanted "always to say something pertinent." It hurt him that some readers found "subtlety where I meant to be sharply indicative," but he said he didn't see any use in trying to be what he wasn't. He liked to suppose that "with familiarity" his readers got along well enough. A lot of them didn't and still don't.

Friends made excuses. They said how "tacit dialogue" was the métier in which he flourished, and how "many of his allegedly difficult essays are readily understood if one intercalates unstated questions and restores an element of that dialogue." The dialogues are essentially monologues, though, and the questions he raises don't always admit of answers. He wasn't simple or lucid. Like Donne, he lived in the prison of his difficult self, a twisted personality. This is impairing, and you see the impairment in his poetry and prose. But also like Donne he put his chisel to the hardest stone. Nobody tried more valiantly than he to take order with disorder. This means that his style is in its difficulty part and parcel of his material. But there is a third thing to say about the hermetic style: if you have the intellectual and sensible tools, you can crack the nut of your material and put the hammered thing on the table; if it isn't plain as plain, it approximates to plainness. Blackmur had the tools and lacked the instinct to accommodate. He didn't care, as Milton says, to expatiate and confer. He liked to keep tight on what he knew. This is partly what it means to call him a mandarin. To read Blackmur with profit, you have to resonate a little to this tight-fisted writer on his mandarin side. Otherwise he will only disgust you. Carlyle says (referring to Dante): "What we want to get at is the *thought* the man had, if he had any: why should he twist it into jingle, if he *could* speak it out plainly?" Good readers of Blackmur won't respond like Carlyle.

The twisted man, the valorous man, and the man in a top hat looking at art and nature through a lorgnette come together in the critic of fiction. Reflecting on "the unscrupulousness of the faithful mind before the inscrutable," Richard said in his youth how "the faithful write better novels than I do because they are not so scrupulous about their feelings and can put their time in on the big emotions: which, being inscrutable, I can do nothing but distrust." When he wrote these words, he had come to a summit—another birthday, another gloomy occasion for looking backward and forward. But it wasn't a summit so far as he knew, nor even a corner into which he had been driven. He was "in process," only that and no more. Writing fiction himself, he confessed that he didn't know what to put in or leave out, and knowledge of this kind remained forever beyond him—"in life, thought, art." His tenuous hold on the substantiality and relative importance of things weakened his sense of composition. Writing was the only form of architecture which would stand up "without underpinnings." He lacked underpinnings, and his general method of writing was "to write key stones and build on in all directions." Reading his later prose, you feel how you are "in the presence of a mystery—of that from which everything that we are has come."

The exemplary American novelists of his own time—Faulkner, Hemingway, and Fitzgerald—were "more representative than exemplary," he said, and what they represented was only the fortuitous "which lurks in any corner." Contemporary fiction didn't much attract him. There were exceptions: he tipped his staff to Cozzens—"he is so heavenly competent"—and he intended "doing a job on his five or six best novels." Mostly, however, he looked to the past. "It's all right to tell us that James Joyce and Henry James are great writers. Thanks for the news," said Keeley sardonically. "But what about what's happening now?" He didn't turn his attention to what was happening now because it mirrored his own desperate epistemology. He presented in himself those modern artists of

whom incredulous students are told in school and before whose invincible
Pyrrhonism their common sense recoils: he didn't know which end was
up, and he didn't want his bedtime reading to confront an endless replicating of what he didn't know.

The kind of fiction he liked filled the page or the abyss of unknowing
with detail—Smollett from early days, Scott, Dickens, Jane Austen and
her game of manners which constituted for him a deliberate and saving
privation. If you know and honor the rules of a rigidly circumscribed
contest—lawn tennis, the sonnet, the novel of manners—you can turn
your back on the anarchy outside the walls. He called himself, said one
editor, "a 'secret Trollopian,' and he wanted to come clean on that" by
writing a book on the English novel to go with his essays on European
fiction. Still another book, worked up "from his notes of many years," was
in his mind when he died—one on Stendhal, *War and Peace*, Gide's *Counterfeiters*, George Eliot, maybe Conrad the stoic. Gide he loved with
aversion. "He seems to me to have created a rival world for all those not
myself, but to have used part of myself in doing so."

The ability to fabricate this rival world gave the novel its special
primacy. Reading novels, you got rid of your own personality. They immersed you in the lore of closed corporations—the bar, the Church, the
army—and so let you lose yourself. Chaos was always menacing, outside
the walls. The novel at its highest pitch put chaos under ban. Not always.
You can say that Tolstoy and Joyce made works of art rather than moral
tracts as they walked the earth ahead of all they knew, and already Richard in his boyhood is saying just this: "James above all succeeded without
. . . knowing it." He made "somewhat other than he intended." Richard
succeeds in his own critique of fiction as he tells you how his novelists—
Dostoevsky, for instance—"got lost in the rush and momentum of what in
life escapes intention and surpasses motive altogether." But the impulse
that brought him to criticize the novel is the benevolent impulse—to arrest
the rush and momentum, to salute the heroes of art who tried vainly to do
this, to enjoy "the sense of control [which] is perhaps the highest form of
apprehension." Proust advanced the verge of consciousness—"and I don't
know a more precious experience," Richard said. Faulkner and Hemingway denied us this experience. Their minds were marked by "primitive
terror and childhood piety," and their heroes fell in the great grasp of
unreason.

Thinking of these things, aspiring too, sends Richard's mind "astretch
on far questions that have to do with the relation of the individual to his
society in our time." By the end of the forties, when his seminars on the
novel were getting started, his writing revealed to Irving Howe "an uneasy

abandonment of exclusively textual criticism." Impatience marked the writing, as if he wanted to get on to "the general crisis of culture." Critics saw him reaching "toward something like philosophy, perhaps toward prophecy." Longing to be freed from reason, he assumed "the roles of priest to the mysteries and speculative philosopher of literature in its relation to modern life." His friend Dick Lewis called him "the critic as prophet." The novel, you heard him saying, "is ethics in action." He had made himself a moralist and even "a somewhat shamefaced theologian." In this late incarnation, his clerical forebears play an important but equivocal role. All his life they enabled but disabled him, too. Like them, he typified the authoritative presence. Unlike them, he missed the "conviction which is the inward sense of outward mastery." It is tempting to speculate on how the cloth would have become him.

Authority described the "high muckamuck." (The malicious phrase is Sherry Mangan's.) In private, however, he wasn't so sure. He couldn't believe his ears when a stranger inquired if he were not "the Blackmur who is the famous critic." The famous critic was humble, Cincinnatus at his plow, and this wasn't altogether a pose. Shut away from his *locus amoenus* in Maine, he became a passionate gardener. He put down ten guineas for membership in the Royal Horticultural Society, his humility taking a holiday here, and his shrewd suspicions were confirmed when the exotic Himalayan Arisaema of the seed catalogues turned out to be a strain of jack-in-the-pulpit. Horseshit Breese was his steward and brought him manure, and they conversed in monosyllables, being men of the soil. When you grew gentians, did you want sun or shade? Like Saint Augustine, another hero whose pestered life he touches at more than one point, he made his garden his book. Plants and flowers were themselves, they were also instrumental, a means for resolving the riddle of things—as though "you could question the vital force in each root and bud on what it can do, and what it cannot, and why."

A claustrophobic man, he devised for himself a claustrophobic existence. Like Augustine he hated traveling and became a great traveler. He ordered his life in a delicate decorum, and while the decorum held he kept his obsessions at bay. The Theodosian Code was among his obsessions. He saw himself being thrown from the Tarpeian Rock, or being encased in a barrel and thrown alive into the sea. Talking, he seemed to talk to still the noises inside. When he fell silent, what was stirring inside found a tongue or involuntary gesture. Once, late at night, climbing up from some dark place, he cried, "Poor Parnell! my dead king!" and once, at an undergraduate bash in his apartment, he grew suddenly quiet, and, moving away from the literary chitchat, slid down the wall by the door, still holding his drink and the cigarette "his way." When someone was about to walk through the door, he raised his thumb brazenly. "Bite it!" he said.

His self-contempt deepened and nightmares troubled his sleep. He dreamed of himself in the Poetry Room, among black servants and strangers including children, where he was trying in vain to arrange the chairs for a seminar. "There was nowhere a chair for myself, and it was evidently not my seminar. I was the intruder. If I stayed there was no one to understand a word, and besides I was no longer a master of a word to say." Abruptly people from Harrington crowded into the room, "but none whom I liked and none who liked me." The dream said there was nowhere for Richard to go "and nowhere I want to go." This was the year before he divorced.

In the lonely time just after his divorce, he acted out the words he had written to Helen. "At loose ends and vacant," he grew bored with the program in Creative Writing. "He'd given up the ghost on it," Mike Keeley supposed. That wasn't surprising. The first-person pronoun stuck in his throat and it was Bernard Bandler's opinion that if he wrote about himself, it would have to be like Adams in the third person. Criticism seemed to him the only civilized form of autobiography. (He wasn't a son of Oscar for nothing.) His adolescent writers had a different idea and recorded with absorption their short and simple annals. Finally Richard acknowledged that he "didn't want to deal with yet another undergraduate manuscript."

Growing abstractedness went with being bored. One of his assistants being up for tenure: Would he like a ride to the meeting, Keeley inquired. "What meeting?" Richard said. "The what case?" he said. "I don't know the man." Keeley said, "He's been teaching creative writing for five years and you're going to have to make a speech about his role as a writing instructor." "Has he been doing it well?" Richard said.

He wrote his own autobiography at a remove, in the Old Pretender pose that grew native to him in his later years, also in the dark mutterings on poetry and fiction which delivered the Old Pretender to the world. Circular puns in Latin appeared in his writing. He got the Latin wrong. He ran on about writers he hardly knew—like Novalis, who "seems to have been one of our heralds." Portentous phrases dropped from his lips. He told the Rockefellers how "with Justice Holmes I hold . . ." and he lamented "the absence of any competent knowledge of the effect of law as an institution." This hadn't much to do with literary study, but he was after bigger game. He recommended to his colleagues, said Robert Fitzgerald, "indeed, to all concerned," that they "inhale the air" of larger worlds, "getting into relation with other than literary objects—with theology, history, politics, and personal experience." For Alfred Knopf he undertook a 30,000-word essay on the "seminal thinkers" who stand behind modern letters—Freud, Nietzsche, Bergson, etc. (He took the advance but did nothing else; ultimately Knopf canceled the contract.)

His style grew prolix, and sickly shining like the paintings of Douanier Rousseau. He favored titles like "The Language of Silence" (1955)— never a title more misleading than this one. The man who spoke his belief in "the law of parsimony" and used Occam's razor every day of his life had begun to let his beard grow. If he didn't count much in the Princeton Department, he had his pals and protégés all around the country—this meant, to be sure, all around the East Coast and a little way inland—who were willing to indulge him in print. Sometimes his late essays stand on their own feet, sometimes (as he feared) they "fall on their own faces." Marian Adams on Henry James gives the color of these essays where they fall: "It's not that he 'bites off more than he can chaw,' but he chaws more than he bites off."

Department meetings brought him up to full proof, and it was vintage Blackmur on whom you could always rely to "introduce a supreme irrelevancy at the moment of truth," so annulling the chance for getting anything done. Freshmen courses were a problem to the department. He proposed to resolve it by requiring all freshmen to take a year's course in the novels of Anthony Trollope. "Then they will become wise," he said, "they will become devoted, they will be serious students." He recurred to this proposal at the beginning of each academic year. It was how his colleagues knew that the year had got started.

In conversation he ran to ellipses, often to solipsism, and Leslie Fiedler remembered "a mad conversation with him and Allen Ginsberg" on Ulysses. Only after an hour did it become apparent "that Allen was talking about Homer's Ulysses, Blackmur about Joyce's. It made little difference." As the hierarchy had stood to him, this quondam outsider stood to others now. Having visited the Villa Serbellone on Lake Como, he advised the Rockefellers on the kind of person they ought to invite for the future. "Certainly the place should not be turned into a Yaddo or a MacDowell Colony. Such amenities are not for the likes of them." Elevated to his professorship, he cast a fishy eye on Faulkner, a parvenu in Princeton and a novelist of unequal parts. In *The Sound and the Fury* Faulkner "didn't understand Harvard." Colleagues thought, nonetheless, that he might be asked to join the department. Richard dissented. Faulkner, he said, drank too much.

The New Critic cultivated a circumambient eye, and literature made a nexus with whatever rubbed against it in his Harvard green bag. To his poetry students he commended D'Arcy Thompson on the relation of mathematics and biology, or he sent them to the science of "Johnnie" von Neumann. That was where you found the best account of poetics. The universities, he said, should educate their students by offering "a series of courses which you might call laymen's courses." The idea was not to train a man in chemistry or physics "or whatever it may be," but in the "significance" of these studies. Only let him "get the hang of it." This tweedy affability was conspicuously absent in his own teaching. At doctors' orals, his presence set the room on a boil. Placing himself invariably on the candidate's left hand, he put his labyrinthine questions. They were harder to work out than the answers, and the relation between the two didn't always come clear. If no one intervened, he supplied the answers, also labyrinthine. Graduate students flocked to Princeton because of his name. Undergraduates revered him and sometimes they understood him. The courses he gave drew a constant enrollment. They remained peripheral, though. "You didn't ever have to take a Blackmur course, ever." His senior colleagues saw to that.

Remote from the center of the department, he made his own center. He created the Gauss Seminars. It seemed appropriate to him that the Rockefellers put up the money, and already in 1948 he and Francis Fergusson, who had followed Richard at the Institute for Advanced Study, were sending importunate notes to John Marshall. As always, powerful friends stood in his corner. Don Stauffer was in his corner, also Ira Wade, the Chairman of Romance Languages and another uncommon man. Wade called himself a scholar, not a critic, but he acknowledged to Richard that to deal with criticism he needed the help "of a critic like you." The chief proponent of Rockefeller support was the Chairman of the Board of the Rockefeller Foundation. This was Walter Stewart, who thought that Richard ought to have a proper forum. Mike Oates agreed with Stewart. He was Chairman of Classics and he ran the holding company which sponsored Richard's program in Creative Arts. The physical and friendly proximity of this man—his office in Firestone was down the hall and around the corner—contributed a certain pollen for Richard's bloom of discourse. Robert Fitzgerald, remarking "the gentle pressure of assistance from thoughtful people near the central switchboard of society," said he "had now seen how this worked."

It worked very well, and in 1949 a three-year grant got the Seminars started. They were known in the beginning as the Princeton Seminars in Literary Criticism. This bias disappeared as Richard took the whole world for his province. Francis Fergusson chaired the meetings and did all the scut work—Rockefeller money had boosted him into the Romance Languages Department and he taught one course for Richard in Creative Arts—but "Dick provided a lot of the ideas and lots of discussion at meetings." He didn't sit in the audience. Like a gray eminence he sat to one side, carrying on a dialogue with his old patron Dean Gauss. His basic idea was to cultivate high talk among a small group of omnicompetent people, not just university people. In his time at the Institute, Niels Bohr and Bertrand Russell had been fellows in residence. That was the sort of company he wanted to keep.

The method was to organize an annual program, four series of seminars each running six weeks and each to be conducted "by someone with something to say." The collaboration of the Institute, where Oppenheimer reigned as Director, seemed assured. Science and social science were the normal tickets for admission, but the year before T. S. Eliot had been a visitor at the Institute, and the auspices looked quite good for the future. Oppenheimer offered Richard two fellowships a year. The School of Historical Studies, led by the iconographer Erwin Panofsky, made threatening noises, however. Even at the Institute, polymaths like Richard and Oppie were rare. So the offer was withdrawn and it was no to bringing T. S. Eliot back again and no to Herbert Read, and Richard temporarily came to a stand.

More trouble was in the offing. Wanting to know how their money had been spent, the Rockefellers commissioned a full-dress report from Robert Fitzgerald, a visitor in Princeton. This poet and translator intended his report to be "endlessly corrigible by finer minds and better informed ones." That was what he said and Richard took him at his word. Fitzgerald had a sharp satiric eye and a pen dipped in acid. One of his chapters reflected a point of view not wholly affirmative. This chapter "turned out to be mysteriously missing" from the file. "I understood at once that Dick had simply removed it." He was, Fitzgerald said, "capable of Action." The cloud on the horizon having been whisked away, Richard set about concocting a new proposal. He didn't want the Seminars to depend on anyone's vagaries but his, and he asked the Foundation to appropriate enough money—"monies," he always said—to give him room for maneuver. He thought a hundred thousand would do. The officers agreed. During the discussion President Dodds left the room with his fellow trustee Henry Pitney Van Dusen, also a trustee of Princeton University. They were joined by John D. Rockefeller III, who was Princeton, class of '29.

The avowed purpose of the newly titled Christian Gauss Seminars—the Dean having died, he got this posthumous honor—was to clarify the old values of the humanities and bring them "face to face with the complex human situation of today." That was only the avowed purpose, and the heavy hand of the evangelist wasn't always so apparent. "What is the real purpose of the Gauss Seminars?" an outsider inquired. "They make it possible," he was told, "for Blackmur to talk with his friends." Over the years he brought most of them to Princeton. Delmore Schwartz gave a seminar, followed by John Berryman, Kenneth Burke, Sean O'Faolain, V. S. Pritchett. To an American colleague, Richard deprecated study "in that useless institution known as the British Museum." Why go to London? he wanted to know. "We could import the right Britishers for you." It was touch and go with Pritchett, however. "A number of the nasty young Turks who attended his lectures were openly patronizing, even contemptuous toward him." Like Edmund Wilson (who got the same treatment), "he was looked upon as a generalist and popularizer." If he found forgiveness, said one forgiving participant, that was because he belonged "to a different, less sophisticated critical tradition."

The friends composed a secret society in Princeton. Cal and Tom and Ezra were honorary members. Outsiders groped in vain for the key to the hieratic language they employed. René Wellek, a historical scholar, confessed himself "often puzzled" by the questions which Blackmur addressed to the room. The questions were rhetorical, but only initiates knew this. Sometimes Richard did most of the talking, and Pritchett was disconcerted when he stood up and bellowed: "V.P. is with me: he's a Tory anarchist!" Sometimes, however, this loquacity served him well. He had a gift, said Bob Hollander, for turning sows' ears into silk purses, and Hollander remembered gratefully how, after the customary ten-minute break, he "would take up the scattered bits of gristle that our symposiac had served us for an unending hour, and would contrive to have understood him as saying something that was actually interesting." In this roundabout way he achieved "a fairly amusing discussion among some of those in attendance and himself, only broken by a few interventions by the visiting Gausser, who was resolutely determined to turn the purses back irretrievably into sows' ears—which he always managed to do."

In 1952 Francis Fergusson left Princeton, a victim of the hostility of his academic colleagues, and E. B. O. Borgerhoff, a member of the innermost circle of friends, took his place as Director. This was the year Richard went off to Europe "to save the Eastern Mediterranean for Rockefeller and democracy." When he got back he confided to Chet D'Arms that Borgerhoff's direction was "not nearly so successful" as Fergusson's had been, and D'Arms followed this up in his report to the Foundation. "Desultory" was his word for the way things were going, and he decried the "lack of organization and leadership." The Seminars needed a more energetic director. Borge got a sabbatical and Richard supplied the need.

Under his direction the Gauss Seminars were "glowing intellectual occasions," and represented for A. Alvarez "the biggest of all possible deals." Other seminarians took a less respectful view. I.A. Richards (known as Ivor) proposed to talk on "What We Will," and for six painful Thursdays his invertebrate seminar dragged its wounded length along. Harry Levin, his discussion of Stendhal beginning to pall, controverted the question: Could you see the Alps from Parma? For Rosemond Tuve, literary criticism reduced to dry-as-dust, and Kingsley Amis sat in the back of the room and muttered under his breath, "Bloody Oxford!" W. H. Auden, contriving to sound both agonized and indifferent, spoke from scribbled notes on the back of an envelope while the room vibrated with free-floating malice.

There was a lot of malice. The ambience on these occasions, Dwight Macdonald said, was esoteric/academic, and unexpected depth charges kept exploding beneath your craft. "Not a few were detonated by R.P.B. as chairman." Macdonald remembered his own ragged performance ("memories not golden") and how at dinner beforehand—a genial, edgy, suspicious affair—Richard "kept matching me drink for drink and indeed pressing 'one more' on me, which I took (wrongly it turned out) as a sign of fellow-feeling." How wrongly, the rest of the evening disclosed. The stern-visaged scholars knew an exoteric critic when they saw one, and the questions they put were of the variety "When did you stop beating your wife?" Faced with a "choice between venial error and invincible ignorance," Macdonald looked to Richard for support. Managing a rueful smile "(but duty is duty) and before I could answer," he rephrased the questions "in a sharper and, I must admit, more unanswerable form." With this went "a sincere sideglance at the speaker (me) that positively radiated hope, against all the evidence of the past two hours, for enlightenment."

Back at Richard's place "for the usual wake," conversation resumed— at arm's length, Macdonald said—and sometimes it was almost morning when the host bid the friends "Arrivedérla." Vast quantities of bourbon oiled the conversation. The friends were serious drinkers, but "to place with Dick for an evening" was out of the question. He talked fluently and wittily, shrouding himself in words "for their own exquisite sake." As the evening wore on, though, "and he got to one or another degree plastered," the fluent talk became a monologue. This was James Burnham's view, recalling the fuliginous seminar he gave on the way the Western world had gone to hell. It was true that for Richard the monologue loomed just over the horizon, but plastered he never was. "I have seen him," said his colleague Robert Hartle, "wise and foolish, brilliant and boring, usually cheerful, and believe it or not, *never* drunk." There were times when Hartle wondered, but Richard always reported that he found the shoe trees in his shoes the next morning.

Sitting up front, "white-haired, round-stomached and benign," Richard seemed to Alvarez "a highbrow Father Christmas." But you built on the resemblance to Father Christmas at your peril. As he got older, he had begun to look like a mature tomcat, said Malcolm Cowley, and sometimes he showed his retractile claws. "He's a cat!" Hannah Arendt used to say of him. Half asleep behind the podium, that was just what he looked like, and his sleepy look suggested that the lecturers and the questioners were mice. They were unaware of this, and the sleepy look was misleading. An "ok human being," said one of his seminarians, but not the sort you would willingly kid around with.

The touch of the proconsular kept Richard's popularity decently incomplete. His senior colleagues took notice of the outrageous style, but the genuine substance went unremarked and largely unrewarded. Almost alone among them, he wasn't honored with a chair. This hurt him in more than his self-love. Every six months he saw his finances "worsen . . . rather than improve." There was reason for this. At dinner he called for the Château Margaux. "My Scotch blood is of the black extravagant strain," he told the Rockefellers, who didn't have to be told. Money was the great fiction, "and fictions as both James and Eliot say must above all be made actual." In middle age, when the Pullman Company overcharged him for his ticket, he wrote a huffy letter demanding the money back, all $3.19. But the penny-pinching man threw money away with both hands, and it was always a scrambling time between the end of one month and the beginning of another.

To make both ends meet, he went on the lecture circuit. Explaining his frequent absences from Princeton, "I travel to speak for money," he said. His public lectures were like a thicket but alluring with promise, if only you could find your way in. The titles he chose—he was always indifferent to titles—gave no help to the acolytes who sat at his feet. Maybe like Shakespeare he thought that a good wine needed no bush. "I don't have a title at hand," he confessed to the English faculty at one institution. Perhaps they might want to use "what I have many times used no matter what I was going to speak about—namely 'A Lion in the Path.'" Let it go at that, he suggested offhandedly to another sponsor. Later on "we will work out between us what would be the best thing actually to give."

The schedule to which he committed himself, crisscrossing the country from Maine to Texas and back again, would have felled an itinerant huckster. He wasn't a huckster and it wasn't enough to keep him in pocket. On McCosh Circle in Princeton he was building the proper house he had wanted for years. It needed a wine cellar, also a greenhouse ("the most continuing folly in which I have ever engaged"), and the kind of furnishings that go with these things. So he took on extra teaching, and in the fifties he earmarked June and July for the School of Letters at Indiana University. "I am making money for furniture these six weeks in Indiana," he wrote to his cousin. But the place was "an oven and also a rat-race," and he said how he got nothing done.

Indiana in the fifties carried on the tradition of the Kenyon School of English which Richard had persuaded the Rockefellers to finance. The idea, said one critic, was to form a "united front" against the middle class and to cultivate the arts of alienation. Bloomington all by itself in a cornfield seemed the right place for this, "a special form of hell" where "man and woman were pleasing and every natural prospect vile." After that training, Richard wrote to John Marshall, "I could take a post in the Red Sea." There were "the usual mitigations in company," though. In 1952 he roomed with John Crowe Ransom; they made an odd couple, so got along fine. Ransom, Richard said, was "mild sweet middleage: all his force in his writing, a nerveless man with a nervous style, an innocent soul with an ironic sensibility." Later he saw this friend under the aspect of a bottle of Old Crow which they qualified together with talking of Lorca and Donne. Or it was the whiskey that qualified the talk. In 1958 Kenneth Burke shared their quarters. His curiosity was raccoon-like, said Marianne Moore, and the trails on which he followed made difficult going for anybody else. At Bennington College, where Richard came to speak and Kenneth introduced him, they hooked up the microphone to the tape recorder rather than the audience. This appeared not to matter. Neither wanted such students as he could teach.

The half-dozen Fellows were committed by prescript to teaching, however. Their charge was to stimulate graduate students, a downtrodden race, "to concentrate their attention upon problems of evaluation." Leslie Fiedler had them concentrating everywhere else, on sex (mostly aborted), or on an endless round of alcoholic parties. One of Richard's students remembered drinking with Richard "at 10 A.M. one steaming July morning of 1954 in a seedy Bloomington bar." The bibulous professor-in-spite-of-himself is the hero-villain of Fiedler's Indiana story—"Pull Down Vanity!" Fiedler called it, suggesting a point of view. But the point of view is ambivalent, this writer loving Richard as much as he deplored him, and feeling "vaguely tinged with guilt at my own failure to understand early on what a lonely and desperate man he was." The story begins: "Actually, I admire Edward Fenton greatly—even though he is a literary critic; and yet for a long time I have wished him dead." Already the aging critic looks to be tottering on his last legs. He wears a pair of old duck pants that hang from him loosely "as if he had recently grown much thinner." Fiedler's narrator thinks how his "natty, opaque essays" were apt to mislead you, "for he had no style at all in his living, only the vestiges of a shabby, old-fashioned recklessness."

It wasn't recklessness that brought Richard back to Indiana in the fifties. His debts were imperious. But so was his body, an adversary from old times, and he lived "in a state of perpetual behindedness." Just standing up, he found himself sore. One grueling summer put him in the hospital for almost a month, where he contemplated "degrees of sloth" unknown to his experience. "Sono ancora stanco," he wrote, "fegato, fegato, fegato," but that was an old problem and now the wretched liver of his litany grew worse. Liver trouble had plagued him since his first trip abroad, and in the winter of 1953 he had entered the American Hospital in Beirut, complaining of fever and chills. Months later in Bologna, he said how he couldn't do much except sleep. To friends he glorified his illness as the Egyptian disease, but this was untrue "for it began in London" and whatever it was, he acknowledged to Tate, "the doctors can't name it and can't treat it." His friends found him "transformed" on his return from Bologna. He had lost fifty pounds and looked shrunken in size, and was able "only barely to keep up" with his work. The transformation was irreversible and carried him down the hill. Academic colleagues who hadn't seen him for years were taken aback "by the change in his appearance." The "remote and tweedy intellectual, quoting Tocqueville and scoring the mass media," suddenly seemed an old man, self-centered, talking very much about himself. "Now his hair is white."

He liked to joke about his ailments, and it pleased him to say how he could feel his liver palpitate. In 1958 a biopsy of the liver revealed sarcoidosis. He was told to stop drinking. He didn't or couldn't. Vascular disease made it hard for him to walk. He suffered from leg cramps and mild hypertension, he had no pulses in his feet, and when he wanted lunch he could hardly make it down Nassau Street to his table at Lahiere's, only a block or so below campus. His circulation worsened and nicotine didn't help. He was told to stop smoking and he said how he tried. Even in early days, he wasn't much of a patient. In the twenties, tuberculosis had sent him to Maine for a year's convalescence. He grumbled the year away. In the thirties, he was in and out of the hospital three times for sinus operations. The cost of this appalled him and he saved all his bills. With much other junk, they were gathering dust when he died. His operations cost him also a perforated nasal septum and two years out of his life, and they dictated his move from Boston, since his doctors said that the smoky quarters of that city would be perilous to him.

In Princeton, however, he contracted diabetes. His prostate enlarged. Off and on, he was anemic. A heart condition began to afflict him. He might have taken to bed, and much good it would have done. The animal which dared to become a man will end up crippled, he said, if it dared long enough. He was this crippled man and he devoured himself in the struggle to renew himself, "to come on the thing, still alive, that was always there." Paraphrasing a line of his, he put his life at risk to make it precious. If you extend yourself as he did, you surpass the human role but not the human capacity. The happy ending becomes unthinkable and only the chance for tragedy remains. When Richard died at sixty-one, he looked as old as the hills. Perhaps he knew the satisfaction of having used himself up.

How do you step over somebody like him, "willing to pay any cost to be that stumbling block called the individual?" He raised this question himself. The individual at full stretch is the hero, he said, and "hero is the high name we give to those to whom we turn for strength." You didn't deal with this hero as you dealt with a tractable problem. "The thing is, to make use of him." The heroism of a private man is not so open to the eye as that of the great makers and shakers. For this private man it consists in what he wrote. He said toward the end, "one wants one's writings to be used." That is why we go to the hero and his work—"to find ourselves a motive" or create ourselves a conscience. This sounds like the old confusion of art and morality, as if the writer were engaging to show us how a good man can die. In didactic ways his story tells us nothing, however. Only it lifts him from a means to a substance.

In a late essay—Richard called it "The Chain of Our Needles," after Montaigne—he singled out for their special quotient of use three eccentric-seeming works of art: *Lycidas*, Joyce's story "The Dead," and *Antony and Cleopatra*. If you wanted to test the catholicity of your critical ideas, go to these works, he said, for they break all the rules and make triumphant constructions. In the course in Criticism he gave at Princeton, these were the works he employed as his touchstones. On any conventional reading, their utility appears elusive. Art always comes short in this respect, he said. It doesn't tell you what to do but what you have to do with. Shakespeare's tragic heroes instruct us in nothing but the truth of themselves. At the end, however—remembering the line from *Antony and*

Cleopatra—they show the cinders of their spirit through the ashes of their chance.

In 1959 Richard looked forward wearily to "my six weeks in Indiana full of solitude and air conditioning." Many years before, taking the measure of an elderly acquaintance, he had predicted the pass to which the years had brought him. "No home life, no friends, but the library and the liquor . . . the great enclosed gentleman. . . . A man anxious for eternity, lonely in anxiety, ever insatiable, an unpacified friend to himself." Solitude was his refuge—part of a pattern in writers' lives, said Malcolm Cowley. "At first they are happy to roam in bands, then year by year they retire from the herd like old bull elephants."

Solitude was his refuge, never his pleasure. More than most men, he epitomized the uxorious man. He couldn't live without women. But he couldn't live with them either, and this made trouble for him and for them. He was like Shelley, the Platonic poet of the poems with an un-platonic fire in his bowels, and like Shelley he wasn't satisfied with one woman at a time. Even before the divorce he needed one for his vocation, another for his avocation. Friends said how Richard, having eaten his supper, would go across the hall in the apartment house on Princeton Avenue and spend the evening with Margot Cutter, leaving Helen to herself. When Margot wasn't there, he attached himself to her roommate. "A difficult husband," said George Anthony, who had a gift for understatement.

Sometimes he came to a party with Helen, sometimes with Margot, or he brought them both along. "People gossiped endlessly," and this was too much for his friend. Margot decided to get away from Richard. She quit her job at the Princeton Press and took a job with the Foreign Service. "And then, when she got to Bologna, there he appeared again, right on her doorstep. And instead of travelling around Europe and doing his job for Rockefeller," said Ed Cone, "he spent most of his time right there in Bologna." He said he had come to visit for only one week. This stretched to half a year and beyond. He lived alone in the old Baglione Hotel (but it became the Majestic Grand and that was the end of it), and he took his lunches "solito" at the Diana. Breaking this sojourn, he traveled through Europe and the Middle East, and the Rockefellers got their money's worth from his essays and reports. But "the rococco and late Italian nature-worshipping palazzo" on the via Zamboni became his self-appointed home—"my base for the year," he said. He directed all his mail to be sent to him there and he took part with relish, sometimes with abandon, in the enormous parties Margot gave for the USIS. "I firmly believe," said Leslie Fiedler, "that he singlehandedly destroyed my liver that year."

Fiedler was aware of "the strength of Richard's affection" for Margot. But he sensed on her part "affectionate detachment," and he saw how malice in Richard, "probably defensive," put the relation in peril. Richard's drinking and dependency were part of the relation. He frightened Margot, said Allen Tate, who remembered Richard in tears when the two of them came to Rome. Margot, Allen supposed, had refused him.

Richard hung on long after his chances, real or imaginary, had vanished. Bologna, where "he had obviously been romantically happy," remained an oasis in the mind. To beautify Margot's villa and gratify himself, he cultivated a flower garden, picking up where the snails had left off. They were his Italian snails and had planted this garden in 1740, he said. Later on, he reproduced his "giardino americano" at home. He wanted opium poppy, which the American catalogues declined to supply, and he wrote hopefully to an Italian friend: "If you pass by any seed store—anything labelled *Semi e Pianti*—ask for a packet of *papaver somniferum*. . . . I know they had them because I grew them in Bologna." He got the poppy seed he wanted, and in his back yard he did his best to approximate the look and feeling of Bologna. But when he returned to Bologna in 1957, he found new tenants installed on the via Zamboni. They had added a gazebo and the garden was gone.

In his cryptic dedication to *The Lion and the Honeycomb*, Richard remembered Margot Cutter. "M.s. e. s.R." his dedication ran—M for Margot, R for Richard—followed by the phrase from Dante: "at least the tower of the true city." He had settled on this, he wrote to his editor, "but do not ask me what it means." Whatever it meant, "solito e sempre" was what he intended—"a Blackmurism," said Margot Cutter, "since it doesn't quite make it as Italian."

Betty Bredemeier was the friend who put Richard's friends in her debt, as she tried to make him happy in his last years. She was ample and outgoing where Margot Cutter was self-possessed and spare, and in Princeton she worked for the publisher Van Nostrand, who specialized in technical books. Her job was taking order with social-scientific writers who thought they had written a book. But Betty couldn't cope with Richard. Toward the women he depended on, his attitude was contemptuous and cruel, and "he liked to *perform* for an audience." The roots of his hostility friends located in weakness and terror. What he couldn't dispense with, he couldn't abide. Betty he treated "very badly indeed." Francis Fergusson remembered a drunken dinner at his place on Ridge Road and Richard abusing Betty and "shooting off his face" regarding Tate and other friends. "The malice of him," Francis said. It wasn't so much that he drank harder toward the end as that it nourished his blackness and made him, said Rob Darrell, "even mean."

Finally Betty, like Margot, bade him goodbye. Or perhaps with both women he was his shrinking self, and never brought himself to put the question. He didn't marry Betty, George Anthony said, because to the end he stayed faithful to Helen. Faithful or not, his vital time was past and his late romantic attachments have about them the air of too late. Like an unwound clock, his life had begun to run down.

Detached, centerless, and lonely, he set off once again on his travels. This was 1961, he was going to Cambridge, and he hoped like Henry Adams at the same age to find relief for what ailed him in flight. But the devil of restlessness pursued him in his travels, and he dreaded "the solitude of hotels and the weariness of self-self-self." Bleak and disappointed when he took his departure, that was how he seemed when Al Alvarez saw him last, "in the beige gloom of the Park Lane Hotel." Mike Keeley remembered this last time he went abroad. "It was an *extraordinary* day. I think it was the day, or very shortly after, that he'd found out that Helen had married again. And he was shaken by that and a lonely man with his news." They drove to New York to put him on the *Queen Elizabeth,* and after drinks and a dull dinner he began to expand. He went on sentimentally about his early years. "I remember sitting in a cabin on this ship, Mary and I, and Blackmur sitting there talking about the good old days, slurring his speech, and clearly not wanting to go anywhere at all." That Richard loved travel was nonsense, Keeley thought. "He was terrified of it, and what he really wanted was to hear me say: 'Get in the car, Richard, and I'll take you back to Princeton.'"

But Princeton was an empty house and he had his commitments over the water. A few years before this, he had talked on the radio about Lambert Strether, the amphibious hero of *The Ambassadors,* hovering between his two worlds. As James concludes the novel, Strether "has almost nothing left but scruple," Richard said. Then came the familiar resort to the dictionary: "scruple" meant a small stone or a pebble in your shoe, and "he can hardly walk by the end of the book." He had too much of conscience in Joyce's sense, "the again-bite of inwit." It wasn't any wonder that he had to go home, "but he wasn't going home to anything."

CHAPTER TEN

The Critic as Artist

WHY RICHARD didn't take his life, unlike his friends Berryman and Randall Jarrell, had "something to do with the survival of the race itself." He typified the enduring man who preserves the sense that life is precious, and "neither tyranny nor privation—no emptiness" could reduce this sense. "It is how one knows one lives and dies alone." Enduring, he makes you think of Bloom in the essay on *Ulysses*. He is "the everlasting hero of the quotidian: truly protean." This says two things. He went about his business, and he was endlessly resourceful in finding ways to cope. Waning on one side, he grew crescent on another. The void at the center of his life needed filling, and he wrote with greater assiduity than ever before. In the dozen years between 1952 and 1964, he published six books, and his *Primer of Ignorance* and the biography of Adams were waiting on the stocks when he died.

More than twenty years earlier, he had proposed for Adams an "imaginative identity with St. Augustine." Now he made this identification his own. He was old Augustine, correcting syntax as the vandals overran the true city. Like Augustine, he defined the *peregrinus* or resident alien traveling toward a distant land. He had his eye on heaven—for the secular man, this meant the life of art—and like the creator of the city of God he longed to create a polity or unified society on earth. But failure awaits the man who puts on wisdom, and the career as public man or rhetor ended in failure for both. Richard like Augustine was marred in the grain, and of what man or woman could this not be said? So the hero is like the rest of us, but only generically. In the psychic pain or *dolor pectoris* which afflicted him lay the source of his strength. Richard said of Dostoevsky: "The habit of his calling overcame the need of his emotion." In his own case, the need begot the habit.

Language as Gesture (1952), the major work of our best American critic, declares the habit. That is true of all his work. But *Language as*

Gesture is the bottom line for him, *aere perennius,* and the right place to come to conclusions. It points and vivifies the life, however mordant the life, and assures a happy ending. The dejected author had no part in the ending. He went wild into his grave. At the funeral in Pittsfield there was only a single mourner to bid him goodbye, and a preacher who didn't know him and who talked about his own son for want of something to say. His vacated professorship at Princeton went unfilled, not because he was irreplaceable but because they saw no need to replace him, and in a little while his name began to sound unfamiliar. "Blackmur?" they said. "The man who wrote *Lorna Doone?*" When friends proposed that the university seek funds for a chair to keep his memory alive, the vice-president in charge of such things said he "admired Richard Blackmur far too much to risk associating his name with an enterprise doomed to ignominious failure." In his own view he was certainly a failure. His art is happy, though.

Language as Gesture makes a palimpsest in which the early criticism is overlaid by Richard's writing of the forties and early fifties. This is typically thrifty but gives you a sense of the cumulative and varying nature of his achievement. In twenty-one essays, all but one on modern poets, he defines and transcends the New Critical method. Where this method begins is suggested in his account of a woman named Annie, otherwise unremembered. To Rob Darrell he said how her presence had started images flowing in his mind. They had "nothing to do with anything she said, but a great deal to do with how she moved: the language of gesture, or the gesture of being." You know the New Critic by his partiality to this language. He is primarily the connoisseur of form. Poetry he called life at the remove of form and meaning. But the definition made a tautology. The poems of Kenneth Patchen, a friend from Cambridge days, were premorphic, Richard thought. Patchen showed all the world's promise but had yet to get into his poetry "something that stands up on its own feet as form." His egalitarian heart was in the right place, etc. Only he didn't let you feel this. The old cliché was muddled because it put sincerity first. James in *The Golden Bowl* had "deepened his sympathies," Richard reported, "or, one might as well say, perfected his style." Sincerity is style and form is the earnest of feeling.

The equation seemed odious to critics on the Left, and they made Richard a whipping boy for his "lack of concern with LIFE." Laura Riding, an unsympathetic poet, deplored his supposed indifference to the economic and political questions of the day. "Historical location" was her phrase for what he missed. "The antipode of Marxist criticism," said a Marxist critic, "is the 'New Criticism' which declines to examine literature in its social, cultural and philosophical context." For Alfred Kazin, Richard epitomized this insular mode of writing since he made "a criticism so *driven* to technical insights that it virtually conceives the literary mind as a sensibility machine—taste, conscience, and mind working as gears, levers, and wheels." The "hard and purely quantitative" criticism he practiced aimed at hooking the attention of "the men in power." But "more urgent problems" beset them, and Richard's essays-in-a-vacuum were bound to fail of their aim. That was Granville Hicks in a notorious critique of "leisure-class culture," to which he assimilated Blackmur & Co. In 1932 Hicks assumed Richard's failure as a matter of course, and he wondered in what direction this formalist critic would turn.

For the immediate future, the direction he took was toward the "quantitative" thing execrated by his critics. Only a piece of the truth got noticed in the character they gave him, and *Language as Gesture* lives partly because it documents the ampler thing he created. Richard in the thirties wrote his criticism in the conviction that art is for art's sake. But he looked without prejudice at the matter in hand and so found the "central place in criticism where literature and politics cross." Shakespeare is our most observant and hence our most political poet. Fidelity to the actual strengthens a writer, Richard supposed, "and gives his writing its only effect on society." His "severe and scrupulous" essays verge on tedium, though. Quoting Richard on himself: "The judgment that flows from . . . [them] needs hardly be stated; it is judgment by description." Not much humor informs his judgment, and the general tone he achieves is about as suspicious as the tone of Yvor Winters, the critic as custodian. This is a young man's writing, Richard's proving ground. "Entre nous Dick B. takes . . . [his poets] all too seriously," said Sean O'Faolain to Lincoln Kirstein. "Imagine analysing Pound as if he were Keats! He does it very well, does Dick. But Jesus! Pound!"

The analytical habit led critics to call him "a botanist of the stanza, verse, phrase, even of the single word." They remarked his "surgical skill," and said they saw in his criticism "a demonstration of poetic dissection by a master anatomist." He had "the mind of an Ostler," though without "that great physician's gifts of communication." His own gifts were transmitted, said his friend Conrad Aiken, "in a cramped and literal" style. Delmore said that diction was his fatal Cleopatra, but not because he indulged it. "I think maybe it is that helpless strength of yours, that overwhelming consciousness of the possibilities of meaning of single words which if it continues will make you end up like Samson dragging the temple of the whole English language down on your head." He made "the sharpest and closest reader of poetry we have," but much of his first book could be described as little more than "brilliant elucidation."

This judgment didn't distress him. Criticism was self-consuming, the means to an end. "We use analysis properly in order to discard it and return that much better equipped to the poem." He presented the acolyte serving his mystery at a becoming distance. When the service was finished, he folded his tent. Call him a camp follower, not yet the doyen of critics. "There are no statues to literary critics," he said. "Criticism by its nature, and like translation, has to be done over again each generation. Only by accident is it lasting." He didn't aspire to the accidental thing. His essays of the thirties resemble fictions or rival creations "probably less than the work of any other critic now writing in English; they are distinguished by the utmost relevance—the utmost devotion—to the masterwork under consideration."

The appreciative phrase is Robert Fitzgerald's, reviewing *The Double Agent* in 1936. With the publication of this book, said Allen Tate, Richard "probably invented what we call the New Criticism in the United States." He had his progenitors. The term had been around for more than thirty years when Ransom found it in the scholar-critic Joel Spingarn and put it in front of the collection of essays he published in 1941. Before Ransom there was Coleridge, already a New Critic in asserting that existence is its own predicate, and Pound when he tells us how "bad art is inaccurate art." Richard himself pointed to Croce and his dictum that art, expressing feeling through lyric intuition, gives theoretic form to the feelings. Technique communicates the form. It is the vade mecum, as for Henry James, "the grandfather of our particular kind of criticism." Addressing the form was how you got at the content. The executive techniques Richard employed in his own criticism were enough, he supposed, to bring us into connection with everything else. They were at any rate the only matters you could usefully discuss, and it was his faith "that they somehow drag after them into being all other matters."

Buoyed by this faith, he left the matter of content to shift for itself. Maybe that was remiss of him. Picking up on "a somewhat alcoholic discussion," Malcolm Cowley protested mildly that Richard didn't listen hard enough "to *what* an author is saying, in your concern with the *how*." His fanatic concern did wonders for readers of poetry, though, and his remorseless scrutinizing came home with the force of revelation. No one before this critic had looked so intently at the words on the page. Almost "the *only* modern critic to deal not with himself but with poetry," said the poet Paul Oppenheimer, a student of Richard's. William Carlos Williams, mostly an antagonist, was agreeably surprised at Richard's willingness to consider respectfully a viewpoint which wasn't his own. "You actually *looked* at something I wrote, looked at it from inside out and made your statement without prejudice." Richard's essays on modern poets taught F. W. Dupee how to read them. He succeeded where "even so great a critic as Edmund Wilson had failed." Wilson, walking around his poets like a cicerone, made much livelier reading, one reviewer said; but "when Blackmur talks about a poem or a piece of writing without alien (usually humanistic) ideas to grind, he is nearly incomparable in modern criticism."

Ideas, paradoxically, were not what he missed, or not by inadvertence. He understood how ideas are inert in themselves. You made your point *ad hoc* or you made no point at all. Particularity engrossed him and he honored its claims. As a line-for-line critic he was marvelous, Cowley said. Tate called him "a great master of explication of text." The mastery depended for Marianne Moore on his "extreme conscience . . . in the matter of detail." In his own phrase, he practiced "the humility of complete attention." Young John Berryman wanted him to look at Dickinson's poetry and "tell the ignorant world which poems of the hundreds are good and which are not . . . say *what* she is saying, *how* she says it." In the criticism that made him famous, that is what he said. He was without rival the critic as taxonomist. Having heard a medical man assert that all medicine lay in an up-to-date medical dictionary, he drew the analogy to his own trade. Know your vocabulary and you could objectify your knowledge, he thought. "It is the same thing with poetry, and with as much responsibility for life and death." This was the faith that sustained him early on, and it still quickens in *Language as Gesture*. He lost his faith as his skepticism deepened. But in his unknowing he found another faith and the means to a new departure. This was the work of his age.

In Richard, faith was always qualified, the man who entertained it not being a fool. "Criticism never gets you to intimacy," he said. What we make in our criticism is "a fiction to school the urgency of reading; no more." Analysis merely distinguished particulars. After that you confronted the unassayable thing. Definition enveloped but didn't render this thing. In his earliest essays Richard said how analysis, like going to the dictionary, figured as "a preparatory school to good criticism." It served the critic's turn without comprising his function. (He is reviewing I. A. Richards in 1929.) Already at nineteen he was catechizing his cousin: "The surd of this letter is apprehensible and impeculiar." That is how the letter begins. The terms are outlandish but make a coherence, also a paradox, and the paradoxical coherence or contradiction in terms casts a long shadow. Richard's letter concludes: "At bottom, it is probably 'finality of utterance' that my plan subtends"—but this finality wasn't open to the cavils of reason.

Richard all his life lusted after *obiter dicta,* but he wanted them coming out of a cloud, as if he were the great God Himself. He wrote in his youthful journal: "Avoid explanations if what you want is a mutual understanding." (He had been reading Diderot.) He liked playing God and he lived in a cloud of unknowing. With respect to the intellect and what it could tell you, his last word was failure. The feeling in poetry, he perceived as a young man, "is not exactly in the words, it is because of them." Trying for the sense of his elusive contingency, he moved beyond analysis. He became, said one critic, "a poet of criticism." He sought to imitate the poem itself by creating in his prose a "semblance of the essential experience" it offered. By the beginning of the fifties, his criticism aspired to the lineaments of art. To a fellow poet he confessed that criticism was a chore "except when, occasionally, I can write it as if it were a poem"—a sentence that speaks profoundly to the best and worst of his critical prose.

The line from Wallace Stevens was dinning in his ears: he wanted to write "the prose that wears the poem's guise at last." Robert Lowell thought he succeeded. "In his prose, every sentence struggles to be poetry, form ringing on rock. He was a good poet, weird, tortured, derivative, original—and more a poet in his criticism." This criticism, said Joseph Frank, "has the gnomic quality of the great, late works of art and literature." In his lengthy meditation or peregrination on *Four Quartets,* he makes us feel how there are depths and conundrums in experience which mere analysis can never elucidate. He makes us feel, but not discursively. His subjects are "evoked, incanted into existence." The stuff of poetry is its own meaning, and for dealing with this stuff intuition counts more than cerebration.

On a hostile view, Richard was most a critic when he approximated most nearly the psychology of Hemingway's hero: "Abstract words such as glory, honor, courage, or hallow were obscene beside the concrete names of villages, the numbers of roads, the names of rivers, the numbers of regiments and the dates." Getting on in years, he yearned for glory, honor, courage. He became the Old Pretender. There is another way to put this, however. Everything he wrote was authentic, Frederic Prokosch observed of him, and the delimiting word defines the New Critic. But this poet went on to say how Richard's writing engendered in the reader a certain "esprit de corps." The writing shows as whimsical, melancholy, or ribald. It speaks of the man who made it. You remember the man and the point of view peculiar to him. Sometimes the text recedes and this, if a fault, is also a kind of triumph. No doubt the triumph is equivocal. The evoking of personality participates in the critic's job of work, as the criticism longs to make a rival creation.

In his "Anni Mirabiles" lectures, comparing qualities of poets which didn't cry out for comparison, Richard hoped only for "some creative virtue" in his analogies. He said he preferred this virtue to the critical "in any case." Expressing this preference, he harks back to his master Flaubert. Critics used to be grammarians, Flaubert said dismissively. In the nineteenth century, they took on themselves the historical role. "When will they be artists—really artists?" he wanted to know. The later essays of *Language as Gesture* address themselves to this question. In these essays, criticism "has become a part of literature or literature . . . has become a part of criticism."

In 1948 Richard and some friends gathered for a symposium at Johns Hopkins University on the great critics of the past. Allen Tate, whose subject was Longinus, wondered if there could be "a criticism of convincing objectivity which approaches the literary work through the analysis of style and which arrives at its larger aspects through that aperture?" The larger aspects were judgmental, and Tate thought that the New Criticism answered his question in the affirmative. Ransom agreed. Richard enters his agreement in the early essays from *Language as Gesture*, on Pound, Stevens, Hart Crane. There are others. Already time had overtaken his agreement, however. Henri Peyre, a dove among these eagles, didn't mean to be rude. New Criticism, even as Richard consigned it to the dustbin, was still a wild surmise for him. A critic, he supposed, "should above all be humbly conscious of his duty to serve the creator and the public." This proper humility shut him off forever "from any aspiration to true greatness." Just here late Blackmur enters, like the God of the Creation. You wouldn't call him invisible, though.

"A good work of criticism," said the poet Karl Shapiro (like Richard, an autodidact or self-begotten man), "is a work of art about another work of art." Take this view of criticism and you will find yourself saying that criticism is superfluous—great works of art supplying their own critique— "unless it is itself a work of art . . . [and] independent of the work" it endeavors to criticize. Creative criticism, like the New Criticism, begins with the Romantics. In the twentieth century its time has come round. "Criticism . . . *is* creation; it gives birth!" That is Margaret Anderson, announcing the *Little Review* in 1914. Let this proposition stand as a rubric for Richard in his last phase, the critic as artist.

He grew to manhood, so he said, in an age of critique, but critique was a means of creation. The famous empiric wore his empiricism loosely, and when it didn't suit him he put it away. Like Gide in *The Counterfeiters*, he accepted reality as validating his thought but not as coming before it. At seventeen he told his cousin how he desired to imitate no one, "no matter how much above me he may be—I must be original in the juxtaposition of words." Cultivating originality, he made his supreme fictions. They aren't wholly off the point, nor intended wholly to school the urgency of our reading. If you don't like him, you will say how, like Oscar, he renders the thing in itself as it isn't. But the thing in itself was always mysterious. As the sense of mystery deepened, his poets began to afford him not a text to elucidate but a point of departure. In his last avatar "Blackmur matches his poets and novelists," said Harold Bloom. This isn't to say that late Blackmur comes out of the blue. Unity in diversity describes his work from the beginning, and *Language as Gesture* exemplifies this mingled yarn. Already the Double Agent is the critic as artist. He makes "his criticism an art, and demonstrates his art while he applies it." In the later criticism, analysis isn't scanted, exactly. But it goes to the back of the class.

Not everyone was tickled by the emergence of the vates, resplendent or comic in his singing robes. His prose that wants to be poetry conveyed to Murray Borish, the friend of Richard's youth, a sense of "painful compression." Murray inquired: "How much of the pregnancy of poetry can prose bear?" For the English novelist John Wain, Richard's late mannered prose abides this question. Criticism, Wain insisted, can never have authority. "It is only art that can have authority." That your prose should "wear the poem's guise at last" wasn't "a thing to be proud of." Sometimes, said one reader of *Language as Gesture*, "Mr. Blackmur is more interesting than his subjects," and sometimes what he writes "trembles on the edge of turning itself into an extrinsicality—a house, say, or a kangaroo." Richard had his answer pat: "In life we do what we can and what we must; in literature and the arts (and sometimes in our daydreams and what we call our thought) we make a kind of rival creation." Does this differ from mere daydream? Yes, it differs, he thinks, as in our creations, responding to actuality, "we alter that actual life."

This permanent altering is the ultimate harvest we barn from his work as a critic. The nourishing ground isn't certitude, though. Creative doubt is the unlikely ground of the harvest. "I was in a brown study, a scholar looking towards the dark." That is Richard at the end. In the dark, however, he learned to see again, "with greater difficulty but also with more penetrating vision." Seeing in the dark was the natural condition but like the fortunate fall, and as we were provident we turned it to account.

His youthful poetry says this. And so do his early essays insofar as he meant them for "provisional and incomplete." In his late twenties he wanted the *Hound & Horn* to let him review *Seven Types of Ambiguity*. This was a book he said he couldn't keep away from. In Empson he met himself and his growing conviction that ambiguity is "the *explicit* virtue of poetry." This didn't mean obfuscation. "The clearest possible definition of things essentially ambiguous leaves ambiguity." The poem wasn't a blueprint nor yet a portmanteau, and he said how he was willing "to bring everything I can to bear on the ambiguous content." But precision of meaning remained in the poem, not in subsequent anagogy.

His friend Jacques Barzun called him "an exclusionist in criticism." This is flat-out misunderstanding. His mind was medieval, like that of the makers of the *multiplex intelligentia*, which is one reason he wrote a great book when he wrote about Adams and the High Middle Ages. The multiform world was the world in which he lived, always uneasily but resolutely, too. Stasis wasn't regnant there nor canonized belief, but the mutual trespass of belief and disbelief. This trespass made a conflagration and he walked by its light. A great writer, said he, in *Language as Gesture*, "always holds conflicting ideas in shifting balance . . . with victory only the last shift." In his most intimate recesses, he betrays "the duplicity of every thought, pointing it out, so to speak, in the act of self-incrimination, and showing it not paled on a pin but in the buff life." Confronting the buff life, this particular writer adopted "an attitude of provisional skepticism; where, imperatively, you must scrutinize and scrutinize until you have revealed, if it is there, the inscrutable divination, or, if it is not, the void of personal ambition." There was no vicar on earth for poetry or anything else.

Frustrated by his failure to close with the truth, he elevated his frustration until it became a point of honor. Only recognize frustration as a fundamental condition of life and it took on the aspect of "fate, tragedy, damnation, the Cross, the other side of every infatuation." Analyzing poetry drove you on despair. He read Robert Frost and saw how in this poet "the analogies multiply and deepen into surds of feeling." But he wasn't hamstrung by what he saw, and he learned to live equably with the indeclinable thing. "What, should we get rid of our ignorance, of the very substance of our lives, merely in order to understand one another?" A major image obsessed him, he told Allen Tate. This was "the *gap* between moments, between words, between breaths, between the particles of thought or sensation, the *gap* that strikes—so much worse than the gulf that swallows—whenever any instance of the discontinuity of experience is felt going, or rather leaping, its way through all our habitual continuums." At sixteen, reading Bertrand Russell's description of Planck's quantum theory, he said how the principle of discontinuity had struck him as a remarkable adventure. When he was twice as old, it had become "the very soup stock of all adventure." Growing to relish the taste of this adventure, he made himself in his age the critic of esthetic Pyrrhonism.

In his late fifties he discovered "a kind of mutilating self-determinism about what we call form." You sensed this, for example, in the novels of Henry James. Old idols were shaking. He discovered in darkness unexpected reserves of strength, and he connived at "the entrance of the dark and uncanny into the service of the gods." He went down into the darkness not to lose himself but to refresh himself. He was looking to find succor in remote forces that seemed at least as menacing as they were propitious. It wasn't to vanquish his enemies that he sought a new access of strength, but to vanquish his own weakness. Like the bourgeois humanist of whom he wrote in Thomas Mann, he was looking to rediscover, now that the order by which he lived was failing, "what all that turbulence was which he had put in order."

This late exploration shows the protean hero. As his life approached its term, he was still growing and changing. The dread he felt before the dark chthonic underground—he called it the daemonic, signifying "the indwelling power, or spirit, or genius in things, whether for good or evil"—explains his abhorrence of the new mass culture he thundered against in the didactic essays of *The Lion and the Honeycomb*. He feared the purport of this eruption of the dark into the light "because you are afraid of yourself." Two of his students, less abashed than the others, didn't hesitate to say so. He drew back, they told him, "out of a fear of your own daring . . . or out of a fear of discovering that you are normal." If he feared the discovery, he had reason. He was one of the sons of darkness. He made a truce with his fear, however, and this is one measure of his greatness. Like Dostoevsky, "he not only gave the devil his due; he knew that the devil lived in his own heart unexorcisably," and he knew that you had to deal with the devil in order to reach the daemonic.

Dreams absorbed him and terrified him, too. They reminded reason "of what it is the servant" and he called them "the most terrible burden" with which reason had to cope. But he knew that the libido was of the whole mind, including reason. "*That* is why it raises hell with 'mere' reason." In his sixtieth year he disclaimed all relation "with people who think that Christianity is to be found in the *Summa* of Aquinas or in the *De Doctrina* of St. Augustine. Bonaventura is more helpful." More idols going down here. Aquinas, he used to say, had made the most profoundly satisfying intellectual system the world had ever known. Augustine, the systems-maker, counted among his enduring heroes. But for Richard as the shades deepened, Bonaventura, the great Franciscan and the antagonist of Saint Thomas, epitomized the central truth of Christianity. Bonaventura deprecated reason, knowing how the heart has its reasons. You can say that Richard outpaced morbidity and fear as he gave increasing credit—the word is his—"to the nonrational aspects of our thinking." A memorable phrase from his *Eleven Essays* is on the point: "His imagination went beyond the mistake of his intellect and overwhelmed it."

In the last decade of his life, primitive culture, magic, and fairy tales began to earn his respectful attention. He called them "a necessary part of the education of our own actual contemporary minds." Already in the forties he had become a student of Jung. The renewed popularity of this occulted stuff was traceable, he said scornfully, to "the delight we find in inventing fresh techniques of trouble." But the moment of outward catastrophe coincided for him with the moment of inward breakthrough, and new understanding challenged his old scorn. All his life he had shunned and denied the base on which Humanism stands. At the end of his life he forced himself out upon this base in darkness. When he expatiated on "The Techniques of Trouble"—his title for the second essay in his "Anni Mirabiles" lectures—he saw how the taint of the artist who explored the dark underbelly of things raised the heroes of modern fiction to heroic proportions. It was just that taint which compelled them "to take stock of the sick and ailing, to seize on the unseemly, to expect the equivocal, and to rejoice in the problematic." Heroes like Hans Castorp and Felix Krull were outsiders who participated in their society. They were "all daemonic people redeemed from the diabolic by the human, but they would not have been daemonic had they not gone in for all the upsetting, all the low-grade relations we have in human nature."

This passage gives the self-portrait of Richard—as always, an oblique portrait—which his friend John Walcott, so many years before, had urged him to compose. The portrait makes a unity of disparate things, and that befits the many-sided man. Richard on one side presents the morbid systematizer, taking order with the myriad of incidental fact. On another side, however, he is the great accommodator, footloose, even headloose, who says in his own poetry: "There is no choice, severalty is all." Equating love of God with knowledge of His creation, he saw how this knowledge had to be plenary. Winnowing and sifting—the province of form—"cuts the options." He exacted a look at the best and the worst and gave to either his "qualitative assent." The quality of his giving is the warrant for calling him happy.

The comprehensive knowledge which informed his yea-saying he located in "that stirring of the flesh, that prospering of deep excitement—as a poppy prospers when its pod rends and falls." Or it was the access of felt being, he said, the carnal equivalent for landscape seen, great thinking conned, a face really discerned. "That stirring, that prospering, that access"—his criticism and poetry are figured in this triad. He called it "the very substance and home of the bodiless eddying faith upon which my life depends and must conclude." He was writing to himself, so he allowed himself to say: "In these moments the Almighty breathes." Knowing such moments, he knew a kind of happiness most men and women are innocent of. This pulled him up from the dead.

But "his triumph was personal and therefore tragic." Life defined itself for him as it ended in failure. The definition is hardly morbid unless the great religious dispensations are morbid. Laforgue, whom he had quoted in his young manhood and never relinquished, had said this best without any but poetic logic to blister his cry: "La Vie est vraie et criminelle!" The act of life is the crime. In his first journal entries the young man had insisted on the truth of his gloomy proposition, his own birth being "the crime of birth," etc. Now at the end he caught the deeper sense of what he had been saying all along. He said how "none are guilty and all are guilty," and how you achieved salvation—or wholeness or integration—as you submitted yourself to the suffering of life at the expense of the act of life.

For Richard, racial dreaming antedated conscious thought, and this was another of his early fixations. "The practice must begin before birth and must linger in the last bone." Toward the end the great soul was still dreaming in him "the anonymous and communal dream of human hope and its cost." The hope was a wan hope and the cost nothing less than extinction. The value of what he showed was worth the cost, however. As death took him, he was still gathering leaves—"those fallen and those about to fall—against a winter work yet to come that will never come since, for all the halcyon summer in the heart, it is already that winter now."

Reason likes the finished job, he said, mocking himself in this knowledge, and what is Richard on one side if not the type of the rational man? "Poetry is a rational and objective art"—that was how he defined it, prosecuting his critic's job of work—"and most so when the theme is self expression." He tried in his own poetry to objectify self-expression, and he wanted to believe that he had "closed the gap between conception and shadow." Sometimes he did this. But his success was intermittent, and failure participates in his achievement. The failure attests our radical imperfection. "Thus in a great man we often find inextricably combined the success which was his alone . . . with the failure which as we feel it is also our own in prospect." But poetry, his best medium when he wrote it himself or when he wrote about it, lent a different perspective to failure. Poetry cared nothing for the finished job. It liked the new job, Richard said, "the living process rather than the vital purpose." In his last years, resuming the living process, he was satisfied to let the purpose alone.

The last years were auspicious in every outward way. Honors fell in the lap of the inauspicious man. The National Institute of Arts and Letters elected him to membership. Eight years later the American Academy of Arts and Sciences did the same. Rutgers gave him the degree of Doctor of Letters. He became a fellow of the Library of Congress. Cambridge named him Master of Arts. Did he think of himself as Ben Jonson, the bricklayer's son, who received this same honor three hundred years before? His undergraduates at Princeton chose him to deliver the coveted Witherspoon Lectures "for his outstanding scholarship and popularity with the students." His publisher got the idea of bringing out his complete works. He was so famous he might have been dead.

Like Henry Adams, he called himself dead long before he died. But like Adams he cultivated steadiness of nerve, "and no quarter to exaggerating trouble." A hundred things were wrong with him, chiefly heart disease, but he didn't show himself affected. Sometimes in company he stiffened with pain and held hard to the arms of the elegant armchair his summer teaching at Indiana had paid for. That was when he thought that no one was looking. Complaining was beneath him. He understood, however, that his time was abridged, and he didn't conspire to make tolerable what ought to remain intolerable. When he came to departmental meetings, it was like death coming into the room. Except at the end, being conscientious was never his strong suit. Now at the end, the more it cost him to come, the more he willed himself to come. Walking was an act of will, and he walked in shoes of lead. A colleague remembered the "shambled hump of flesh" framed in Hulit's window, the shoestore in Palmer Square. He didn't speak, he didn't turn, and looking at his tired back, this colleague supposed that his eyes didn't turn but strayed in fixed proportion to his thought. "His eyes were in his pocket with Pascal."

In March of 1963 he was hospitalized. He found himself short of breath and fluids began to accumulate in his body. After his death the autopsy revealed that he had had a coronary thrombosis. So toward the end there was only the one coronary left. Getting up in the morning, he took a long shower to nerve himself for the day. Putting on his clothes was a major event. His sister Betty came to visit, and with wry humor he told her how he had been trying to rig a contraption for holding his shirt at the ready. Taking off his shirt was too much for him, though, and he turned to Betty for help. "He looked so thin," she said, "but he was still Dick." In the mornings he dozed a little, after breakfast and the *Times*. Everyone should read the *Times*, he said. In the early afternoons he had another nap. He didn't lie down on the leather couch in his living room, because he didn't dare lie down. Instead he napped in a chair, keeping himself in an upright position. He couldn't eat, he couldn't drink. Drinks, he said ruefully, didn't taste the way they used to. Friends persisted in having him over for dinner. Making apologies, he toyed with his food. One painful evening, a little girl at the table wanted to know what was wrong with the dreadful old man. In 1964 he lost the feeling in his limbs. When he couldn't cope, he took to his bed. He got up again, however. Medication kept him going. To help him through the day, he hired a practical nurse. "That whole last six months was very trying," said one of his friends.

Gertrude Buckman, Delmore's wife, was a friend he hadn't seen for years. She came down to Princeton when she heard he was ill. "Very sad, very depressed, he was." She remembered seeing in the garden the bales of peat he was never to use. He talked about his flower bulbs around the trees in the garden. He talked about money, and he worried that there wouldn't be enough to see him through. This worry, poignant and comical, had dogged him all his life. After he died, friends got together to choose a coffin for the funeral, and one of them spoke of a deal of "wry humor about what Blackmur himself would have thought appropriate and how much he would have been willing to spend." The friends chose a plain wooden coffin.

Beleaguered in the present, Richard lived in the past. In the kitchen of his house he had hung the painting called "Blackmur's Rum." Waldo Peirce had made this painting one summer in Maine. To friends he talked about Waldo, a different and more flamboyant type of the hero. Under the painting stood the butcher's block table which Ansel had given him. Ansel and Viola had lived on Oak Point, down the road from Richard and Helen. That was half a lifetime ago. Dozing in his chair or swapping recollections with his sister Betty, he went back in mind to early days in Cambridge. Every Sunday for years, until he was into his teens, he had sung in the choir at Christ Church Episcopal, "rolling out the words" of the great Protestant hymns. "A Mighty Fortress Is Our God" was one of his favorites. This fortress was a refuge, also a privation. His mother and her disappointed view of the world and its business had made sure of that for him. She was buried beneath the elms in the family plot in Pittsfield, near his brother Ted. Up the road from the cemetery lay the little town of Lanesboro where the Reverend Charles James Palmer had preached for sixty years. Richard evoked in memory summer holidays with Grandpop and the way this muscular Christian had made them toe the line. When Helen Palmer Blackmur died in 1963, he said how early sorrow had predicted the whole course of her life. He was his mother's son, but he was also the maker who made shapes from early sorrow at the remove of meaning and form.

The winter term loomed and he said how the prospect of teaching dismayed him. He wondered if he could carry it off. He wanted to get back to his teaching, however, and until he could do this he held informal seminars in his living room. Students remembered on the living room wall the Piranesi engraving of Ara Coeli and Campidoglio. His skin was white beneath the skin, said one of his students. But "inside the white head moved a golden mouth." He said himself that he wanted to live.

For years a secretary had helped him with his correspondence, duplicating what he wrote, and that is why so many of his letters survive. In his last illness he was still writing letters. To an early student he wrote laconically about his illness, and how as a result he had done nothing worth spitting at for almost a year. The rigid diet they imposed on him made travel impossible when meals were involved. If only they might transport him back to the eighteenth century "and give me an equipage of servants including cooks and the contents of a kitchen." This was what he had always wanted, good health or bad.

Richard dated his letter January 25, 1965. On this day he turned sixty-one. As time flies he wasn't old, and his Blackmur and Palmer forebears had lived to a far greater age. He knew better than to take comfort from the auspices, though. He told his sister that someday soon an embolism would block the flow of blood to his brain. The doctor had said that the end would come quickly. February 2 fell on a Monday and the new term at Princeton was getting under way. It was the dead of winter and the flat terrain of Mercer County looked like the winter scene imagined by John Berryman in his poem after Brueghel. Richard said, however, that he was ready to teach and he insisted that the department schedule him for classes. He spent the day doing errands. He went to the barber's and he went for lunch to Lahiere's. For a long time he hadn't had the energy to do this. In the late afternoon Harold Stein dropped by for a visit. This old friend was dying and both of them knew it. The visit got his mind off himself, Richard said. In the evening after dinner, he packed his briefcase for class. He left it ready on the table to pick up in the morning, then went to bed. During the night he suffered a heart attack and somewhere near morning he died.

Abbreviations

AMN   Autograph MS notebook, begun 12/18/25 and extending to the mid-1930s; Box 29, folder 13, Princeton

DP   R. D. Darrell Papers

GFA   Guggenheim Foundation Archive, New York City

HA   Henry Adams manuscript, in the author's possession

HBP   Harcourt Brace Papers

H&H   The *Hound and Horn*

IFAS   Institute for Advanced Study, Princeton

LHUS MS   "Henry James" MS for *A Literary History of the United States,* ed. Robert Spiller (1948), IFAS

NDA   New Directions Archive

PP   Palmer Papers, Houghton Library, Harvard

RFA   Rockefeller Foundation Archive, Tarrytown, New York

ZP   Zabel Papers, Box I, folder 8, University of Chicago

Notes

1. Past and Present

Page

3 his Cambridge childhood . . . : Drawing on RPB to Walcott, 6/28/42, Princeton Univ.; Jay Laughlin, 10/31/45, NDA; John Marshall, 8/30/49, Marshall Papers; Richard Johns, [ca. 1930], Univ. of Delaware; Gyde Shepherd, 8/30/55, Princeton.

an ancestral part . . . : To J. R. Weagant, 6/27/57, Princeton.

on your sleeve . . . : To Lee Anderson, 6/1/60, Princeton.

have no biography . . . : Biographical notes to Oscar Williams's anthology *New Poems: 1940* (New York, 1940).

entirely in longhand . . . : To Frank V. Morley, Labor Day 1939, HBP.

4 my own thoughts . . . : AMN, pp. 107, 14, 15.

or other convention . . . : Black notebook, 1/21/23, Box 29, folder 15, Princeton.

speak and see . . . : AMN, p. 107.

present *should* be . . . : Black notebook, 11/22.

much to seed . . . : Interview (Boston), 3/77.

de l'enfer . . . : For example AMN, p. 104.

5 house "next door" . . . : To the author, 9/77.

in "Norton's Woods" . . . : Betty Blackmur to the author, 10/31/78.

appropriated him, too . . . : RPB to Robert Penn Warren, 12/11/35, Beinecke Library, Yale.

and which Babbitt's . . . : 10/22/42, Princeton.

I inherited wealth . . . : Box 31, folder 27, Princeton.

and well bred . . . : Review of Aldous Huxley's *Do What You Will* in *New Republic*, 25 Dec 1929, p. 149.

same public school . . . : Drawing on Cummings's *Six Non Lectures* (Cambridge, Mass., 1942).

in English tweeds . . . : Malcolm Cowley, *Second Flowering* (New York, 1973), p. 90.

in the garret . . . : Tessa Horton, interview (Harrington, Maine), 9/76.

acquire and preserve . . . : To George Anthony Palmer, 2/4/23, PP.

a jay bird . . . : To RPB, 1/21/31, 2/23/31, Princeton.

6 coast of Maine . . . : Kenneth Wiggins Porter to the author, 7/25/77.

was it Gloucester . . . : To the author, 2/1/77.

was British, born . . . : RPB's visa questionnaire, 3/26/61, Princeton; RPB to Robert Giroux, 2/15/52, HBP.

at his funeral . . . : Mary Blackmur Waterbury to the author, 10/15/77, 10/30/78; Betty Blackmur to the author, 10/30/78. (Horace is buried in Greenwood Cemetery.)

about the title . . . : To Lambert Davis at Harcourt Brace, 1/11/43, HBP.

287

7   in his story . . . : Account derives from Waterbury to the author, 10/15/77;
and Betty Blackmur, n.d. Allen School records show George Edward
Blackmur as entered there in 1872.

    sight or mind . . . : *The Education of Henry Adams* (Boston and New York,
1918), p. 291.

    A. & A. Lawrence . . . : Allen School records place him there 1881–95. Bishop
Lawrence was, coincidentally, Helen Palmer's favorite clergyman and a
lifelong friend of her father's, with whom he attended the Protestant
Episcopal School in Cambridge in the 1870s. Amos Adams Lawrence, the
merchant and philanthropist, was his father. *DAB*; William Lawrence, *Life
of Amos A. Lawrence* (Boston and New York, 1899).

    next ten years . . . : Betty Blackmur to the author, 10/31/78.

    making children's toys . . . : *Boston Herald*, 31 Oct. 1920; Helen (Blackmur)
Van Eck to the author, 12/78.

8   sparkled a little . . . : Horton, interview, 9/76.

    sell fireworks anyhow . . . : 8/23/29, Princeton. ("He did *not* sell fireworks":
Helen Van Eck, 12/78).

    spoke very nicely . . . : Interview (Cambridge), 3/77.

    Richard didn't speak . . . : Rob Darrell to the author, 1/19/77; Richard de
Rochement to the author, 7/8/76.

    of the floor . . . : "A Necessary Gesture," MS dated 12/26, Princeton.

9   "live and wait" . . . : Two typed pages in Box 63, folder 3, Princeton.

    he will die . . . : Box 46, folder 2, Princeton.

    and chew gum . . . : Helen to RPB, 8/9/29, Princeton.

    Her family tree . . . : From "Ancestral Chart" compiled by William Lincoln
Palmer (a younger brother of Helen's father), 1/1/21.

    James Monroe Palmer . . . : Betty Blackmur to the author, 10/27/76. He was
still alive in 1892, when his son George applied to Harvard, and was living
on Berkeley St. in Boston.

10   Following his ordination . . . : 6/19/1878.

    herd of cows . . . : T. Horton, interview, 9/76.

    tragic and absurd . . . : To RPB, 8/6/29, Princeton.

    his best story . . . : Recited by Bishop Lawrence at the funeral in St. Stephen's
Church, Pittsfield, Mass. (Rev. Palmer died in Albany, N.Y.). Details derive
from material in Special Collections branch of Bowdoin College Library.

11   for a preacher . . . : Darrell to the author, 3/13/79.

    rest is fantasy . . . : To the author, 10/27/76.

12   linguist, a traveler . . . : George Monroe Palmer's application for graduate
study at Harvard.

    as Radcliffe College . . . : Dudley Allen Sargent, *An Autobiography*
(Philadelphia, 1927).

    roommate, Mary Blackmur . . . : Mary B. Waterbury to the author, 10/30/78,
places Mary Blackmur, Horace's daughter by his third wife, at Dr. Sargent's; and as a graduate nurse at Corey Hill Hospital and Children's
Hospital in Boston. "At one of these schools her roommate was Helen
Palmer." Betty Blackmur to the author, 10/30/78: "My mother went to
boarding school at a young age, eleven or twelve, and had as a roommate a
Mary Blackmur, cousin of Pop." This was at a private school in Boston
"run by a 'genteel' lady."

13 and at Harvard . . . : William W. Whalen (Harvard Univ. Archives) to the
author, 11/27/78.

he was born . . . : His birth was not recorded until 1931 (Rose A. Pollard, City
Clerk, to the author, 1/10/79).

wasn't a cure . . . : Two typed pages, n.d., Box 63, folder 3, Princeton.

wrote popular fiction . . . : Like *Friendly Doorways* (1931) and *Lotta's Last
Season* (1940).

in the city . . . : Betty Blackmur to the author, 5/4/77, and 10/30/78.

was pregnant again . . . : Edward Benson (Ted) b. NYC 8/30/06; George
Watson b. NYC 12/30/08.

14 a short story . . . : "The Cut," *larus*, July 1922.

a whimsical postcard . . . : Dated 9/21/09, from "J. W. Rockefeller."

in Felton Hall . . . : The site is now occupied by the Cambridge High School
Memorial pool and gym.

paying the rent . . . : Helen to RPB, 8/6/29, Princeton.

care for him . . . : 7/19/29, Princeton.

as "high-class chambermaid" . . . : To RPB, 8/13/29, Princeton.

effects of malnutrition . . . : T. Horton, interview, 9/76.

fresh and girlish . . . : Darrell to the author, 1/19/77.

15 time this month . . . : Box 63, folder 3, Princeton.

spent her days . . . : Helen to RPB, 8/23/29, Princeton; George Orrok, interview, 3/77.

letter to Richard . . . : N.d., Princeton.

eyes are bothered . . . : Helen to RPB, 8/23/29, Princeton.

he couldn't do . . . : Helen to RPB, 8/13/29, Princeton.

16 at for *every*thing . . . : The same.

and open doors . . . : Helen to RPB, 3/20/39 (from 53 Wendell St.), Princeton.

In a letter . . . : To G. A. Palmer, 5/6/21, PP.

himself from shame . . . : Box 46, folder 2, Princeton.

from his mother . . . : 7/15/40 (to Oak Pt.), Princeton.

him to herself . . . : Betty Blackmur to the author, 10/27/76.

17 wrote his mother . . . : To Edward T. Cone; Betty Blackmur to the author,
10/30/78, says at least once or twice a week; also Dorothy Persons, quoted
in Stow Persons to the author, 12/15/77.

my ancient mother . . . : RPB to Anderson, 9/9/60, Washington Univ., St.
Louis.

of the week . . . : 4/2/55, Princeton.

still my baby . . . : 7/12/29, 8/6/29, n.d., Princeton.

include you, entirely . . . : 3/20/39, Princeton.

and his friends . . . : To the author, 10/31/78.

own works published . . . : 9/15/58, from "Mr. Young Thomas Taylor, Jnr.,"
Princeton.

18 his wife left . . . : Later George married again.

When he died . . . : 1/6/58.

awake until evening . . . : Darrell to the author, 1/19/77.

He sold out . . . : Cambridge City Directory still lists him as proprietor of
Amee Bros. News Service in 1939.

and the Celtics . . . : S. Persons to the author, 12/15/77.

our great metaphor . . . : AMN, p. 76

object of criticism . . . : AMN, p. 77.

to be illusion . . . : To G. A. Palmer, 4/9/21, PP.

19   gap of birth . . . : Balance of this discussion draws on AMN, pp. 11–15, 17,
      18, 21, 22.

20   of the night . . . : Black notebook, 9/3/22.

      remembering Wallace Stevens . . . : Blackmur uses this quotation to make a
      similar point in AMN, p. 77 .

21   they recollect him . . . : Henry W. Hardy to the author, 10/20/78; classmate
      Edwin D. Sage to Hardy. RPB studied at Peabody Grammar School,
      Sept. 1912–June 1916; his record there was "excellent" (Mrs. Dussett).

      but no face . . . : Leland F. Perkins to the author, 2/1/77.

      Richard de Rochemont . . . : Interviewed by Alan Wald, 5/27/76.

      In his reading . . . : RPB to G. A. Palmer, 10/8/22, 2/4/23, 9/28/21; PP;
      Box 31, folder 27 (1921–22), and Box 29, folder 15 (1/21/23 and 8/22),
      Princeton.

      much in evidence . . . : De Rochemont to the author, 7/8/76.

      of the smoke . . . : Betty Blackmur to the author, 10/31/78.

22   rest of mankind . . . : RPB to G. A. Palmer, 7/9/22, PP.

      of intelligent life . . . : Box 29, folder 15 (1/21/23), Princeton.

      who crossed himself . . . : RPB to Conrad Aiken, 4/16/31, Princeton.

      speak the truth . . . : Box 31, folder 27 (summer 1920), Princeton.

      to his cousin . . . : 10/8/22, PP.

      sense of relief . . . : The same.

      live vividly, vitally . . . : 4/9/21, PP.

      Mrs. Eberhart thought . . . : To the author, 9/25/76.

      of my life . . . : Box 29, folder 15 (1/21/23), Princeton.

      him home again . . . : Betty Blackmur to the author, 10/27/76.

      15 to 17 . . . : AMN, p. 87.

      was his cousin . . . : To the author, 1/17/77.

      wanted to write . . . : Interview, 3/76.

24   "Portrait: R.P.B." . . . : *Harvard Advocate* 110 (June 1924), 393.

      said Tessa Horton . . . : Interview, 9/77.

      that he died . . . : 3/29/76.

      very good friend . . . : Interview, 3/77.

      home and curse . . . : "Politikon," *H&H* 2 (1928), 52.

      a lady chaser . . . : RPB to G. A. Palmer, 10/29/24, PP.

      said de Rochemont . . . : To the author, 7/27/76.

25   We saw Pavlova . . . : Orrok, interview, 3/77.

      have the dancers . . . : To G. A. Palmer, 4/12/23, PP.

      Margery the Medium . . . : The Boston psychic, Mina Stinson Crandon.

      Foster Damon explained . . . : 2/15/21, quoted by B. L. St. Armand in
      "S. Foster Damon: Demonologist," *Michigan Quarterly Review* 16
      (summer 1977), 308–14.

      at Frank Locke's . . . : RPB to G. A. Palmer, 3/30, PP.

      good," Betty said . . . : To the author, 5/4/77.

      on your ass . . . : Darrell to the author, 4/24/79.

      produce sore thumbs . . . : 7/2/35, PP.

      like Lewis MacKay's . . . : T. Horton to Betty Blackmur, quoted in Betty
      Blackmur to the author, 5/4/77.

crowded with ghosts . . . : RPB to Darrell, 6/13/38, DP.

with him ever . . . : To Darrell, 5/30/40, DP.

27 mother was right . . . : Betty Blackmur to the author, 10/31/78.

years her senior . . . : Betty was born 12/27/14.

28 his own fastness . . . : *Eleven Essays in the European Novel*, p. 115 (on *Doctor Faustus*).

they were adults . . . : Elinor Rowe to the author, 8/78; Cummings, *Six Non Lectures*; May Sarton, *I Knew a Phoenix* (New York, 1954).

to summer school . . . : Transcript reads 1919 for 1918. RPB studied at CHLS 1916–18.

told Allen Tate . . . : Tate, interview (Nashville), 8/9/77.

he was expelled . . . : Because of difficulties involved with his writing of the school paper, J. Marshall thought (interview, 12/20/75).

on the doorstep . . . : T. Horton, interview, 10/8/78.

me. He did . . . : Inserted sheets headed "A Change of Attitude," Blue notebook, 3/19/23, Box 29, folder 15, Princeton.

29 I was mad . . . : Box 31, folder 27, Princeton.

category as 'honoraries' . . . : To the author, 2/10/78.

Richard "really intuitive" . . . : To Margaret Marshall, 9/26/40, Bogan Letters.

than correspondence schools . . . : To Wesley S. Hartley, 10/29/58, Princeton.

in *The Possessed* . . . : To the author, 2/1/77.

of the autodidactic . . . : To the author, 9/76.

30 and earlier depression . . . : 1/22/33, ZP.

to his cousin . . . : 9/28/21, PP.

of particular knowledge . . . : To G. A. Palmer, 4/9/21, PP.

a stack boy . . . : "two or three nights a week" (RPG to G. A. Palmer, 8/18/22, PP); "dusting enormous tomes in the Harvard Library" (Black notebook).

found excitingly pornographic . . . : Wald interview, 5/27/76.

walking her home . . . : Betty Blackmur to the author, 5/4/77.

he bought me . . . : To the author, 7/16/76.

He was strapped . . . : RPB to G. A. Palmer, 12/4/24, PP.

lack of funds . . . : 2/13/21, PP.

31 have fallen apart . . . : Black notebook, 10/19/22. Mañach, later famous as a critic, political journalist, and biographer, tried to preserve the friendship. There are letters from him to RPB at Princeton and Yale. He died in exile in Spain at age sixty-three (Cedomil Goic to the author, 3/15/77).

$125 a month . . . : To G. A. Palmer, 3/3/25, PP.

of obtaining any . . . : 1/13/21, PP.

luck *may* change . . . : To G. A. Palmer, 4/9/21, PP.

and my shawl . . . : 1/19/25, PP.

friend James Leonard . . . : RPB describes to G. A. Palmer, 9/28/21, PP. Further details in Tessa Horton to the author, 11/17/78, and Anna Walsh (Cambridge Latin School) to the author, 10/27/78.

inevitable, and irrevocable . . . : To G. A. Palmer, 9/28/21, PP.

cunt of Mary . . . : To G. A. Palmer, 7/9/11, PP.

a perpetual disaster . . . : To G. A. Palmer, 10/21/21, PP.

also a lie . . . : Discussion drawn on AMN, pp. 13, 21.

despise them all . . . : Box 31, folder 27 (summer 1920), Princeton.

haunted by women . . . : RPB to G. A. Palmer, 2/22/23, PP.

32   has its value . . . : Black notebook, [ca. 9/3/22].

remain a stranger . . . : AMN, p. 49.

think like that . . . : 4/28/29, Princeton.

to be 'attractive' . . . : Black notebook, 1/21/23.

passion in another . . . : The same.

beloved Essex bitch . . . : 2/4/23, PP.

to the trouble . . . : RPB to G. A. Palmer, 7/9/22, PP.

33   salivary or seminal . . . : AMN, p. 25.

war in him . . . : Discussion follows AMN, pp. 19, 20, 25.

student at Princeton . . . : Green notebook, 11/22/40, Princeton: I told him "of my uncle George (not his suicide though)."

Lawrence Scientific School . . . : Subsequently the Harvard Engineering School. G. M. Palmer attended 1880–82; thereafter for a year at Harvard College (1882–83) and a year in the Graduate School (1892–93).

wife was dead . . . : Annie Wildes Brown died in 1912 (Phoebe Palmer to the author, 11/5/78).

still wrenched heavily . . . : Black notebook, 9/3/22.

34   himself to bear . . . : *Education*, p. 287; and paraphrasing in what follows pp. 288–89.

to Conrad Aiken . . . : 4/16/31, Princeton.

their own meaning . . . : AMN, p. 100.

fire love man . . . : AMN, p. 115.

than write essays . . . : To G. A. Palmer, 10/8/22, PP.

wanted to write . . . : To G. A. Palmer, 1/13/21, 4/9/21, 9/28/21, PP.

prospect is frightful . . . : Black notebook, 8/22.

of efficient imbecility . . . : To G. A. Palmer, 9/10/22.

idle young man . . . : The two free years have grown to five, in RPB to G. A. Palmer, 3/3/25, PP.

35   ahead of me . . . : Black notebook, 1/21/23.

2. Breaking Out

36   of our nature . . . : AMN, p. 92.

opened the Mermaid . . . : Probably in late 1923: first bill dated 1/9/24, and preserved in Wallace Dickson's scrapbook, "The Citadel of Fame," in Rose Dickson's possession.

most anything new . . . : George Orrok, interview, 3/77.

37   take a share . . . : To RPB, 8/23/27, Princeton (reflecting a later enterprise, subsequent to Dickson & Blackmur).

join the firm . . . : RPB to George Anthony Palmer, 1/22/24, PP (and reciting details of the Crucible House).

of the Mermaid . . . : Sold by 12/30/24 (Dickson, "Citadel of Fame").

Mount Auburn Street . . . : Correspondence dated 6/24/26 so headed, Box 58, folder 3, Princeton. Palmer details his debt to Dickson & Blackmur for books, 4/30/26. Probably the bookstore opened in late 1925. The Cambridge City Directories for 1925, 1926, and 1927 fail, however, to list D&B. In

1925, in any case for most of that year, the Harvard Cooperative Society Bookstore occupied the property at 87 Mt. Auburn St.; in 1926–27 the site was occupied by William Tutin Books, RPB's former employer. Evidently D&B lived briefly and without recording a business certificate in late 1925 and 1926. (Sigmund Roos [Cambridge Historical Commission] to the author, 2/13/79.)

few beautiful books . . . : Interview, 3/77.

38   necessary as breathing . . . : HA II, 215.

poor man's club . . . : George T. Goodspeed to the author, 1/15/79, on RPB coming in "to talk about Henry Adams . . . after we moved to Beacon Street in 1935."

they came in . . . : Louise Solano (Grolier Book Shop) to the author, 2/15/78.

with my class . . . : To Nancy Russ (Bollingen Foundation), 3/6/? [mid-1950s], RFA.

unofficial, the unregulated . . . : HA II, 215.

was an annex . . . : Robert Kent to the author, 7/25/77.

half his talents . . . : HA, p. 239.

the finest mind . . . : G. A. Palmer, interview, 3/76.

with Robert Hillyer . . . : Hillyer to RPB, 5/15/28, Princeton.

couldn't ask Murray . . . : Orrok, interview, 3/77.

Britannica went wrong . . . : Palmer, interview, 3/76.

always an A . . . : Betty Blackmur to the author, 10/27/76.

like a cadaver . . . : Interview, 9/76.

Boring to her . . . : Kate Foster Kurzke to Alan Wald, 9/11/76.

39   cherrywood blocks" in . . . : To RPB, 9–10/8/26, Princeton (from the Univ. of Missouri, where Murray taught while taking the Ph.D. at Harvard).

not enjoying myself . . . : To RPB, 10/20/31, Princeton.

Read him in . . . : AMN, pp. 100, 101.

which it surpasses . . . : Paraphrasing AMN, p. 123.

a little longer . . . : 5/25/28, 6/13/28, Princeton.

full of duplicity . . . : AMN, p. 126.

at being women . . . : Tessa Horton, interview, 9/76.

get a woman . . . : AMN, p. 105.

a short story . . . : "The Invitation," autograph MS dated 7/23/28, Princeton.

40   be a blessing . . . : 6/26/27, 10/28/27, 2/2/28, 4/6/28, Princeton.

lost at sea . . . : 1/29/43.

Symposium, the *Magazine* . . . : E.g., RPB to Palmer, 7/25/30, 7/2/35, PP.

of unpopular standards . . . : To David H. Stevens, 2/5/44, RFA.

ceased to function . . . : To RPB, Lionel Trilling, and Malcolm Cowley, 11/6/46, Princeton Tate Collection.

and his friends . . . : E.g., Sherry Mangan, Palmer, Foster Damon.

mention of it . . . : Quoted in G. A. M. Janssens, *The American Literary Review; A Critical History 1920–1950* (The Hague and Paris, 1968), p. 25.

on the *Dial* . . . : Palmer, interview, 3/76.

blessedly be early . . . : RPB in a 43-page report to the Rockefeller Foundation: "Memorandum on American Literary and Critical Magazines" (1944), p. 10, RFA.

41   make a profit . . . : *New York Times*, 31 May 1929.

a renascent period . . . : RPB, quoted in Frederick J. Hoffman, Charles Allen, Carolyn F. Ulrich, *The Little Magazine: A History and a Bibliography* (Princeton, 1947) p. 87.

was Creighton Hill . . . : To RPB, 10/3/27, 10/19/27, Princeton.

reader be damned . . . : The last of Eugene Jolas' Twelve Propositions, on which *transition* was founded.

the Stock Exchange . . . : Cowley, *Exile's Return* (1934; 1951), p. 276.

of the artist . . . : Review of Wyndham Lewis's *Time and Western Man* (1927) in *H&H* 1 (1928), p. 273.

want journalistic comment . . . : Damon to RPB, 12/3/28, Princeton.

part of them . . . : RPB, Rockefeller report, p. 10.

the world inhabitable . . . : *Exile's Return*, pp. 202–03 (winter 1923–24).

right after publication . . . : To RPB, 5/14/27, 7/13/27, Princeton; RPB to Palmer on Pound's *Personae*, 1/15/27, PP.

are on nobody . . . : To his former student Gerald Dryansky, then at Harvard, 10/29/59, Princeton.

strictly from nowhere . . . : To the author, 6/28/76. Mangan to Kate Foster, 7/17/54, Houghton Library, Harvard: "The idea that Dicky Blackmur was included in the expatriates of the '20s makes my hair stand on end: nothing was more pro-Eliot and anti-Dome than Dicky in those days."

42   fragile but intense . . . : AMN, n.d.

and very fine . . . : To Palmer, 12/24, PP.

literary or otherwise . . . : John Marshall, interview, 12/20/75.

Borish called him . . . : To RPB, 10/25/27, Princeton.

or in gaiters . . . : Marshall to RPB, 7/17/28, Princeton.

bill as aspirin . . . : Rob Darrell to the author, 5/20/79.

remembered Mr. Dick . . . : RPB to Robert MacGregor (New Directions), 9/18/61, Princeton.

were living high . . . : Interview, 9/76.

forever surround yourself . . . : 8/15/27, Princeton.

43   just a succedaneum . . . : AMN, p. 105.

we three consumed . . . : To Palmer, 12/24, PP.

instance of vitality . . . : Delmore Schwartz to RPB, 10/23/41, Princeton.

by studied ennui . . . : AMN, p. 122.

the alienated man . . . : AMN, p. 126.

was a baby . . . : Bernard Bandler, interview, 3/77.

in her train . . . : To RPB, 10/23/43, Princeton.

"Tutti-frutti," he said . . . : Schwartz to RPB, 1/28/43, Princeton.

44   for a fiver . . . : 12/24, PP.

a melodramatic dismissal . . . : To Palmer, 9/13/26, PP.

didn't meet again . . . : To RPB, 7/16/26, Princeton.

with Molly himself . . . : Interview, 7/76.

canceled, "probably forever" . . . : To Palmer, 9/13/26, PP.

mangy fur hat . . . : Darrell to the author, 2/79, 2/24/79.

down the dictation . . . : AMN, p. 100.

at the establishment . . . : Darrell, "The Music of Henry F. Gilbert," *New World Records Recorded Anthology of American Music*, No. 228, p. 2.

to the ground . . . : Elinor Rowe to the author, 8/78.

the fair Yolanda . . . : RPB to Palmer, 12/4/24, PP.

45 be a cad . . . : RPB to Palmer, 1/9/25, PP.
one of them . . . : Darrell to the author, 4/24/79.
of them feasible . . . : RPB to Palmer, 1/9/25, PP.
with Madam G . . . : 1/13/25, PP.
her put-upon husband . . . : Insert page in Black notebook, 4/18/24.
eunuchs of literature . . . : Hemingway in the *Transatlantic Review*, 1924.
English madrigals together . . . : Horton to the author, Thanksgiving 1976.
training in music . . . : Edward T. Cone to the author, 9/23/76.
of the *jalousies* . . . : Darrell uses this passage from *The Magic Mountain* as
     epigraph to his preface to *The Gramophone Shop Encyclopedia of Recorded
     Music* (New York, 1936).
extra, nothing false . . . : To Palmer, 3/3/25, PP.

46 go yachting by . . . : 8/10/30.
Phonograph Monthly Review . . . : (Hereafter *PMR*.) Letters bearing on re-
     views: RPB to Darrell, 4/3/28, 6/18/30; Darrell to RPB, 7/30. DP.
whenever you want . . . : 7/31/30, DP.
have no responsibility . . . : To Darrell, 6/18/30, DP.
they were doing . . . : *PMR*, May 1930, p. 351.
water and grass . . . : *PMR*, June 1930, p. 313, on Julian Carillo's "Preludio a
     Cristóbal Colón."
that bred it . . . : *PMR*, Nov. 1930, p. 45.
what was old . . . : Cone to the author, 9/23/76; RPB to Darrell on Palestrina,
     Victoria, Gregorian chant, 1/31/37; on Bach and Handel, 8/10/30, DP;
     Byron A. Vazakas to RPB on his criticism of plain chant recordings,
     6/1/37, Princeton.
It demands hospitality . . . : *PMR*, June 1930, p. 313 (on Carillo). Conrad
     Aiken, knowing of Richard's interest, tried at least three times to get him
     to call on Walter Piston, then a member of the Harvard faculty, at his
     house in Belmont (to RPB, 12/25/32, Princeton).

47 "modern" and "poetic" . . . : *PMR*, Apr. 1931, p. 224.
morphology and statistics . . . : RPB, "T. S. Eliot," *H&H* 1 (1928), 293.
is actually inaccessible . . . : *PMR*, Sept. 1930, pp. 430–31.
Edna St. Vitus . . . : Aiken to RPB, [ca. 1931], Princeton.
imitation of nature . . . : RPB, "Phoenix in Ashes," intended for *PMR* but
     unpublished (the author's copy).
man, had seen . . . : HA, p. 270.
of the soul . . . : *PMR*, Jan. 1931, pp. 121–22.
feeling, and emotion . . . : To Darrell, 8/30, DP.

48 are sometimes divine . . . : Review of *Selected Poems by Conrad Aiken* (1929)
     in *New Republic*, 22 Jan. 1930, p. 255.
forced into being . . . : "T. S. Eliot," p. 202.
words have stopped . . . : HA, p. 271.
stand aghast at . . . : HA, p. 28. "T. S. Eliot," p. 189: The object counts more
     than interpretation; we can say, "by stretching language a little, the object
     is the interpretation."
of his substance . . . : Review of *Personae* in *Saturday Review*, 30 Apr. 1927,
     p. 784.
the Seven Dwarfs . . . : Marshall, interview, 12/75.

49 Tessa Horton said . . . : Interview, 9/76.

for the Mermaid . . . : Dickson, "Citadel of Fame," records purchases, 2/24.

very slippery individual . . . : Maurice Firuski, interview, 9/30/76. Darrell's
    opinion tallies (to the author, 4/24/79).

the initial outlay . . . : Palmer, interview, 3/76.

at minimum cost . . . : Large collection of receipts from Firuski, beginning
    1926 and acknowledging small payments from RPB into 1928, in Box 68,
    folder 3, Princeton.

couldn't pay them . . . : Scribner's duns Dickson & Blackmur for 83¢, 8/11/27.
    RPB annotates: "Paid 24 Aug. 1927."

it was both . . . : To the author, 8/10/76; interview, 9/30/76.

working for Brentano's . . . : RPB to Palmer, 9/13/26, PP.

a nickel apiece . . . : Horton, interview, 9/76.

power of attorney . . . : Witnessed by M. E. Borish, 4/28/26, Box 59, folder 4,
    Princeton.

two thousand dollars . . . : Palmer, interview, 3/76.

at forty dollars . . . : RPB's (unsuccessful) Guggenheim application, 11/32.

remember his handwriting . . . : Interview, 9/30/76.

50 said Bernard Bandler . . . : Interview, 3/77 (on which subsequent discussion
    draws).

The building itself . . . : Firuski opened the Dunster House Book Shop in 1919
    at 26 Holyoke St. The building was demolished in 1927. (Firuski to the
    author, 8/10/76; Arthur J. Krim [Cambridge Historical Commission] to
    the author, 6/24/76.)

never saw Richard . . . : Larsen to the author, 1/12/77.

blank on RPB . . . : To the author, 1/24/77.

unloading heavy drums . . . : AMN, p. 73.

was in him . . . : To the author, 3/77.

51 the only book . . . : Interview, 9/30/76.

over your reviews . . . : To RPB, 2/25/31, Princeton.

next five months . . . : 4/27/31 (in Hugh McMillan's possession, Salisbury,
    Conn.).

the "exceptional honesty" . . . : To the author, 8/10/76.

will and honesty . . . : HA, "The Family Go-Cart," p. 100.

shabbiness was groomed . . . : Albert J. Guerard, Jr., to the author, 11/8/76.

another acquaintance thought . . . : Kenneth Wiggins Porter to the author,
    7/25/77.

Adams, Mr. James . . . : Bandler, interview, 3/77.

52 and John Clement . . . : Who later assisted Pell (to the author, 1/24/77) in
    his research for the life of Ethan Allen.

looking for work . . . : To Palmer, 9/13/26, PP.

to his cousin . . . : 11/18/26, PP.

to South Street . . . : RPB records move to 20 South St. and Dunster, 4/9/28,
    Princeton.

in Elliot Paul . . . : RPB to Paul, 6/23/27, Columbia Univ.; Paul to RPB (from
    Paris), 4/23/27, Princeton.

Wallace said scornfully . . . : "Citadel of Fame."

they reached Montreal . . . : Palmer disputed this story, interview, 3/76.

suggested by him . . . : "The *Hound & Horn*, 1927–1934," *Harvard Advocate*
    121 (Christmas 1934), 7.

a proper fire . . . : Darrell to the author, 4/24/79.

T. S. Eliot's mother . . . : 1/24/27, Red notebook, Box 29, folder 16, Princeton.

53 in personal rage . . . : RPB to N. Mindlin (editor of a quarterly report on
world censorship), who wants to reprint "Dirty Hands," 1/11/65, Princeton. Reprinted Folcroft Press, 1969 (quotation from p. 15). Betty Blackmur
to the author, 5/4/77, represents RPB as writing his tract in defense of
Firuski's employee Al Delacy. The original title of Richard's tract,
"Dirty Fingernails," was altered by the *New Republic*.

tickled Ezra Pound . . . : 1/22/29, Princeton.

on Firuski's letterhead . . . : E.g., "She Did," [ca. 1927], Princeton.

à l'outrance . . . : AMN, pp. 100, 102.

nothing but read . . . : 11/18/26, PP.

of a soul . . . : AMN, p. 69.

developing a donnée . . . : To Palmer, 11/18/26, PP.

equal to vision . . . : "Robert Frost," *New Criticism in the United States*, pp.
69–70.

Scientific writing engaged . . . : Like Lewis's *The Anatomy of Science*, on
which he comments at length to Palmer, 11/18/26, PP. One of the ten
books which had most influenced him was W. B. Cannon's *Wisdom of the
Body*, on the relation of the autonomic system to the self-regulation of
physiological processes. (RPB to Frances Steloff [Gotham Book Mart],
5/23/42, Berg Collection, N.Y. Public Library.)

wholly into him . . . : To Palmer, 2/4/23, PP. Santayana's *The Life of
Reason* also made the Steloff list.

in our time . . . : AMN, p. 97.

but only intuited . . . : After RPB's critique of Bonamy Dobrée's *The Lamp
and the Lute; Studies in Six Modern Authors* (1929) in *New Republic*, 11
Dec. 1929, p. 75.

Returning to Conrad . . . : AMN, pp. 187–88.

54 were meant for . . . : 7/12/29, Princeton; interview, 9/30/76.

went to writing . . . : Firuski to the author, 8/10/76.

keep the books . . . : To Darrell, 4/3/28, DP.

at Miss Beck's . . . : Betty Blackmur to the author, 5/4/77.

here I am . . . : 1/7/29, Yale.

was "editing manager" . . . : Cambridge Directory, having listed him as
student, 1925–27, and as clerk, 1928, gives him this title in 1930.

next five years . . . : 1/3/28 (letter reads erroneously 1929), Yale.

read in 1940 . . . : 1/4/29, Yale.

a partial list . . . : "The list can be expanded to include almost every literary
figure who was prominent or who was coming into prominence between
1927 and 1934" (Leonard Greenbaum, "The *Hound & Horn* Archive,"
Yale University Library Gazette, vol. 39 [Mar. 1965]).

it perfectly well . . . : 12/3/28, Princeton.

or "something else" . . . : 10/5/29, Newberry Library.

55 grateful when Cowley . . . : The letter in the Newberry is incomplete and
undated.

and Allen Tate . . . : From whom RPB solicits work, 10/5/29, Yale.

promised a story . . . : 10/28/29, Princeton.

did Jean Toomer . . . : 3/28/29, Princeton.

he was "freshened" . . . : To W. Stevens, 12/2/31, Huntington Library.

getting to know . . . : To Darrell, 10/22/41, DP.

T. S. Eliot . . . : Gordon Fraser (who is publishing a series of pamphlets and books on matters of contemporary interest, and wants to do "Dirty Hands"), 8/9/30, Princeton.

in my generation . . . : To RPB, 2/28/32, Princeton.

of its kind . . . : To Lincoln Kirstein, 5/7/43, Beinecke Tate Collection, Yale.

masterpiece," Kirstein said . . . : "The *H&H*," p. 92.

said how the . . . : Review of her "Hippolytus Temporizes" (1927) in *H&H* 1 (1927), 48.

only "fancy flatulence" . . . : Review of E. E. Cummings's *Him. A Play* (1927) in *H&H* 1 (1927), 173.

metabolism it expresses . . . : Review of Read's *Prose Style* (1928), *H&H* 2 (1928), 93.

Reviewing Wyndham Lewis . . . : *Time and Western Man* (1928), *H&H* 1 (1928), 271.

history of art . . . : Robert Flint to RPB, 2/17/55, Princeton.

56 plans or blueprints . . . : Pseudonymous review (as Perry Hobbs) of Bertrand Russell's *The Analysis of Matter* (1927), *H&H*, p. 155. The same ideas are expressed in RPB's review of David Garnett's *No Love* (1920), *H&H* 3 (1929), 125: "It is not a question of totalled virtue but of the quality of being."

and wrote Kirstein . . . : 4/10/31, Yale.

damned much after . . . : Hemingway, concluding *Death in the Afternoon*.

the something else . . . : 12/25/32, Princeton.

infers no truths . . . : RPB on Stein's *The A-B-C- of Aesthetics* (1927), *H&H* 1 (1927), 170.

liked him personally . . . : To the author, 2/1/77.

be "quite swell" . . . : To Wilson, 4/8/29, Yale.

'atmosphere' and personality . . . : To RPB, 11/14/29, Princeton. The particular point is to book-reviewing, but it seems to encompass critical writing as a kind.

is written about . . . : RPB's judgment of Thornton Wilder's *The Woman of Andros*, *H&H* 3 (1930), 589.

57 but with words . . . : Review of *The Double Agent* in *New York Herald Tribune*, 10 May 1936.

in their terms . . . : Warren Carrier's review of Wilson's *Shores of Light* in *Western Review* (Iowa), summer 1953.

exegesis tout court . . . : To Morton D. Zabel, 1/25/32, ZP.

to Wallace Stevens . . . : 11/11/31, Huntington.

the imagination takes . . . : "T. S. Eliot," p. 195.

58 in poetry is . . . : To W. Stevens, 12/2/31, Huntington.

directly we met . . . : Interview, 3/77 (followed in subsequent discussion).

Richard told Cowley . . . : 11/12/29, Newberry.

for two days . . . : "The *H&H*," p. 7.

poetry, your review . . . : 5/14/29, 8/5/28, Princeton.

this family's ability . . . : Firuski, interview, 9/30/76.

59 in New York . . . : After Bernhard Taper, *Balanchine* (New York, 1963), pp. 159–60.

to be Kirstein . . . : Mangan to Johns, 11/13/30. "Solstice" is in *A Return to Pagany*, ed. Stephen Halpert and Richard Johns (Boston, 1969), p. 162.

said Richard's friend . . . : Interviewed by Alan Wald, 5/27/76.

'Alice in Wonderland' . . . : "The Swan in Zurich," *A Primer of Ignorance*, p. 131.

of the ballet . . . : RPB to Zabel, 7/12/34, ZP. Kirstein and MacLeish were rooming together in the early thirties (Kirstein to RPB, 6/4/32, Princeton). RPB's characterization recalls his hostile review of MacLeish's *Hamlet* (1932) in *H&H* 2 (1929), 167–69.

anybody I know . . . : 9/4/27, Princeton.

I feel deserted . . . : From Berlin and Munich, 8/30/27 and ?/9/27, Princeton.

the letters stopped . . . : RPB to Kirstein, 9/26/35, Yale, wants "a few spare words of your own," while acknowledging that "Mine dwindle."

so amazingly well-educated . . . : "The *H&H*," p. 7; To the author, 6/28/76.

60 quite a standing . . . : To the author, 4/1/78. Belgion, in an unpublished memoir (in his widow Helen Belgion's possession), tells of meeting with Bandler and RPB, and of Bandler's enthusiasm for Irving Babbitt (Ch. 17, pp. 21–22).

magazine of techniques . . . : Kirstein, "The *H&H*," p. 10.

it can command . . . : This manifesto of 1929–30 (*H&H* 3 [1929], 5–6) is unsigned but was probably written by RPB.

the accidental good . . . : Bandler's phrase.

edited the magazine . . . : To Cowley [summer 1929], Newberry (incomplete).

Scribner's or *Harper's* . . . : Kirstein, "The *H&H*," p. 9.

61 to replace it . . . : 4/20/31, Yale.

any in America . . . : Jan. 1930 issue, p. 372.

than the whole . . . : Darrell to the author, 4/24/79.

I ever had . . . : To Firuski, 4/27/31, McMillan Collection.

Fry . . . hated him . . . : Interview, 12/26/76.

out of art . . . Quoted in RPB's "T. S. Eliot," p. 298.

thin, and subdued . . . : Interview, 8/1/76.

force under compression . . . : To the author, 2/2/77.

62 joined the staff . . . : Mrs. William Hamovitch (reflecting conversation with Kirstein) to the author, 1/16/77; Kirstein, interview, 12/26/76.

with, a super-intellectual . . . : To Mrs. Hamovitch, 7/75.

to learn Sanskrit . . . : Kirstein, interview, 12/26/76.

makes me *sick* . . . : To the author, 9/18/76.

Bandler had another . . . : Interview, 3/77.

as an administrator . . . : Marshall to the author, 2/2/77: "I doubt that Dick was exactly the model editor." Kirstein might have "become disillusioned."

63 money and intentions . . . : To Cowley, 11/12/29, Newberry.

the fifteen-minute merger . . . : Interview, 12/26/76.

been most unpleasant . . . : 1/23/30, Yale.

be called off . . . : Burnham to the author, 12/8/77.

classmate, Alan Stroock . . . : Stroock to the author, 3/31/77, on RPB: "a warm, scholarly and obviously brilliant person."

for no salary . . . : Bandler, interview, 3/77.

critical for Richard . . . : Orrok, interview, 3/77.

$2,340 a year . . . : RPB's Guggenheim application, 1932; Code to Kirstein,

3/27/33, Yale; Patchen to Kirstein, n.d., Yale. Darrell, writing to his sister immediately after Richard had been "let go," reported Bandler's promise of regular salary "until you get another job, and then some small sum —say ten dollars a week—until the expiration of our five years' agreement" (10/24/29). This promise, so far as Darrell knew, wasn't honored. (To the author, 4/24/79.)

      you so ill . . . : Aiken to RPB, 2/14/31, 10/17/31, Princeton.

64   or other attenuation . . . : To Cowley, 11/12/29, Newberry. RPB writes of losing "my job a month ago."

    criticism of consequence . . . : Genevieve Taggard to RPB, 3/2/35, Princeton.

    said Kenneth Patchen . . . : 1/11/38, Princeton.

    the very best . . . : 5/4/27, Princeton.

    going to be . . . : Quoted in Elva dePue Matthews to RPB, 2/9/41, Princeton.

    of our time . . . : Quoted in Guerard to RPB, n.d., Princeton; Winters to RPB, 2/29/32, Princeton.

    of the magazine . . . : "The *H&H*," p. 7.

3. Good *and* Evil

65   the one lump . . . : HA I, "The Family Go-Cart," p. 14.

    have need of . . . : Quoted in Helen to RPB [post-1949].

    a negative rejoinder . . . : RPB to George Anthony Palmer, 11/25, PP.

    a la PLO . . . : Tessa Horton to the author, 1/26/79.

66   Rob Darrell said . . . : To the author, 12/15/79.

    under Tessa's nose . . . : George Orrok, interview, 3/77.

    and elementary way . . . : Murray Eden, quoted in Pat Eden to the author, 8/25/77.

67   the Brookline section . . . : Following newspaper clipping (*Boston Herald?* n.d.), Box 61, folder 2, Princeton. Helen, her sister Katharine, and their widowed mother moved from Brookline to Belmont, fall 1926 (Katharine Brown to the author, 5/27/79).

    for a lark . . . : Betty Blackmur to the author, 10/30/78.

    who ever did . . . : R. Darrell to the author, 12/15/76.

    concealment of motive . . . : 9/13/26, PP.

68   than polished mediocrities . . . : To Palmer, 1/13/21/, PP.

    the lover's infinite . . . : The same.

    therefore enjoy themselves . . . : "She Did."

    as a husband . . . : To George and Elizabeth Orrok, 4/30, in the Orroks' possession.

    or our hands . . . : To Palmer, 3/30, PP.

    brakes or gas . . . : 5/31/28, Princeton.

    from marrying her . . . : 5/18/28, Princeton.

    the suicidal talk . . . : 7/6/26, Princeton.

    marriage with Helen . . . : 5/18/28, Princeton.

    Francis Fergusson said . . . : Interview, 8/1/76.

    of psychological exploration . . . : Review of Lord David Cecil's *The Stricken Deer* in *New Republic*, 10 Sept. 1930, p. 105.

    in the parlor . . . : Interview, 8/9/77.

a sadistic fashion . . . : To the author, 7/2/76, 4/1/78.

69 adorable and sexy . . . : Leslie Westoff to the author, 6/8/77.

kind of woman . . . : Horton, interview, 9/76; Darrell to the author, 4/24/79; P. Eden to the author, 8/25/77; *Boston Herald* article.

really earning money . . . : To the author, 5/27/79.

never admit it . . . : Eileen Simpson, interview, 8/3/76.

wife for him . . . : To Alan Wald, 9/11/76.

it was solved . . . : R. Darrell, 12/6/42, to the Employment Manager of the Eastern Aircraft Division of General Motors (Trenton, N.J.), Helen's wartime employer, DP.

Monster of Sloth . . . : RPB to Prof. J. W. Clark at the Univ. of Minnesota, 4/19/61, Princeton.

fun than wit . . . : To the author, 12/17/77.

toads fell out . . . : Quoted in Kate Foster to Wald, 9/11/76.

summed her up . . . : Interviews: Willard Thorp, 7/76; P. Eden, 8/25/77; Betty Blackmur, 10/30/78.

70 and deny it . . . : R. J. Kaufmann to the author, 10/15/76.

be almost beautiful . . . : To the author, 1/19/77, 7/24/77.

which it wasn't . . . : To the author, 7/25/77.

with her toes . . . : E. D. H. Johnson to the author, 9/26/76; interview, 5/77.

71 sensitive of detail . . . : Review of *The Letters of Marian Adams 1868–1883*, ed. Ward Thoron, in *Virginia Quarterly Review* 13 (spring 1937), 292–93.

or divination reasonable . . . : "Henry and Brooks Adams: Parallels to Two Generations," *Southern Review* 5 (1939), 309.

in the night . . . : R. Darrell to the author, 7/24/77.

his women *woolen* . . . : The same.

sincerity and grace . . . : To R. Darrell, 1/8/45, DP.

outside museum paint . . . : 8/7/40, Princeton.

was endlessly destructive . . . : John Marshall, interview, 12/75.

to commit suicide . . . : R. Darrell to the author, 9/1/79.

sadness and resignation . . . : Stow Persons to the author, 2/1/80.

he told her . . . : Mr. and Mrs. A. Lincoln Pattee, interview, 9/76.

72 in my sleep . . . : To the Orroks, 4/30.

two husky lassies . . . : RPB's mother to RPB, 7/12/29, Princeton.

They were married . . . : Conflating: Lincoln Kirstein to the author, 6/28/76; RPB to the Orroks, 4/30; Betty Blackmur to the author, 5/4/77; Conrad Aiken to RPB, 2/14/31, Princeton; R. Darrell to RPB, Princeton, and to the author, 2/10/79; Katharine Brown to the author, 8/29/79.

big bare house . . . : Interviews: T. Horton, 9/76; G. Orrok, 3/77.

73 and live alone . . . : Brown to the author, 5/27/79.

After three years . . . : RPB's Guggenheim application, 10/30/32, still puts him at 332 Waverly St., Belmont.

next six years . . . : RPB to R. Darrell, 11/25/39, DP: "Mrs. D. has moved out."

what I write . . . : 5/16/35, Yale.

painted . . . ballroom dancing . . . : P. Eden to the author, 8/25/77; Marshall, interview, 12/75; T. Horton, interview, 9/76; Brown to the author, 5/27/79; R. Darrell to the author, 4/24/79; RPB to R. Darrell, 8/12/36, 3/27/37, DP; RPB to Frank Morley, Labor Day 1939, HBP; mimeo headed "WPA for Mass. Federal Arts Project," 4/7/39, Princeton.

74 poor as rats . . . : To Palmer, 3/30, 7/25/30, PP.

on the edge . . . : 9/30/35, 10/28/30, PP.

bring it up . . . : 2/15/31, Princeton Tate Collection.

to get drawn . . . : R. Darrell to the author, 10/24/79.

waited in anguish . . . : To Palmer, 9/30/35, PP.

to one editor . . . : To Robert Penn Warren, 3/2/36, *Southern Review* Papers, Yale.

for my books . . . : 8/30/37 to Miss McLeod of the Maine State Library, Augusta.

behavior was "scriminess" . . . : To R. Darrell, 4/29/35, DP.

who have advantages . . . : To R. Darrell, 1/31/37, DP.

Richard after that . . . : E. Orrok to the author, 2/18/80, disputes this account.

would cut him . . . : R. Darrell to the author, 7/24/77.

75 Richard responded cautiously . . . : 10/2/29, *H&H* Archive, Yale (assigned to RPB on internal evidence).

Pound feasted hugely . . . : As in the Apr.–June 1930 issue of *H&H*.

other 'little' magazines . . . : "The *H&H*," p. 8.

Tate and Blackmur . . . : To Kirstein, 10/10/33, *H&H* Archive; Greenbaum, "The *H&H* Archive," pp. 144–45.

about as good . . . : To Kirstein, 2/1/32, *H&H* Archive.

matter with him . . . : To Bandler, 5/16/32, *H&H* Archive.

funnel of talent . . . : Bandler and Mayor left in fall 1932; Winters became regional editor for the Pacific seaboard in 2/32, and first editor in all but name in 1933.

a dead one . . . : 10/16/33, Princeton.

of slipshod elegance . . . : *H&H*, Apr.–June 1935, p. 538.

a traveling salesman . . . : To Kirstein, 11/25/32, Yale.

by his heels . . . : To *H&H*, 4/8/30, Yale.

Eliot has done . . . : To Kirstein, 11/24/29, Yale.

creatures is implied . . . : D. C. Allen to RPB, 11/12/58, Princeton.

Sears Roebuck suits . . . : Interview, 8/77.

Conrad Aiken inquired . . . : To RPB, 10/17/31, Princeton.

tissue of bluster . . . : Stanley Edgar Hyman, *The Armed Vision* (New York, 1952), p. 263.

showed his teeth . . . : Florence Codman to RPB, 9/20/37, Princeton.

76 as its master . . . : To Warren, Yale, 10/10/36.

data of experience . . . : "A Note on Yvor Winters," *The Expense of Greatness* (1940), p. 167.

good *and* evil . . . : Review of *The Oxford Anthology of American Literature*, ed. William Rose Benét and Norman Holmes Pearson, *Southern Review* 5 (1939), 198.

to that experience . . . : "Notes on the Criticism of Herbert Read," *larus*, vol. 1 (Apr.–June 1928).

carried to excess . . . : *Pagany* 2 (winter 1931), 101–02.

77 'ought' to be . . . : *American Criticism* (1928). Discussion draws on Hoffman, *The Twenties*, pp. 166–67, 170–71.

Bandler's pet project . . . : Humanism "was Bandler's interest, not mine" (Kirstein, "The *H&H*," p. 7).

found positively painful . . . : Belgion's unpublished memoir (in Mrs. Belgion's possession) ch. 17, pp. 21–22.

the golden mean . . . : "The Discipline of Humanism" in *The Critique of Humanism*, ed. C. H. Grattan (New York, 1930), p. 245.

flock of scabs . . . : 11/12/29, Newberry.

were closely akin . . . : Review of Morley Callaghan's *A Native Argosy* (1929) in *H&H* 2 (1929), 439.

with moral bias . . . : RPB to R. Darrell, 4/29/35, DP: "I had to write a synopsis of it [his novel, *The Greater Torment*] the other day, and I never read anything so revoltingly moral in my life."

letter to Wheelwright . . . : 3/16/29, John Hay Library.

religion—myself especially . . . : 2/13/29, Yale, *H&H* Archive.

be too much . . . : To T. S. Eliot, 3/20/29, Yale.

of diligent talent . . . : To Aiken, 4/16/31, Huntington.

and expansive desires . . . : *Humanism in America* (1930).

78 Ford's assembly belt . . . : "Angry Professors," *New Republic*, 9 Apr. 1930.

approved by one . . . : 26 Mar. 1930, 153.

are not there . . . : "Anni Mirabiles," *Primer of Ignorance*, p. 7.

humanistically transcended it . . . : "The Discipline of Humanism," p. 239.

amount of transcendence . . . : After T. S. Eliot, in "Anni Mirabiles," p. 72.

work in hand . . . : "The Discipline of Humanism," p. 247.

control at all . . . : AMN, pp. 64–65.

79 of squash blossoms . . . : 8/3/31, DP.

why not I . . . : To Palmer, 7/24/46, PP.

ignorance—expanding itself . . . : Review of Aiken's *The Coming Forth by Day of Osiris Jones* and *Preludes for Memnon* in *Poetry*, vol. 40 (1932).

with blueberry blossom . . . : 4/16/31, Huntington.

neither was purple . . . : To Palmer, 9/8/48, 6/25/49, PP.

on the bay . . . : To R. Darrell, 8/10/30, DP.

fight or retreat . . . : To Palmer, 9/8/48, PP.

80 for his wedding . . . : R. Darrell to the author, 12/15/76; Lewis MacKay to Darrell, 5/6/30, DP.

against the weather . . . : To Palmer, 10/16/35, PP.

servants and retainers . . . : To Palmer, 7/2/36, PP.

woods were magnificent . . . : To Palmer, 10/16/35.

didn't see this . . . : Persons to the author, 12/15/77.

suits me better . . . : To R. Darrell, 8/3/31, DP.

two part song . . . : 7/10/37, Hay.

One friend thought . . . : P. Eden to the author, 8/25/77.

be "spiritual salvation" . . . : To Allen Tate, 5/4/34, Princeton Tate.

81 of Cape Cod . . . : To the publisher Peter Smith, 12/10/59, Princeton.

on the tack . . . : *LHUS* MS, p. 35.

a fine line . . . : To the author, 5/20/79.

the Wind's Eye . . . : To RPB, 7/25/29, Princeton.

in a fog . . . : To Mrs. Ward Thoron, 8/2/41, Harvard.

in shared convictions . . . : *Exile's Return*, p. 213.

82 discussed literary matters . . . : T. Horton, interview, 9/76.

fond of him . . . : To John McCormick, 10/15/59, Princeton.

a spontaneous phrase . . . : To the author, 10/5/76.

of harness rein . . . : To R. Darrell, 9/30, DP.

of five inches . . . : To Palmer, 6/24/49, PP.

lot together again . . . : To Palmer, 9/8/48, PP.

way to China . . . : 7/5/49, PP.

of the ground . . . : To Robert Spiller, 7/28/46, Univ. of Pennsylvania.

woods, and rare . . . : 25 Nov. 1936, p. 114.

for the philosopher . . . : Review of Robert Neumann's *Flood*, in *New Freeman* 2 (Oct. 1930), 70.

83   straw was new . . . : To the author.

of large cities . . . : To U.S. Information Agency, 9/24/59, Princeton.

my own stuff . . . : To Palmer, 7/5/49, PP.

History of Literature . . . : To Spiller, 9/4/46, Pennsylvania.

hand grew heavy . . . : To J. Kerker Quinn, 9/20/45, Univ. of Illinois, Quinn Papers.

on the keys . . . : To G. A. and Marjorie Palmer, 7/13/48, PP.

what I see . . . : To Palmer, 7/28/49, PP.

84   and steaming day . . . : 6/22/37, Hay.

the vegetable garden . . . : To R. Darrell, 7/12/32, 8/5/33, DP; to the Palmers, 7/21/49, PP.

was colding through . . . : In *From Jordan's Delight* (here and hereafter).

85   lovely though bleak . . . : Christine Weston to RPB, 3/9/41, Princeton.

misanthrope, he thought . . . : Persons to the author, 12/15/77.

in that family . . . : To Wald, 9/11/76.

richness she is . . . : AMN, p. 122.

86   read poetry aloud . . . : The painter Richard Carline to Wald, [ca. 1976]. (RPB "wasn't much at home with the visual arts.")

a diffident painter . . . : Kaufmann to the author, 10/15/76.

owls obsessed her . . . : Sherry Mangan to Foster, 7/17/54, Harvard.

one innocent guest . . . : Bruce Berlind to the author, 8/24/77.

out to hunt . . . : Johnson, interview, 5/77.

a ramshackle barn . . . : Persons to the author, 12/15/77. RPB to Albert R. Erskine, business manager of *Southern Review*, wants an advance to help pay for the moving and rebuilding, 8/24/37, Yale.

with Guggenheim money . . . : R. Darrell to the author, 12/15/76.

87   the maggot school . . . : RPB to R. Darrell, 8/12/36, DP.

and comic genius . . . : The same.

she'd ever had . . . : Libby (Zimmerman) Derby to RPB, 4/15/42, Princeton.

88   measured her hurt . . . : Richard's perception, AMN, p. 122.

the debacle upstairs . . . : AMN, p. 62.

an adolescent fool . . . : To R. Darrell, 3/27/37, DP.

ship or train . . . : Box 46, folder 2, Princeton. ("Codman" is scribbled among other names on the back of the page, hence the conjectured date.)

death was ominous . . . : AMN, p. 120 [ca. age 32].

radium into lead . . . : AMN, p. 185.

in desiring more . . . : AMN, pp. 126–27, age 33.

89   ethics, Richard said . . . : AMN, p. 101.

his own lapses . . . : AMN, pp. 61–62.

ourselves in for . . . : 4/29/35, DP.

His married friends . . . : T. Horton, interview, 9/76.

and brutal stupidity . . . : AMN, p. 90.

had her reservations . . . : Persons to the author, 12/15/77.

and go away . . . : To Emmie Darrell, 5?/34, DP.

well was another . . . : P. Eden to the author, 8/25/77.

90   in the leg . . . : T. Horton, interview, 9/76 (and hereafter).

the enervated man . . . : AMN, p. 122.

a sterile personality . . . : AMN, pp. 114-45.

the ejaculating penis . . . : To R. Darrell, 8/12/36, DP.

substance in marriage . . . : AMN, p. 54 [ca. 1933].

in her eyes . . . : AMN, p. 118.

I am ready . . . : AMN, pp. 126-27.

the drama actual . . . : "T. S. Eliot," *Double Agent*, p. 208.

91   stream of composition . . . : "The Critical Prefaces of Henry James," *Double Agent*, p. 241.

cannot be repaired . . . : After T. S. Eliot, quoted in Richard's *Double Agent* essay, p. 186.

the tap-roots below . . . : "A Critic's Job of Work" (*Double Agent*, p. 301), from which all quotations hereafter derive unless otherwise noted.

and so ashamed . . . : AMN, p. 103.

offered him instead . . . : 7/17/35, Princeton.

a religious convert's . . . : To the author, 2/12/77.

case, Blackmur's book . . . : *The Armed Vision*, p. 249.

92   acquired innate validity . . . : Review of *Poems and Sonnets* in *Nation*, 12 Dec. 1934, pp. 688-89.

action in reaction . . . : Review of Allen Tate's *Reactionary Essays on Poetry and Ideas* in *Columbia University Review*, Apr. 1936, p. 30.

93   but support it . . . : 11/21/35, Princeton Tate.

4. The Witnessing Art—Blackmur at Poetry

even a lifetime . . . : To George Anthony Palmer, 4/12/23, PP.

I can find . . . : Black notebook, 10/9/22.

poems, 52 good . . . : 8/8/24, Princeton.

a long poem . . . : 2/15/31, Princeton.

write slowly enough . . . : 9/30/35, PP.

water flow again . . . : Box 29, folder 13, p. 109, Princeton.

so stopped writing . . . : Robert V. Keeley to the author, 3/9/77.

sums remained miracles . . . : To Harriet Monroe, 4/28/26, 4/2/31.

95   first person singular . . . : Harold Norse, *Tiger's Eye*, p. 73.

who trooped in . . . : 9/26/41, DP.

doing so again . . . : 2/25/58, Univ. of Chicago.

trembling into stone . . . : From "Scarabs for the Living," *From Jordan's Delight*, p. 46 (Princeton edition).

a long time . . . : 10/3/35, Chicago.

poetry in public . . . : Interview, 3/4/78. Warren to RPB, 2/9/39, Yale, acknowledges their first meeting.

a few myself . . . : To Rob Darrell, 5/14/40, 7/11/40, DP.

96 do give up . . . : 3/11/40, 3/28/40, Minnesota; Berryman to RPB, 4/4/40, Princeton.

the Cooper Unions . . . : RPB to Darrell, 3/31/41, DP.

of my verse . . . : 8/3/42, Washington Univ.

said John Walcott . . . : 10/22/41, Princeton. Perhaps Walcott was assassinated (Tessa Horton, interview, 9/76). RPB to Darrell, 12/24/42, DP, describes his work in military intelligence; Christine Weston to RPB, 12/12/43, Princeton, reports his death. In 1941 Richard had reviewed Walcott's MS novel for Harcourt, and was paid to help revise it. In 1952 Richard's editor, Catharine Carver, reopened the question of publication, but unsuccessfully.

and excellent poet . . . : 12/19/42, Princeton.

another small volume . . . : 3/28/46, Yale.

burdens of poetry . . . : Weldon Kees, *New York Times*, 1947.

97 hold on it . . . : 3/21/51.

have to bear . . . : To John McCormick, 10/15/59, Princeton.

he got ready . . . : Meredith to Margaret Marshall, 3/18/65, HBP.

their first dreams . . . : To the author, 9/18/76.

its own light . . . : "Of Lucifer," *From Jordan's Delight*, p. 14.

some of it . . . : To Lee Anderson, 8/3/42, Washington Univ.

an important exception . . . : RPB to Palmer, 7/17/22, PP.

98 Poe and . . . Symons . . . : To Palmer, 4/9/21, 7/13/21, 10/18/21, PP.

deadly sweet beauty . . . : To Palmer, 5/6/21, PP.

wicked and wild . . . : "A Dream." His undated juvenilia, headed as from 52 Irving St., were given by Palmer to Houghton Library, Harvard, 3/27/72.

at a clip . . . : RPB to Palmer, 7/17/22, PP.

Webster and Ford . . . : To Palmer, 10/12/21, 4/12/23, PP.

Bishop Henry King . . . : 1/20/27, *Poetry* Archive, Chicago.

our achieved ends . . . : "The Composition in Nine Poets: 1937," *Expense of Greatness*, p. 205.

99 pretty high class . . . : To Palmer, 7/17/22, PP.

of Adelaide Crapsey . . . : To Palmer, 4/12/23, PP.

a great story . . . : RPB to the author. He retells the story in a BBC talk of 1956 (Box 33, folder 1, Princeton).

since Emily Dickinson . . . : To RPB, 4/3/37, Princeton.

100 of voice effects . . . : To Palmer, 7/17/22, PP.

or, dans Ecbatane . . . : 7/13/21, PP.

with beautiful . . . sounds . . . : To Palmer, 1/13/21, PP.

power unto itself . . . : Peter Putnam and Robert Fuller to RPB, 3/31/? (1950's), Princeton.

side of God . . . : After Putnam and Fuller.

an irreducible surd . . . : "Examples of Wallace Stevens," *Double Agent*, p. 73.

101 gap is absolute . . . : "A Critic's Job of Work," *Language as Gesture*, p. 381.

of the form . . . : Black notebook, 11/22.

his own poetics . . . : To Jacques Barzun, 12/12/57, Princeton.

at a conference . . . : Columbia Univ. Bicentennial Conference, 10/27–10/30/54. Lewis Leary, ed., *The Unity of Knowledge* (New York, 1955), pp. 157–64, abridges von Neumann's remarks. Complete version exists in IFAS

Archives, Princeton. Marina von Neumann Whitman to the author, 7/7/76, and Oskar Morgenstern to the author, 9/8/76, describe RPB's relation to von Neumann, tenuous except in his own eyes.

said Isidore Rabi . . . : To the author, 5/30/77.

own lecture notes . . . : Box 33, folder 2, Princeton.

were itself opportunistic . . . : 12/8/54, Princeton.

102 some profound level . . . : To the author, 2/16/77.

ad lib forever . . . : 12/19/42, Princeton.

rackings of desperation . . . : HA II, 274.

Hugh Kenner supposed . . . : "Inside the Featherbed," in *Gnomon* (New York, 1958), pp. 242–48.

at the table . . . : To Henry Nims, ed. of *Poetry*, 7/23/46, *Poetry* Archive, Box II, folder 10, Series I, Chicago.

upon our generation . . . : To Palmer, 4/12/23, PP.

perfection of rhythm . . . : To Palmer, 7/17/22, 8/18/22, PP.

103 Robinson, and Bodenheim . . . : To Palmer, 1/13/21. In addition he cites Joyce, Colum, Sassoon, Rupert Brooke, James Stephens, Richard Aldington.

in the work . . . : 1/25/25, Yale.

of the world . . . : 11/11/24, Yale.

what they are . . . : 6/15/33, ZP.

sometimes an afterthought . . . : In *Poetry*, Oct. 1938.

to heed him . . . : *New Republic*, 21 July 1937, p. 316.

the inner form . . . : 12/20/36, Yale.

104 feel both myself . . . : To Alfredo Rizzardi, 9/12/55, Princeton.

the "jewelled Monstrosities" . . . : RPB to Palmer, 7/17/22, PP.

against my ruins . . . : Epigraph of notebook of poems dated 8/26/23, Princeton.

of sixty years . . . : From an untitled autograph sonnet dated 2/25–2/27/27 in Maurice Firuski's possession.

literature to *twelve* . . . : RPB to Monroe, 10/3/36, Chicago.

to make serene . . . : AMN, p. 25 (11/4/32).

of the poems . . . : To Morton D. Zabel, 1/12/33, 1/22/33, ZP.

on Richard's discipleship . . . : Following RPB's introduction of Eliot in Perry Ellis, *Major American Writers* (1962), pp. 761, 763, 760.

105 position is secure . . . : AMN, pp. 30–31 (11/10/32).

to lyric poetry . . . : To John Crowe Ransom, 1/23/51, Kenyon College.

has yet come . . . : "The Composition in Nine Poets: 1937," p. 223.

Eliot has done . . . : To Palmer, 9/30/35, PP.

more "profoundly exciting" . . . : To Monroe, 10/3/36, Chicago.

form, *felt* thought . . . : 7/30/26, Princeton.

outside the poems . . . : 6/11/29, Delaware.

106 it became him . . . : RPB to Palmer on reading Yeats at seventeen, 10/18/21, PP.

indubitable major poet . . . : "T. S. Eliot," *Double Agent*, p. 186.

have tackled do . . . : 8/18/41, Yale.

read the plays . . . : MS notebook, 8/22, Box 31, folder 27, Princeton.

as withstand disorder . . . : AMN, p. 68.

feel as alien . . . : "T. E. Lawrence," *Expense of Greatness*, p. 18.

107   and the attitude . . . : Black notebook, 8/22.

poems he reviewed . . . : *Reading the Spirit* in *Partisan Review* 4 (Feb. 1938), 56.

sincerity will do . . . : 3/38, Princeton.

imagination, into emotion . . . : "T. E. Lawrence," p. 13.

108   really solid meal . . . : To the author, 7/22/79.

kept a file . . . : MS notebook, 8/8/24, Box 31, folder 27, Princeton.

them entirely 'successful' . . . : To Palmer, 1/13/21, PP.

stands equally alone . . . : To Darrell, 7/12/32, DP.

feeling—a discipline . . . : 4/29/35, DP.

worse, of pause . . . : 11/3/36, ZP.

overstressing of method . . . : 2/16/27, Chicago.

by vitiated convention . . . : "Nine Poets: 1939," *Expense of Greatness*, p. 230.

109   still love best . . . : Quoted in Alan Wald, "The Pilgrimage of Sherry Mangan," *Pembroke Magazine* 8 (spring 1977), 85.

a special sort . . . : Wald, "Sherry Mangan," p. 86.

acting as witness . . . : HA, "The Burial of My Grandfather's Doctrine," p. 28.

is probably nil . . . : To Palmer, 3/2/27, PP.

the mere idea . . . : Review of *The Notebooks and Papers of Gerard Manley Hopkins*, ed. Humphry House in *Virginia Quarterly Review* 13 (summer 1937), 452.

toward the visual . . . : Review of *Further Letters of Gerard Manley Hopkins*, ed. C. C. Abbott in *Kenyon Review* 1 (winter 1939), 96.

ends of politics . . . : Review of Gregory's *No Retreat* in *Poetry* 42 (July 1933), 220.

110   end no soap . . . : Review of Kenneth Fearing's *Dead Reckoning* in *Partisan Review* 6 (winter 1939), 109.

day as another . . . : To Robert MacGregor (New Directions), 9/18/61, Princeton.

a sad waste . . . : To Wald, 8/20/74.

George Anthony said . . . : To Wald, 4/25/75.

taking a breath . . . : Murray Borish to RPB, 10/20/31, Princeton.

so many steaks . . . : Horton, interview, 9/76.

list of necessities . . . : Kate Foster to Wald, 9/20/74.

Wintergreen for President . . . : Palmer to Wald, 9/1/74.

the ticket won . . . : Foster to Wald, 9/1/74.

111   great a Fall . . . To the author, 9/1/79.

His sister-in-law thought . . . : Greville Droescher, Kate's sister (Foster to Wald, 2/20/74; Jay Laughlin to Wald, 12/23/76).

pseudonyms for Sherry . . . : Palmer to Wald, 9/1/74.

the Armed Forces . . . : Wald to the author.

and amazing things . . . : 3/2/27, PP.

in on Sherry . . . : Austin Warren to the author, 9/76, recalls meeting RPB at the Mangans in Lynn.

they dined together . . . : RPB to MacGregor, 9/18/61, Princeton.

a close set . . . : To Wald, 9/11/76. There are sixteen Mangan letters, beginning 1926, and other correspondence bearing on their friendship, in the Blackmur Archive, Princeton.

from my own . . . : To Zabel, 9/7/34, ZP.

the worst things . . . : RPB to Palmer, 3/2/27, PP.

112 are our beginnings . . . : Review of *The Ground We Stand On* in *Decision* 2
   (Oct. 1941), 80.

   have been experienced . . . : Review of Allen Tate's *Reactionary Essays* in
   Columbia Review 17 (Apr. 1936), 30.

   large cosmopolitan gull . . . : Mangan explains his choice of title in a brochure
   of 1927, announcing the Lone Gull Press.

   a swell guy . . . : Review of Mangan's *"No Apologie for Poetry" and Other
   Poems Written 1922–31* (1934) in *Sewanee Review* 44 (Jan.–Mar. 1936).

   Virgil Thomson said . . . : To Wald, 1/16/76.

   thoroughly selfish life . . . : AMN, p. 114.

   brought to bear . . . : Review of *A Further Range* in *Nation*, 24 June 1936, p.
   818.

   of his verse . . . : Kirstein to Tate, 5/12/31, Tate Collection, Yale.

   New England Poets . . . : *New Republic*, 14 Aug. 1935, p. 14; RPB to Winfield
   T. Scott, 12/29/34, Hay.

   of the epigram . . . : *New Republic*, 21 July 1937, p. 315.

113 *Hound & Horn* . . . : 5/1/34, Princeton.

   ribbon of craft . . . : Review of *No Retreat* in *Poetry* 42 (July 1933), 217,
   219–20.

   have a locus . . . : Review of Kay Boyle's *A Glad Day* in *Partisan Review* 6
   (winter 1939), 110.

   presence somewhere upstairs . . . : Howard Nemerov to Wald, 9/1/77.

114 or Delmore Schwartz . . . : Kenneth W. Porter to Wald, 7/25/77.

   both shall live . . . : To Zabel, 6/19/34, ZP.

   somewhat by counting . . . : Review of W. C. Williams' *The Wedge* in *Kenyon
   Review* 7 (1945), 341.

   is . . . recogniseably sound . . . : 4/23/34, Brown.

   full of holes . . . : Review of *Rock and Shell* in *Poetry* 44 (1934), 283.

   man of variety . . . : RPB in John Brooks Wheelwright's self-promoting
   brochure, n.d.

   them or not . . . : RPB's "Note" on Wheelwright for New Directions, Princeton.

   this a symbol . . . : To Wald, 2/6/76.

115 stream is Fascist . . . : 8/15/40, Princeton.

   and to Fascism . . . : [1936?], Princeton.

   the "unregenerate outsider" . . . : "Heresy within Heresy," *Double Agent*, p.
   221.

   our limiting humanity . . . : "The Dangers of Authorship," *Double Agent*, p.
   179.

   in my place . . . : To Wald, 2/18/77.

   of the frivolous . . . : RPB's review of Carl Van Doren's *Anthology of World
   Prose* in *New Republic*, 11 Sept. 1935, p. 137.

   under the rug . . . : Richard Eberhart to Wald, 2/6/77.

116 the Old Howard . . . : Malcolm Cowley, *Second Flowering*, p. 78.

   Harvard Poetry Society . . . : John Marshall to the author, 2/2/77.

   The Signet Club . . . : Following *Third Catalogue of the Signet* (Boston, 1903).

   a useful animal . . . : To the author, 7/22/79.

   some excellent Bacardi . . . : RPB to Palmer, 12/24, PP.

   called the Bards . . . : Which included at various times Robert Fitzgerald,

Howard Blake, RPB, and the physicist Cuthbert Daniel.

wrote a history . . . : 1915–31, typed MS, Box 64, folder 14, Princeton. Subsequent discussion draws on this MS.

and Grant Code . . . : At 18, RPB is sought out by Grant Hyde Code, then teaching at Harvard: "an author by right of publication as well as by private accomplishment" (Black notebook, 11/22). Dudley Fitts in his autobiographical statement for *American Authors* owes his literary education "to my association, as an undergraduate, with John Wheelwright, Foster Damon, Grant Code, and Richard Blackmur." In Yvor Winters's opinion (*Uncollected Essays and Reviews of Yvor Winters*, ed. Francis Murphy, p. 124), Code "is one of the most distinguished poets living."

Twice he declined . . . : Following Guggenheim application, 1932.

was Carl Sandburg . . . : On whom Amy Lowell spoke as the last of six lectures.

117   to put in . . . : "Note" on Wheelwright.

of excellent poetry . . . : To Carver, 9/16/52, HBP.

to Malcolm Cowley . . . : 10/10/57, Newberry.

subject of Wheelwright . . . : 1/15/37, Yale.

sometime, to turn . . . : To Laughlin, 8/15/40, NDA.

didn't mean assimilation . . . : Dudley Fitts in *Saturday Review*, 20 Mar. 1948, p. 28: "not that I mean to imply that Mr. Blackmur derives from Wheelwright (the debt, if it exists, must surely be reckoned the other way around)."

syllable by syllable . . . : RPB to R. P. Warren, 12/20/36, Yale.

obfuscation of purpose . . . : Review of Edward Duro's *Shiloh* in *Poetry* 50 (June 1937), 168.

freer the content . . . : Review of Norman Macleod's *Horizons of Death* in *Poetry* 46 (1935), 112.

utmost in craft . . . : Review of *Reading the Spirit* in *Partisan Review* 4 (Feb. 1948), 54–55.

mind's sufficient grace . . . : Review in *Partisan Review* 6 (1939), 110.

118   give disorder room . . . : Review of C. H. Ford's *The Garden of Disorder* in *Partisan Review* 6 (winter 1936), 111.

substance of order . . . : Review of Allen Tate's *The Winter Sea* in *Kenyon Review* 7 (1945), 343.

above all death . . . : *Nation*, 1 May 1937.

119   eddying of order . . . : 12/30/36, Yale.

120   looking at them . . . : AMN, pp. 111–12.

Judas who betrays . . . : After Allen Tate's review of the poems, in *Southern Review* 3 (1937), 194.

121   merely a vagary . . . : 4/22/29, Delaware.

grasp its reality . . . : Review of Charles Morgan's *Sparkenbroke* in *Nation*, 13 May 1926, p. 618.

find her solace . . . : Black notebook, 10/5/20.

strength but anxiety . . . : The playwright Carty Ranck quoting Robinson's reaction, and adding his own similar reaction and that of the poet Nancy Bird Turner, in a letter to RPB from Peterborough, 8/30/25, Princeton. RPB to Zabel, 9/23/33, ZP: "Years ago I went to the MacDowell Colony as a week's guest." (RPB doesn't say how he came to be invited or when, but probably the Gilbert family took him there when the composer—as often

—was in residence (Horton, 7/22/79, and Darrell, 9/1/79, to the author).

from Oscar Williams . . . : *Nation*, 10 Oct. 1942, p. 354.

122   of self-expression . . . : Review of *Collected Poems of Joseph Trumbull Stickney* in *Poetry* 42 (June 1933), 160.

attribute your arrival . . . : 5/18/28, PP.

he will be . . . : *larus* 1 (May 1927), 26.

wrote to Zabel . . . : 2/10/36, ZP.

123   of the sea . . . : RPB to R. P. Warren, 12/20/36, Yale.

condition of idiom . . . : "The Composition in Nine Poets: 1937," pp. 199–200.

out for yourselves . . . : To Janet Gersten and Stephen Palery (Queens College, N.Y.), 4/17/57, Princeton.

5. A Failure Worth Making—The Life of Henry Adams

124   in scattered notes . . . : Guggenheim application, 10/26/36, GFA.

thinking it inexorable . . . : HA I, iii, 85.

turned hocus pocus . . . : II, 58.

125   not a book . . . : 7/12/48, Princeton Tate.

mind and character . . . : To Henry Allen Moe, 10/4/32, GFA.

his brother Brooks . . . : To George Anthony Palmer, 9/28/21, PP.

raised the veil . . . : HA I, "The Burial of My Grandfather's Doctrine," 43. Adams' poem is called "Buddha and Brahma."

as his own . . . : II, 249.

my critical biography . . . : To Rob Darrell, 8/12/36, DP.

to 20 months . . . : 5/12/36, Princeton Tate.

eastern United States . . . : To Jay Laughlin, 11/25/40, NDA.

was "positively mountainous" . . . : To Charles A. Pearce, editor-in-chief at Harcourt, 1/16/36, HBP.

to become omnivorous . . . : To Moe, 3/9/37, GFA.

126   he had dreamed . . . : To Moe, 9/16/37, GFA.

than it was . . . : To Darrell, 8/13/42, DP.

fruitless, seedless blades . . . : 10/30/42, Univ. of Iowa Library.

trespass or dull . . . : To Palmer, 9/10/42, PP; to Lambert Davis, (5/12/42, HBP), re 80,000 publishable words written "since last September."

complied in detail . . . : To Davis, 5/43, HBP.

another Harcourt editor . . . : Catharine Carver, who describes the review at length to J. H. McCallum, 4/22/55, HBP.

127   by the award . . . : To Moe, 3/19/37, GFA; Moe to RPB, 3/18/37, GFA.

except waste time . . . : To Darrell, 4/19/36, DP.

entirely useless work . . . : To Allen Tate, 3/21/37, Princeton Tate.

luck would change . . . : To Darrell, 1/31/37, DP.

essays and reviews . . . : Guggenheim application, 1936, GFA, on which subsequent discussion draws.

sought a fellowship . . . : To Moe, 10/30/32, GFA, asking first for support for the Adams book, then for the critical essays.

wrote the essays . . . : He said his say on Hopkins in reviews.

128   signed a contract . . . : As with New Directions (RPB to Laughlin, 8/15/40, NDA.

conspicuously forgot it . . . : RPB to J. H. Kyle at Johns Hopkins Univ., 11/10/55, Princeton.

it for spring . . . : To G. A. and Marjorie Palmer, 12/12/45, PP.

succubus and incubus . . . : RPB to Charlotte Kohler (*Virginia Quarterly Review*), 4/1/59, Princeton.

work a day . . . : Edward T. Cone, interview, 7/76.

has been written . . . : Mrs. Ward Thoron to RPB, 7/26/49, Princeton, re the 700 pages he has delivered to Harcourt.

just to live . . . : [Ca. 12/39], GFA; RPB to Pearce, 1/16/36, HBP.

been slowed down . . . : To Mrs. Thoron, 7/15/40, Harvard.

steadily on Adams . . . : To Frank V. Morley (Harcourt), Labor Day 1939, HBP.

putting things off . . . : To Morton D. Zabel, 4/29/31, ZP.

you write anything . . . : 10/18/43, Princeton.

129   dealings with him . . . : To the author, 2/16/77.

a permanent undercurrent . . . : To Charles Scribner, 3/1/61, Princeton.

guilt and sloth . . . : To Wayne Andrews (Scribner's), 11/9/62, Princeton.

in the Psyche . . . : To Pat (Hartle) Eden, 8/27/55, in her possession.

to Philip Rahv . . . : 5/25/44, *Partisan Review* Papers, Rutgers Univ.

to Harcourt Brace . . . : RPB to John Berryman, 5/12/36, Minnesota.

a modest advance . . . : of $400 (RPB to Moe, 5/10/36, GFA; to Tate, 5/12/36, Princeton Tate.

Giroux recorded another . . . : 6/8/51, HBP.

deadline" has passed . . . : William B. Goodman to RPB, 10/13/60, HBP.

the common scold . . . : Goodman to RPB, 5/11/60, HBP.

his own autobiography . . . : "The Techniques of Trouble" in "Anni Mirabiles," *Primer of Ignorance*, pp. 21–37.

book was his . . . : To Laughlin, 10/23/39, NDA; Berryman to RPB, 4/4/40, Princeton.

carried a bankroll . . . : Edmund L. Keeley, interview, 5/14/77.

130   wring an advance . . . : Carver to RPB, 10/5/55, HBP.

with New Directions . . . : RPB to Cleanth Brooks, 11/6/39; to Robert Penn Warren, 2/11/40, Yale; Robert M. MacGregor (New Directions) to RPB, 11/25/59, Princeton.

the very last . . . : Laughlin to RPB, 7/5/40, Princeton.

on that date . . . : 8/15/40, NDA.

have taken on . . . : 9/30/41, NDA.

the James' book . . . : 11/17/49, NDA.

lifetime to wait . . . : 11/25/49, NDA. RPB to MacGregor 9/18/61, Princeton, is in the same vein.

notions of immediacy . . . : To RPB, 12/22/55, NDA.

now and then . . . : To Laughlin, 12/29/55, HBP.

for another advance . . . : MacGregor to RPB records it, 11/25/29, NDA.

himself "ever eager" . . . : 12/7/64, NDA.

increase in hardship . . . : HA II, 165.

the book done . . . : To Moe, 3/22/38, GFA; Box 58, folder 3, Princeton.

131   for serial chapters . . . : Harry A. Bull of *Town & Country* to RPB, 6/23/37, Princeton; the managing editor of the *Virginia Quarterly Review* to RPB,

4/24/45, IFAS. Lincoln Kirstein's letters of 1937 to RPB comment on the book.

volunteered his correspondence . . . : To RPB, 12/30/37, Princeton. Also Worthington C. Ford, who is editing Adams's letters, to RPB, 11/25/37 and thereafter, Princeton.

Florence Codman . . . inquired . . . : 3/18/36, Princeton.

the same question . . . : 9/28/37, Princeton.

year after that . . . : 10/11/38, Princeton.

A friend remembered . . . : Darrell to the author [ca. 5/21/79].

waste of time . . . : N.d., Princeton.

early next winter . . . : To Pearce, 1/16/36, HBP.

then another winter . . . : RPB to Moe, 5/10/36, GFA.

time is needed . . . : To Pearce, 2/19/38, HBP.

deadline kept receding . . . : RPB to Pearce, 8/23/39, HBP; to Havens at Johns Hopkins, 10/10/39, Johns Hopkins; to Laughlin, 12/6/39, NDA; to Morley, Labor Day 1939, HBP.

finished by summer . . . : To Moe, 6/3/42, GFA.

of the year . . . : To Davis, 8/17/42, HBP.

me up entirely . . . : To Mrs. Thoron, 3/6/41, Harvard.

"impede" his progress . . . : To Morley, 6/14/40, HBP.

a strange place . . . : RPB to Mrs. Thoron, 12/12/40, Harvard.

His teaching job . . . : RPB to Mrs. Thoron, 7/15/40, Harvard.

count on me . . . : To Davis, 2/4/42, HBP.

sure any longer . . . : To Davis, 3/16/42, HBP.

132   bread and butter . . . : RPB to Morley, 5/14/40, HBP.

case of appendicitis . . . : RPB to Warren, 4/26/38, Yale; to Darrell, 3/23/38, DP.

tissue and bone . . . : To Berryman, 4/27/39, Minnesota.

to the hospital . . . : RPB to Darrell, 1/31/37, 2/8/40, DP; to Warren, 2/15/39, 2/22/39. Yale.

in the East . . . : To RPB, 3/14/[39?], Princeton.

I've been punk . . . : 4/24/39, DP.

face and jaw . . . : To Pearce, 1/16/36, HBP.

this trouble recurred . . . : RPB to Morley, Labor Day 1939, HBP.

and with justification . . . : To Davis, 1/19/45, HBP.

to get him . . . : To Davis, 8/17/42, HBP.

published in wartime . . . : To Palmer, 9/15/39, PP.

to take it . . . : To Mrs. Thoron, 7/15/40, Harvard.

finished this spring . . . : To Palmer, 2/18/43, PP.

or early winter . . . : 6/15/43, Minnesota.

What about it . . . : 5/6/43, HBP.

to you by . . . : 5/10/43, HBP.

touched near bottom . . . : To Davis, 9/7/43, HBP.

finish after all . . . : To Davis, 1/9/45, HBP.

133   actually in sight . . . : To Mrs. Thoron, 6/5/46, Harvard; to Davis, 11/14/46, HBP.

was "nearing birth" . . . : 1/25/52, HBP.

the same thing . . . : Quoted in Mrs. Thoron to RPB, 1/30/52, Princeton.

reticent and unwilling . . . : RPB to Pearce, 1/16/36, HBP.

to finish up . . . : 5/9/55, Kenyon; to Carver, 3/14/55, HBP; to Gyde Shepherd at McGill Univ., 10/13/55, Princeton.

what he said . . . : To Lee Anderson, 7/15/55, Washington Univ.

had hoped for . . . : RPB to Carver, 10/12/55, HBP.

poor Adams book . . . : To Richard Eberhart, 6/23/55, Princeton.

than the verge . . . : To the librarian at Houghton Library, Harvard, 11/24/54, Princeton.

and . . . in morals . . . : Recapitulated in RPB to Davies, a Cambridge don, 10/13/60, Princeton.

literature and history . . . : To the author, 10/4/76.

on Henry James . . . : To Davies, 11/12/58, Princeton.

many years ago . . . : To Christof Wegelin at the Univ. of Oregon, 12/11/58, Princeton.

only "vague hopes" . . . : To Peter Smith, 5/17/61, Princeton.

134 of getting ahead . . . : To Richard H. Rupp, who is writing a thesis on Adams at Indiana Univ., 5/3/61, Princeton.

a hundred pages . . . : RPB to Vern Wagner at Wayne State Univ., 3/11/58, Princeton.

the final chapter . . . : Goodman to RPB, 2/7/61, HBP.

had a photostat . . . : Goodman to William Jovanovich, 2/26/65, HBP.

everything goes well . . . : To Wagner, 2/6/61, Princeton.

year at Cambridge . . . : To Anderson, 11/29/62, Washington Univ.

going to finish . . . : To the author, 9/13/76.

didn't travel well . . . : To Alan Wald, 9/11/76.

said Graham Hough . . . : Mark L. Krupnick, Hough's tutee, to the author, 3/27/77.

John Wain's opinion . . . : *Essays on Literature and Ideas* (1963), pp. 145–55.

two former students . . . : Walter Clemons (to the author, 12/76) and A. Walton Litz.

135 lecture on Adams . . . : Leslie Fiedler to the author, 9/13/76.

to Cambridge students . . . : David Daiches to the author, 10/4/76.

Three public lectures . . . : Goodman to the author, 6/29/77.

consciously rejected him . . . : Goodman to the author, 3/23/79.

under his hand . . . : The same.

sense of purpose . . . : HA II, 55.

a watery mirror . . . : Paraphrasing Adams in *Education*, p. 429.

his great myth . . . : "The Later Poetry of W. B. Yeats," *Expense of Greatness*, p. 105.

to any description . . . : "The Method of Marianne Moore," *Double Agent*, p. 153.

bottomlessness of knowledge . . . : "Examples of Wallace Stevens," *Double Agent*, p. 91.

136 of his work . . . : Guggenheim application, 1936.

137 failure worth making . . . : The same.

spring the nails . . . : HA III, 58.

its present expression . . . : III, 57.

an evident fact . . . : *Education*, p. 373.

advance of you . . . : To RPB, 9/14/36, Princeton.

138 emptiness without terror . . . : "Adams: Images: Eidolon," a 6-page autograph
meditation found in Richard's papers at Princeton.

its own meaning . . . : HA II, 190.

in rational imagination . . . : Guggenheim application, 1936.

139 cannot be given . . . : To Pearce, 1/16/36, HBP.

of American intelligence . . . : Guggenheim application, 1936.

in the wilderness . . . : "A Feather-Bed for Critics," *Expense of Greatness,*
p. 298.

scholarship bemused him . . . : Interview, 8/76.

No *Paradise Lost* . . . : Interview, 3/77.

enlargement of detail . . . : 2/18/09, Harvard, quoted in Mrs. Thoron to RPB,
8/1/49, Princeton.

are our beginnings . . . : 10/8/58, Princeton.

ground before him . . . : To Davis, 5/43, HBP.

140 make an emphasis . . . : Guggenheim application, 1936.

unity in motion . . . : To Palmer, 11/25, PP.

this won't do . . . : 5/43, HBP.

141 of felt value . . . : "Notes on the Novel," *Expense of Greatness,* p. 187.

what it makes . . . : *Partisan Review* 10 (1943), 298.

as high priest . . . : To Davis, 5/43, HBP.

where you began . . . : After HA II, 208.

ice protected him . . . : III, 26, 29.

completed by 1938 . . . : Veronica Makowsky to the author, 11/9/79, 1/7/80;
Mrs. Thoron to RPB, 7/5/38, Princeton.

discipline for that . . . : HA III, 70–71.

142 a rational imagination . . . : I, 27.

every good thing . . . : I, 101, 103.

own twentieth-century life . . . : II, 199.

a collapsing world . . . : I, 102.

and an aggravation . . . : II, 150.

ladder of doubt . . . : [Ca. 1961], found among Richard's books in Firestone
Library, Princeton, 1979.

of radical imperfection . . . : HA I, 73.

of great men . . . : I, 26.

have this conviction . . . : I, 81.

my cateyes climb . . . : To Darrell, 7/1/40, DP.

143 and place prospered . . . : HA I, 63.

everything, when found . . . : I, 55.

condition of 1942 . . . : I, 38.

think of FDR . . . : I, 80.

its very seat . . . : I, 34.

time and ours . . . : I, 38.

is an Individual . . . : To Davis, 5/43, HBP.

144 anarchist on principle . . . : HA I, 91.

by producing types . . . : To Davis, 5/43, HBP.

is discovered "today" . . . : HA I, 93.

the immediate present . . . : I, 21.

did not exist . . . : I, 2.

did actually survive . . . : "The Politics of Human Power," *The Lion and the Honeycomb*, p. 35.

and American history . . . : Guggenheim application, 1936.

can be finished . . . : HA III, 31.

book "in petto" . . . : To Darrell, 4/19/36, DP.

145　momentum of mass . . . : RPB to Moe, 5/18/36, GFA.

challenge and fascination . . . : HA II, 88.

in the *Education* . . . : P. 263.

believe in nothing . . . : Review of *Education* in *Athenaeum*, 23 May 1919.

ardent speculative intelligence . . . : 8/13/29, Brown.

faith was live . . . : HA II, 195.

146　they were felt . . . : II, 161.

on them all . . . : II, 211.

justice and law . . . : II, 231.

into the works . . . : I, "Return," iv, 3.

meant for purification . . . : Autograph meditation.

experienced an emotion . . . : HA II, 247.

stability is death . . . : II, 254.

not yet discerned . . . : "A Note on Yvor Winters," *Expense of Greatness*, p. 175.

a tragic fall . . . : HA II, 209, 231.

147　to protect him . . . : II, 233.

which we stand . . . : II, 231.

destructive to it . . . : II, 163.

not in view . . . : III, 21.

148　to poor Henry . . . : To Lizzie Boott, 1/7/1886. RPB asked Leon Edel for a copy of this letter and received it, 2/6/56, Princeton.

finished my dinner . . . : To Rebecca Gilman Rae, 12/21/1897.

we are not . . . : To Mrs. Thoron, 1/17/45, Princeton.

of Adams' life . . . : Guggenheim application, 1936.

is all sex . . . : To RPB, 1/22/43, Princeton.

his own reaction . . . : Autograph meditation.

149　back to life . . . : To her niece Ellen Gurney (unposted), copied and sent to RPB by Mrs. Thoron, 1/28/47, Princeton. I have transposed the sentences.

the finishing touches . . . : To Pearce, 1/16/36, HBP.

150　to his story . . . : To Davis, 5/43, HBP.

order to live . . . : HA II, 62.

combine with force . . . : To Smith, 5/17/61, Princeton.

to write biography . . . : 5/12/37, Princeton.

the whole system . . . : To RPB, 10/2/36, Princeton.

151　wishes to destroy . . . : HA I, vii, 19–20.

hope is born . . . : II, 226.

one short paragraph . . . : 1/17/45, Princeton.

my poor book . . . : 7/1/51, Harvard.

6. Diabolus in the Scale—Blackmur at Fiction

154　imaginative and prophetic . . . : HA I, "Five of Hearts," 28.

abstinence from jobs . . . : RPB to Jay Laughlin, 6/21/40, NDA.

to a friend . . . : Rob Darrell (Darrell to the author, 3/13/79).

self-driven, and self-complete . . . : "Henry James" (*LHUS* MS), p. 20.

on a novel . . . : 8/30, DP.

155   of new material . . . : RPB to Richard Johns, 5/14/30, Delaware.

draft was ready . . . : RPB to Johns, 3/31/32, Delaware.

than a novelist . . . : John Hall Wheelock to RPB, 5/16/32, Princeton.

money losing novel . . . : RPB to Darrell, 7/12/32, DP.

Kenneth Patchen inquired . . . : N.d., from Warren, Ohio, Princeton.

one of supererogation . . . : To Darrell, 7/12/32, DP.

abeyance and servitude . . . : To Rob and Emma Darrell, 8/5/33, DP.

the same minute . . . : To RPB, 12/25/32, Princeton.

to publish it . . . : 9/6/34, Brown.

written—and overwritten . . . : William Soskin, quoted in Bernice Baumgarten
    (of Brandt & Brandt) to RPB, 11/24/36, Princeton.

156   Tessa Horton recalled . . . : Interview, 9/76.

all the others . . . : To RPB, 7/28/35, Princeton.

on personal experience . . . : Baumgarten to RPB, 6/19/35, Princeton.

King Pandar forever . . . : To George Anthony Palmer, 11/25, PP.

Adams ever had . . . : "The Pedagogue of Sensibility," *Chimera* 2 (1944), 6.

157   in the offing . . . : To RPB, 7/28/35, Princeton.

comparative arouses interest . . . : 5/2/32, Princeton.

as by enema . . . : To Darrell, 4/29/35, DP.

Florence Codman's words . . . : To RPB, 10/30/35, Princeton.

of irreparable loss . . . : RPB, Synopsis, Princeton.

concern with death . . . : 10/30/35, Princeton.

adjustment to Helen . . . : 12/6/36, Princeton.

his own bowels . . . : Synopsis.

an objective consciousness . . . : Synopsis.

only the drama . . . : 4/29/35, DP.

plug the holes . . . : To Palmer, 9/30/35, PP.

much less vivid . . . : Anonymous reader, quoted in Codman to RPB, 10/30/35,
    Princeton.

the pulp stage . . . : 10/30/35, Princeton.

most tremendously glad . . . : To RPB, 1/6/36, Princeton.

158   Crime, Punishment, and Penance . . . : Synopsis.

of literary forms . . . : Echoing James in "The Critical Prefaces of Henry
    James," *Double Agent*, p. 266.

keep it buried . . . : Bruce Berlind to the author, 7/22/77.

saved from himself . . . : HA I, ii, 60.

promote his fiction . . . : Delmore Schwartz to RPB, 5/2/40, Princeton;
    Laughlin to RPB re Schwartz's praise of *King Pandar*, 5/2/40, NDA;
    Walcott, in praise, to RPB, 11/21/41, Princeton. Laughlin, 7/5/40, NDA,
    hopes to read the novel soon. At least three times, RPB sought to persuade
    Laughlin to publish (10/12/39, 6/21/40, 8/15/40, NDA).

his "fierce desire" . . . : E. D. H. Johnson, interview, 5/77.

peculiar but pressing . . . : "The Undergraduate Writer As Writer," *College
    English* 3 (Dec. 1941), 251.

Queen of Tarts . . . : RPB to Darrell, 7/12/32, DP.

own "best prospect" . . . : 2/14/41, PP.

159 of great distinction . . . : 5/16/32, Princeton.
that "seeing eye" . . . : [Ca. 1942–43], Princeton.
of their own . . . : "The Undergraduate Writer," p. 251.
to render it . . . : AMN, p. 78.
the values rendered . . . : *LHUS* MS, p. 19.
lacks "tolerable proportion" . . . : To RPB, 7/28/35, Princeton.
seduce, nor persuade . . . : 10/9/41?, Princeton.

160 stock personal emotions . . . : "Notes on the Novel: 1936," *Expense of Greatness*, p. 195.
illusion of form . . . : "Notes on the Novel," pp. 182–83.
bit that way . . . : [Ca. 1942–43], Princeton.
hidden, utter dreariness . . . : "Above the Stream," autograph MS dated 4/16/23, Princeton.
of mine undisguise . . . : AMN, pp. 102, 116.

161 a unique situation . . . : Review of Sacheverell Sitwell's *Doctor Donne and Gargantua* in *Poetry* 38 (June 1931), 165.
solicit a story . . . : RPB to Johns, 5/14/30, Delaware.
published "The Cut" . . . : *larus* 1 (July 1927).
Tate and Winters . . . : To Jack Wheelwright, 3/3/33, Brown.

162 or anybody else . . . : Review of *Doctor Donne and Gargantua*, p. 165.
almost factual realism . . . : To RPB, 5/16/32, Princeton.
Florence Codman's word . . . : To RPB, 7/28/35, Princeton.
the Jacobean patter . . . : To J. Kerker Quinn (*Accent*), 2/15/45, Illinois.

163 and Henry James . . . : AMN, p. 79.
novel begot it . . . : To RPB, 10/30/35, Princeton.

164 consciousness of sex . . . : The same.
its segregation horrible . . . : To RPB, 12/6/32, Princeton.
their own dishonesty . . . : *The Greater Torment*.
in New York . . . : Soskin, quoted by Baumgarten to RPB, 11/24/36, Princeton.

165 substance of interest . . . : "The Sacred Fount," *Kenyon Review* 4 (1942), 344.
and the voices . . . : To RPB, 4/29/39, Princeton.
to Elliot Paul . . . : (Salutation reads "Dear Elliot") 7/8/27, Columbia.
to my neck . . . : 2/8/46, Princeton Tate.
the fairy tale . . . : *LHUS* MS, p. 10.

166 of rational art . . . : Review of Joseph Roth's *Tarabas: A Guest on Earth* in *Nation*, 19 Dec. 1934, p. 717.
perspective and direction . . . : "Notes on the Novel," p. 190.
gesture is inexplicable . . . : Review in *Nation*, 22 Aug. 1934.
of contingent reality . . . : *LHUS* MS, p. 3.
your rational responsibility . . . : "Notes on the Novel," p. 190.
every other individual . . . : Laurel edition of *The Wings of the Dove*, p. 6.

167 private and impregnable . . . : AMN, p. 24.
popular well-made play . . . : *LHUS* MS, p. 37.
Wilson encouraged Richard . . . : 2/25/31, Princeton.
read future scripts . . . : To RPB, 4/15/31, Princeton.
assurance of being . . . : AMN, p. 55.
without moral compassion . . . : Laurel edition, p. 1.
reading at eighteen . . . : Black notebook, 9/19/42.

Avis and Joseph . . . : "The Taking of Avis" in two versions, MS dated
  10/29/23.

168   Aiken had commended . . . : To RPB, 2/14/31, Princeton.

play of reality . . . : 4/15/31, Princeton.

involved in it . . . : The same.

the last cadence . . . : "Twelve Poets," *Southern Review* 7 (1941), 191.

169   get on with . . . : Lecture notes, 1/11/49, Box 30, folder 36, Princeton.

no doubt deserved . . . : 4/16/31, Huntington.

with the next . . . : 5?/31, Princeton.

thing about Lindbergh . . . : "With the stylistic influence of Cocteau's *Orphée*"
  (Lincoln Kirstein to the author, 5/1/80).

anarchistic and treasonable . . . : Alfred S. Shivers, *Maxwell Anderson* (Boston,
  1976), p. 106.

swell subject anyway . . . : To Conrad Aiken, 4/16/31, Huntington.

then complete silence . . . : RPB to Darrell, 8/3/31, DP.

down the drain . . . : Darrell to the author, 1/27/80, on RPB's emotional
  investment in this play, "originally . . . to be titled, *Eagles Fly High*."

170   composition of fullness . . . : AMN, pp. 95–96.

171   to have been . . . : *LHUS* MS, pp. 13–14.

of the individual . . . : "The Sacred Fount," p. 335.

base are irreconcilable . . . : HA I, iv, 93.

Francis Fergusson . . . thought . . . : Interview, 8/1/76.

172   any other world . . . : To Palmer, 9/28/21, PP.

symbols or fables . . . : HA I, "Five of Hearts," 2.

minds, James won . . . : To Palmer, 7/9/22, PP.

art was enough . . . : Paraphrasing RPB's conclusion to "The Prefaces of Henry
  James," first appearing in last issue of *H&H* and reprinted in *Double Agent*.

Cowley told him . . . : 4/28/34, Princeton.

in his diary . . . : *Shadows of the Sun*, published posthumously in 3 vols. by
  Crosby's Black Sun Press in Paris (Geoffrey Wolff, *Black Sun* [New York,
  1976], p. 12).

his best poem . . . : Wheelwright, "Wise Men on the Death of a Fool," *H&H*
  4 (1931), 401–02.

Richard had corresponded . . . : Thayer to RPB, 1/18/24, Princeton.

173   sank with him . . . : William Wasserstrom, *The Time of the "The Dial"*
  (Syracuse, N.Y., 1963), pp. 1, 64, 80, 86; Nicholas Joost, *Scofield Thayer and
  "The Dial"* (Carbondale, Ill., 1964), p. 258.

touch at parting . . . : *Exile's Return*, p. 119.

paths still open . . . : 4/28/34, Princeton.

for six years . . . : RPB, "Economy of the American Writer," *Sewanee Review*,
  (Apr. 1945), pp. 3, 6.

expert in alcoholism . . . : Review of Mark Schorer's *Sinclair Lewis* in *New
  Republic*, 20 Nov. 1961, p. 18.

or went abroad . . . : "The Economy of the American Writer," p. 5.

174   most easily destroyed . . . : Review of Wyndham Lewis's *The Role of the Hero
  in the Plays of Shakespeare* in *H&H* 1 (1927), 43.

of this prophet . . . : Quoting Berryman's poem, "Olympus."

end is highbrow . . . : *The Freedom of the Poet* (New York, 1976).

catering to it . . . : To the editor of the *New York Times Book Review*, 4/21/47.

wrote to Richard . . . : 10/18/43, Princeton.

could not make . . . : "Economy of the American Writer," p. 2.

keep my vertigo . . . : AMN, pp. 121–22.

175   precarious bodily states . . . : "Chaos Is Come Again," *Southern Review* 6 (spring 1941), 658–74.

role of artist . . . : "Economy of the American Writer," p. 11.

by literary means . . . : "The Enabling Act of Criticism," *American Issues*, ed. W. Thorp (Philadelphia, 1941), vol. II.

savage and mendacious . . . : Palmer, interview, 3/76. Review appeared 12/30/40.

supposed a friend . . . : RPB to Palmer, 2/14/41, PP.

virtues of Joyce . . . : To RPB, 12/19/42, Princeton.

ingenuity and foolishness . . . : Schwartz to RPB, 9/16/43, Princeton.

as Gilbert Osmond . . . : To RPB, 1/28/43, Princeton. Elsewhere (Schwartz to RPB, 4/6/43, Princeton), his prototype "must be Karenin."

of the review . . . : Malcolm Cowley to RPB, 2/24/41, Princeton: "I didn't assign your book for review either, and wouldn't in any case have given it to Levin."

course believe that . . . : RPB to Palmer, 2/14/41, PP.

to me, probity . . . : [Ca. 1941], NDA.

been quite deliberate . . . : To Palmer, 2/14/41.

at full speed . . . : To the author, 9/1/79.

176   felt the knife . . . : Interview, 3/76.

feel with satisfaction . . . : AMN, p. 125 [ca. 1937].

regrets and griefs . . . : 2/14/41, PP.

he wrote plaintively . . . : 9/28/42, Princeton.

littered with mementoes . . . : Darrell to the author, 4/24/79.

her famous wager . . . : Darrell to the author, 5/20/79.

Poetry," *Southern Review* 7 (spring 1971), 510.

said Matthew Josephson . . . : "Improper Bostonian: John Wheelwright and His

177   forget the parties . . . : T. Horton, interview, 9/76.

I not failed . . . : *New and Selected Poems* (Garden City, N.Y., 1967), pp. 135–36.

in the mail . . . : "For Certain Sectionalists," the poem RPB chose for the *New Republic* anthology, "Eight New England Poets," 14 Aug. 1935, p. 15.

have I done . . . : Sonnet II, *Collected Poems, 1937–1962* (New York, 1962), p. 103. Scott Donaldson, *Poet in America: Winfield Townley Scott*, Austin, Texas and London, 1972.

178   the alien himself . . . : AMN, p. 126.

is thenceforth haunted . . . : AMN, p. 78.

of thought, dead . . . : AMN, p. 66.

179   of this age . . . : Quoted in Codman to RPB, 4/28/39, Princeton.

of my bones . . . : 9/14/44, RFA.

sort of work . . . : Morton D. Zabel (quoting a previous letter) to RPB, 1/18/33, Princeton.

of the money-colour . . . : RPB to Darrell, 4/29/35, DP.

and pressing responsibilities . . . : To RPB, 2/21/? [mid-1930s], Princeton.

in New York . . . : RPB to Darrell, 4/19/36, DP.

God for that . . . : To RPB [late 1930s], Princeton.

that primary character . . . : To Henry Allen Moe, 4/19/38, GFA.

a "peripatetic pedagogue" . . . : RPB to Aiken, 4/16/31, Huntington.

180   with existing institutions . . . : "Economy of the American Writer," p. 11.

for him there . . . : To Darrell, 4/29/35, DP.

for an interview . . . : RPB to Zabel, 4/6/35, ZP; to Palmer, 7/2/35, PP.

she was there . . . : Francis Fergusson, interview, 8/1/76.

the minimum living . . . : To Frank Morley, Labor Day 1939, HBP.

Allen Tate's insistence . . . : RPB to Morley, 6/14/40, HBP.

save my skin . . . : 6/21/40, NDA.

his first choice . . . : P. Horton, interview, 3/76.

a different way . . . : 7/1/40, Princeton Tate.

much enjoy it . . . : 10/6/40, Princeton.

evangelical, almost apocalyptic . . . : John F. Sullivan, *Commentary*, 13 May 1955, p. 159.

181   lose our responsibilities . . . : To Michael Jamieson, 6/5/64, Princeton.

persons," Cowley wrote . . . : *Second Flowering*, pp. 252–53.

7. The Pedagogue of Sensibility

182   on in Maine . . . : Stow Persons to the author, 12/15/77.

under a bushel . . . : 9/30/41, Princeton.

take the risk . . . : To George Anthony, 7/24/46, PP.

fingers in air . . . : "Religion and the Intellectual," *Partisan Review* 17 (1950), 221 and 223.

counterparts in Europe . . . : Clark, *Einstein*, p. 529.

183   victim to this . . . : To Christian Gauss, 5/15/44, *The Papers of Christian Gauss*, (New York, 1957).

it too much . . . : Interview, 5/77.

handsome minor successes . . . : 3/16/43, Princeton.

but not envious . . . : Report on the Princeton Seminars in Literary Criticism, 1951, RFA.

184   myself also was . . . : 10/1/58, Princeton.

185   who grows grapes . . . : Interview, 7/76.

186   kind of club . . . : Wilson to Gauss, 2/24/50, Wilson Letters.

186   in a hotel . . . : To Mrs. Ward Thoron, 12/12/40, Harvard.

and windless lands . . . : To Lee Anderson, 8/3/42, Washington Univ.

him head on . . . : Frederick Buechner to the author, 10/5/76.

187   of "small-town feller" . . . : Irving Howe to the author, 11/22/77.

to tell him . . . : Bruce Berlind to the author, 7/22/77.

an inch rule . . . : 7/1/40, Princeton Tate.

Tate had hunted . . . : Richard to Allen Tate, 7/1/40, Princeton Tate.

own sexual antics . . . : Persons to the author, 12/15/77.

as K. Burke . . . : 5/15/41, Princeton.

Burke had mellowed . . . : To Rob Darrell, 5/14/41, DP.

the cyanotic blue . . . : RPB to Arthur Efron, 11/9/64, Princeton.

same bar sinister . . . : Burke in "R. P. Blackmur" (a booklet published by the *Nassau Literary Magazine*, May 1965), p. 6.

of lamb chops . . . : Buechner to the author, 10/5/76.
188   them put together . . . : Berlind to the author, 7/22/77.
their rival Ph.D.'s . . . : To the author, 8/2/76.
met in conversation . . . : To Darrell, 5/14/41, DP.
other in public . . . : RPB to Efron, 11/9/64, Princeton.
But they do . . . : To Darrell, 5/14/41, DP.
it as here . . . : [Ca. early winter 1941], NDA.
his ornate tweeds . . . : Franklin Reeve to the author, 6/21/78.
closed behind them . . . : Howell, interview, 8/10/76.
a Blackmur cult . . . : Willard Thorp, interview, 7/76.
said Mike Keeley . . . : Interview, 5/77.
189   his philological inadequacies . . . : Robert Hollander to the author, 8/76.
Irving Howe's sense . . . : To the author, 1/22/77.
betrayed the abyss . . . : To Tate, 8/11/41, Princeton Tate.
less talented infants . . . : To Darrell, 7/24/41, DP.
glittering than twinkling . . . : Buechner to the author, 10/5/76.
Eileen Simpson remembered . . . : To the author, 9/12/78.
your water lines . . . : Berlind to the author, 7/22/77.
passed endless hours . . . : Persons to the author, 5/5/80.
190   argued Socialist politics . . . : Howe to the author, 1/22/77.
remembered what rhymed . . . : To Jean Garrigue, 10/30/42, Iowa.
weren't many academics . . . : Barr to the author, 6/9/78.
he went canoeing . . . : RPB to Darrell, 6/6/45, DP.
ran the library . . . : RPB to J. Kerker Quinn, 3/14/44, Illinois.
Drive in Virginia . . . : RPB to John Marshall, 5/1/46, RFA.
on Easter Sunday . . . : To the author, 12/15/77.
the same campus . . . : Berlind to the author, 7/22/77.
in his charge . . . : "San Giovanni in Venere: Allen Tate as Man of Letters,"
        Primer of Ignorance, p. 174 (originally appeared in *Sewanee Review*, 1959).
the English department . . . : To George Havens, 2/29/41, Johns Hopkins.
of their history . . . : "Christian Gauss and the Everlasting Job," *American
        Scholar*, 17, no. 3 (summer 1948), 343.
condition of living . . . : "Christian Gauss," p. 342.
191   any such feeling . . . : To the author, 1/22/77.
lives of others . . . : "Origins," *Papers of Christian Gauss*, p. 12.
Richard said this . . . : "San Giovanni," p. 175.
open to him . . . : "Origins," pp. 6, 21.
Fred Wahr remembered . . . : Interview, 1/22/77.
192   powers of initiative . . . : "Origins," pp. 24–25.
souls I know . . . : Diary entry, 1/12/42 (to David Stevens of the Rockefeller
        Foundation), *Papers of Christian Gauss*.
his first choice . . . : Gauss to Wilson, 2/21/39, *Papers of Christian Gauss*.
corresponding in 1929 . . . : RPB to Tate, 8/5/29, Princeton Tate.
was Paean General . . . : Dudley Fitts to Lincoln Kirstein, 11/11/29, Yale Fitts
        Collection.
in her bowels . . . : 4/17/37, Princeton Tate.
an inferior race . . . : To Kirstein, 5/10/33, Yale.
193   detached from it . . . : "San Giovanni," p. 169.

grows increasingly urban . . . : Review of *I'll Take My Stand* in *H&H* 4 (1931), 438.

around the world . . . : *"The Fugitive,* 1922–25*," Princeton University Library Chronicle* 3 (Apr. 1942), 82.

against the stranger . . . : Quoted in George Core, "A Naturalist Looks at Sentiment," *Virginia Quarterly Review* 3 (summer 1977), 459.

this quarter century . . . : "San Giovanni," p. 166.

perfect a review . . . : To RPB, 5/5/36, Princeton.

called worthless pastiche . . . : To staff of *H&H*, 7/31/33, Yale.

he esteemed handsomely . . . : Morton Zabel to RPB, 1/12/32, Princeton.

the same age . . . : 5/5/36, Princeton.

level of experience . . . : To Tate, 5/12/36, Princeton Tate.

of received philosophy . . . : "San Giovanni," p. 170.

powers of *elucidation* . . . : Tate (quoting John Ransom) to RPB, 5/5/36, Princeton.

194   preferred the quicksands . . . : To Palmer, 2/14/41, PP.

fall of 1938 . . . : Tate to RPB, 3/26/38, Princeton.

Richard called him . . . : To Delmore Schwartz [early 1940s], Yale.

Allen persuaded Richard . . . : Harry Duncan to the author, 8/15/77.

Allen put it . . . : To Eileen Simpson (Simpson, interview, 8/76).

orders and aids . . . : To Tate, 6/13/40, Princeton Tate.

a Nazi sympathizer . . . : Interview, 8/9/77.

said to Tate . . . : ?/10/38, Princeton Tate.

job for himself . . . : Interview, 8/76.

had undercut him . . . : To the author, 8/2/76.

and to me . . . : 12/7/41, PP.

195   short of it . . . : Interview, 8/1/76.

expressed "complete satisfaction" . . . : E. F. D'Arms minute on interview with Harold Dodds, 12/21/48, RFA.

into the program . . . : 10/5/42, Princeton Tate.

essay on Baudelaire . . . : 9/23/43, Princeton.

about the war . . . : Tate to RPB, 9/30/42, Princeton.

sent for training . . . : Tate to RPB, 10/8/42, Princeton.

in Richard's phrase . . . : "San Giovanni," p. 161.

Yours and Caroline's . . . : 12/18/48, Princeton Tate.

of being dishonest . . . : Joan Jurow to the author, 12/11/77.

on most everybody . . . : Louis Rubin to the author, 10/31/77.

to invite me . . . : To the author, 11/5/76.

made partial amends . . . : To the author, 5/6/77.

196   up disliking him . . . : To the author, 10/3/76.

of his contentiousness . . . : "San Giovanni," p. 168.

best American critic . . . : Interview, 8/9/77.

of its content . . . : "San Giovanni," p. 163.

in the world . . . : Tate to RPB, 5/5/36, Princeton.

The "new overlord" . . . : RPB to Darrell, 9/12/42, DP.

decent chap personally . . . : To Tate, 10/5/42, Princeton Tate.

a "stud writer" . . . : Interview, 8/9/77.

197   I was there . . . : To the author, 1/20/77.

a scheme afoot . . . : 2/18/43, PP.

friend, Mike Oates . . . : Marshall to the author, 6/11/80.

Hodder Fellow exulted . . . : To Quinn (*Accent*), 5/17/43, Illinois.

of my society . . . : Green notebook [ca. 10/1/41], Princeton.

the heart's action . . . : To Darrell, 7/11/40, DP.

across the water . . . : To Mrs. Thoron, 8/14/40, Harvard.

kink and country . . . : 1/29/42, Princeton.

the Marine Corps . . . : RPB to Mrs. Thoron, 9/4/42, Harvard.

oversize tuberculosis scar . . . : To Jay Laughlin, 11/17/42, NDA; to Darrell, 12/24/42, DP; to Tate, 3/16/43, Princeton Tate.

job in Maryland . . . : 2/18/43, PP.

bed of uncertainty . . . : The same.

198   Tessa Horton said . . . : Interview, 9/76.

ax to fall . . . : To Tate, 10/5/42; to Darrell, 8/13/42, DP.

drafted was preferable . . . : To Mrs. Thoron, 9/4/42, Harvard.

Washingtonian other-other land . . . : Tina Weston to RPB, 2/3/42, Princeton.

in the ranks . . . : To Darrell, 9/12/42, DP.

his other ailments . . . : RPB to Tate, 10/7/42, Princeton; to Darrell 10/13/42, DP.

in a factory . . . : To Darrell, 12/24/42, DP.

new torpedo planes . . . : RPB to Mrs. Thoron, 6/19/44, Harvard.

her body rebelled . . . : RPB to Palmer, 11/22/44, PP.

out in Princeton . . . : RPB to John Berryman, 10/12/43, Minnesota; to Palmer, 11/22/44, PP.

let herself off . . . : 3/14/44, Princeton Tate.

Sleeplessness afflicted her . . . : Schwartz to RPB, 4/6/43, Princeton.

yearned to hear . . . : To RPB, 1/28/43, Princeton.

which she wears . . . : To Palmer, 2/18/43, PP.

in or out . . . : To Laughlin, 11/17/42, NDA.

199   in all senses . . . : To Havens, 10/3/40, Johns Hopkins.

half my time . . . : To Palmer, 2/18/43, PP.

of a professor . . . : RPB, "A Statement with Respect to the Creative Writing Section of the CAP," 6/13/57, Princeton.

the leaves off . . . : Green notebook, 11/12/40, Princeton.

his own bellows . . . : Green notebook, 11/18/40, Princeton.

friends and equals . . . : Sidney Monas, in *Princeton Alumni Weekly* tribute to RPB, 4 May 1965, p. 10.

a remarkable teacher . . . : Interview, 8/9/77.

work and presence . . . : Franklin Reeve, *PAW* tribute, p. 9.

Merely his presence . . . : Geoffrey Wolff to the author, 2/20/77.

is this campus . . . : Michael Fried, quoted by Paul Oppenheimer to the author, 9/10/76.

200   kind of conscience . . . : Wolff to RPB, 8/2/61, Princeton.

want to be . . . : Reeve, *PAW* tribute, p. 9.

wrote my fiction . . . : Edmund Keeley, *PAW* tribute, p. 10.

I did not . . . : To the author, 7/22/77; *PAW* tribute, p. 10.

in your way . . . : Reeve, *PAW* tribute, p. 9.

you come from . . . : The same.

spell he cast . . . : *PAW* tribute, p. 9.

country of letters . . . : *PAW* tribute, p. 9.

a little terrible . . . : Buechner to the author, 10/5/76.

less inspired students . . . : Rosenwald to the author, 10/24/77.

little boys here . . . : To Garrigue, 10/30/42, Iowa.

much time altogether . . . : Interview, 8/9/77.

201   results and rewards . . . : Reeve to the author, 6/28/78.

years, he said . . . : Reeve to the author, 6/28/78.

than you do . . . : Keeley, interview, 5/77.

a student poll . . . : *Nassau Sovereign* Course Evaluation Poll, Jan. 1948.

the sand dried . . . : HA II, 173.

virile and uninhibited . . . : Joseph Bennett, *PAW* tribute, p. 10.

of personal possibility . . . : To the author, 10/15/76.

202   an unceasing experiment . . . : Michael Kelley, *PAW* tribute, p. 10.

perhaps he tried . . . : Monas, *PAW* tribute, p. 9.

in the poem . . . : To the author, 9/13/76.

talking the other . . . : To the author, 9/13/76.

powerful critical methodology . . . : To the author, 2/6/77.

203   have produced it . . . : To Richard Coulson, 6/24/55, Princeton.

bestow "my blessing" . . . : To Lowell, 11/14/46, Princeton.

for Mr. Steiner . . . : To the Institute, 9/19/57, IFAS file.

of your criticism . . . : 8/16/42, Princeton.

said Leon Edel . . . : To the author, 9/28/76.

a hopeless student . . . : Merwin to the author, 12/1/76.

was his tailor . . . : RPB to Darrell, 12/20/44, DP.

a Blackmurian choice . . . : To RPB, 7/7/43, Princeton.

small fry bills . . . : To RPB, 11/10/42, Princeton.

the eyes especially . . . : Berlind to the author, 7/22/77.

foreskin in jeopardy . . . : Geoffrey Wolff, *The Duke of Deception* (New York, 1979), p. 244.

processes and preoccupations . . . : Theodore Holmes, *PAW* tribute, p. 9.

204   one disapproving critic . . . : John Wain, *Essays on Literature and Ideas* (London, 1963), pp. 145–55.

in Dan Seltzer . . . : Seltzer, *PAW* tribute, p. 10.

poet, that matters . . . : Berlind to the author, 7/22/77.

was Geoffrey Wolff . . . : To the author, 2/20/77.

perhaps retarded, boy . . . : To the author, 6/22/78.

at a distance . . . : Peter Putnam to the author, 2/11/77.

Merwin revered him . . . : Merwin to the author, 10/7/77.

further than Richard . . . : To the author, 10/5/76.

in the act . . . : Interview, 5/77.

role of myself . . . : Eleven insert pages, Green notebook, 11/5/45–1/14/46, Princeton.

205   were Clyde Beatty . . . : Reeve to the author, 6/28/78.

to his flock . . . : Robert Fuller and Peter Putnam to RPB, 3/31/? [1950s], Princeton.

with religious intensity . . . : Putnam to the author, 2/11/77.

Thomas Love Peacock . . . : Lecture notes on *Heartbreak House*, 1/1/49, Box 30, folder 22, Princeton.

were "altogether terrible" . . . : Fuller and Putnam.

by your fingernails . . . : Reeve to the author, 6/28/78.

seriousness of frivolity . . . : Green notebook, 11/12/40, Princeton.

privation of intelligence . . . : HA I, iii, 73.

to be earned . . . : II, 197.

up before us . . . : Fuller and Putnam.

sign of compromise . . . : The same.

one felt capable . . . : Dan Seltzer, *PAW* tribute, p. 10.

they did not . . . : Putnam to the author, 11/1/78.

206   less than yourself . . . : Green notebook, 11/5/45–1/14/46, Princeton.

to the honour . . . : 3/30/36, Minnesota.

altogether ungracious dishabille . . . : To Havens, 10/10/39, Johns Hopkins.

a lousy lecturer . . . : Keeley, interview, 5/77.

the armchair method . . . : Tate to RPB, 10/8/42, Princeton.

was "most gratifying" . . . : To the chairman of the Committee on the CAP, 5/5/42, Princeton Tate.

Senator from Maine . . . : Schwartz to RPB, 8/25/34, 9/16/43, Princeton.

never talked about . . . : 2/25/41, Yale.

207   from levelling down . . . : Barbara Long, 2/12/58, Princeton.

have ever encountered . . . : To the author, 8/76.

208   the symbol made . . . : HA II, 119.

and articulate fancy . . . : To the author, 9/13/76.

but fascinating mumble-from-notes . . . : Robert Kent to the author (on RPB's J. W. Beach lecture at Minnesota, early 1960s), 7/25/77.

Northrop Frye remembered . . . : To RPB, 2/5/60, Princeton.

sort of prospectus . . . : To Palmer, 2/18/43, PP.

Blackmur moral speech . . . : Keeley, interview, 5/77.

anarchy in him . . . : Green notebook, 11/12/40, Princeton.

which is sin . . . : The same, 11/13/40.

me too much . . . : The same [ca. 11/40].

209   off against another . . . : To the author, 2/16/77.

was "by osmosis" . . . : Quigg to the author, 1/18/77.

shortens my audience . . . Green notebook, 11/18/40, Princeton.

noses into him . . . : Fuller and Putnam.

210   most necessary order . . . : To Newton P. Stallknecht, 12/17/58, Princeton.

in practical charades . . . : Green notebook, Princeton.

in the Lebanon . . . : "Toward a Modus Vivendi," *Lion and the Honeycomb*, p. 4.

8. A Lion in the Path

211   "at home" nights . . . : Eileen Simpson, interview 8/3/76, and to the author, 9/12/78.

complicated an experience . . . : John Haffenden, "Berryman in the Forties," *New Review*, Oct., Nov. 1976. Citations of Berryman come from these articles, unless otherwise noted.

most devoted admirers . . . : Florence Codman to RPB, 4/26/36, Princeton.

a good teacher . . . : To RPB, 4/6/43, Princeton.

instructorship at Princeton . . . : RPB to Berryman, 10/7/43 and 10/9/43, Minnesota.

simple as fingers . . . : RPB to Berryman, 10/12/43, Minnesota.

of the piece . . . : RPB to Berryman, 10/7/43, Minnesota.

in Creative Writing . . . : Dodds to RPB, 4/15/46, Princeton.

Israel from Cambridge . . . To RPB, n.d., Princeton.

212   a dreary success . . . : To George Anthony Palmer, 4/9/51, Harvard.

the irate proprietor . . . : To the author, 10/4/76.

in its inception . . . : Quoted in Robert Giroux's preface to Berryman's *The Freedom of the Poet*, New York, 1976.

213   talked about them . . . : Edmund L. Keeley, interview, 5/77.

the first person . . . : Berryman in his preface to *The Dream Songs*.

had been deprived . . . : "Anni Mirabiles," *A Primer of Ignorance*, p. 33.

belly growing stout . . . : Codman to the author, 2/12/77.

old simple give-and-take . . . : To the author, 11/26/76.

dust and ashes . . . : To Sir Frederick Pollock, 6/27/19.

can have ideas . . . : Quoted in Schwartz to RPB, 10/30/42, Princeton.

of the actual . . . : To RPB, 11/30/42, Princeton.

seem absolutely impinging . . . : RPB to Palmer, 12/7/41 (on hearing the news of Pearl Harbor), PP.

like a sunrise . . . : Green notebook, 11/18/40, Princeton.

214   his poetic soul . . . : Keeley, interview, 5/77.

to a Jeffrey . . . : To the author, 9/18/76.

is also true . . . : "Anni Mirabiles," p. 41.

our own children . . . : "Ara Coeli and Campidoglio," *Primer of Ignorance*, p. 113.

in its transformations . . . : The same, p. 119.

teaching in universities . . . : "The State of American Writing, 1948: Seven Questions," *Partisan Review* 15 (1948), 855, 861–65.

that of isolation . . . : To Palmer, 10/8/22, PP.

of a substance . . . : HA I, "Return," 3.

215   only two decimations . . . : "Anni Mirabiles," p. 26.

for every dispute . . . : HA I, "Henry Adams and Foreign Policy," 52.

remedy the failure . . . : The same, p. 59.

of trying again . . . : The same, p. 96.

is describing it . . . : To the author, 9/18/76.

conditions of society . . . : IFAS memorandum, 3/12/45, IFAS Archives.

and the arts . . . : RPB, "A New Criticism" (lecture at Johns Hopkins), 4/15/48.

took appreciative notice . . . : 26 Apr. 1948.

an *aesthetic* experience . . . : "State of American Writing," p. 865.

deform our culture . . . : The same, p. 861.

216   than crowns experience . . . : HA II, "Indian Summer," 116.

the modern mind . . . : Ruth Nanda Anshen, ed. of series of books on "Religious Perspectives," to RPB, 1/6/60; RPB to Anshen, 3/7/60, Princeton.

and no man . . . : "Anni Mirabiles," p. 74.

and the Moha . . . : To John W. Aldridge, 5/27/52, in Aldridge's possession.

majesty and obliviousness . . . : Aldridge to the author, 2/19/77.

217   the wrong way . . . : "The King over the Water," *Princeton University Library Chronicle* 9 (1948), 127.

look at it . . . : "For a Second Look," *Kenyon Review* 11 (1949), 8.

the artist himself . . . : "State of American Writing" p. 861.

society really are . . . : The same, p. 863.

area of knowledge . . . : IFAS memo, 3/9/45, IFAS.

and into Princeton . . . : "Comments on Blackmur's 'Two Proposals for the Advance of Integration of Knowledge,' " 1/12/44, IFAS.

rather than tamp . . . : The same, 3/12/45, IFAS.

action and judgment . . . : The same, 3/23/45, IFAS.

and its unity . . . : The same, 3/9/45, IFAS.

and impossible style . . . : Robie Macauley, review of *A Primer of Ignorance* in *New York Times Book Review*, 12 Feb. 1967, p. 5.

218   It's extremely interesting . . . : Johns Hopkins Conference, 4/14/48, Box 35, folder 4, Princeton.

understand—the creator . . . : At Princeton, 5/27–5/28/44, Box 35, folder 3, Princeton.

of the particular . . . : To Robert Spiller, 3/2/46, Pennsylvania.

late evenings now . . . : 9/14/44, RFA.

and monetary policy . . . : *New Criticism in the United States*, p. 98.

thick as thieves . . . : Interview, 12/75.

my affairs prosper . . . : 5/9/45, PP.

219   the Poetry Chair . . . : RPB to Tate, 1/31/45, Princeton Tate.

to Bennington College . . . : To Tate, 2/9/45, Princeton Tate.

the close stone . . . : RPB to George Havens, 11/27/44, Johns Hopkins.

for another year . . . : To David H. Stevens, 2/5/45, IFAS.

like Richard Blackmur . . . : The same.

in literary criticism . . . : 4/24/45, RFA.

the necessary funds . . . : To Frank Aydelotte, Director of IFAS, 4/16/45, RFA.

said Alfred Kazin . . . : To the author, 12/76.

postponed too long . . . : 3/29/45, RFA.

all good Americans . . . : To Rob Darrell, 8/12/36, DP.

was no question . . . : To Edward D'Arms and John Marshall, 2/6/52, RFA.

Europe, Marshall observed . . . : Rockefeller Foundation memo, 4/4/52, RFA.

of anima semplicetta . . . : To Pat and Bob Hartle, 9/17/52, in Mrs. Pat Eden's possession.

records in Italian . . . : RPB to Darrell, 5/4/52, DP.

unfamiliarity with German . . . : *The Armed Vision* (1952), p. 260.

220   other than English . . . : To the author, 9/13/76.

my rightful language . . . : To Rizzardi, 2/3/61, Princeton.

figured as "Maestro" . . . : Alfredo Rizzardi to RPB, 9/29/53, 4/29/60, Princeton.

of Italian grammar . . . : RPB to Sergio Perosa, 11/28/58, Princeton.

than the T.L.S. . . . : To Catharine Carver, 12/20/54, HBP.

in my spirit . . . : To Carver, 9/3/52, HBP.

mountains made me . . . : To the Hartles, 9/17/52.

loss of mystery . . . : RPB to D'Arms, 12/29/52, RFA.

translator presented him . . . : Emilio Scarlatti in preface to RPB's "Introduzione alla Mostra del Libro Americano" (Bologna, Oct. 1952).

am an Italian . . . : To Darrell, 9/27/53, DP.

than he did . . . : To Carver, 9/3/52, HBP.

on the roadside . . . : To the Hartles, 9/17/52.

you feel free . . . : The same.

221 of the motorcycles . . . : The same.

possible without virtue . . . : "Anni Mirabiles," p. 74.

Bologna to Salzburg . . . : RPB to Darrell, 9/27/53, DP; to Tate, 8/1/53, Princeton Tate.

summer explaining Blackmur . . . : Cone to the author, 6/21/77.

week or two . . . : 5/7/54, RFA.

on Henry James . . . : Interview, 12/75.

dollars in debt . . . : RPB to Darrell, 9/27/53, DP.

to travel abroad . . . : Interview, 5/77.

hotels and restaurants . . . : D'Arms's diary, 7/30/53, RFA.

know not when . . . : To Marjorie Palmer, 12/16/55, PP.

in the Dogana's . . . : To Pat Hartle, 1/26/57.

222 a "communal relationship" . . . : To Franklin Reeve, 5/28/59, Princeton.

his sumptuous hotel . . . : Items on Hotel Amzoo from Box 59, folder 6, Princeton.

afternoons at Nido's . . . : Robert Penn Warren and Eleanor Clark, interview, 3/78; Albert Erskine to the author, 3/28/78.

have been Modena . . . : 10/9/59, Princeton.

took for me . . . : To Parker Taylor (*Art News Annual*), 2/25/59, Princeton.

he added Japan . . . : Invited to participate in seminar at Nagano by State Dept., 2/28/56, responded, 6/1/56 (U.S. File, Princeton).

on an elephant . . . : RPB to John Hartle [summer 1956], in Mrs. Pat Eden's possession.

add another thousand . . . : As earlier, 1/19/53, when "travel and living expenses exceeded his original estimate" (RFA).

patronized, and was . . . : Stow Persons to the author, 12/15/77.

found good ears . . . : To Aldridge, 7/7/51, in Aldridge's possession.

the *London Times* . . . : 16 Jan. 1955, p. 5.

it were true . . . : To Frank Fetter in Surrey, 2/4/55, Princeton.

up your name . . . : To Darrell, 11/2/44, DP.

in this country . . . : RPB to Havens, 11/27/44, Johns Hopkins.

perfection of work . . . : "The American Literary Expatriate," *Lion and the Honeycomb*, p. 75.

223 new intellectual proletariat . . . : RPB, note appended to papers on USIS and "The Literary Scene," RFA.

the intellectual enterprise . . . : Rockefeller Foundation memo, 4/4/52, RFA.

hardly ever why . . . : To George Anthony Palmer, 11/22/44, PP.

have yet taken . . . : The same.

as a whole . . . : "The Anthropology of Leading Ideas," IFAS.

their underlying sameness . . . : Colin Franklin (Routledge) to RPB, 8/11/60, Princeton.

his triangulating point . . . : RPB to Marshall, 6/27/55, Princeton; notes for his project in Box 32, folder 30, Princeton.

224 a fresh voice . . . : HA II, 32.

employ that power . . . : IFAS memo, 3/23/45, IFAS.

all my life . . . : To Darrell, 7/10/37, DP.

yet probably visionary . . . : 8/13/45, IFAS. RPB gives genesis of his scheme in
  IFAS memo, 4/27/44.

to Jay Laughlin . . . : 10/23/39, NDA.

I had lost . . . : "Ara Coeli and Campidoglio," p. 109.

our intended reach . . . : Memo, RPB and Lucius Wilmerding, 3/21/46, in the
  author's possession.

a "propitious time" . . . : Pell to Wilmerding, 4/12/46, in possession of the
  author; Julian Boyd to Charles Trynan (Pell's lawyer), 8/24/45, IFAS
  Archives.

225 argument of policy . . . : RPB to J. Kerker Quinn (*Accent*), 3/14/44, Illinois.

close, and closer . . . : 3/8/44, RFA.

than advocating views . . . : Paraphrasing Wilmerding to RPB, Boyd, and
  Walter Stewart, 11/13/46, in the author's possession.

of its readers . . . : IFAS memo, 4/27/44 IFAS; Rockefeller Foundation report,
  3/8/44.

the ancient way . . . : To RPB, Boyd, and Stewart, 11/13/46.

laceration from showing . . . : AMN, p. 99.

226 more generous editors . . . : To Brooks and Warren, 3/9/42, Yale.

in the world . . . : Lambert Davis to RPB, 11/23/46, HBP.

thousand a year . . . : Doris R. Levine (who ran the office when the *H&H*
  moved to NYC) to RPB, 3/25/42, Princeton.

and Florida combined . . . : Erskine to Tate, 3/29/39, Yale.

his letters said . . . : E.g., to Warren, 3/14/42, Yale.

he should be . . . : "Reflections of Toynbee," *A Primer of Ignorance*, p. 149.

to gather statistics . . . : RPB to Lambert Davis (formerly of *Virginia Quarterly
  Review*), 3/16/42 HBP; Davis to RPB, 3/25/42, HBP; RPB to Quinn,
  3/14/44, Illinois.

227 into the night . . . : Boyd to H. L. Mencken, 4/17/46, Seeley G. Mudd MS
  Library, Princeton.

followed Lucius' precedent . . . : Boyd to Stewart, 9/18/46, Mudd.

go any further . . . : Quoted in Boyd to Stewart, 6/11/46, Mudd.

and intelligent magazine . . . : To Boyd, 4/1/46, Mudd.

a smaller audience . . . : Boyd to Mencken, 3/29/46, Mudd.

to forget it . . . : Boyd to the author, 1/20/77. The lunch for Mencken was held
  in Princeton 6/3/46.

of the mind . . . : "Between the Numen and the Moha," *Lion and the
  Honeycomb*, p. 299.

discussion have failed . . . : Boyd to Stewart, 6/11/46, Mudd.

sneered at Christianity . . . : Black notebook, 1/21/23, Princeton.

life without religion . . . : AMN, p. 82.

waste within us . . . : AMN, p. 108.

228 of his doubt . . . : "Ara Coeli and Campidoglio," p. 109.

on old purpose . . . : "Toward a Modus Vivendi," *Lion and the Honeycomb*,
  p. 25.

of early doom . . . : Quinn's phrase to RPB [3/44], Illinois.

importunate letters began . . . : E.g., 5/4/45, seeking subvention for *Sewanee*
  and *Partisan*, GFA.

of literary advance . . . : Rockefeller Foundation memo, 9/11/46, RFA.

to Richard's satisfaction . . . : RPB to Irving Kristol, 10/29/59, Princeton.

the new illiteracy . . . : "The Economy of the American Writer," *Lion and the Honeycomb*, p. 56.

population and education . . . : "Toward a Modus Vivendi," p. 27.

maintenance of standards . . . : Rockefeller Foundation report, 3/8/44, p. 8.

to John Marshall . . . : 1/22/41, RFA.

229 pray for you . . . : 9/22/55, Kenyon.

for Swiss publishers . . . : Elisabeth Schnack from Zurich to RPB, 10/21/54, Princeton.

use to literature . . . : E.g., to Randall Jarrell, 10/25/46, Princeton.

was "in order" . . . : Marshall to RPB, 7/17/46, RFA.

included pure wheat . . . : Rockefeller Foundation in-house document, 11/55, pp. 4–5, RFA.

spending its money . . . : RPB to Rockefeller Foundation, 9/18/46, RFA.

of final judgment . . . : CAP Report.

writer in America . . . : In-house memo, 5/18/46, RFA.

of his material . . . : RPB to Malcolm Cowley (quoting Tate to him), 4/27/34, Newberry.

a "hoitsy-toitsy" reply . . . : To Cowley, 11/18/46, Newberry.

230 believe, to you . . . : 11/4/46, Princeton.

to make money . . . : 11/12/46, Princeton.

a disagreeable necessity . . . : Quoting Adams to Lodge, 1881.

did not make . . . : 8/13/45, IFAS.

231 makes aspiration necessary . . . : HA II, 77.

Primer of Ignorance . . . 4/6/45, IFAS and RFA.

go with it . . . : To Marshall, 5/7/54, RFA.

thinking up recently . . . : To Carver, 5/7/54, HBP.

signed a contract . . . : 2/21/56, HBP.

I would do . . . : To J. H. McCallum, 9/19/57, HBP.

an unfinished ruin . . . : RPB's preface to *Eleven Essays in the European Novel*.

who will read . . . : To Marshall, 6/27/55, RFA.

the Rockefeller Foundation . . . : RPB to Marshall, 5/7/54, RFA.

thought becoming action . . . : 6/27/55, RFA.

anything but itself . . . : "The Everlasting Effort," p. 112.

232 the complete scholar-critic . . . : "The Lion and the Honeycomb," *Lion and the Honeycomb*, p. 183.

platitude of statement . . . : "The Critical Prefaces of Henry James," p. 244.

or underlying form . . . : "The Loose and Baggy Monsters of Henry James," p. 268.

editor at Harcourt . . . : To Carver, 8/24/54, HBP.

Essays in Institutions . . . : To Carver, 9/15/54, HBP.

evils without them . . . : From notes found among his books, 1979; probably dating from 1961, Princeton.

Letters and Society . . . : To Carver, 9/15/54, HBP.

life of Adams . . . : HA II, 72–73.

the American animal . . . : To William Phillips, 6/5/58, Rutgers.

in a dozen countries . . . : RPB to Wystan Curnow, 2/5/64 (reflecting his "research" of the fifties), Princeton.

they can do . . . : 7/14/55, Princeton.

233   he may devour . . . : "The Logos in the Catacomb," p. 87.

cannot be corrected . . . : To RPB, 10/20 and 10/30/42, Princeton.

of it, evangelical . . . : "A Burden for Critics," *Lion and the Honeycomb*,
p. 212.

opening before me . . . : 6/27/55, RFA.

Mangan likened him . . . : In "Matthew Arnold B_____, Man of Letters,"
Fantasy 3, no. 1, (1938), 28. In a later version of this poem Mangan changed
the title to "Matthew Arnold Doone," playing on Blackmuir, the author
of *Lorna Doone.*

with "that half-hero" . . . : "Anni Mirabiles," p. 72.

has become moribund . . . : "RPB: The Later Phase," *The Widening Gyre*
(New Brunswick, N.J., 1963).

234   substitute for religion . . . : To Roy P. Basler, Associate Director of the Library
of Congress, 9/2/55, Princeton.

the year 1922 . . . : RPB to Ted Brown of McGill Univ. (5/23/55, Princeton),
where Blackmur's lecture of 10/28/55 makes a first version of the Library
of Congress lectures.

the literature itself . . . : "Anni Mirabiles," p. 67.

proud of it . . . : "Anni Mirabiles," p. 8.

on a man . . . : To the author, 9/24/76.

and fifty years . . . : "The Lion and the Honeycomb," p. 196.

his bedtime reading . . . : "Ara Coeli and Campidoglio," p. 122.

to the subject . . . : "The Swan in Zurich," *Primer of Ignorance*, p. 129.

of Margaux 1925 . . . : "Ara Coeli and Campidoglio," p. 106.

235   outskirts of Palermo . . . : The same, p. 108.

at home there . . . : "The Logos in the Catacomb," p. 103.

in his imagination . . . : "The American Literary Expatriate," p. 72.

of stairs between . . . : "The Logos in the Catacomb," p. 83.

passed among enemies . . . : "The Great Grasp of Unreason," p. 9.

made it necessary . . . : The same, p. 12.

236   his own wishes . . . : The same, p. 17.

freed from Reason . . . : "The Artist as Hero: A Disconsolate Chimera," *Lion
and the Honeycomb*, p. 47.

role at all . . . : HA I, "Five of Hearts," 16.

emperor to clown . . . : "The Logos and the Catacomb," p. 98.

of the mind . . . : Review of H. H. Watts's "The Artifice of Our Century," a
MS submitted to the Univ. of Michigan Press; RPB to E. Watkins,
12/17/57, Princeton.

his title wrong . . . : E. E. Hamer to RPB, 9/5/57, RPB to Hamer, 9/19/57,
Library of Congress.

name I know . . . : "Between the Numen and the Moha," pp. 293–94.

Richard's friend Oppenheimer . . . : "Well, he met Bob, I think, first in
Cambridge" (Bernard Bandler, interview, 3/77).

237   William Jennings Bryan . . . : To Hans Nathan, 3/17/59, Princeton.

if I say . . . : "Humanism and Symbolic Imagination," *Lion and the Honeycomb*, p. 152.

and the Japanese . . . : The same, p. 153; "The Lion and the Honeycomb,"
p. 188.

speak of friends . . . : "The Lion and the Honeycomb," p. 195; "Anni Mirabiles," p. 33.
238 yet become real . . . : "Ara Coeli and Campidoglio," p. 104.
we call miracle . . . : The same, pp. 107, 109; "Reflections of Toynbee," p. 147.
a green study . . . : "Ara Coeli," pp. 109, 110; "Reflections," pp. 148, 149.
239 in his bones . . . : Inserted in notebook for "Anni Mirabiles" lectures, Box 30, folder 23, Princeton.
of administrative order . . . : "Ara Coeli in Campidoglio," p. 115.
beat of history . . . : The same, p. 126.

9. Through the Ashes of this Chance

240 out at Princeton . . . : To Morton Zabel, 3/20/48, *Letters of Louise Bogan*, p. 260.
to save himself . . . : Fiedler to the author, 9/13/76.
excess of charity . . . : Hyman, *Armed Vision*, p. 244.
together every day . . . : John Marshall to the author, 12/20/75.
241 reference to Blackmur . . . : To D. H. Stevens, 2/5/45, RFA.
defeat of Germany . . . : 1/31/45; RPB to Allen Tate, 2/9/45, Princeton Tate.
were good coin . . . : Green notebook, 11/5/45–1/14/46, Box 32, folder 30, Princeton.
of the world . . . : Fuller and Putnam to RPB, n.d., Princeton.
make everything plain . . . : Green notebook, p. 28 (2/1/50).
242 use it up . . . : Irving Howe to the author, 1/22/77.
forgotten it all . . . : Frederick Buechner to the author, 10/5/76.
happens in response . . . : Green notebook.
a final review . . . : D'Arms memo, 2/25/51, RFA.
parent of despair . . . : Green notebook, 11/14/40.
243 a public lecture . . . : RPB to J. Kerker Quinn, 5/17/43, Illinois.
professor at Princeton . . . : To the author, 8/12/76 (telephone); Willard Thorp, interview, 7/76; G. E. Bentley, interview, 8/76; Harold Dodds to the author, summer 1976.
244 draw on together . . . : Green notebook, inserted pages, n.d.
as an infant . . . : To the author, 6/15/78.
honey to flow . . . : Green notebook, inserted pp.
attractive to men . . . : E. L. Keeley, interview, 5/77.
livelier Slater Brown . . . : Mangan to George Anthony Palmer, 4/9/51, Harvard.
potatoes to peel . . . : Tessa Horton to the author, 7/7/78; Malcolm Cowley to the author, 4/1/78.
245 Ingmar Bergman film . . . : Eileen Simpson, interview, 8/3/76.
been for years . . . : Simpson to the author, 9/12/78.
best tiger rodomontade . . . : RPB to Palmer, 2/18/43, PP.
his own chop . . . : Simpson, interview, 8/3/76.
contemned or dreaded . . . : Green notebook, p. 28, (1950).
is no escape . . . : Green notebook, 11/5/45–1/14/46.
more than that . . . : To Lambert Davis, 8/17/42, HBP.
'crowd' had children . . . : Pat Eden to the author, 8/25/77.

him different ways . . . : Joan Jurow to the author, 10/21/77.
246 best of all . . . : To John Holmes, 12/5/57, Princeton.
Human and tender . . . : Eden to the author, 7/20/78.
you're very beautiful . . . : Pattee, interview, 10/76.
measured the fault . . . : "Beauty out of Place: Flaubert's *Madame Bovary*,"
    Eleven Essays in the European Novel, p. 71.
a long letter . . . : [Post 1949], Princeton.
248 have left her . . . : Simpson, interview, 8/3/76; Palmer, interview, 3/76.
for that woman . . . : Keeley, interview, 5/77.
her his books . . . : RPB to Catharine Carver, 9/16/52, HBP.
I know nothing . . . : 11/26/57, PP.
a former wife . . . : 1/26/53, Yale.
attracting young men . . . : Interview, 9/76.
with the man . . . : Interview, 5/77.
very good friend . . . : Charles Rosen to the author, 10/17/77.
a *nasty* man . . . : George Orrok, interview, 3/77.
249 and married again . . . : Palmer, interview, 3/76.
man twenty years . . . : Horton, interview, 9/76.
so little *joy* . . . : Eden to the author, 8/25/77.
she destroyed it . . . : Horton, interview, 9/76.
succes d'estime . . . : Robert Fitzgerald to the author, 6/29/78.
if not sounder . . . : To Rob Darrell, 4/29/35, DP.
the ten books . . . : To Frances Steloff (Gotham Book Mart) on the verso of
    her inquiry of 5/23/42, Berg Collection, New York Public Library.
Dusty the Drifter . . . : To Palmer, 2/18/43, PP.
most 'important' book   . . . : To Carver, 5/7/54, HBP. The allusion is to *The*
    Lion and the Honeycomb, which RPB ranks just below the Adams and
    Dostoevsky.
then sugar off . . . : To Quinn, 3/2/46, Illinois.
was nearly finished . . . : To Quinn, 6/1/43, 3/2/46, Illinois; to J. C. Ransom,
    5/23/51, Kenyon.
book on Joyce . . . : To Carver, 5/7/54, HBP.
the devil creates . . . : "*Crime and Punishment*: Murder in Your Own Room,"
    Eleven Essays, p. 136.
of great proverbs . . . : Delmore Schwartz to RPB, 3/16/43, Princeton.
250 talking to himself . . . : A. F. Schwarz to the author, 11/28/76.
This unmeditated performance . . . : Eden to the author, n.d.; F. D. Reeve,
    Princeton Alumni Weekly tribute to RPB, 4 May 1965, p. 9.
was never better . . . : J. W. Aldridge to the author, 2/19/77.
Tuesday night explorations . . . : R. J. Kaufmann to the author, 10/15/76.
his supreme moment . . . : E. D. H. Johnson, interview, 5/77.
library of Alexandria . . . : To the author, 12/1/76.
the little magazines . . . : Voluminous correspondence regarding publication at
    Kenyon and Illinois (*Accent*).
a former student . . . : Reeve at Wesleyan.
qualities of Propertius . . . : 9/23/33, Princeton.
with Latin pronunciation . . . : Box 33, folder 2, Princeton.
to read Maritain . . . : *Humanisme intégral*, 1936, from which RPB quotes
    extensively in French, Box 31, folder 28, Princeton.

perceptions of reality . . . : The Whorf-Sapir hypothesis. RPB to Davis wants Sapir's *Language*, 2/4/42, HBP.

point them out . . . : E.g., Edmund Wilson (Mary McCarthy to the author, 2/1/77); René Wellek, "R. P. Blackmur Re-Examined," *Southern Review* 7 (1971), 825–45.

251 into the texture . . . : *"The Idiot*: A Rage of Goodness," *Eleven Essays*, pp. 159–60.

or deliberate obfuscation . . . : Wellek, "Blackmur Re-Examined," p. 839.

to his remarks . . . : Schwarz to the author, 11/28/76.

of my life . . . : Interview, 5/77.

Bogan called it . . . : To Wilson, 9/23/28, *Letters*, p. 174.

252 functions is tragic . . . : "A Critic's Job of Work," *Language as Gesture*, p. 376.

own best antonym . . . : "On Sickness of Office," Princeton.

than catching them . . . : To the author, 1/11/77.

circles of qualification . . . : Memo, 4/14/31, HBP.

children under 18 . . . : To Robert Scher (*March Monthly*), 1/18/60, Princeton.

of one syllable . . . : To Jay Laughlin, 9/30/41, n.d., NDA; to Davis, 4/23/42, HBP.

along well enough . . . : To Robert Spiller, 7/24/46, 9/4/46, Pennsylvania.

of that dialogue . . . : Kaufmann to the author, 10/15/76.

253 nothing but distrust . . . : AMN, p. 45 (1/13/33), Princeton.

in all directions . . . : RPB to Laughlin, 6/21/40, NDA.

are has come . . . : Walter Sutton, *Modern American Criticism* (Englewood Cliffs, N.J., 1963), p. 141.

representative than exemplary . . . : "The Politics of Human Power," *Lion and the Honeycomb*, p. 38.

six best novels . . . : To Davis, 7/31/42, 8/17/42, HBP.

what's happening now . . . : Interview, 5/77.

254 fiction he liked . . . : To Palmer, 7/28/49, PP; to Northrop Frye, 6/9/60, Princeton.

clean on that . . . : W. B. Goodman to the author, 3/23/79.

of many years . . . : W. B. Goodman to J. H. McCallum, 4/8/63, HBP.

in doing so . . . : "Anni Mirabiles," *Primer of Ignorance*, p. 29.

your own personality . . . : " *Madame Bovary*," p. 49.

than he intended . . . : To Palmer, 7/17/22, PP.

form of apprehension . . . : "The Craft of Herman Melville: A Putative Statement," *Lion and the Honeycomb*, p. 132.

more precious experience . . . : To Darrell, 8/28/28, DP.

and childhood piety . . . : "Politics of Human Power," p. 34.

in our time . . . : "The Jew in Search of a Son: Joyce's *Ulysses*," *Eleven Essays*, p. 27.

255 crisis of culture . . . : "Magazine Chronicle," *Partisan Review* 16 (1949), 416–27.

critic as prophet . . . : R. W. B. Lewis, quoted in Richard Foster, *The New Romantics* (Bloomington, Ind., 1962), p. 104 (and pp. 84–85, 91, 103).

ethics in action . . . : "Between the Numen and the Moha," *Lion and the Honeycomb*, p. 289.

somewhat shamefaced theologian . . . : Wellek, "Blackmur Re-Examined," p. 841.

is Sherry Mangan's . . . : To Palmer, 4/9/51, Harvard.

the famous critic . . . : James Harrison to the author, 2/18/78.

jack-in-the-pulpit . . . : To Katharine White, 1/23/58, Bryn Mawr College.

cannot, and why . . . : Quoted in Peter Brown, *Augustine of Hippo* (London, 1969), p. 143.

256 for a seminar . . . : Green notebook, 2/3/50.

ghost on it . . . : Interview, 5/77.

Bernard Bandler's opinion . . . : Interview, 3/77.

puns in Latin . . . : F. J. Friend-Pereira from Calcutta, 4/15/57, calls his attention to misspelling of Latin tags in *The Lion and the Honeycomb*; RPB, responding, 7/18/57, confesses "a trick that failed," Princeton.

of our heralds . . . : Recommending Frederic Prokosch to the Bollingen Foundation, 5/23/55, Princeton.

Holmes I hold . . . : To K. W. Thompson at the Rockefeller Foundation, 10/16/58, Princeton.

257 and personal experience . . . : "Enlarging the Change: The Princeton Seminars in Literary Criticism 1949–1951," prepared by Fitzgerald for the Rockefeller Foundation.

canceled the contract . . . : Johnson, interview, 5/77.

law of parsimony . . . : "For a Second Look," *Kenyon Review* 11 (1949), 10.

their own faces . . . : Preface to *Eleven Essays*.

he bites off . . . : Quoted in "The Letters of Marian Adams," *Expense of Greatness*, p. 249.

moment of truth . . . : Keeley, interview, 5/77.

Leslie Fiedler remembered . . . : To the author, 9/13/76.

likes of them . . . : To Chadbourne Gilpatrick, Chairman of the Villa Serbellone Committee, 10/4/62, Princeton.

drank too much . . . : Fiedler to the author, 9/13/76.

258 supplied the answers . . . : Thorp, interview, 7/76.

Blackmur course, ever . . . : Keeley, interview, 5/77.

to John Marshall . . . : E.g., RPB to Marshall, 11/15/48, RFA; and Francis Fergusson to the author, 2/13/77; Marshall, interview, 12/20/75.

critic like you . . . : Marshall reports this in a Rockefeller Foundation memo, 1/15/47, RFA.

how this worked . . . : Rockefeller Foundation report, ch. vi.

a three-year grant . . . : Awarded 2/18/49 (J. William Hess, Associate Director of RFA, to the author, 12/28/76).

259 discussion at meetings . . . : Fergusson to the author, 2/13/77.

to one side . . . : Joseph Frank, interview, 8/76; Ludmilla Turkevich to the author, 7/19/77.

something to say . . . : Fitzgerald report.

to a stand . . . : Discussion draws on RFA.

a full-dress report . . . : 10/51, RFA.

simply removed it . . . : To the author, 6/23/77.

The officers agreed . . . : 4/2/52 (Hess to the author, 12/28/76).

260 situation of today . . . : Memo, 4/2/52, RFA.

with his friends . . . : Princeton faculty tribute by E. T. Cone, A. S. Downer, and Keeley, *Princeton Alumni Weekly*, 4 May 1965, p. 7.

Britishers for you . . . : To Kaufmann, 10/25/63, Princeton.

sophisticated critical tradition . . . : Aldridge, *New York Times Book Review*,
  24 Aug. 1977, p. 26.
questions which Blackmur . . . : To the author, 3/7/77.
a Tory anarchist . . . : V. S. Pritchett to the author, 2/27/77.
managed to do . . . : To the author, 8/76.
took his place . . . : RPB to Carver, 9/16/52, HBP.
Rockefeller and democracy . . . : Frye to RPB, 1/14/60, Princeton.
nearly so successful . . . : Quoted by D'Arms in 1/26/54 memo, RFA.
261 organization and leadership . . . : 2/18/54 memo, RFA.
all possible deals . . . : A. Alvarez, "W. H. Auden A Memoir," *American
  Review 23: The Magazine of New Writing*, ed. Theodore Solotaroff
  (Toronto, New York, and London, 1975), pp. 144–56.
R.P.B. as "chairman" . . . : To the author, 12/7/77.
place with Dick . . . : Darrell to the author, 7/24/77.
own exquisite sake . . . : Pritchett to the author, 2/27/77.
James Burnham's view . . . : 10/31/77 to the author.
262 the next morning . . . : To the author, 7/6/77.
highbrow Father Christmas . . . : "Richard Palmer Blackmur (1904–1965),"
  The Review, 1967; *Beyond All This Fiddle* (New York, 1969), pp. 274–78.
his retractile claws . . . : To the author, 7/2/76.
He's a cat! . . . : Quoted in McCarthy to the author, 2/1/77.
kid around with . . . : Clement Greenberg to the author, 7/10/76.
popularity decently incomplete . . . : Fitzgerald report.
the Château Margaux . . . : Leslie Westoff to the author, 6/8/77.
black extravagant strain . . . : To Marshall, 1/23/53, RFA.
be made actual . . . : To Davis, asking payment for his revision of John
  Walcott's novel, 6/15/42, HBP.
a huffy letter . . . : 4/29/58, Princeton.
speak for money . . . : To G. A. Palmer (and Marcia), 3/27/48, PP.
in the Path . . . : To Robert G. Elliott at Ohio State Univ., 11/7/58, Princeton.
actually to give . . . : To Newton P. Stallknecht at Indiana Univ., 2/10/58,
  Princeton.
263 an itinerant huckster . . . : Lecture schedule for 1958 in Box 46, folder 2,
  Princeton.
have ever engaged . . . : To the reprint publisher Peter Smith, 12/10/59,
  Princeton.
weeks in Indiana . . . : To G. A. Palmer (and Phoebe), 6/29/58, PP.
got nothing done . . . : To Pat and Bob Hartle, 7/29/52, in Pat Eden's
  possession.
said one critic . . . : William Wasserman, *The Time of "The Dial*," p. 138.
form of hell . . . : RPB to Carver, 8/26/54, HBP.
the Red Sea . . . : 8/3/54, RFA.
mitigations in company . . . : To Carver, 8/26/54, HBP.
an ironic sensibility . . . : Green notebook, 11/13/40; RPB to Ransom, 5/30/58,
  Kenyon; RPB to D. C. Allen, 6/22/58, Johns Hopkins.
Lorca and Donne . . . : Sergio Perosa to the author, 7/19/77; RPB to Michael
  Burr, 1/22/64, Princeton.
than the audience . . . : Howard Nemerov to the author, 1/20/77.
problems of evaluation . . . : Introduction to "The School of Letters IU

Twentieth Anniversary 1968" (Bloomington, 1968).

seedy Bloomington bar . . . : Phillip Leininger to the author, 12/7/76.

264   man he was . . . : To the author, 9/13/76.

of perpetual behindedness . . . : RPB to Palmer, 3/29/59, PP.

fegato, fegato, fegato . . . : To William Arrowsmith, 5/5/59, Princeton.

the wretched liver . . . : To William Van O'Connor, 5/13/59, Syracuse; to Robie
    Macauley, 10/22/63, Kenyon.

fever and chills . . . : Marshall diary, 2/23/53, and memo, 2/27/53, RFA.

much except sleep . . . : To Tate, 8/1/53, Princeton Tate.

found him "transformed" . . . : Simpson, interview, 8/76.

to keep up . . . : RPB to Quinn, 3/5/54, Illinois.

hair is white . . . : Conflating James V. Baker (discussing the New Criticism,
    summer 1959, Box 61, folder 1, Princeton) and Irving Howe (to the
    author, 1/22/77).

his liver palpitate . . . : Simpson, interview, 8/76.

liver revealed sarcoidosis . . . : Marvin Blumenthal, Blackmur's physician,
    interview, 5/77.

that he tried . . . : Fitzgerald to the author, 6/29/78.

265   for sinus operations . . . : RPB to Tate, 6/26/39, Princeton Tate; to Laughlin,
    12/6/39, NDA; to John Berryman, 3/11/40, Minnesota; Ranson to RPB,
    2/4/39, Kenyon; Green notebook, 11/14/40; Elva de Pue Matthews to
    RPB, 4/19/39, Princeton.

all his bills . . . : Box 58, folder 3, Princeton.

dared long enough . . . : "The Artist as Hero: A Disconsolate Chimera,"
    Lion and the Honeycomb, p. 46.

was always there . . . : "The Lord of Small Counterpositions: Mann's *The
    Magic Mountain*," *Eleven Essays*, p. 80.

Paraphrasing a line . . . : "Crime and Punishment," p. 129.

called the individual . . . : Green notebook, 1950.

turn for strength . . . : "The Artist as Hero," p. 45.

use of him . . . : Green notebook, 1950.

to be used . . . : To Michele Murray, 8/8/58, Princeton.

ourselves a conscience . . . : "The Artist as Hero," pp. 45–46.

as his touchstones . . . : Schwarz to the author, 11/28/78.

to do with . . . : "The Brothers Karamazov," *Eleven Essays*, p. 215.

266   and air conditioning . . . : To O'Connor, 5/13/59, Syracuse.

friend to himself . . . : His characterization of Conrad Aiken's uncle Alfred
    Potter, AMN, pp. 71–72.

old bull elephants . . . : *Second Flowering*, p. 247.

Helen to herself . . . : Palmer, interview, 3/76; Fergusson, interview, 8/1/76;
    Simpson, interview, 8/3/76.

People gossiped endlessly . . . : Eden to the author, 8/25/77.

said Ed Cone . . . : To the author, 6/21/77.

half a year . . . : RPB to Schwartz, 1/26/53, Yale. Simpson, interview, 8/3/76.

He lived alone . . . : RPB to the Hartles, 9/17/52; Alfredo Rizzardi, interview
    (telephone), 4/79; Margot Cutter to the author, 3/2/79.

Italian nature-worshipping palazzo . . . : RPB to the Hartles, 9/17/52.

for the year . . . : To Carver, 9/3/52, HBP.

all his mail . . . : To Tate, 8/1/53, Princeton Tate.

parties Margot gave . . . : RPB to Carver, 9/16/52, HBP.

267   liver that year . . . : To the author, 9/13/76.

had refused him . . . : Interview, 8/9/77.

Richard hung on . . . : Fergusson, interview, 8/1/76.

been romantically happy . . . : Pritchett to the author, 2/27/77.

planted this garden . . . : To his former student Irving A. Portner, 2/3/60,
    Princeton; Betty Blackmur to the author, 10/27/76.

wanted opium poppy . . . : To Alvarez, 6/4/59, 3/7/60, Princeton; to Perosa,
    11/12/58, Princeton.

what it means . . . : To Carver, 9/15/54, HBP.

it as Italian . . . : To the author, 1/3/78.

very badly indeed . . . : Fiedler to the author, 9/13/76.

Francis Fergusson remembered . . . : Interview, 8/1/76.

268   said Rob Darrell . . . : To the author, 7/24/77.

faithful to Helen . . . : Interview, 3/76; Eden to the author, 7/20/77.

to run down . . . : Greenberg to the author, 7/10/76.

weariness of self-self-self . . . : After J. C. Levenson's *Adams*, pp. 208, 219, 221.

Park Lane Hotel . . . : "Richard Palmer Blackmur," *The Review*, p. 23.

Mike Keeley remembered . . . : Interview, 5/77.

about Lambert Strether . . . : Taped broadcast, 1956, Univ. of Massachusetts.

10. The Critic as Artist

269   and dies alone . . . : Green notebook, Princeton.

with St. Augustine . . . : Quoted in Louisa Thoron to RPB, 8/8/44, Harvard;
    HA III, 26.

the true city . . . : HA III, 49.

of his emotion . . . : *"The Possessed*: In the Birdcage," *Eleven Essays in the
    European Novel*, p. 165. . .

270   a single mourner . . . : Betty Blackmur (to the author, 5/4/77).

to ignominious failure . . . : Edgar M. Gemmell to the author, 6/28/77;
    E. D. H. Johnson, interview, 5/77.

gesture of being . . . : 10/22/41, DP.

form and meaning . . . : "A Critic's Job of Work," *Language as Gesture*, p. 372.

feet as form . . . : To Jay Laughlin, 10/12/39, NDA.

perfected his style . . . : Taped radio broadcast, 1956, Massachusetts.

concern with LIFE . . . : Florence Codman on the critics to RPB, 6/17/36,
    Princeton.

of the day . . . : Codman to RPB, 2/13/36, Princeton.

and philosophical context . . . : A. Anikst, "Twentieth-Century American
    Literature: A Soviet View" (Moscow, 1976), p. 192.

271   levers, and wheels . . . : *On Native Grounds* (1942), p. 440.

of "leisure-class culture" . . . : "Inheritance Tax," *New Republic*, 20 Apr. 1932,
    pp. 278–79.

and politics cross . . . : Following the citation he wrote for Irving Howe,
    honored by the National Institute of Arts and Letters (RPB to Felicia
    Geffen, 4/20/60, Archives of the American Academy and Institute of Arts
    and Letters, New York).

effect on society . . . : "A Feather-Bed for Critics," *Language as Gesture*, p. 412.

severe and scrupulous . . . : Morton D. Zabel's review of *The Double Agent* in
New York Herald Tribune, 10 May 1936.

But Jesus! Pound! . . . : N.d., *H&H* Archives, Yale.

the single word . . . : W. T. Scott's review of *Language as Gesture* in *Saturday
Review*, 21 Mar. 1953.

his "surgical skill" . . . : Will Wharton's review of *Language as Gesture* in
St. Louis Post-Dispatch, 15 Feb. 1953.

a master anatomist . . . : Milton Rugoff's review of *Language as Gesture* in
New York Herald Tribune, 28 Dec. 1952.

gifts of communication . . . : Edward Fiess's review of *Language as Gesture* in
New Leader, 30 Mar. 1953.

cramped and literal . . . : To Maxwell Perkins, 12/17/29, Scribner Collection,
Princeton (quoted in Carol K. Scholz's Pennsylvania dissertation on Aiken,
1977).

his fatal Cleopatra . . . : To RPB, 1/28/43, Princeton.

poetry we have . . . : Hyman, *Armed Vision*, p. 270.

than "brilliant elucidation" . . . : The same, p. 244.

272   to the poem . . . : "Examples of Wallace Stevens," *Double Agent*, p. 71.

is it lasting . . . : Handwritten pages in Box 36, folder 1, Princeton.

masterwork under consideration . . . : *New Republic*, 17 June 1936, p. 184.

the United States . . . : Responding to RPB's paper, "A New Criticism," Johns
Hopkins Symposium, 4/15/48, Box 35, folder 4, Princeton.

is inaccurate art . . . : "The Serious Artist," 1913.

pointed to Croce . . . : *New Criticism in the United States*, p. 3.

kind of criticism . . . : The same, p. 11.

all other matters . . . : The same, p. 30.

with the *how* . . . : To RPB, 11/22/41, Princeton.

but with poetry . . . : To the author, 9/10/76.

273   Wilson had failed . . . : To the author, 3/28/77.

in modern criticism . . . : Warren Carrier's review of *Language as Gesture* in
Western Review, summer 1953.

marvelous, Cowley said . . . : To the author, 7/2/76.

Tate called him . . . : Interview, 8/9/77.

matter of detail . . . : To Codman (quoted in Codman to RPB, 10/26/36,
Princeton).

of complete attention . . . : "The Craft of Herman Melville: A Putative
Statement," *Lion and the Honeycomb*, p. 132.

she says it . . . : To RPB, 10/8/36, Princeton.

life and death . . . : *Expense of Greatness*, p. 232.

you to intimacy . . . : *New Criticism*, p. 11.

reading; no more . . . : "The Method of Marianne Moore," *Double Agent*,
p. 141.

render this thing . . . : "Anni Mirabiles," *Primer of Ignorance*, p. 78.

Richards in 1929 . . . : *Practical Criticism* in *H&H* 3 (1929), 455.

apprehensible and impeculiar . . . : 4/12/23, PP.

274   a mutual understanding . . . : Notebook entitled "Topica," Princeton.

because of them . . . : "Examples of Wallace Stevens," p. 75.

poet of criticism . . . : Foster, *New Romantics*, p. 205.

were a poem . . . : To Lee Anderson, 8/3/42, Washington Univ.

in his criticism . . . : "A Conversation with Ian Hamilton," *American Poetry Review*, Sept./Oct. 1978, pp. 25–26.

art and literature . . . : *The Widening Gyre*, p. 247.

incanted into existence . . . : Foster, *New Romantics*, p. 204.

esprit de corps . . . : To RPB, 6/30/[60?] and n.d., Princeton.

its own meaning . . . : "Anni Mirabiles," p. 53.

275 artists—really artists . . . : To Georges Sand, 1869.

part of criticism . . . : "Anni Mirabiles," p. 79.

through that aperture . . . : *Lectures in Criticism*, p. 52.

to true greatness . . . : *Lectures in Criticism*, p. 125.

of the work . . . : Friedrich Schlegel, *Athenäum*, 1798.

276 means of creation . . . : "Anni Mirabiles," p. 14.

coming before it . . . : The same, p. 32.

juxtaposition of words . . . : 4/9/21, PP.

poets and novelists . . . : *New York Times Book Review*, 5 Feb. 1978, p. 9.

he applies it . . . : John Holmes's review of *The Double Agent* in *Boston Transcript*, 8 Aug. 1936.

can prose bear . . . : To RPB, 4/6/28, Princeton.

be proud of . . . : *Essays on Literature and Ideas* (London, 1963), pp. 145–55.

or a kangaroo . . . : Hayden Carruth, *Nation*, 10 Jan. 1953; anon. review of *Language as Gesture* in *Harper's*, Dec. 1952.

that actual life . . . : "Anni Mirabiles," p. 22.

more penetrating vision . . . : "Reflections of Toynbee, *Primer of Ignorance*, pp. 150, 153.

277 provisional and incomplete . . . : To Julian Sawyer, 7/27/34, Univ. of Iowa.

virtue of poetry . . . : To Wallace Stevens, 12/2/31, Huntington.

Barzun called him . . . : To the author, 10/5/76.

or anything else . . . "A Critic's Job of Work," pp. 375–76, 398–99, 381.

of every infatuation . . . : "Anni Mirabiles," p. 12.

surds of feeling . . . : The same, p. 42.

understand one another . . . : "Lord Tennyson's Scissors: 1912–1950," *Language as Gesture*, p. 428.

278 of all adventure . . . : 4/17/37, Princeton.

we call form . . . : "*The Brothers Karamazov*," *Eleven Essays*, p. 103.

of the gods . . . : "Parody and Critique: Mann's *Doctor Faustus*," *Eleven Essays*, p. 103.

put in order . . . : The same, pp. 98–100.

good or evil . . . : The same, p. 100.

you are normal . . . : Fuller and Putnam, n.d., Princeton.

reach the daemonic . . . : "*The Possessed*," p. 171; "*Doctor Faustus*," p. 100.

with 'mere' reason . . . : Green notebook, pp. 28–29.

is more helpful . . . : To Arthur Efron, 11/9/64, Princeton.

279 of our thinking . . . : "*The Idiot*: A Rage of Goodness," *Eleven Essays*, p. 142.

actual contemporary minds . . . : To Criterion Books, 7/22/55, reviewing a prospectus submitted by Hyman for a book on myth and ritual.

student of Jung . . . : RPB to Lambert Davis, 10/21/41; to Catharine Carver, 6/30/55, HBP.

techniques of trouble . . . : Review of Hyman prospectus.

of His creation . . . : AMN, p. 99.

cuts the options . . . : "*The Brothers Karamazov*," p. 193.

280   the Almighty breathes . . . : AMN, p. 82.

and therefore tragic . . . : Describing John Quincy Adams in HA "The Family Go-Cart," p. 101.

act of life . . . : "*Crime and Punishment*: Murder in Your Own Room," *Eleven Essays*, pp. 120, 123; "*The Brothers Karamazov*," p. 187.

the last bone . . . : Green notebook, 1950.

and its cost . . . : Thomas Mann, quoted in "The Lord of Small Counterpositions: Mann's *The Magic Mountain*," *Eleven Essays*, p. 90.

that winter now . . . : "Reflections of Toynbee," p. 147.

is self expression . . . : "Emily Dickinson," *Language as Gesture*, p. 49.

conception and shadow . . . : To Tate, 2/14/46, Princeton Tate.

281   own in prospect . . . : "Three Emphases on Henry Adams," *Expense of Greatness*, p. 255.

the vital purpose . . . : "Anni Mirabiles," p. 44.

him to membership . . . : 2/6/56.

Doctor of Letters . . . : 6/4/58.

with the students . . . : 1963.

his complete works . . . : J. H. McCallum to RPB, 12/21/59, HBP.

to exaggerating trouble . . . : Thoron to RPB, 7/5/38, Harvard.

into the room . . . : Willard Thorp, interview, 7/76.

pocket with Pascal . . . : Conflating two poems by Robert Hollander, "Blackmur's Ghost" and "A Death Six Months Distant."

282   was still Dick . . . : Betty Blackmur to the author, 10/30/78.

was very trying . . . : E. L. Keeley, interview, 5/77.

never to use . . . : To the author, 12/23/78.

willing to spend . . . : Keeley, interview, 5/77.

out the words . . . : Betty Blackmur to the author, 5/4/77.

283   a golden mouth . . . : After Hollander.

of a kitchen . . . : To F. D. Reeve, Princeton.

Index